Yamada-kun and the Seven Witches

10

MIKI YOSHIKAWA

...

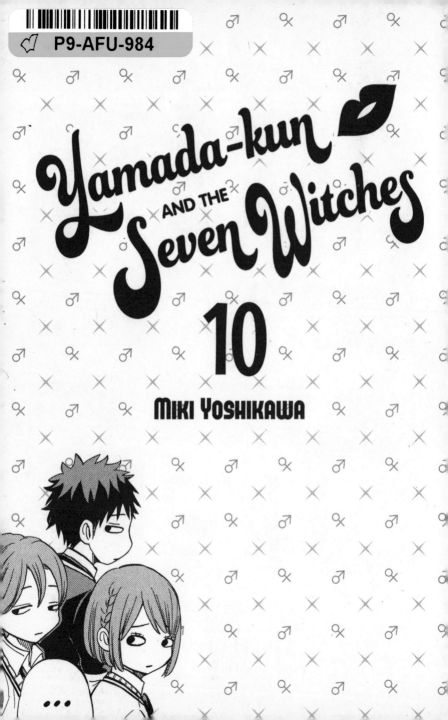

Ryu Yamada

A second-year at Suzaku High School and part of the Supernatural Studies Club. He's loathed by his schoolmates for some reason. He's known as the "Copy Guy" and possesses the ability to copy the power of whichever witch he kisses.

Urara Shiraishi ★

A second-year at Suzaku High School and president of the Supernatural Studies Club. A coolheaded girl who's always studying. She's known as the "Switch Witch" and switches bodies with the person whom she kisses. Her smile, which she shows from time to time, is so cute that it should be illegal.

★ Currently has no memory of Yamada from the time that he entered high school until now.

Toranosuke Miyamura ★

A second-year at Suzaku High School. He's the vice-president of the Supernatural Studies Club and Student Council. The polar opposite of Yamada, he's the most popular kid in school. He's very curious and sharp, but his perverted streak is a problem.

Miyabi Itou ★

A second-year at Suzaku High School and part of the Supernatural Studies Club. She's the only member of the club who's into the occult. She's surprisingly popular with boys.

Leona Miyamura

A third-year at Suzaku High School and Toranosuke Miyamura's older sister. One year ago, she had investigated the witches but almost had her memory erased after discovering the name of the seventh witch. She escaped but hasn't been to school since then. She speaks sort of like a warrior.

Meiko Otsuka ★

A second-year at Suzaku High School and member of the Manga Studies Club. She is known as the "Thought Witch" and can perform telepathic communication with the person whom she kisses.

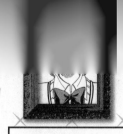

Haruma Yamazaki

A third-year at Suzaku High School and president of the Student Council. He's a crafty guy who holds many secrets. And he has a dirty mind!

Rika Saionji

A third-year at Suzaku High School and the seventh witch. She appears before anyone who knows the identities of all seven witches. She doesn't wear panties and appears and disappears when you least expect it. She's what you might call…"abnormal!"

Nene Odagiri

A second-year at Suzaku High School. She shares the position of Student Council vice-president with Miyamura. She is known as the "Charm Witch" and makes the person whom she kisses fall in love with her.

Noa Takigawa ★

A first-year at Suzaku High School. A little rascal who is infatuated with Yamada. She is known as the "Retrocognition Witch" and by way of dreams can see the past trauma of whomever she kisses.

Mikoto Asuka ★

A third-year at Suzaku High School and vice president of the Student Council. She loves the Student Council president and is super sadistic! She used to be the "Invisible Witch" but had her power erased by Tamaki.

Ushio Igarashi ★

A second-year at Suzaku High School. He is the loyal minion of the cunning Odagiri. He was Yamada's friend in junior high.

Maria Sarushima ★

A second-year at Suzaku High School. She's a kissing-fiend who used to live abroad. She is known as the "Prediction Witch" and can see the future from the perspective of the person whom she kisses.

Shinichi Tamaki

A second-year at Suzaku High School. A guy with an attitude who's aiming to be the next Student Council president. He's known as the "Capture Guy" and steals the power of the witch whom he kisses. He currently possesses the ability to turn invisible.

CONTENTS

CHAPTER 77: Disgraceful!

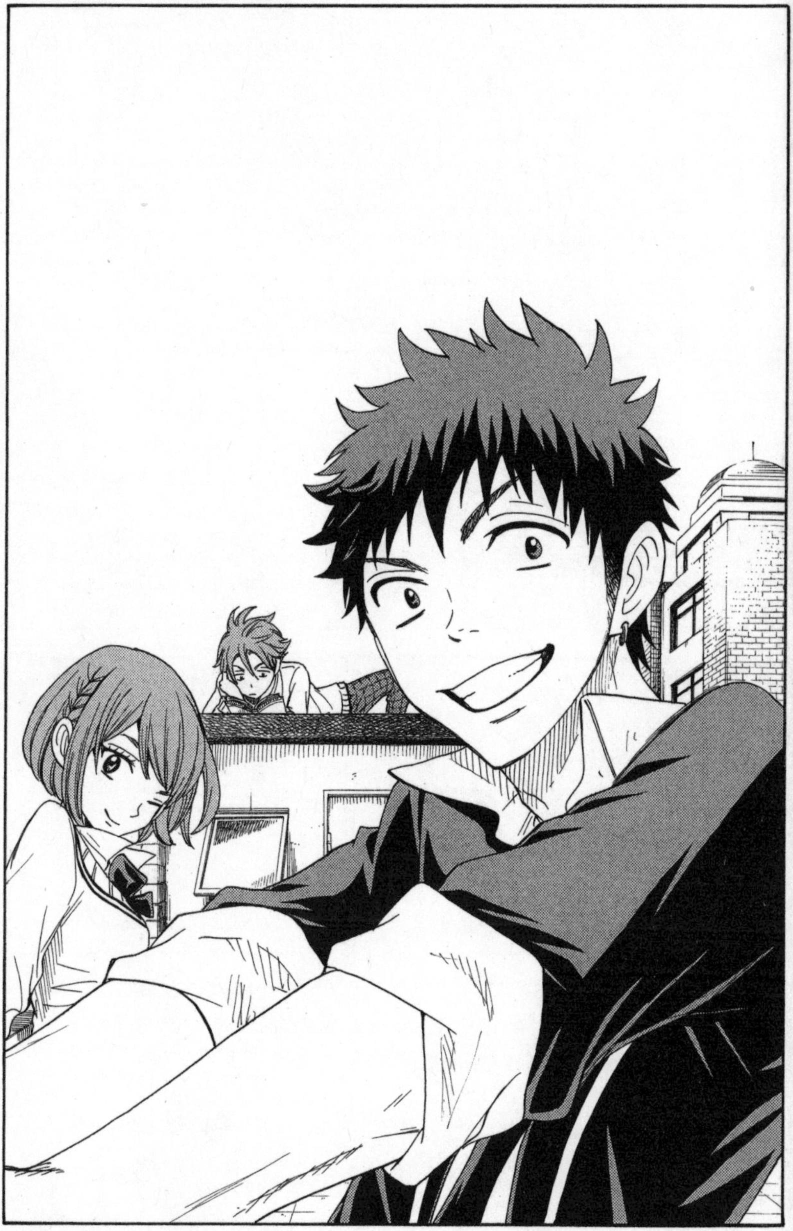

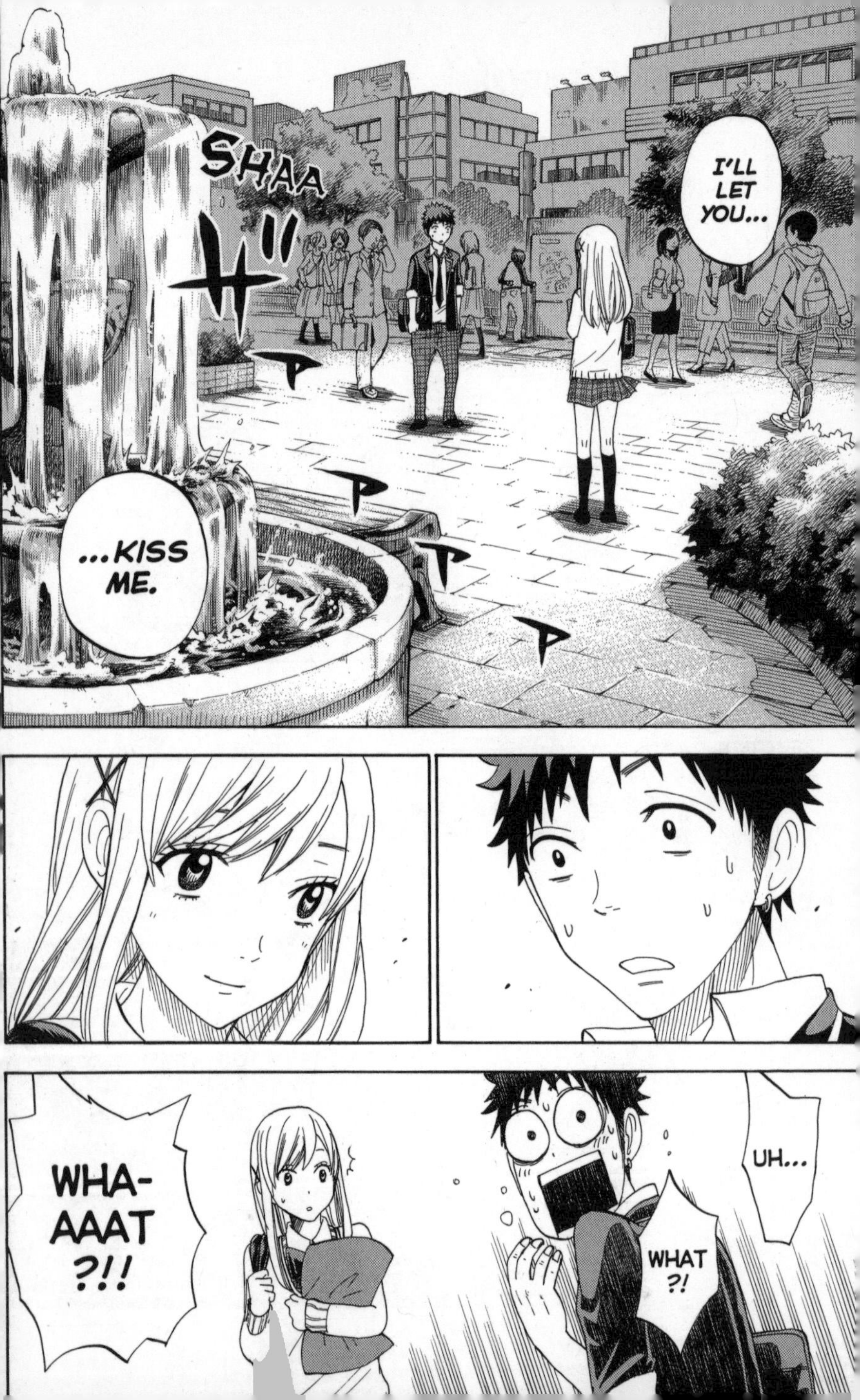
I'LL LET YOU...
SHAA
...KISS ME.
UH...
WHAT ?!
WHA-AAAT ?!!

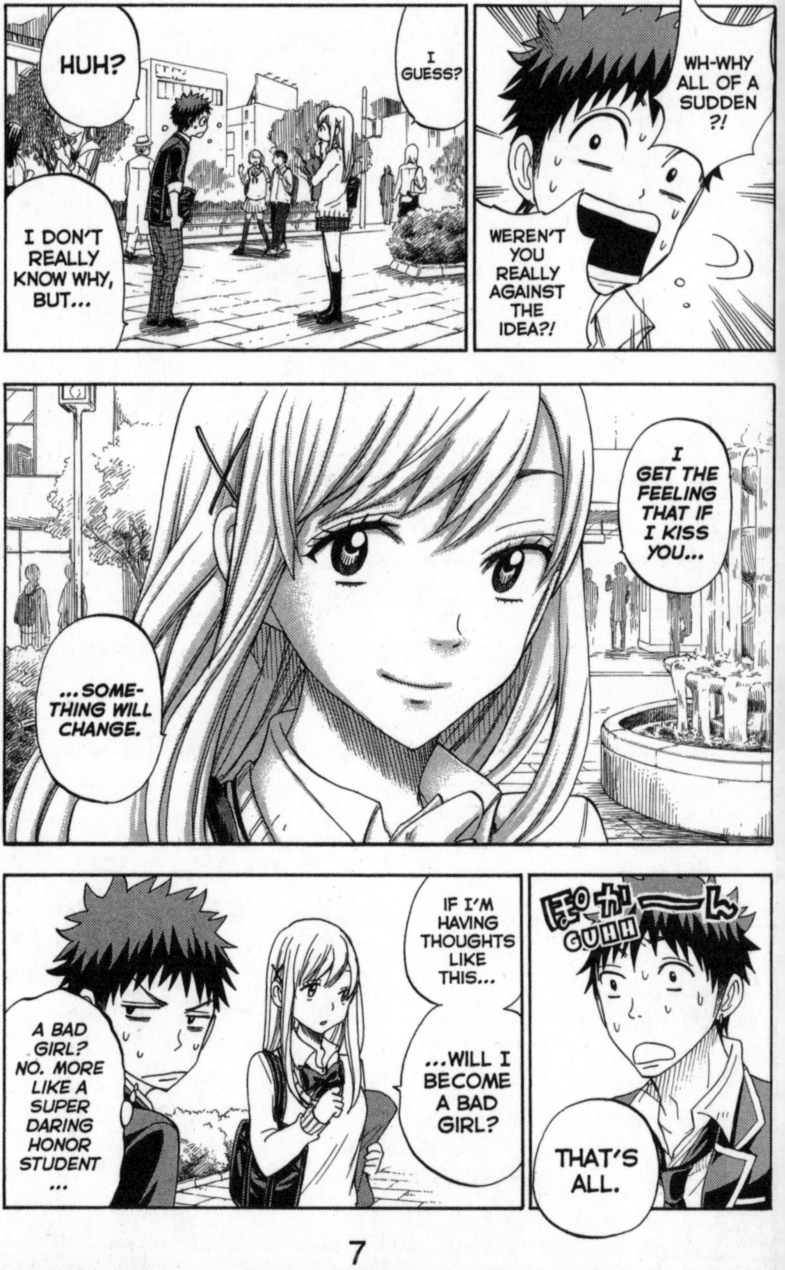
WH-WHY ALL OF A SUDDEN ?!
WEREN'T YOU REALLY AGAINST THE IDEA?!
I GUESS?
HUH?
I DON'T REALLY KNOW WHY, BUT...
I GET THE FEELING THAT IF I KISS YOU...
...SOME-THING WILL CHANGE.
ぽかーーん
GUHH
THAT'S ALL.
IF I'M HAVING THOUGHTS LIKE THIS...
...WILL I BECOME A BAD GIRL?
A BAD GIRL? NO. MORE LIKE A SUPER DARING HONOR STUDENT ...

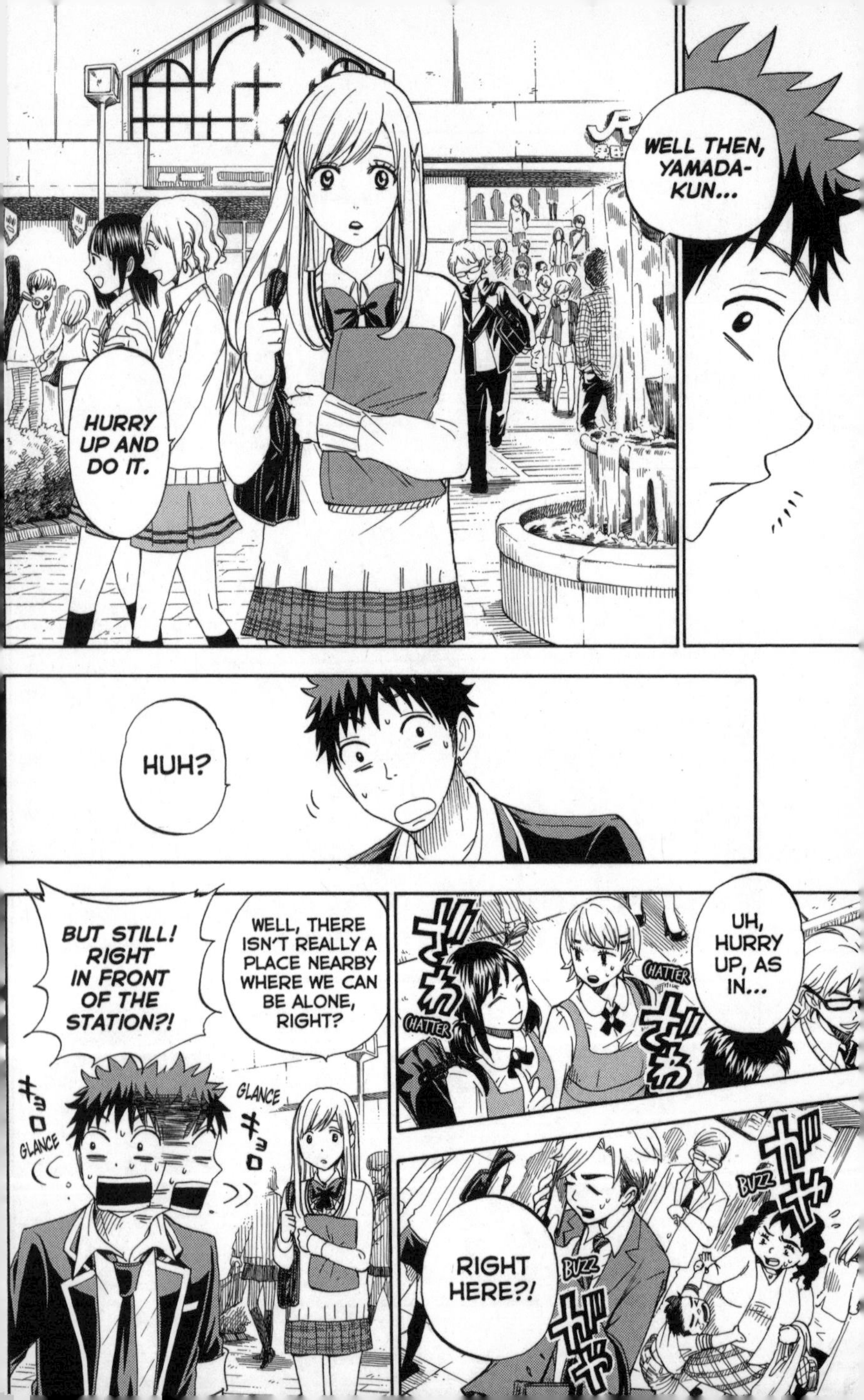
WELL THEN, YAMADA-KUN...
HURRY UP AND DO IT.
HUH?
UH, HURRY UP, AS IN...
ざわ
CHATTER
ざわ
CHATTER
RIGHT HERE?!
ガヤ
BUZZ
ガヤ
BUZZ
WELL, THERE ISN'T REALLY A PLACE NEARBY WHERE WE CAN BE ALONE, RIGHT?
BUT STILL! RIGHT IN FRONT OF THE STATION?!
キョロ
GLANCE
キョロ
GLANCE

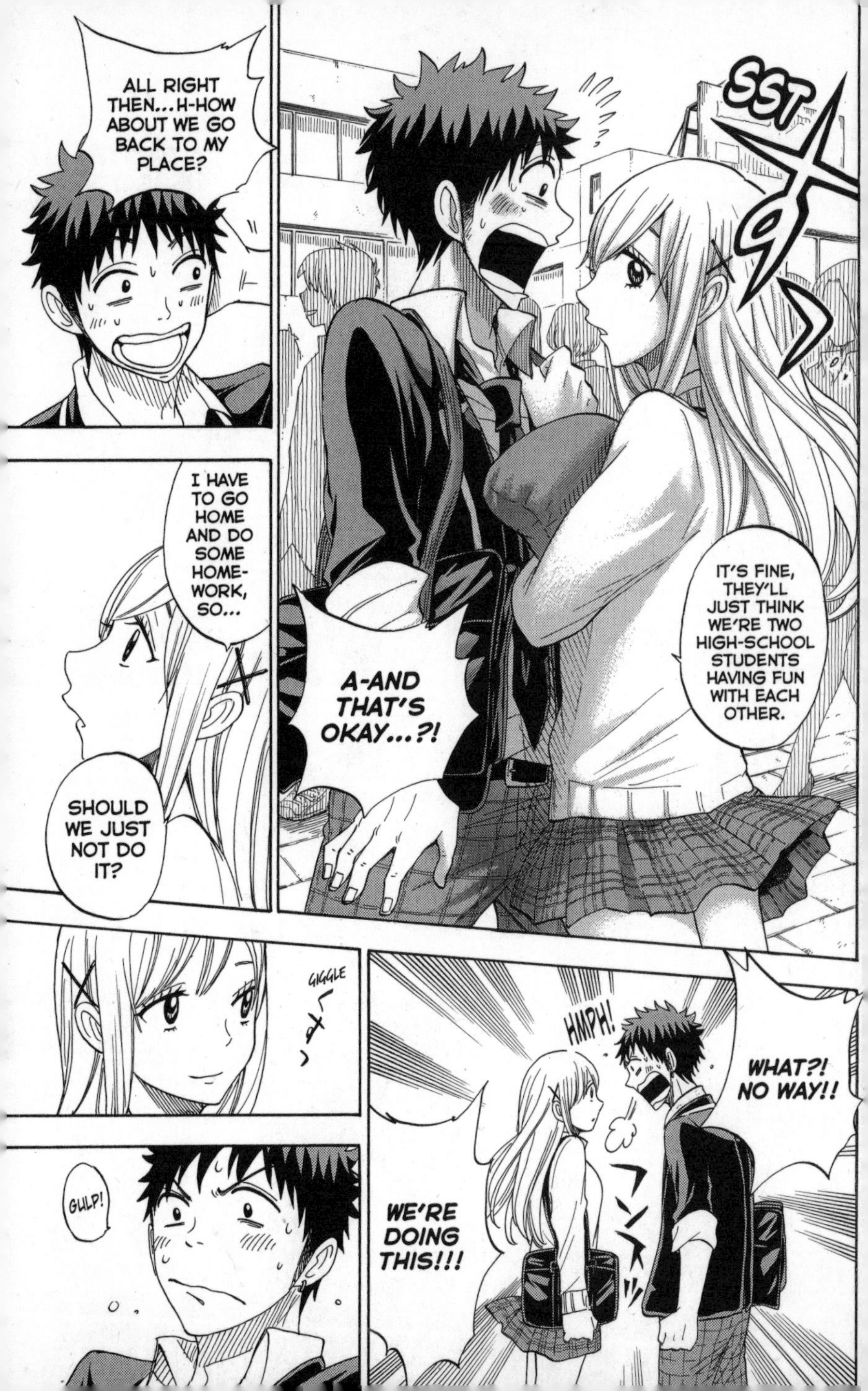
SST
IT'S FINE, THEY'LL JUST THINK WE'RE TWO HIGH-SCHOOL STUDENTS HAVING FUN WITH EACH OTHER.
A-AND THAT'S OKAY...?!
ALL RIGHT THEN... H-HOW ABOUT WE GO BACK TO MY PLACE?
I HAVE TO GO HOME AND DO SOME HOME-WORK, SO...
SHOULD WE JUST NOT DO IT?
WHAT?! NO WAY!!
HMPH!
WE'RE DOING THIS!!!
GIGGLE
GULP!

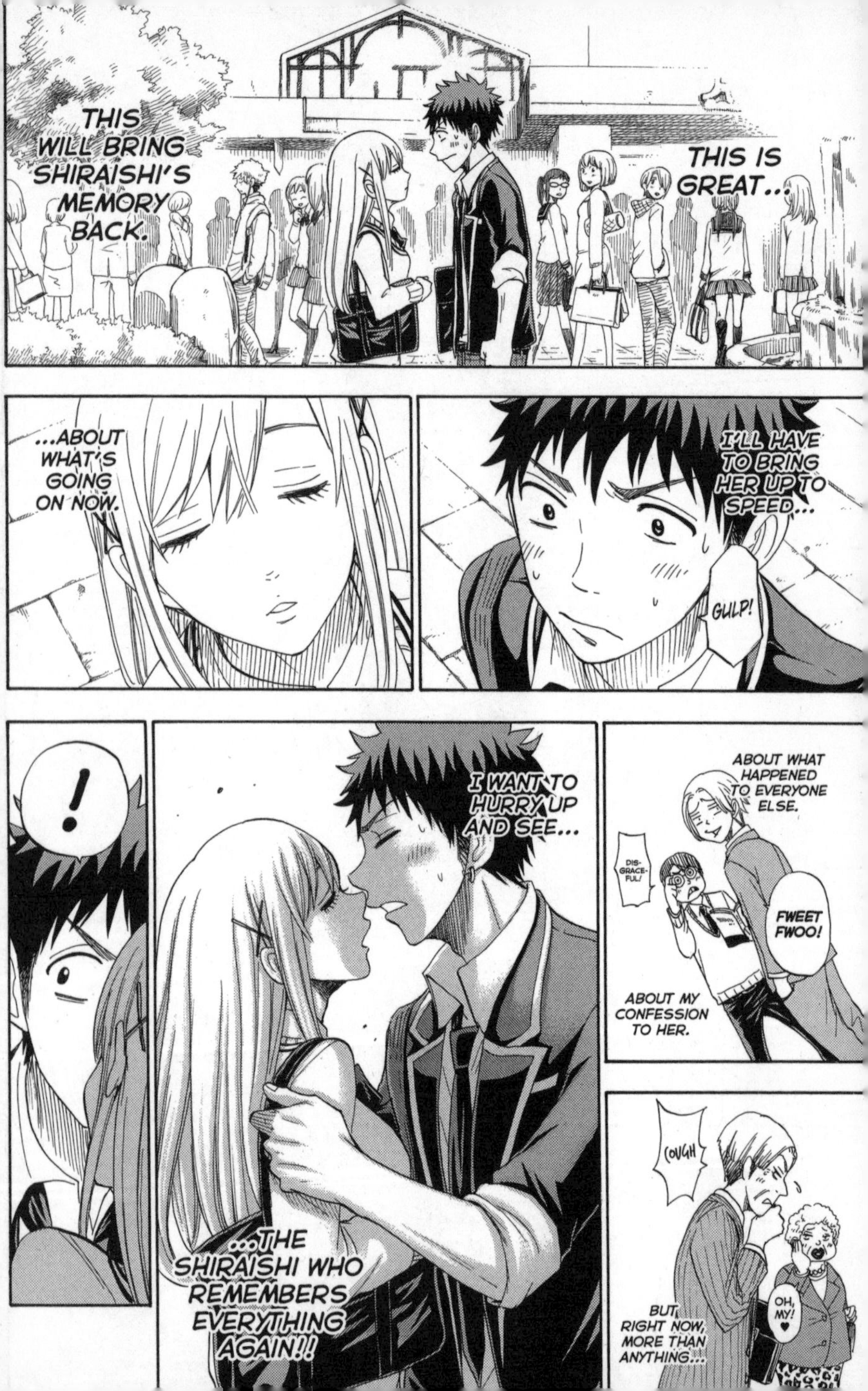
THIS IS GREAT...
THIS WILL BRING SHIRAISHI'S MEMORY BACK.
I'LL HAVE TO BRING HER UP TO SPEED...
GULP!
...ABOUT WHAT'S GOING ON NOW.
ABOUT WHAT HAPPENED TO EVERYONE ELSE.
FWEET FWOO!
DIS-GRACE-FUL!
ABOUT MY CONFESSION TO HER.
COUGH
OH, MY! ♥
BUT RIGHT NOW, MORE THAN ANYTHING...
I WANT TO HURRY UP AND SEE...
...THE SHIRAISHI WHO REMEMBERS EVERYTHING AGAIN!!
!

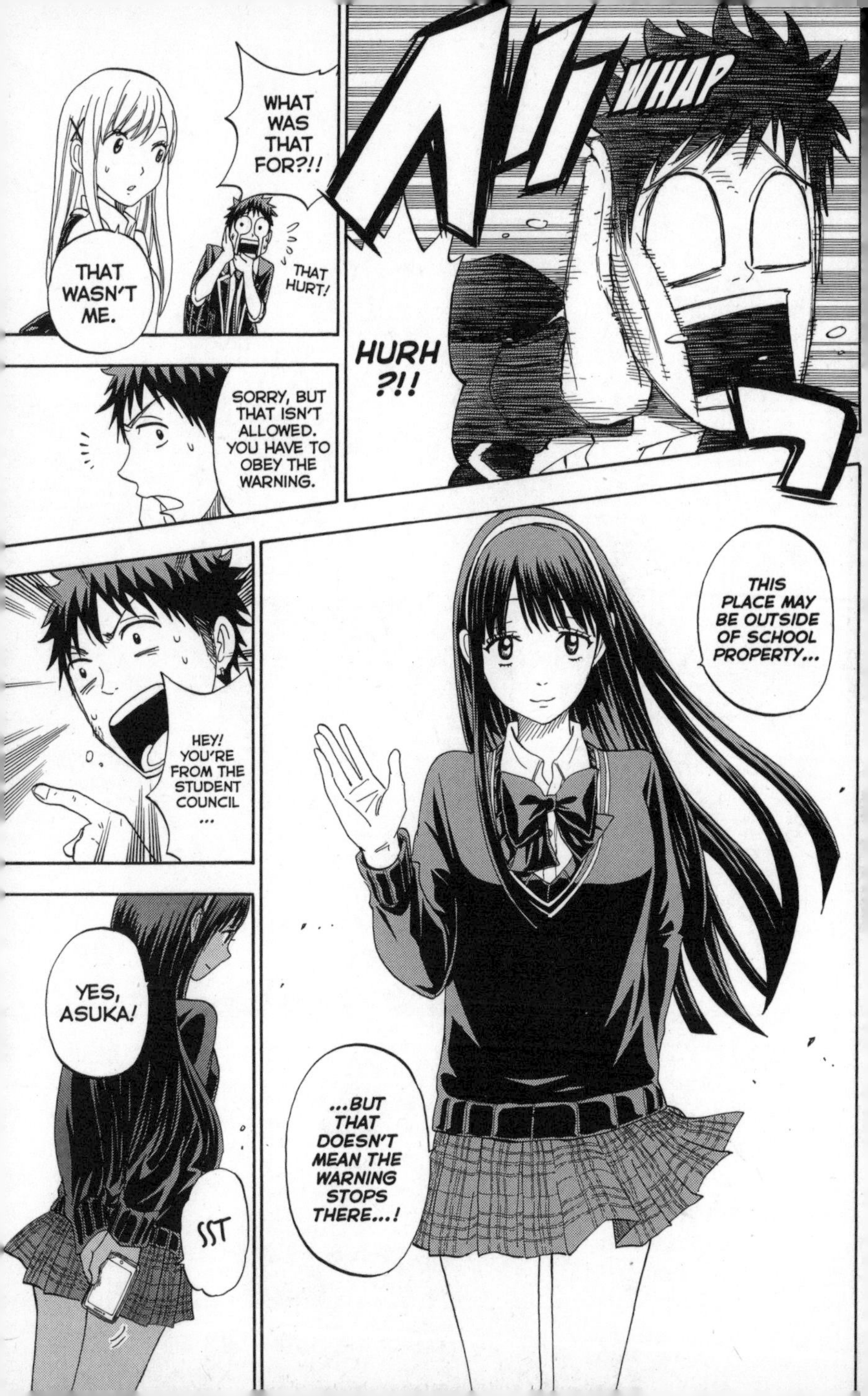
WHAP
HURH ?!!
WHAT WAS THAT FOR?!!
THAT HURT!
THAT WASN'T ME.
SORRY, BUT THAT ISN'T ALLOWED. YOU HAVE TO OBEY THE WARNING.
THIS PLACE MAY BE OUTSIDE OF SCHOOL PROPERTY...
...BUT THAT DOESN'T MEAN THE WARNING STOPS THERE...!
HEY! YOU'RE FROM THE STUDENT COUNCIL ...
YES, ASUKA!
SST

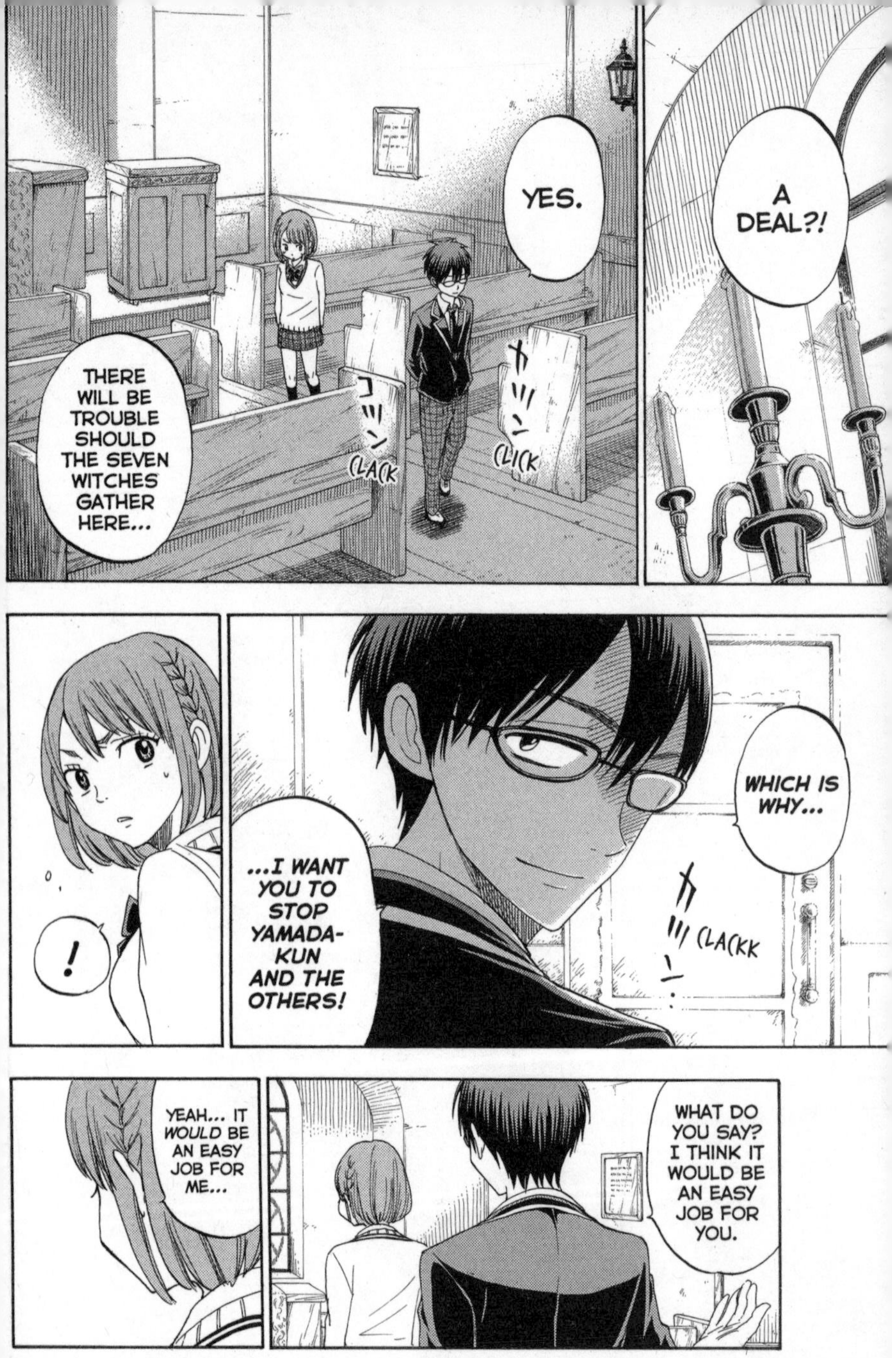

A DEAL?!
YES.
カツン
CLICK
コツン
CLACK
THERE WILL BE TROUBLE SHOULD THE SEVEN WITCHES GATHER HERE...
WHICH IS WHY...
CLACKK
...I WANT YOU TO STOP YAMADA-KUN AND THE OTHERS!
!
WHAT DO YOU SAY? I THINK IT WOULD BE AN EASY JOB FOR YOU.
YEAH... IT *WOULD* BE AN EASY JOB FOR ME...

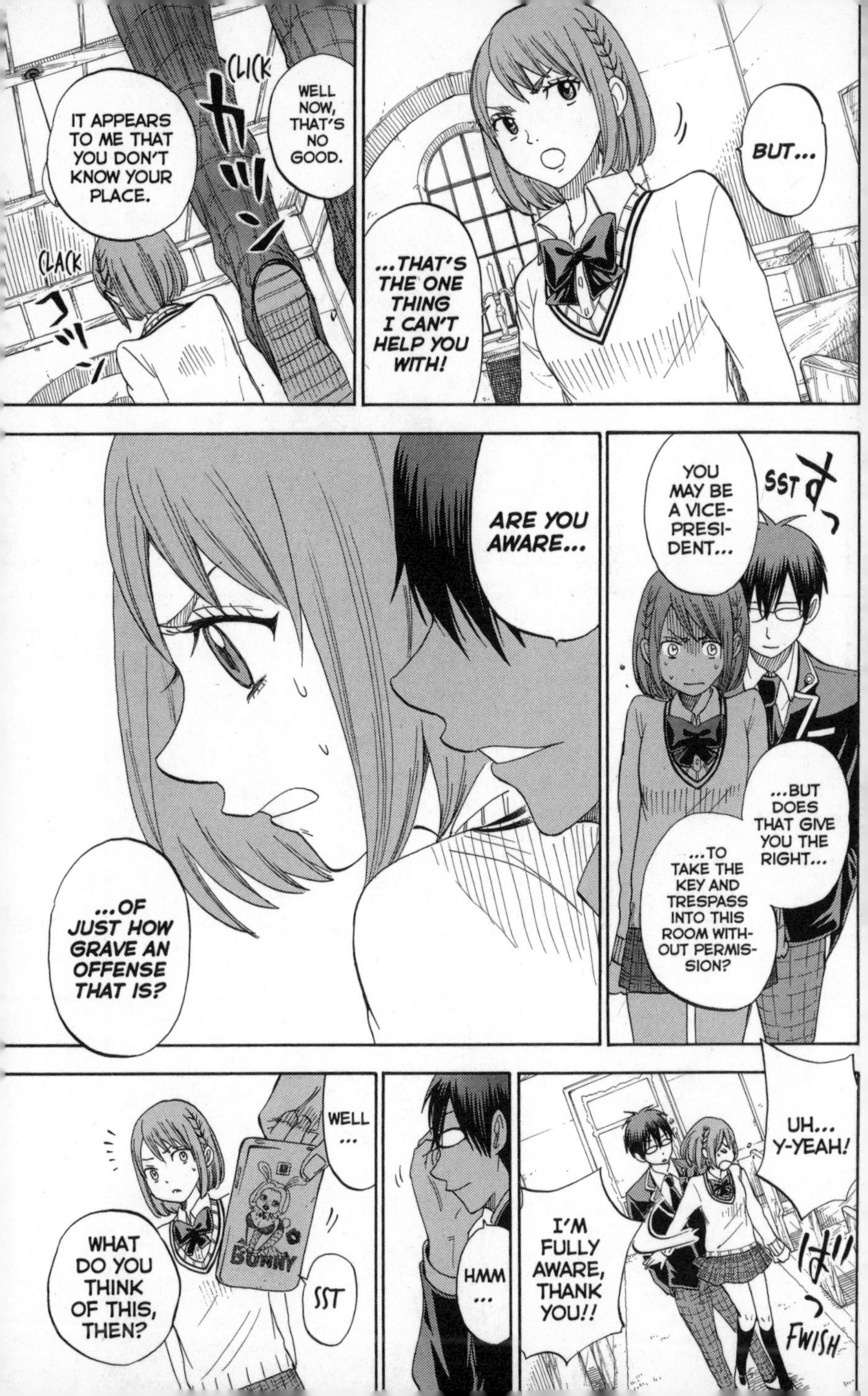
BUT...
...THAT'S THE ONE THING I CAN'T HELP YOU WITH!
WELL NOW, THAT'S NO GOOD.
CLICK
IT APPEARS TO ME THAT YOU DON'T KNOW YOUR PLACE.
CLACK
SST
YOU MAY BE A VICE-PRESIDENT...
...BUT DOES THAT GIVE YOU THE RIGHT...
...TO TAKE THE KEY AND TRESPASS INTO THIS ROOM WITHOUT PERMISSION?
ARE YOU AWARE...
...OF JUST HOW GRAVE AN OFFENSE THAT IS?
UH... Y-YEAH!
I'M FULLY AWARE, THANK YOU!!
FWISH
HMM ...
WELL ...
BUNNY
WHAT DO YOU THINK OF THIS, THEN?
SST

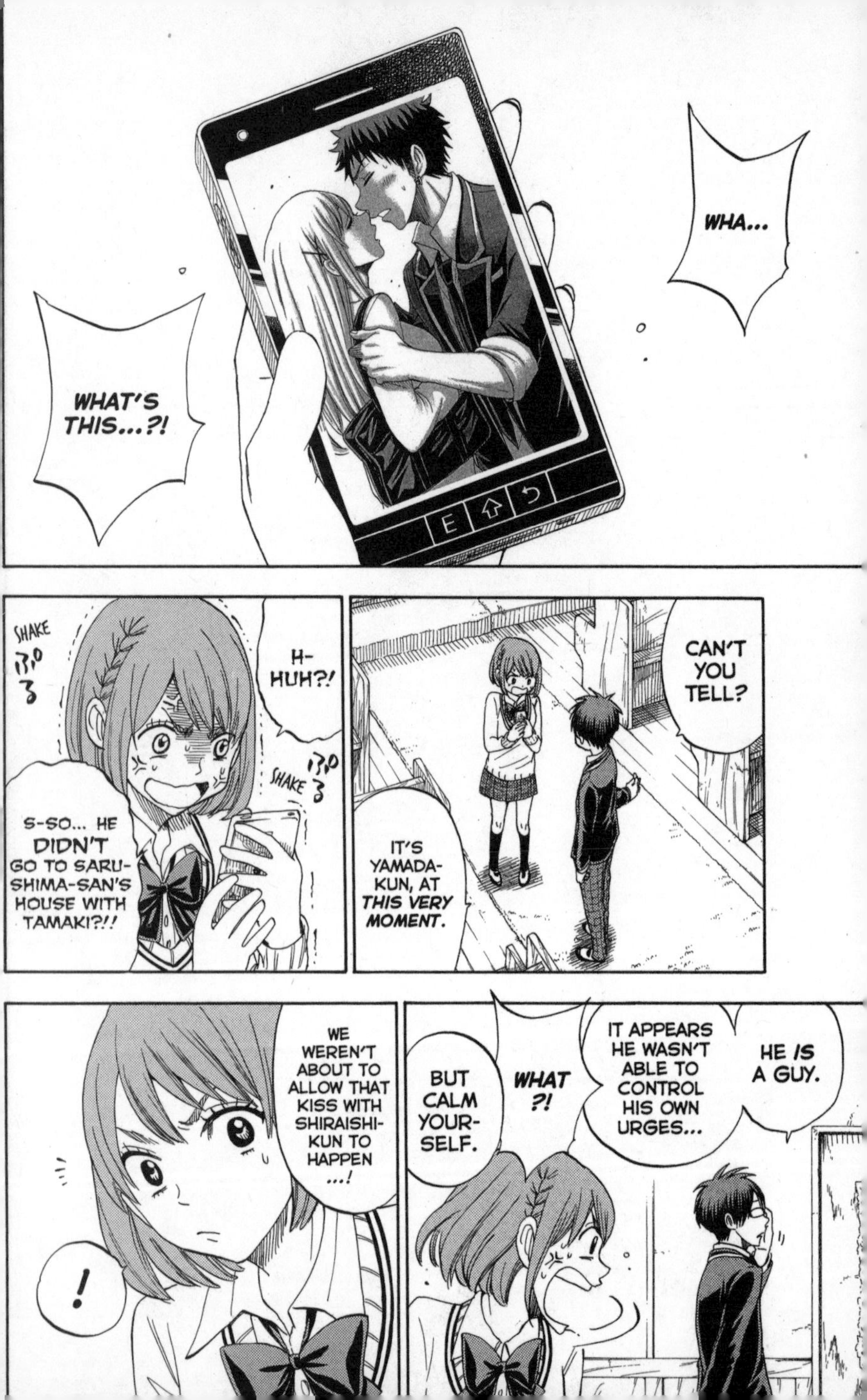
WHA...
WHAT'S THIS...?!
CAN'T YOU TELL?
IT'S YAMADA-KUN, AT THIS VERY MOMENT.
SHAKE
H-HUH?!
SHAKE
S-SO... HE DIDN'T GO TO SARUSHIMA-SAN'S HOUSE WITH TAMAKI?!!
HE IS A GUY.
IT APPEARS HE WASN'T ABLE TO CONTROL HIS OWN URGES...
WHAT?!
BUT CALM YOURSELF.
WE WEREN'T ABOUT TO ALLOW THAT KISS WITH SHIRAISHI-KUN TO HAPPEN...!
!

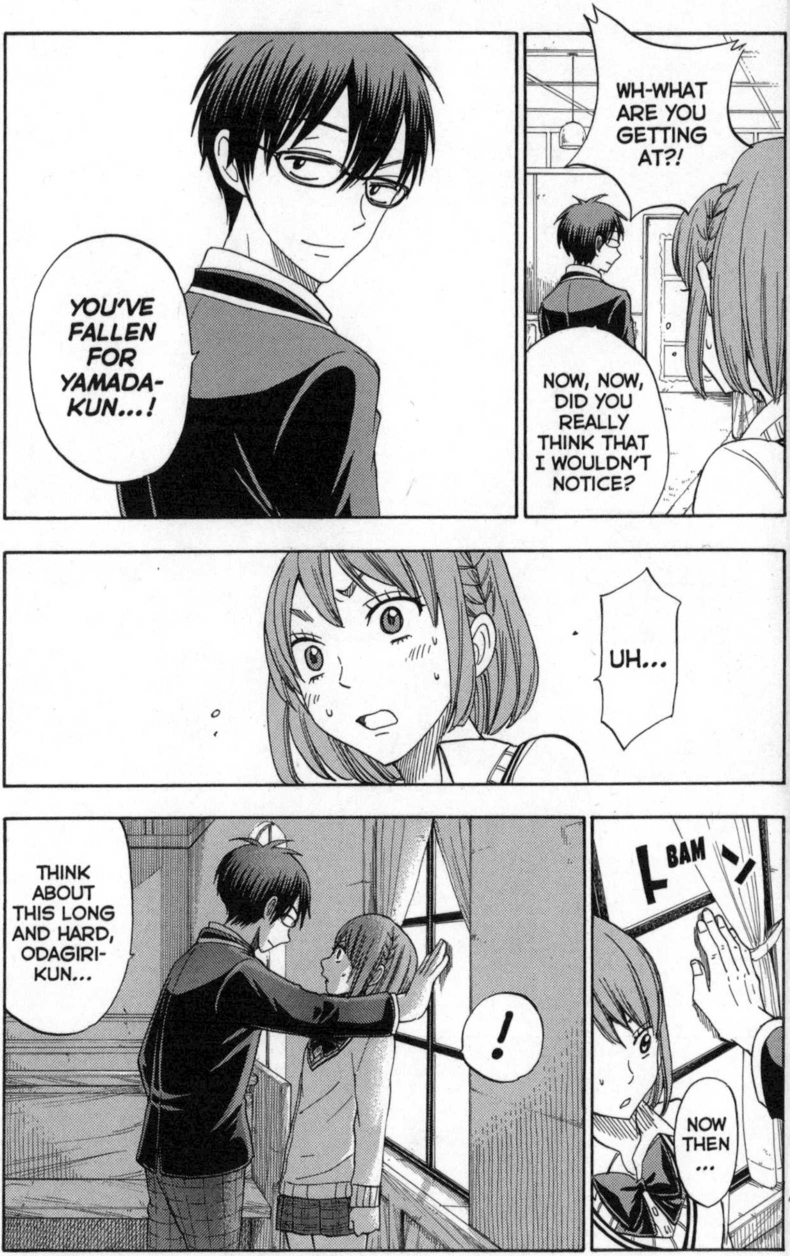
WH-WHAT ARE YOU GETTING AT?!
NOW, NOW, DID YOU REALLY THINK THAT I WOULDN'T NOTICE?
YOU'VE FALLEN FOR YAMADA-KUN...!
UH...
BAM
NOW THEN ...
THINK ABOUT THIS LONG AND HARD, ODAGIRI-KUN...
!

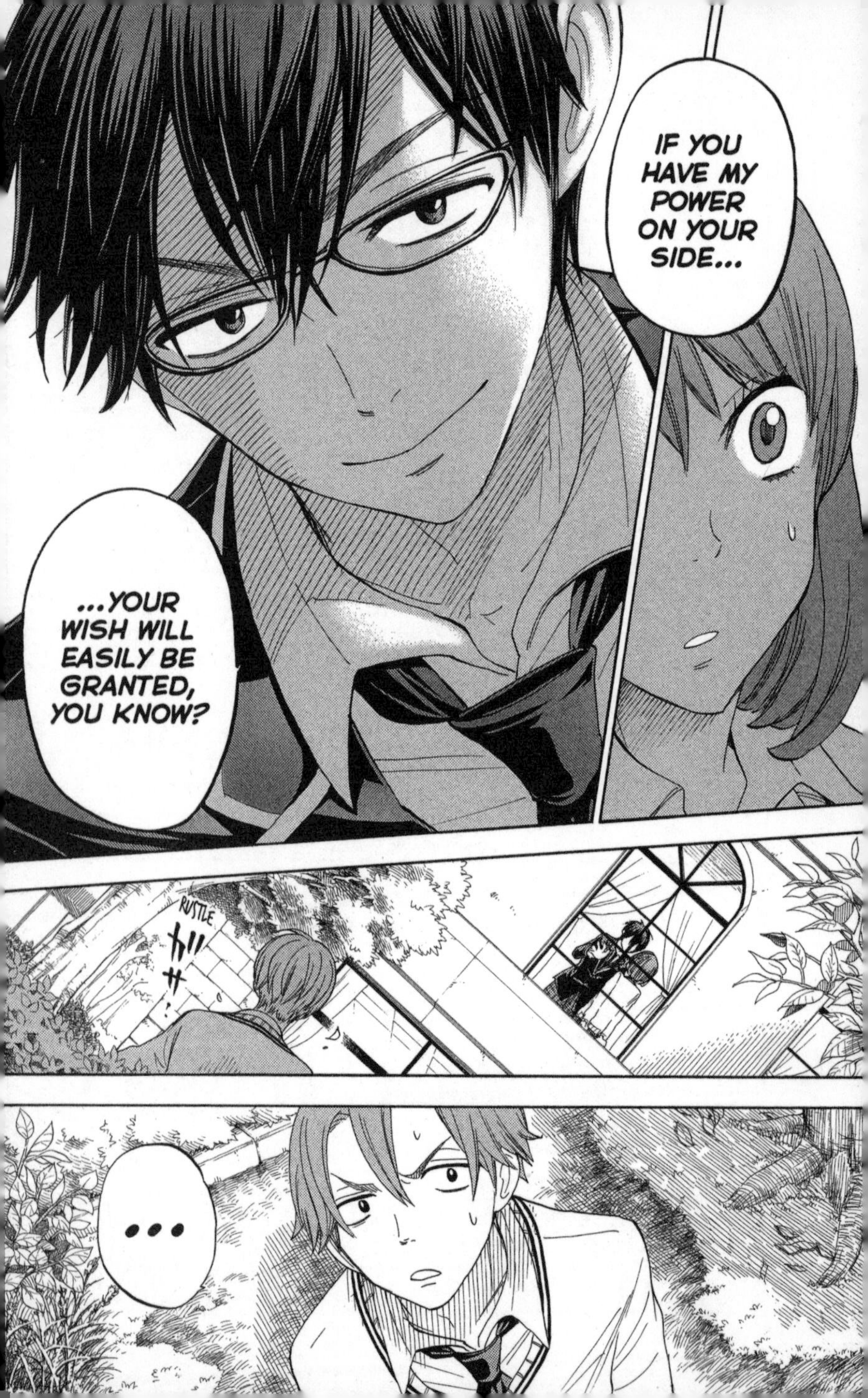
IF YOU HAVE MY POWER ON YOUR SIDE...
...YOUR WISH WILL EASILY BE GRANTED, YOU KNOW?
RUSTLE
...

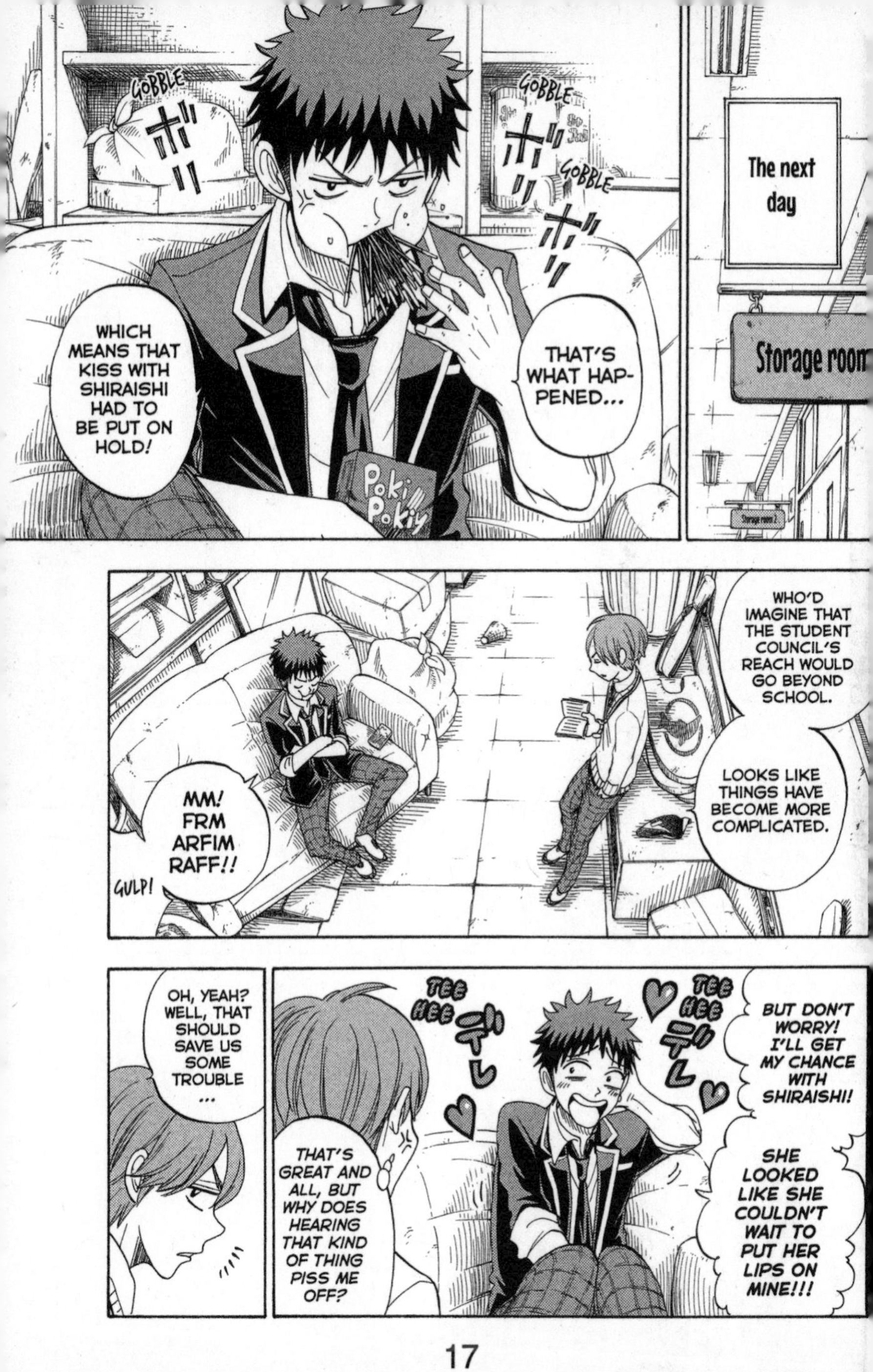
The next day
Storage room
Storage room 2
GOBBLE
GOBBLE
GOBBLE
THAT'S WHAT HAPPENED...
WHICH MEANS THAT KISS WITH SHIRAISHI HAD TO BE PUT ON HOLD!
Poki Pokiy
WHO'D IMAGINE THAT THE STUDENT COUNCIL'S REACH WOULD GO BEYOND SCHOOL.
LOOKS LIKE THINGS HAVE BECOME MORE COMPLICATED.
MM! FRM ARFIM RAFF!!
GULP!
BUT DON'T WORRY! I'LL GET MY CHANCE WITH SHIRAISHI!
SHE LOOKED LIKE SHE COULDN'T WAIT TO PUT HER LIPS ON MINE!!!
TEE HEE
TEE HEE
THAT'S GREAT AND ALL, BUT WHY DOES HEARING THAT KIND OF THING PISS ME OFF?
OH, YEAH? WELL, THAT SHOULD SAVE US SOME TROUBLE...

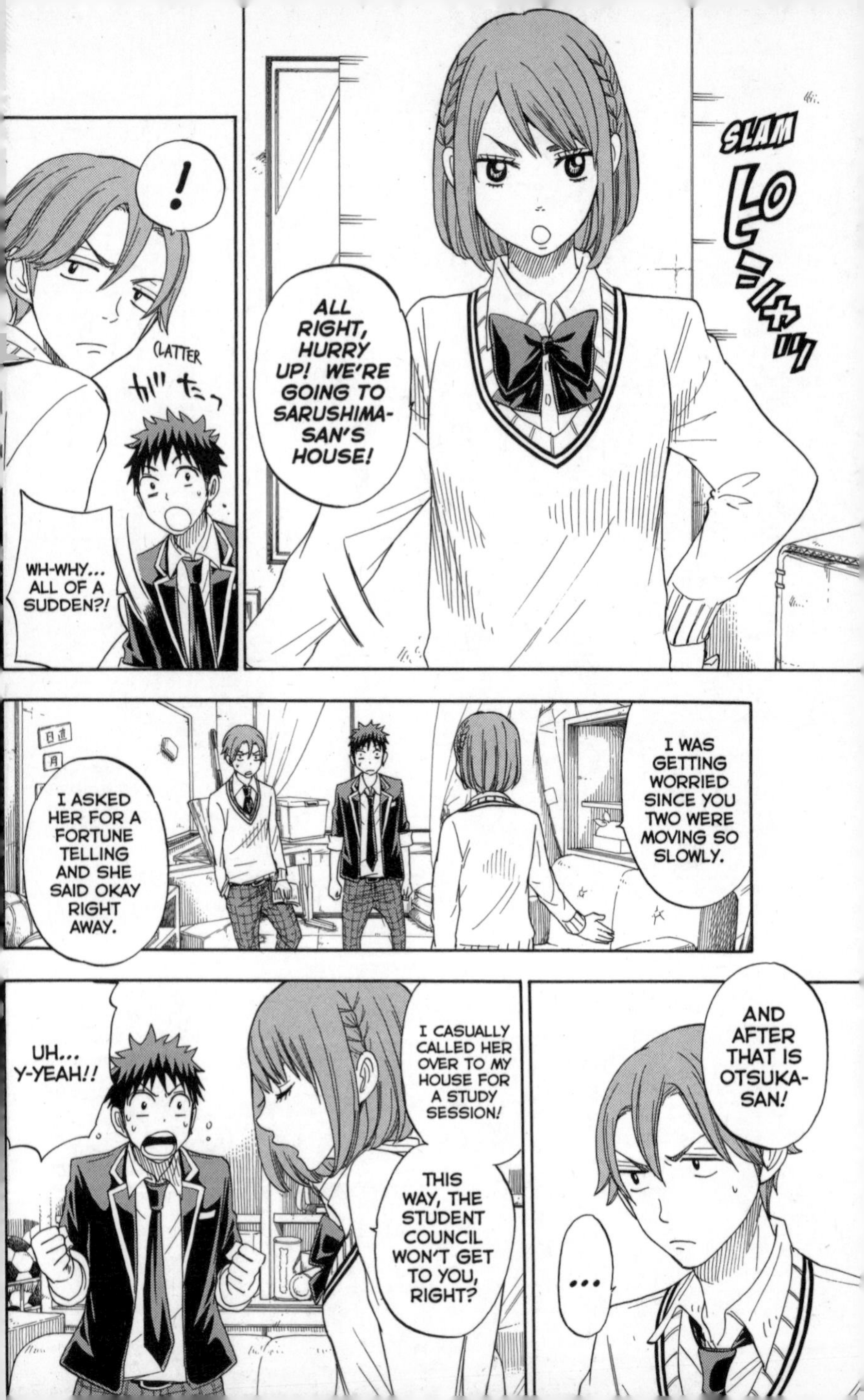
SLAM
ALL RIGHT, HURRY UP! WE'RE GOING TO SARUSHIMA-SAN'S HOUSE!
!
CLATTER
WH-WHY... ALL OF A SUDDEN?!
I WAS GETTING WORRIED SINCE YOU TWO WERE MOVING SO SLOWLY.
I ASKED HER FOR A FORTUNE TELLING AND SHE SAID OKAY RIGHT AWAY.
AND AFTER THAT IS OTSUKA-SAN!
...
I CASUALLY CALLED HER OVER TO MY HOUSE FOR A STUDY SESSION!
THIS WAY, THE STUDENT COUNCIL WON'T GET TO YOU, RIGHT?
UH... Y-YEAH!!

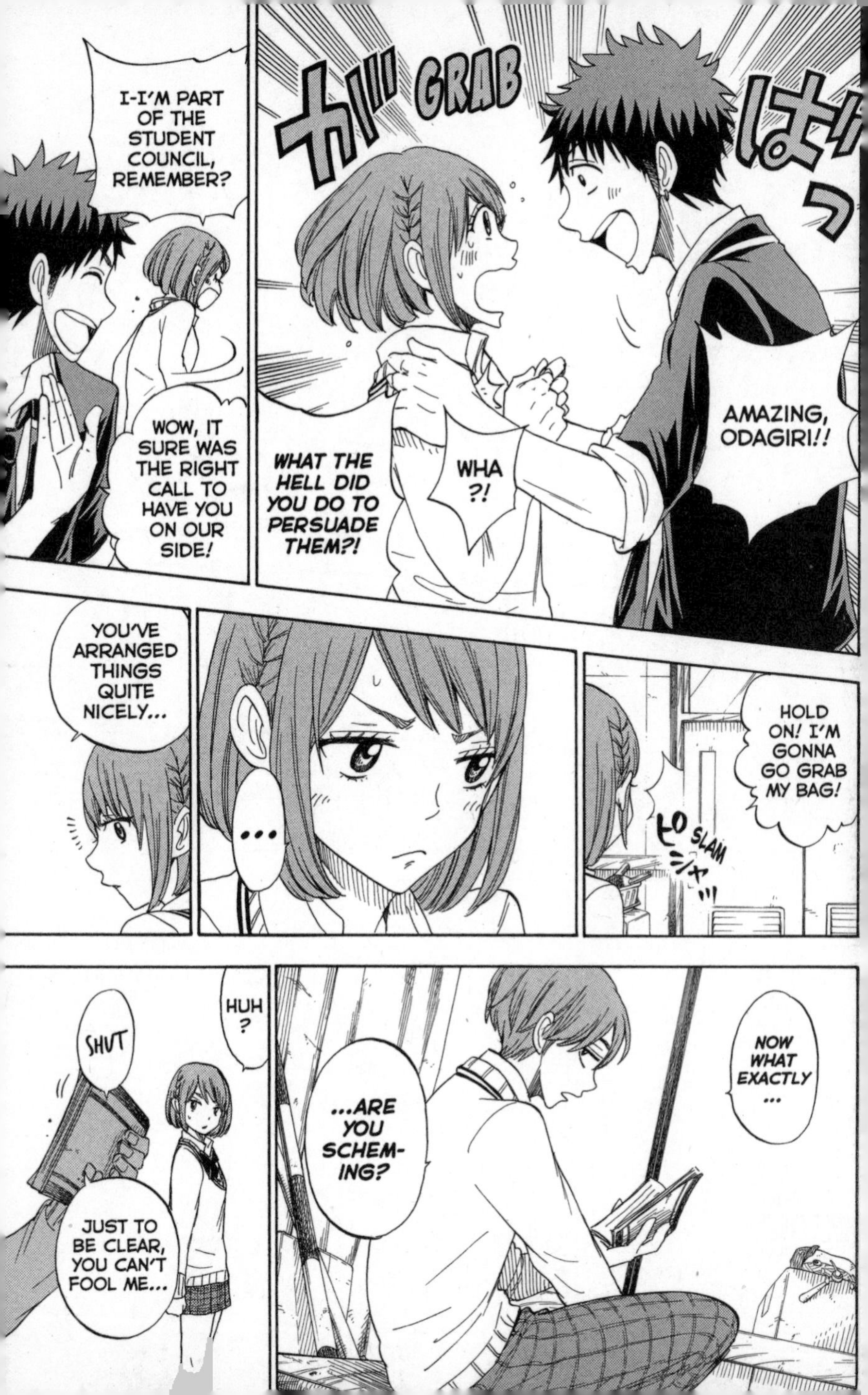
GRAB
AMAZING, ODAGIRI!!
WHA ?!
WHAT THE HELL DID YOU DO TO PERSUADE THEM?!
I-I'M PART OF THE STUDENT COUNCIL, REMEMBER?
WOW, IT SURE WAS THE RIGHT CALL TO HAVE YOU ON OUR SIDE!
HOLD ON! I'M GONNA GO GRAB MY BAG!
SLAM
...
YOU'VE ARRANGED THINGS QUITE NICELY...
NOW WHAT EXACTLY ...
...ARE YOU SCHEM- ING?
HUH ?
SHUT
JUST TO BE CLEAR, YOU CAN'T FOOL ME...

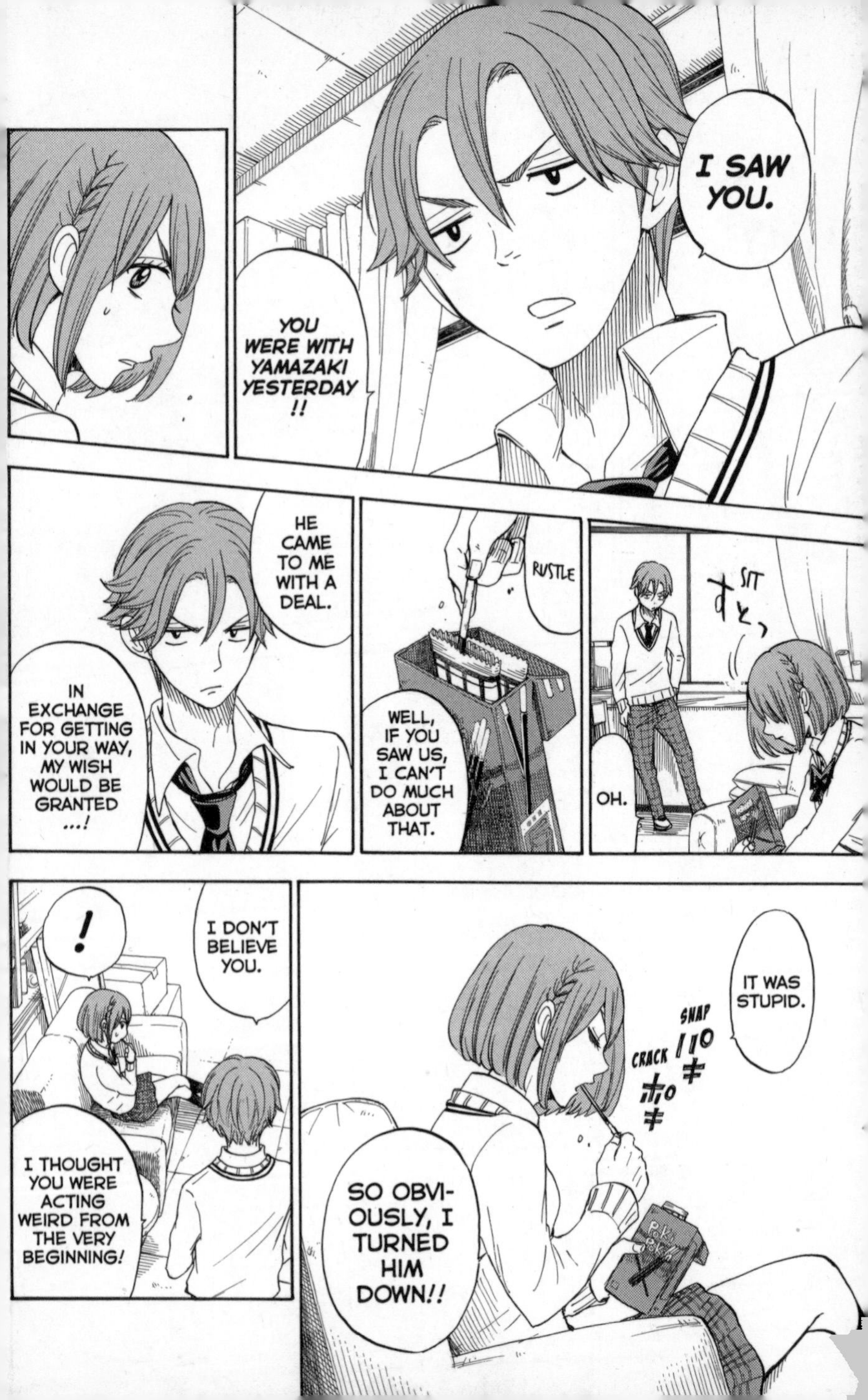
I SAW YOU.
YOU WERE WITH YAMAZAKI YESTERDAY!!
SIT
OH.
RUSTLE
WELL, IF YOU SAW US, I CAN'T DO MUCH ABOUT THAT.
HE CAME TO ME WITH A DEAL.
IN EXCHANGE FOR GETTING IN YOUR WAY, MY WISH WOULD BE GRANTED...!
IT WAS STUPID.
SNAP
CRACK
SO OBVIOUSLY, I TURNED HIM DOWN!!
I DON'T BELIEVE YOU.
!
I THOUGHT YOU WERE ACTING WEIRD FROM THE VERY BEGINNING!

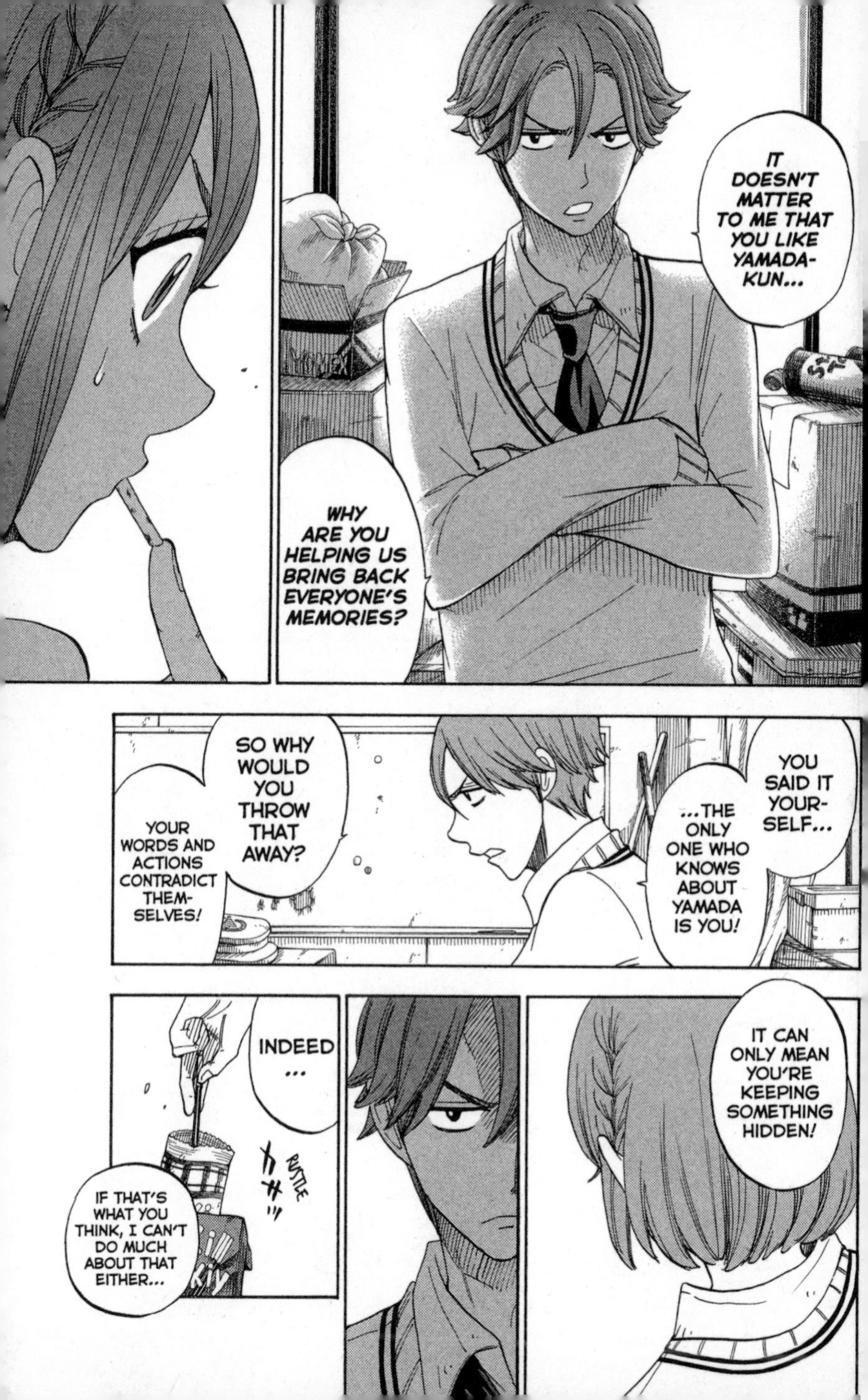
IT DOESN'T MATTER TO ME THAT YOU LIKE YAMADA-KUN...
WHY ARE YOU HELPING US BRING BACK EVERYONE'S MEMORIES?
YOU SAID IT YOURSELF...
...THE ONLY ONE WHO KNOWS ABOUT YAMADA IS YOU!
SO WHY WOULD YOU THROW THAT AWAY?
YOUR WORDS AND ACTIONS CONTRADICT THEMSELVES!
IT CAN ONLY MEAN YOU'RE KEEPING SOMETHING HIDDEN!
INDEED...
RUSTLE
IF THAT'S WHAT YOU THINK, I CAN'T DO MUCH ABOUT THAT EITHER...

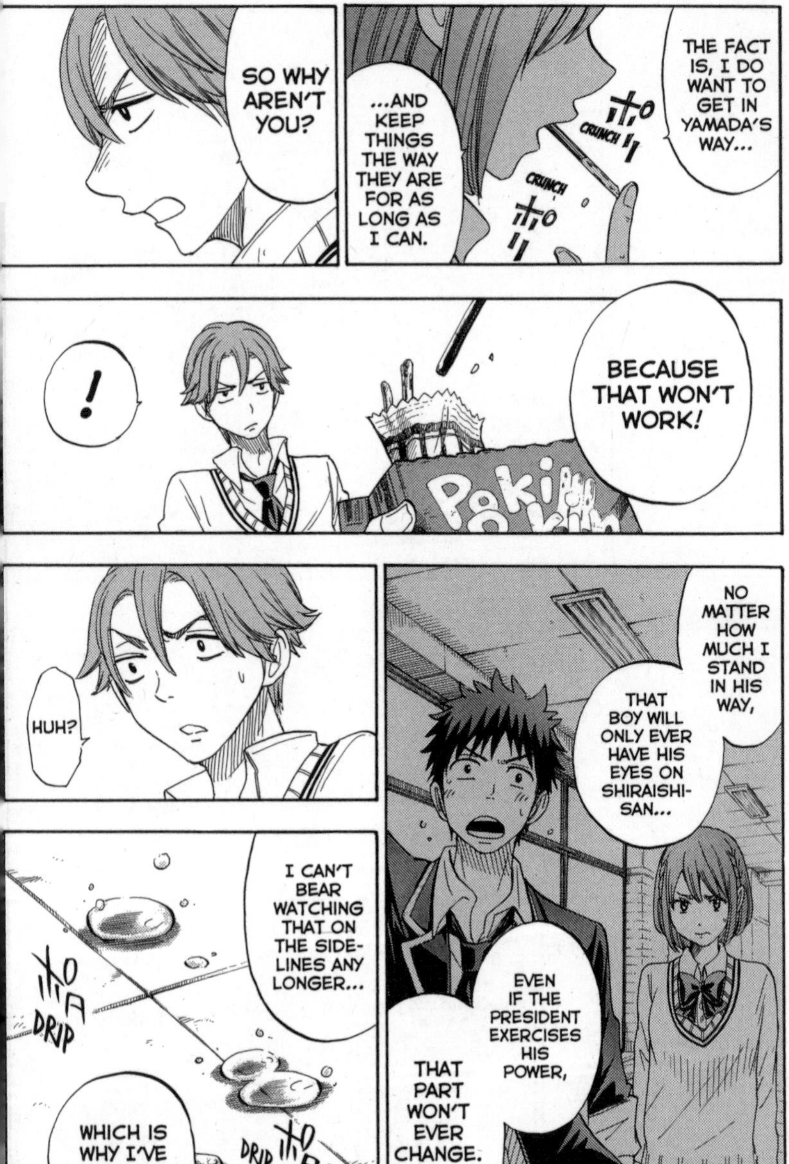
THE FACT IS, I DO WANT TO GET IN YAMADA'S WAY...
CRUNCH
CRUNCH
...AND KEEP THINGS THE WAY THEY ARE FOR AS LONG AS I CAN.
SO WHY AREN'T YOU?
BECAUSE THAT WON'T WORK!
!
NO MATTER HOW MUCH I STAND IN HIS WAY,
THAT BOY WILL ONLY EVER HAVE HIS EYES ON SHIRAISHI-SAN...
EVEN IF THE PRESIDENT EXERCISES HIS POWER,
THAT PART WON'T EVER CHANGE.
HUH?
I CAN'T BEAR WATCHING THAT ON THE SIDE-LINES ANY LONGER...
DRIP
WHICH IS WHY I'VE MADE UP MY MIND...
DRIP DRIP

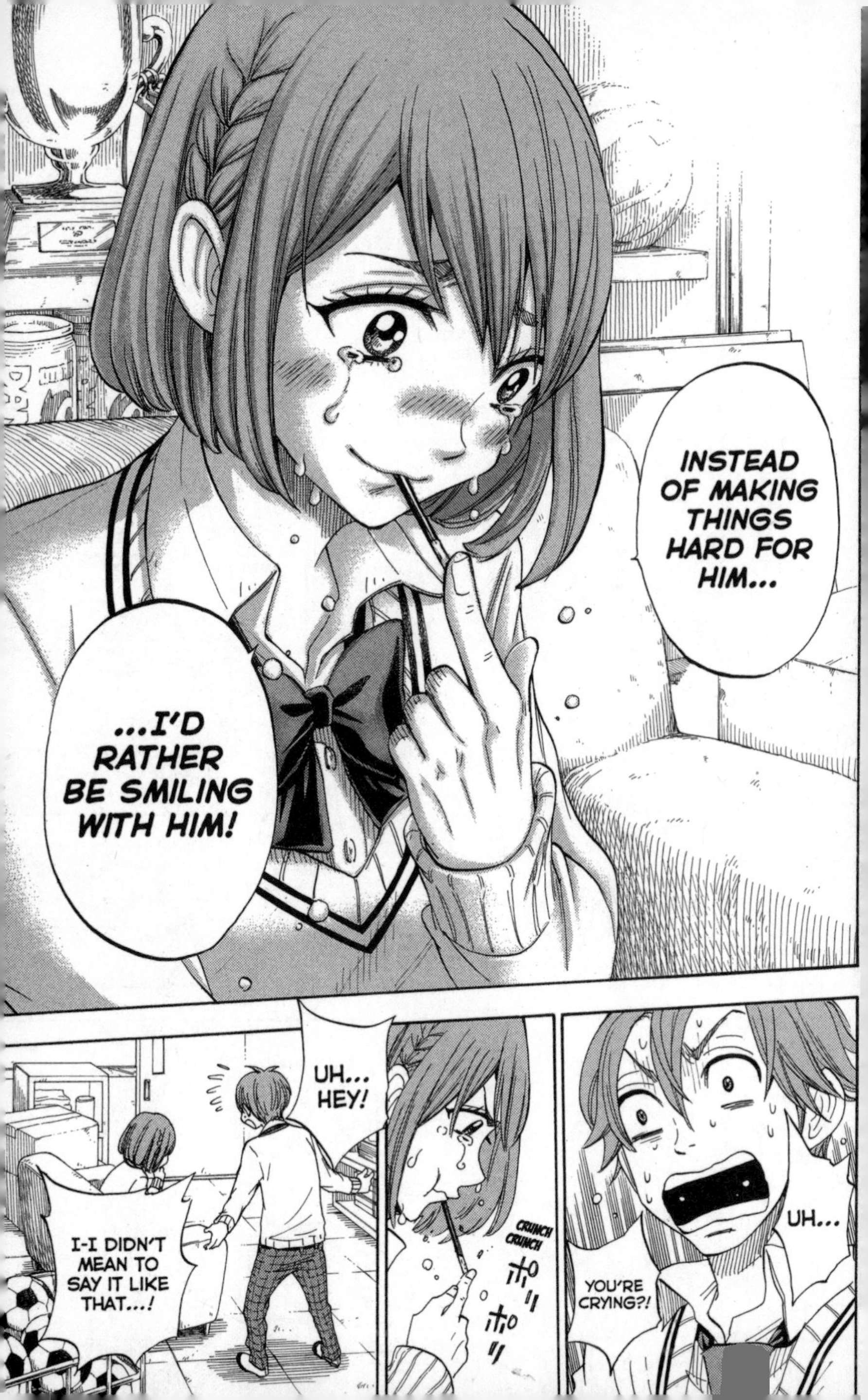
INSTEAD OF MAKING THINGS HARD FOR HIM...
...I'D RATHER BE SMILING WITH HIM!
UH...
YOU'RE CRYING?!
CRUNCH CRUNCH
UH... HEY!
I-I DIDN'T MEAN TO SAY IT LIKE THAT...!

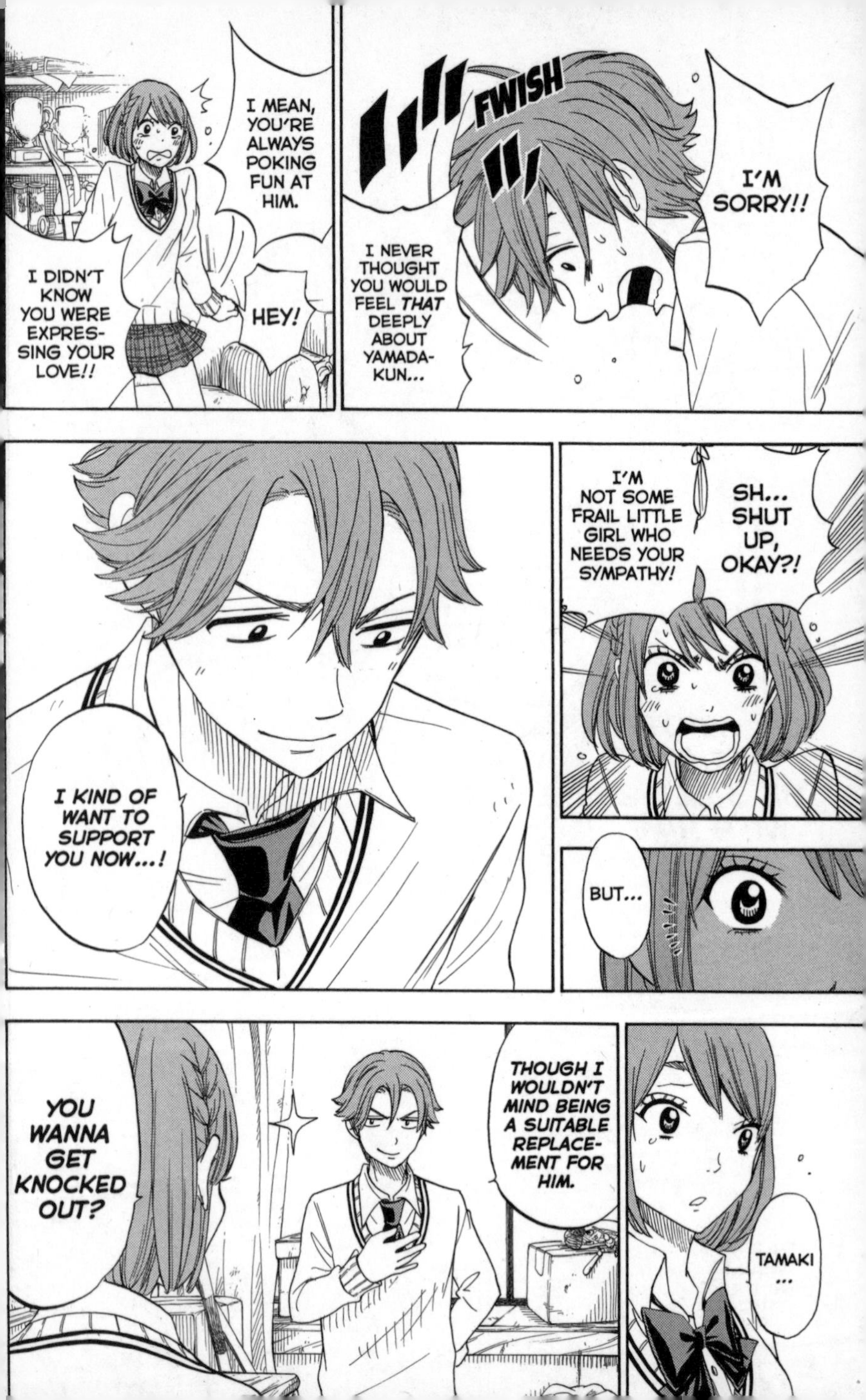
I'M SORRY!!
FWISH
I NEVER THOUGHT YOU WOULD FEEL *THAT* DEEPLY ABOUT YAMADA-KUN...
I MEAN, YOU'RE ALWAYS POKING FUN AT HIM.
HEY!
I DIDN'T KNOW YOU WERE EXPRESSING YOUR LOVE!!
SH... SHUT UP, OKAY?!
I'M NOT SOME FRAIL LITTLE GIRL WHO NEEDS YOUR SYMPATHY!
BUT...
I KIND OF WANT TO SUPPORT YOU NOW...!
TAMAKI ...
THOUGH I WOULDN'T MIND BEING A SUITABLE REPLACEMENT FOR HIM.
YOU WANNA GET KNOCKED OUT?

CHAPTER 78: Always inferior.

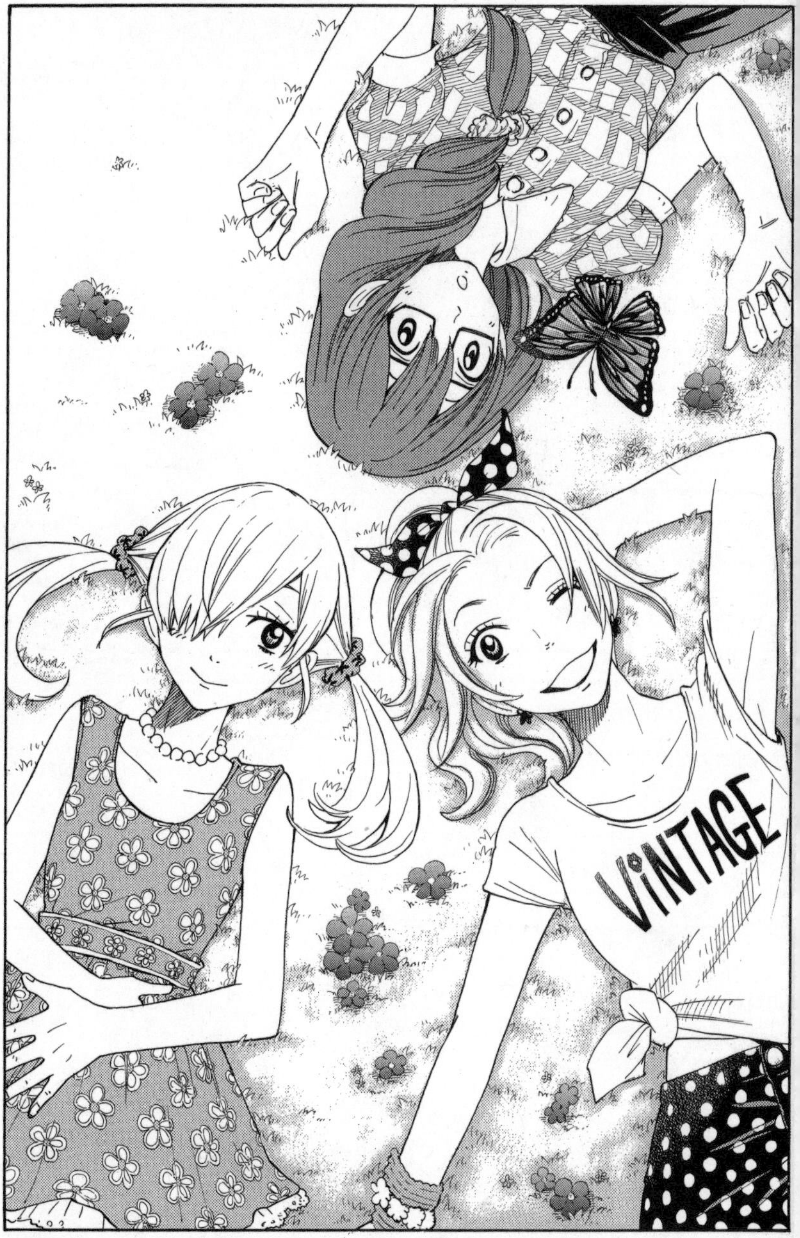
VINTAGE

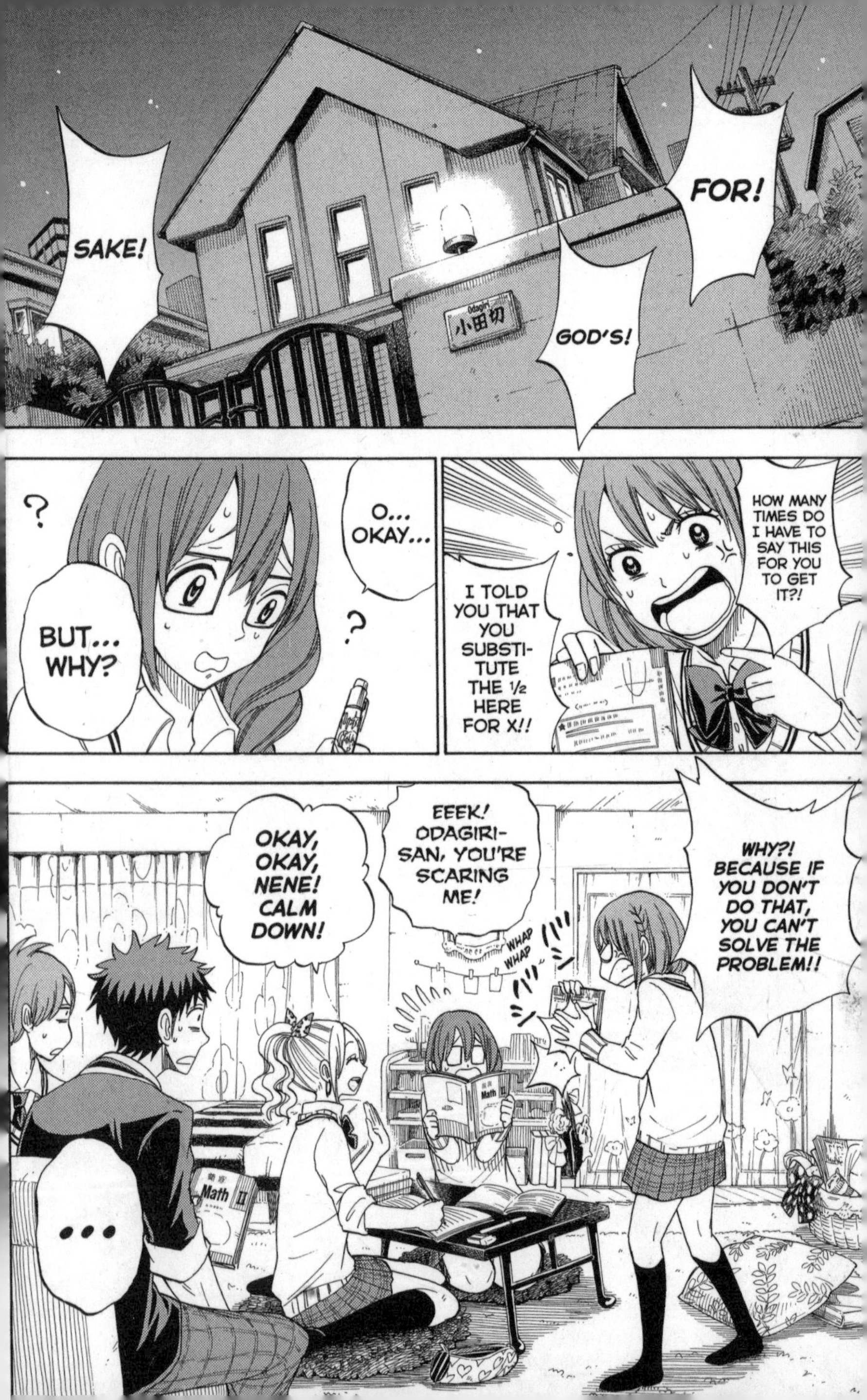
FOR!
GOD'S!
Odagiri
小田切
SAKE!
HOW MANY TIMES DO I HAVE TO SAY THIS FOR YOU TO GET IT?!
I TOLD YOU THAT YOU SUBSTITUTE THE 1/2 HERE FOR X!!
O... OKAY...
BUT... WHY?
WHY?! BECAUSE IF YOU DON'T DO THAT, YOU CAN'T SOLVE THE PROBLEM!!
WHAP WHAP
EEEK! ODAGIRI-SAN, YOU'RE SCARING ME!
Math II
OKAY, OKAY, NENE! CALM DOWN!
Math II
...

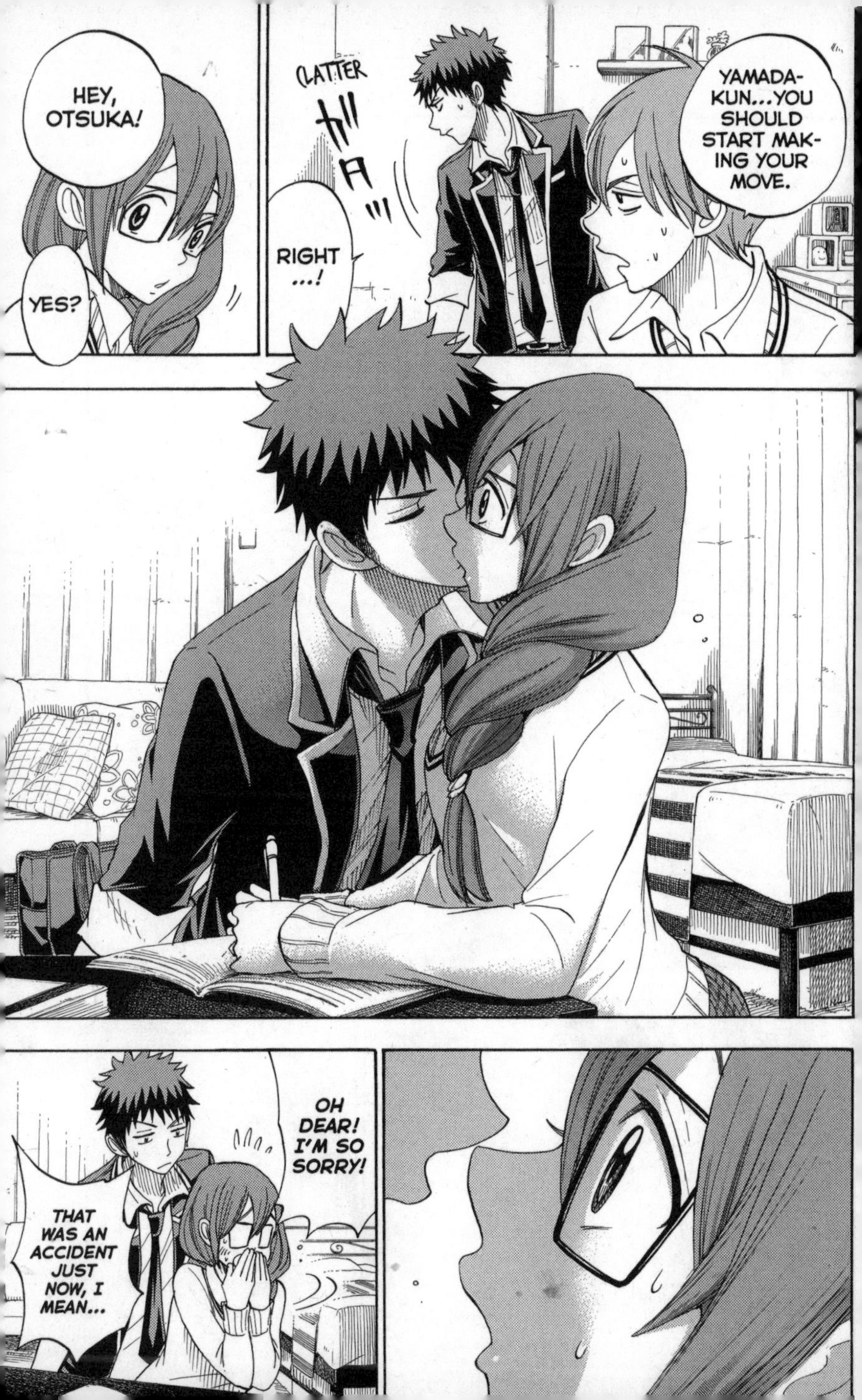
YAMADA-KUN...YOU SHOULD START MAK-ING YOUR MOVE.
CLATTER
RIGHT ...!
HEY, OTSUKA!
YES?
OH DEAR! I'M SO SORRY!
THAT WAS AN ACCIDENT JUST NOW, I MEAN...

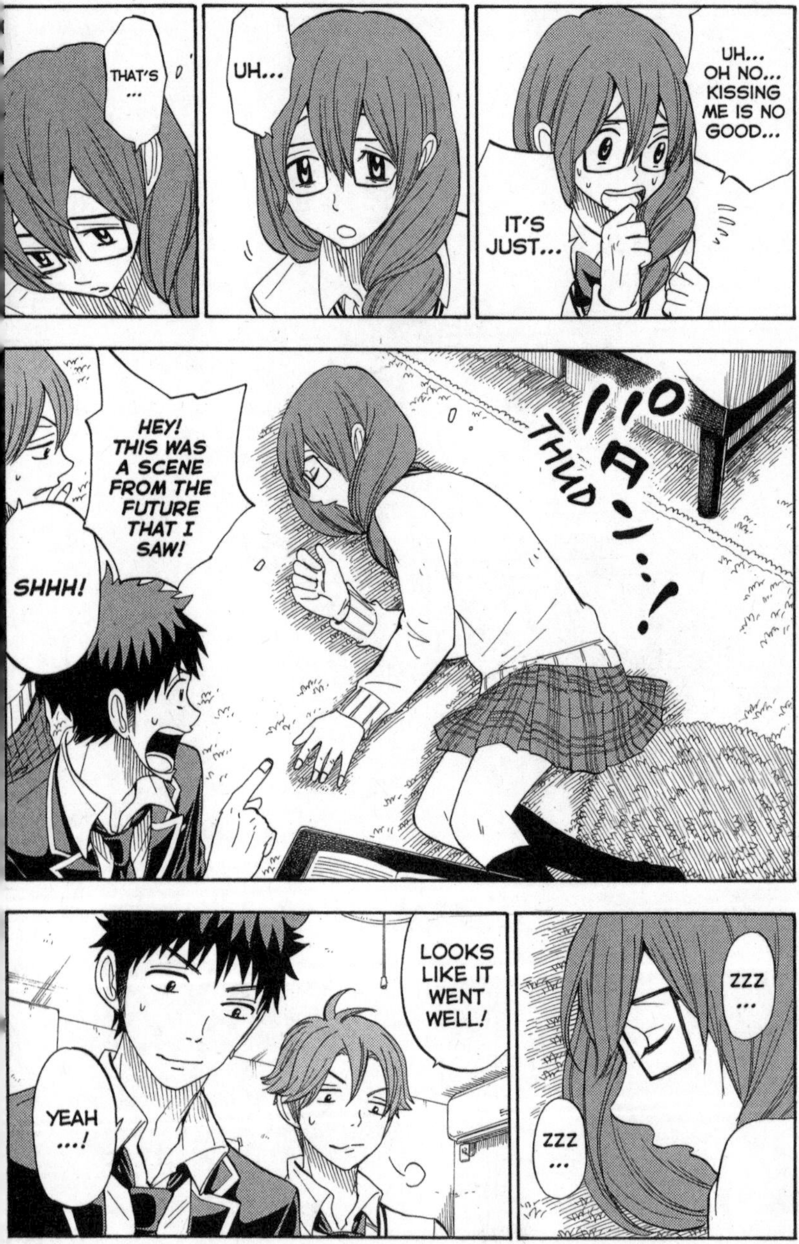

UH... OH NO... KISSING ME IS NO GOOD...
IT'S JUST...
UH...
THAT'S ...
THUD
HEY! THIS WAS A SCENE FROM THE FUTURE THAT I SAW!
SHHH!
ZZZ ...
ZZZ ...
LOOKS LIKE IT WENT WELL!
YEAH ...!

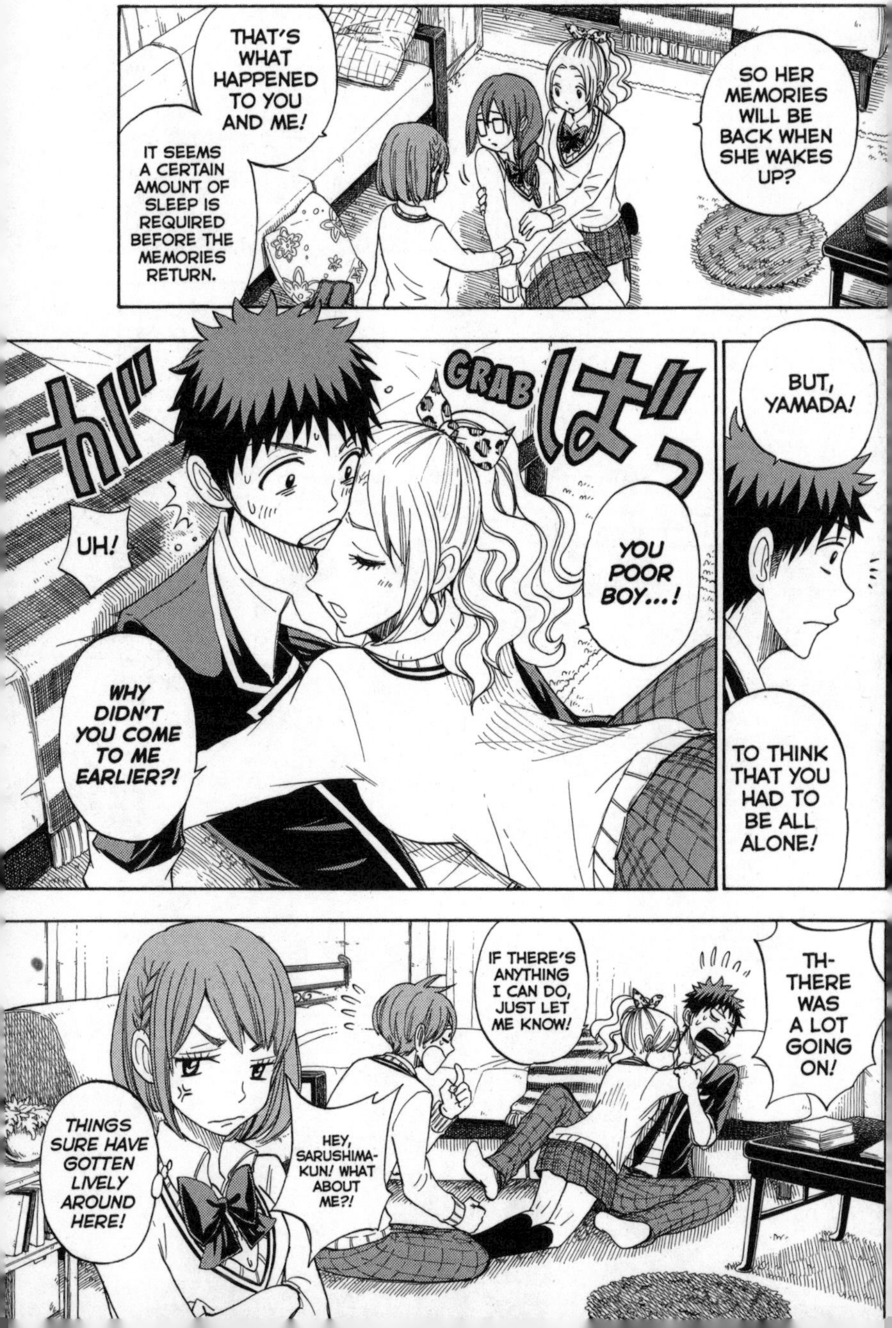
SO HER MEMORIES WILL BE BACK WHEN SHE WAKES UP?
THAT'S WHAT HAPPENED TO YOU AND ME!
IT SEEMS A CERTAIN AMOUNT OF SLEEP IS REQUIRED BEFORE THE MEMORIES RETURN.
BUT, YAMADA!
TO THINK THAT YOU HAD TO BE ALL ALONE!
GRAB
ばっ
YOU POOR BOY...!
UH!
WHY DIDN'T YOU COME TO ME EARLIER?!
が
TH- THERE WAS A LOT GOING ON!
IF THERE'S ANYTHING I CAN DO, JUST LET ME KNOW!
HEY, SARUSHIMA-KUN! WHAT ABOUT ME?!
THINGS SURE HAVE GOTTEN LIVELY AROUND HERE!

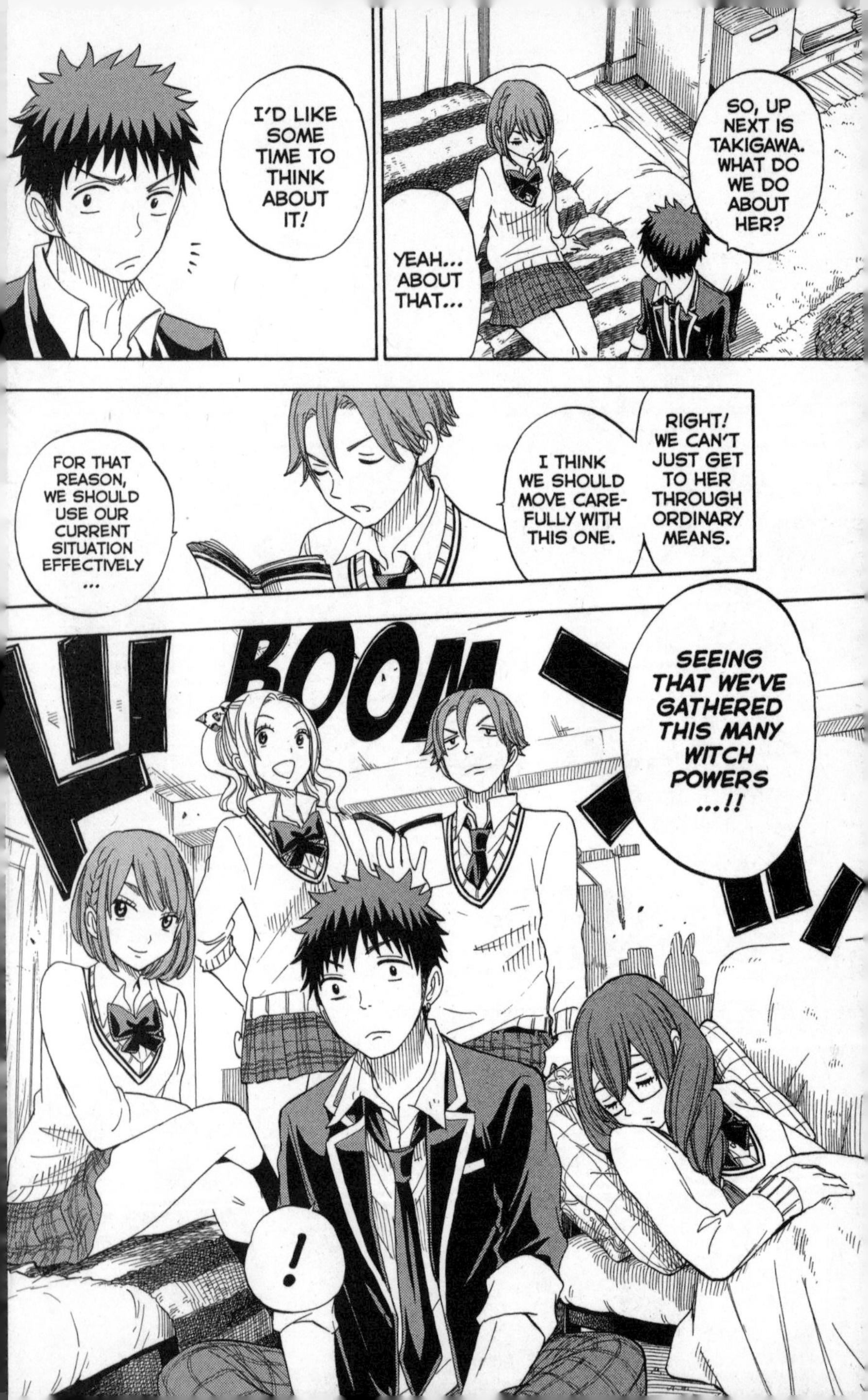
SO, UP NEXT IS TAKIGAWA. WHAT DO WE DO ABOUT HER?
YEAH... ABOUT THAT...
I'D LIKE SOME TIME TO THINK ABOUT IT!
RIGHT! WE CAN'T JUST GET TO HER THROUGH ORDINARY MEANS.
I THINK WE SHOULD MOVE CARE-FULLY WITH THIS ONE.
FOR THAT REASON, WE SHOULD USE OUR CURRENT SITUATION EFFECTIVELY...
SEEING THAT WE'VE GATHERED THIS MANY WITCH POWERS...!!
BOOM
!

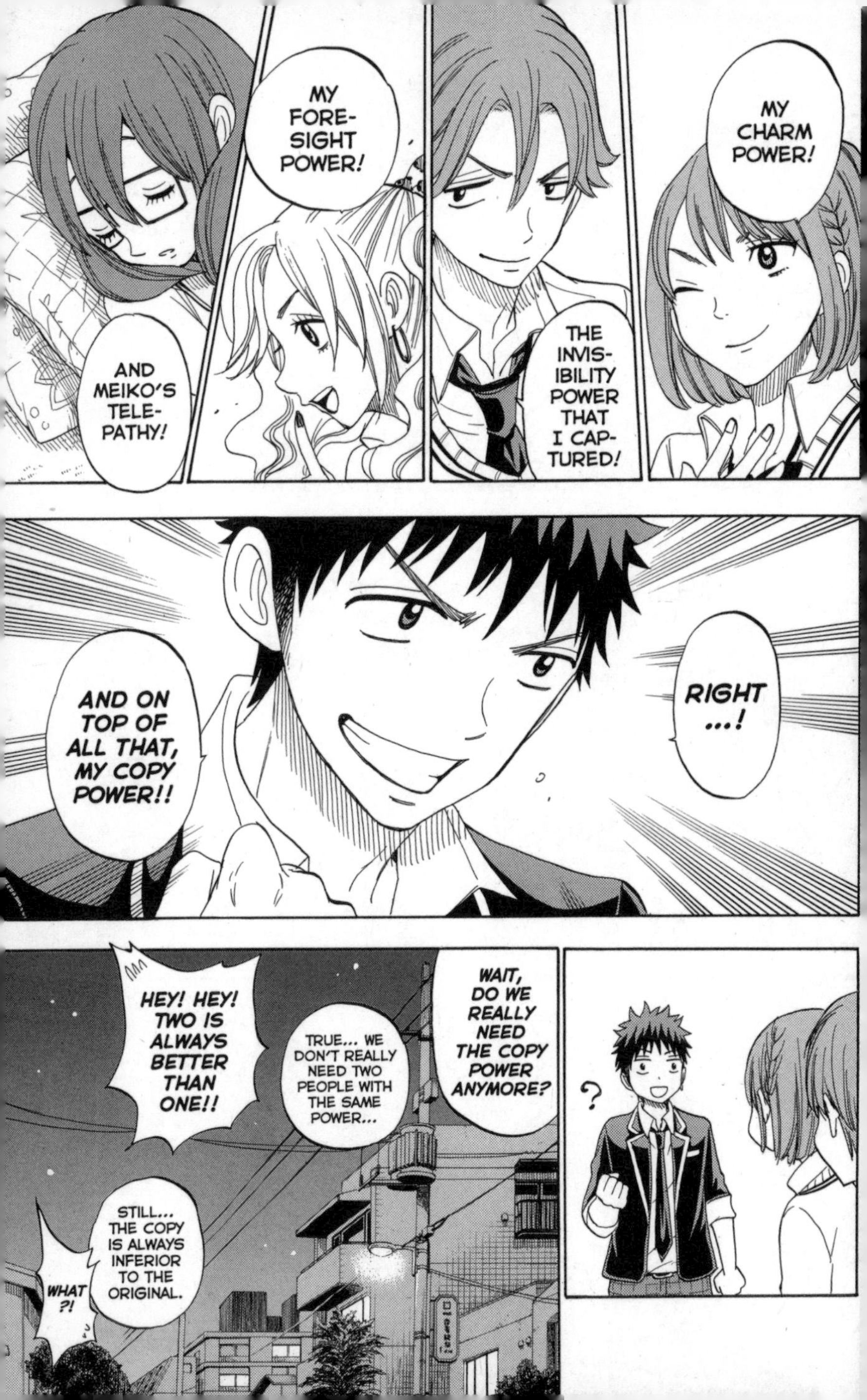
MY CHARM POWER!
THE INVISIBILITY POWER THAT I CAPTURED!
MY FORESIGHT POWER!
AND MEIKO'S TELEPATHY!
RIGHT ...!
AND ON TOP OF ALL THAT, MY COPY POWER!!
?
WAIT, DO WE REALLY NEED THE COPY POWER ANYMORE?
TRUE... WE DON'T REALLY NEED TWO PEOPLE WITH THE SAME POWER...
HEY! HEY! TWO IS ALWAYS BETTER THAN ONE!!
STILL... THE COPY IS ALWAYS INFERIOR TO THE ORIGINAL.
WHAT ?!

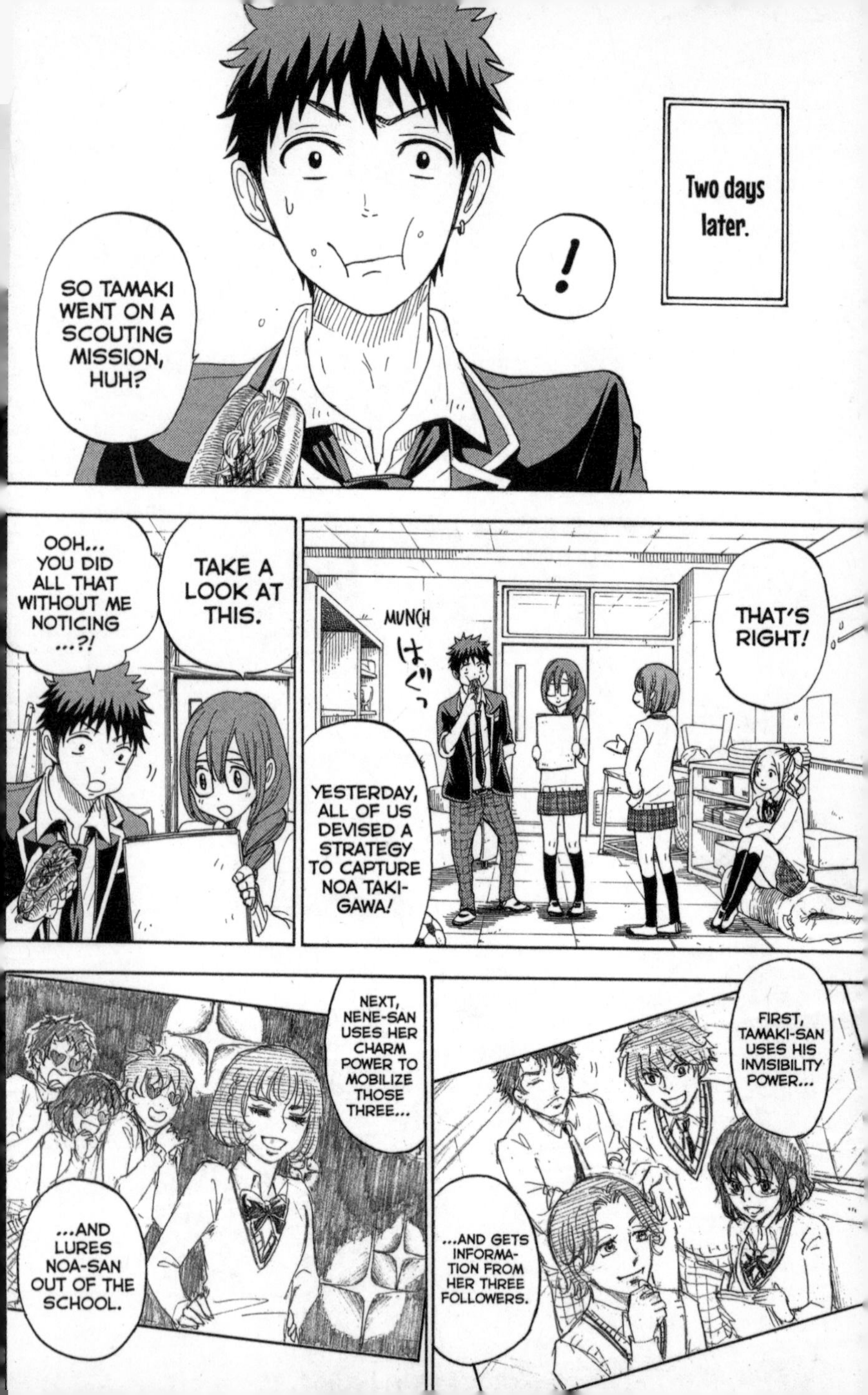
Two days later.
!
SO TAMAKI WENT ON A SCOUTING MISSION, HUH?
THAT'S RIGHT!
MUNCH
はぐっ
YESTERDAY, ALL OF US DEVISED A STRATEGY TO CAPTURE NOA TAKI-GAWA!
TAKE A LOOK AT THIS.
OOH... YOU DID ALL THAT WITHOUT ME NOTICING ...?!
FIRST, TAMAKI-SAN USES HIS INVISIBILITY POWER...
...AND GETS INFORMA-TION FROM HER THREE FOLLOWERS.
NEXT, NENE-SAN USES HER CHARM POWER TO MOBILIZE THOSE THREE...
...AND LURES NOA-SAN OUT OF THE SCHOOL.

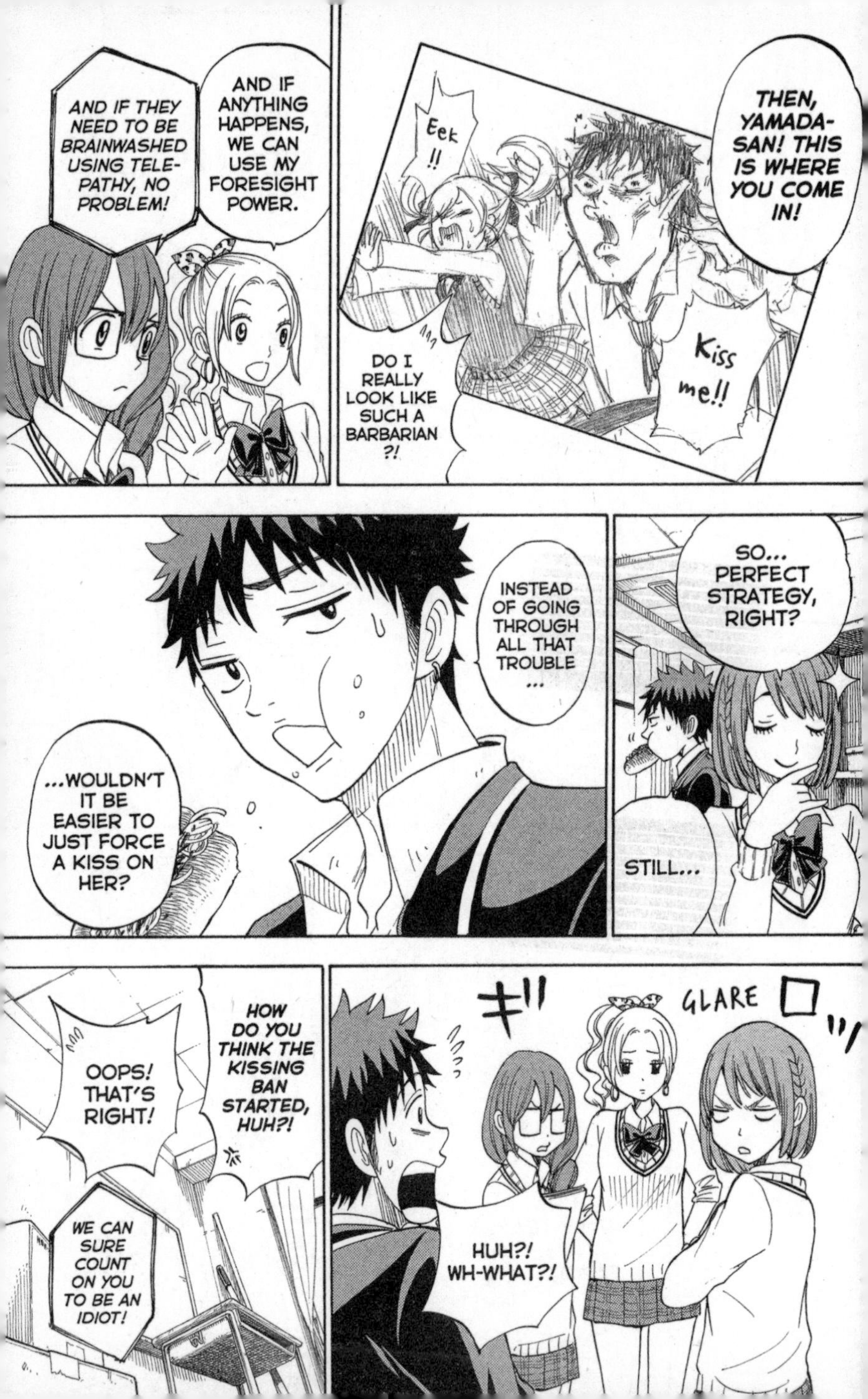
THEN, YAMADA-SAN! THIS IS WHERE YOU COME IN!
Kiss me!!
Eek !!
DO I REALLY LOOK LIKE SUCH A BARBARIAN?!
AND IF ANYTHING HAPPENS, WE CAN USE MY FORESIGHT POWER.
AND IF THEY NEED TO BE BRAINWASHED USING TELEPATHY, NO PROBLEM!
SO... PERFECT STRATEGY, RIGHT?
STILL...
INSTEAD OF GOING THROUGH ALL THAT TROUBLE...
...WOULDN'T IT BE EASIER TO JUST FORCE A KISS ON HER?
ギリ
GLARE
HUH?! WH-WHAT?!
HOW DO YOU THINK THE KISSING BAN STARTED, HUH?!
OOPS! THAT'S RIGHT!
WE CAN SURE COUNT ON YOU TO BE AN IDIOT!

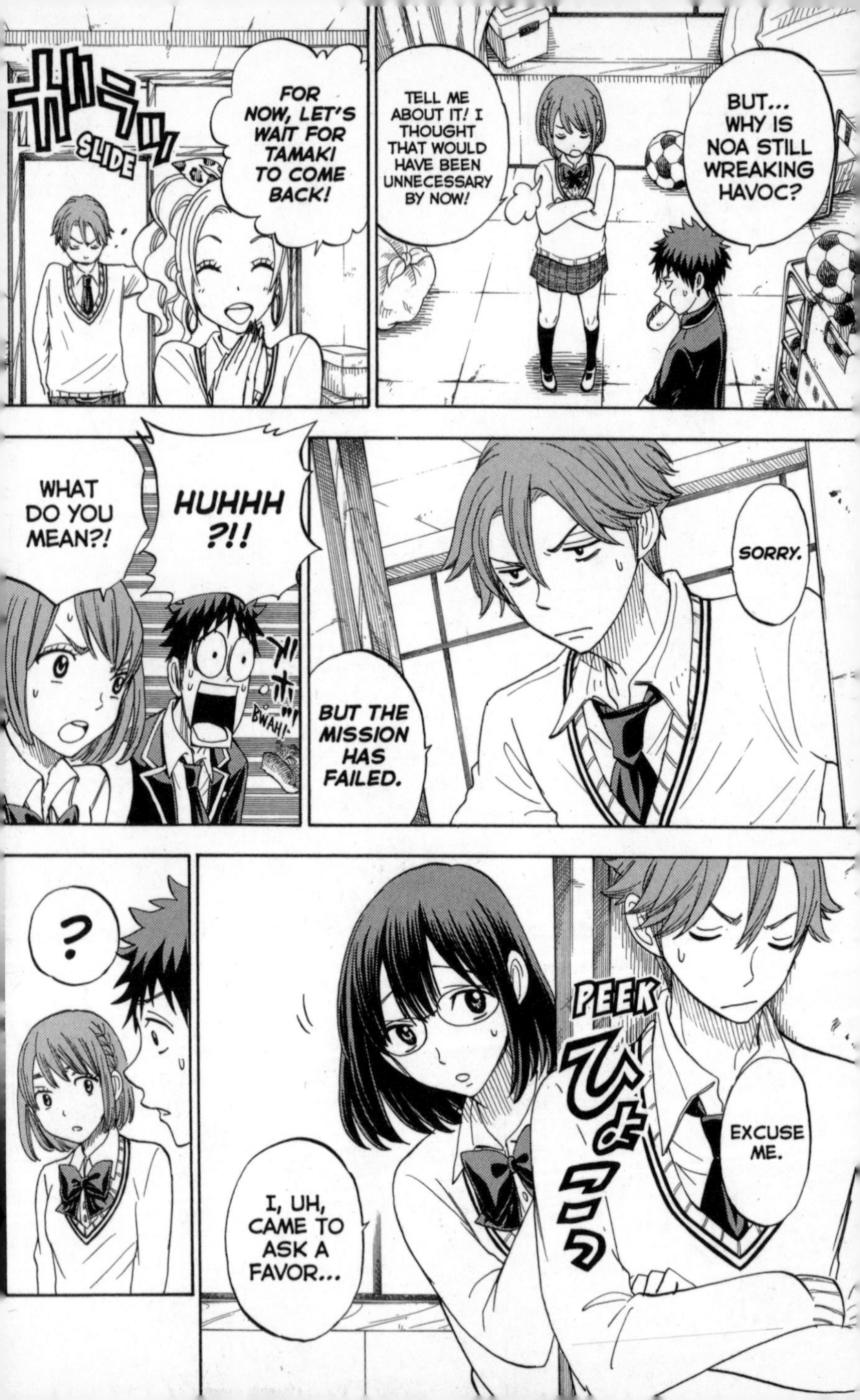
BUT... WHY IS NOA STILL WREAKING HAVOC?
TELL ME ABOUT IT! I THOUGHT THAT WOULD HAVE BEEN UNNECESSARY BY NOW!
FOR NOW, LET'S WAIT FOR TAMAKI TO COME BACK!
SLIDE
SORRY.
BUT THE MISSION HAS FAILED.
HUHHH ?!!
BWAH!
WHAT DO YOU MEAN?!
EXCUSE ME.
PEEK
ひょこっ
I, UH, CAME TO ASK A FAVOR...
?

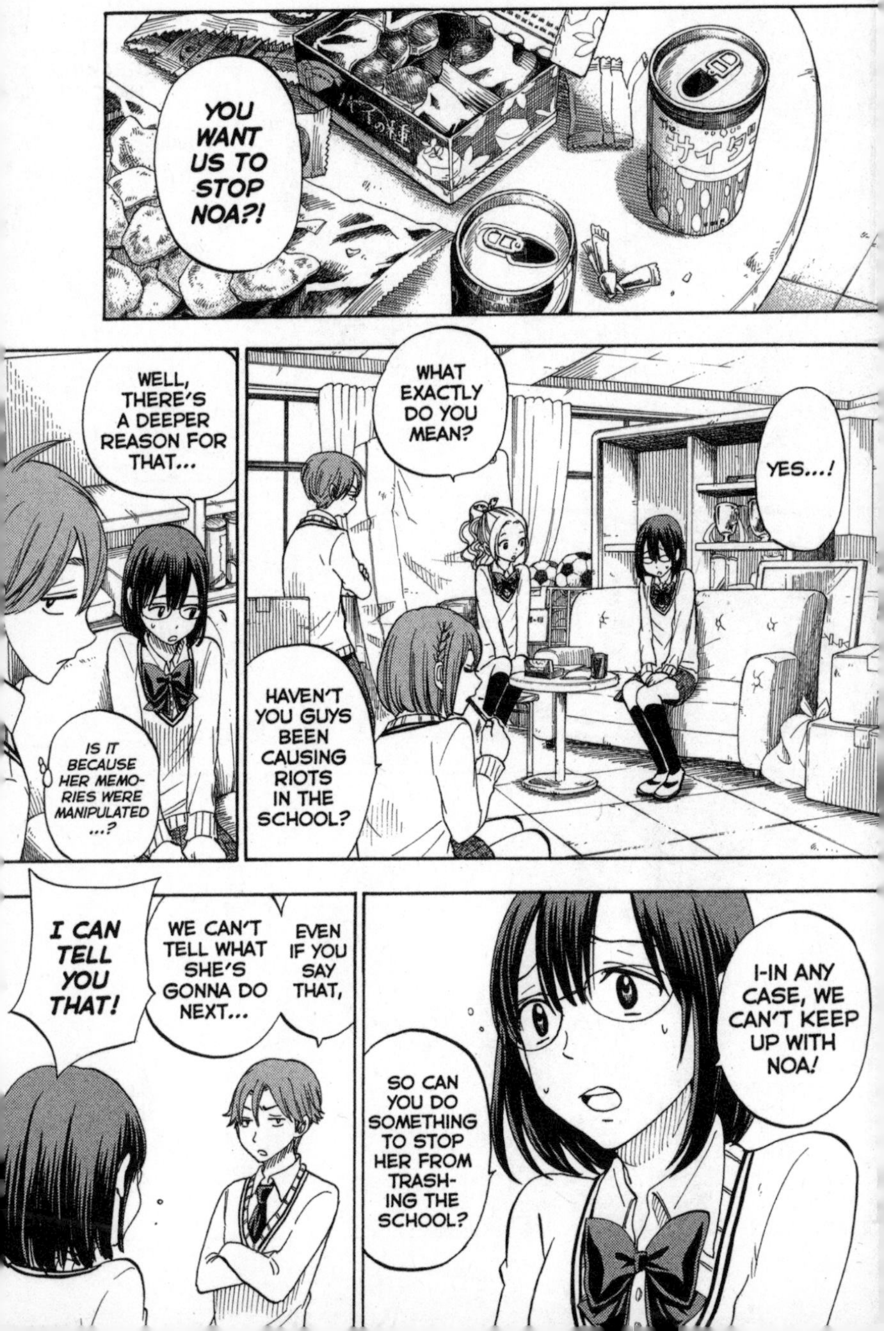
YOU WANT US TO STOP NOA?!
YES...!
WHAT EXACTLY DO YOU MEAN?
HAVEN'T YOU GUYS BEEN CAUSING RIOTS IN THE SCHOOL?
WELL, THERE'S A DEEPER REASON FOR THAT...
IS IT BECAUSE HER MEMORIES WERE MANIPULATED ...?
I-IN ANY CASE, WE CAN'T KEEP UP WITH NOA!
SO CAN YOU DO SOMETHING TO STOP HER FROM TRASHING THE SCHOOL?
EVEN IF YOU SAY THAT,
WE CAN'T TELL WHAT SHE'S GONNA DO NEXT...
I CAN TELL YOU THAT!

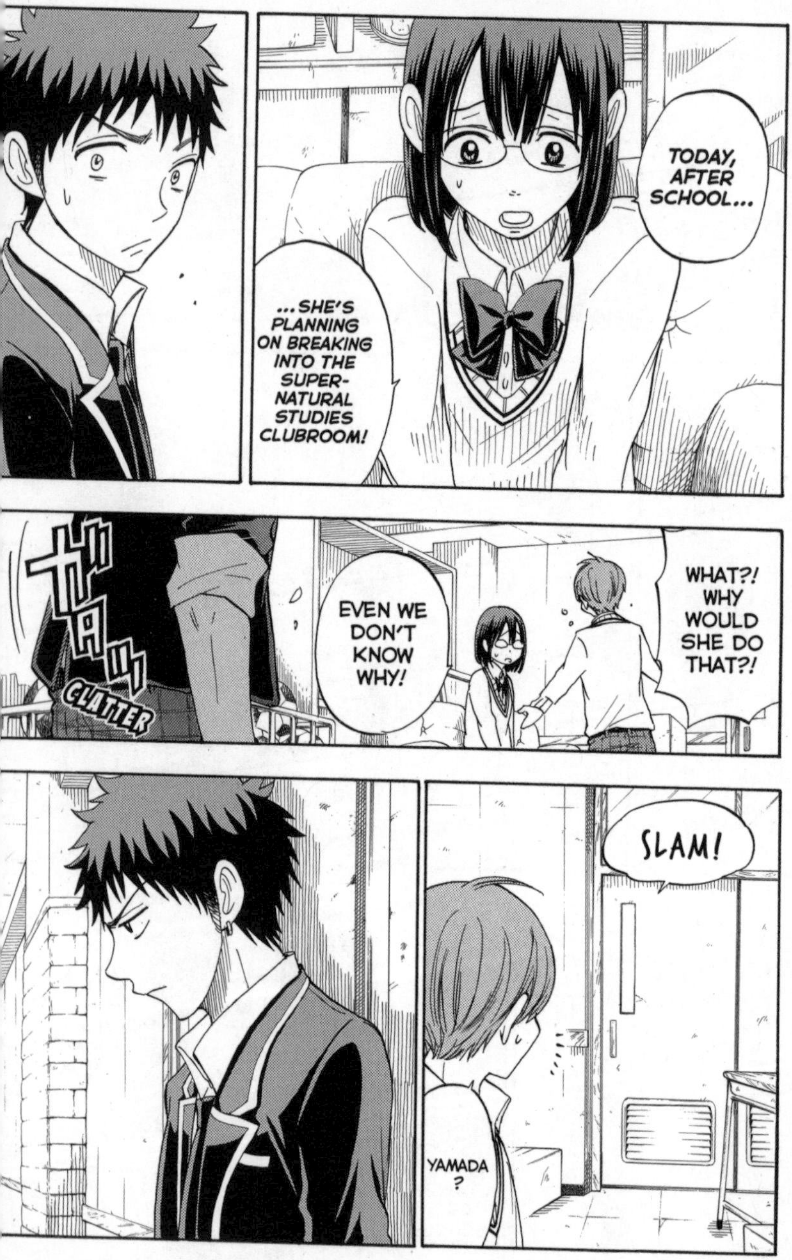
TODAY, AFTER SCHOOL...
...SHE'S PLANNING ON BREAKING INTO THE SUPER-NATURAL STUDIES CLUBROOM!
WHAT?! WHY WOULD SHE DO THAT?!
EVEN WE DON'T KNOW WHY!
CLATTER
SLAM!
YAMADA?

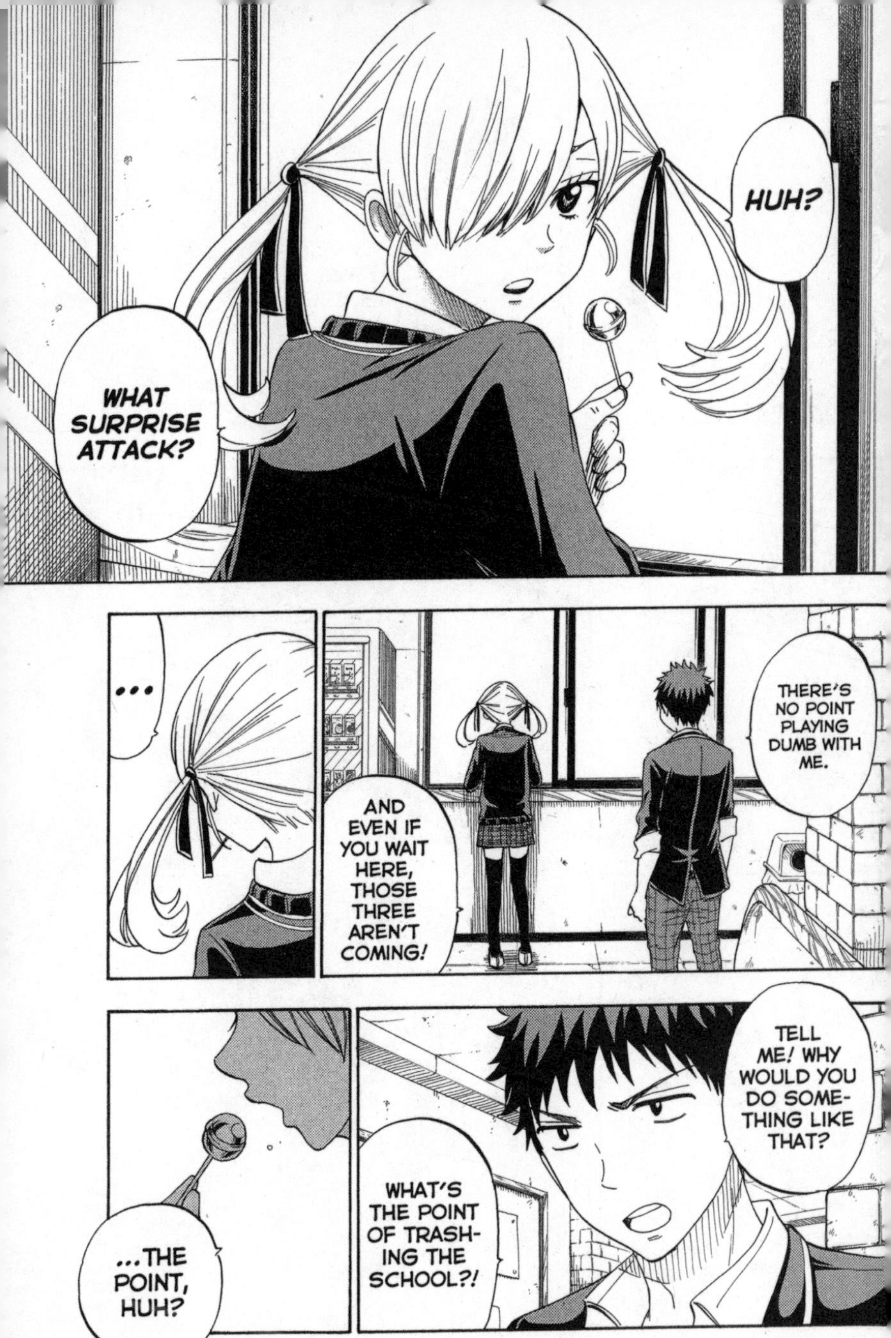
HUH?
WHAT SURPRISE ATTACK?
THERE'S NO POINT PLAYING DUMB WITH ME.
AND EVEN IF YOU WAIT HERE, THOSE THREE AREN'T COMING!
...
TELL ME! WHY WOULD YOU DO SOMETHING LIKE THAT?
WHAT'S THE POINT OF TRASHING THE SCHOOL?!
...THE POINT, HUH?

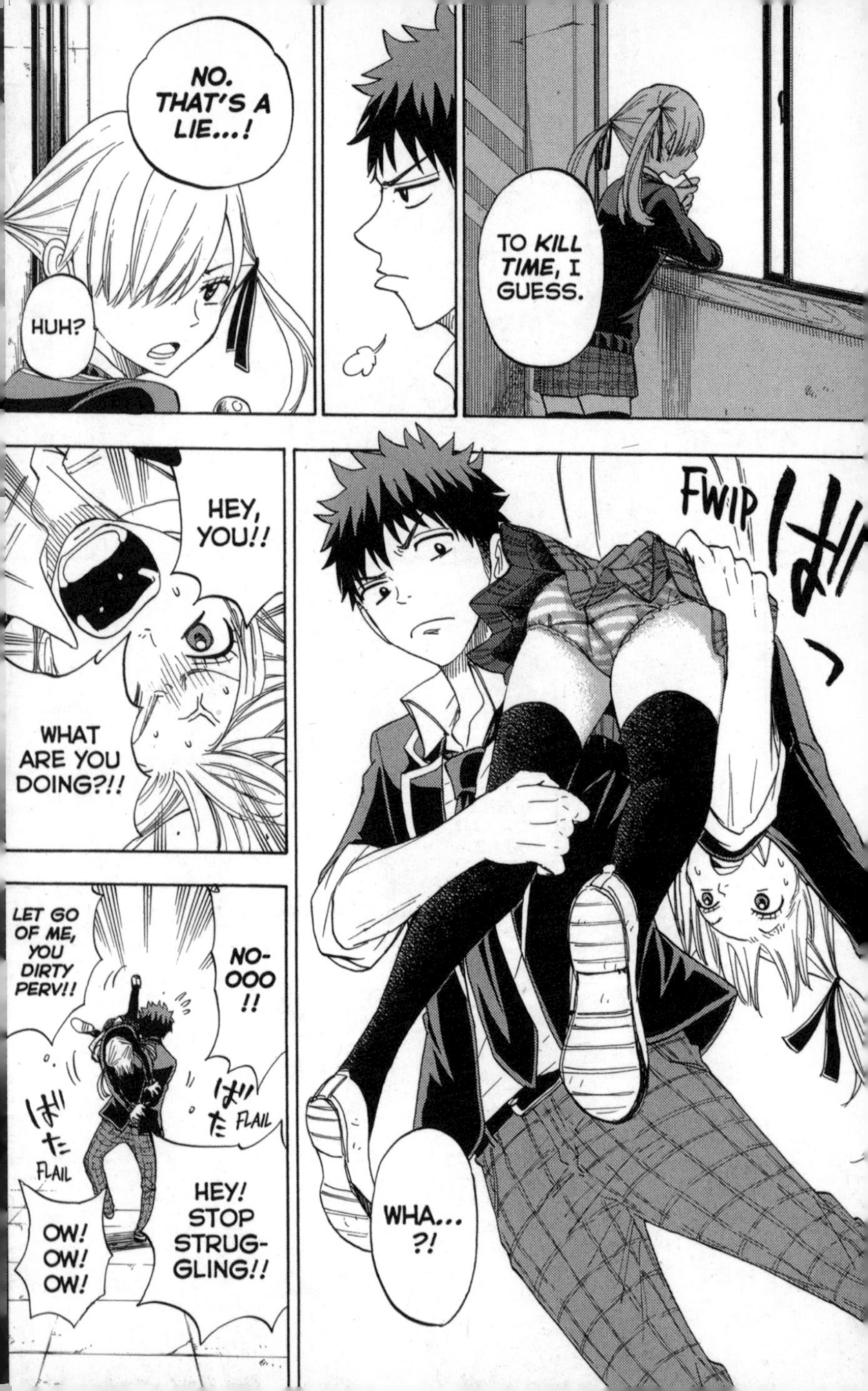
TO KILL TIME, I GUESS.
NO. THAT'S A LIE...!
HUH?
FWIP
WHA... ?!
HEY, YOU!!
WHAT ARE YOU DOING?!!
NO-OOO!!
LET GO OF ME, YOU DIRTY PERV!!
FLAIL
FLAIL
HEY! STOP STRUG-GLING!!
OW! OW! OW!

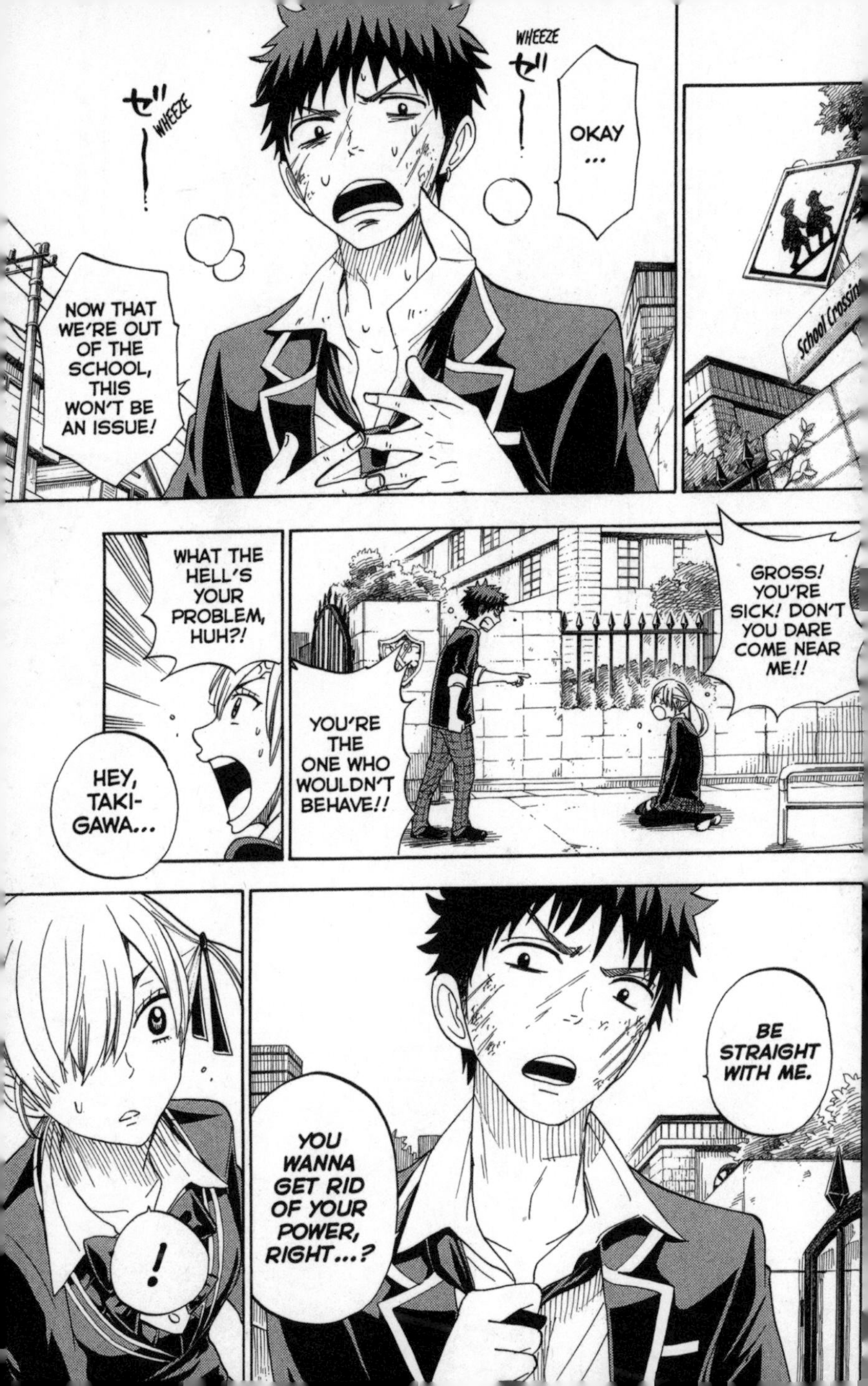
WHEEZE
ゼー
OKAY ...
ゼー
WHEEZE
NOW THAT WE'RE OUT OF THE SCHOOL, THIS WON'T BE AN ISSUE!
GROSS! YOU'RE SICK! DON'T YOU DARE COME NEAR ME!!
YOU'RE THE ONE WHO WOULDN'T BEHAVE!!
WHAT THE HELL'S YOUR PROBLEM, HUH?!
HEY, TAKI-GAWA...
BE STRAIGHT WITH ME.
YOU WANNA GET RID OF YOUR POWER, RIGHT...?
!

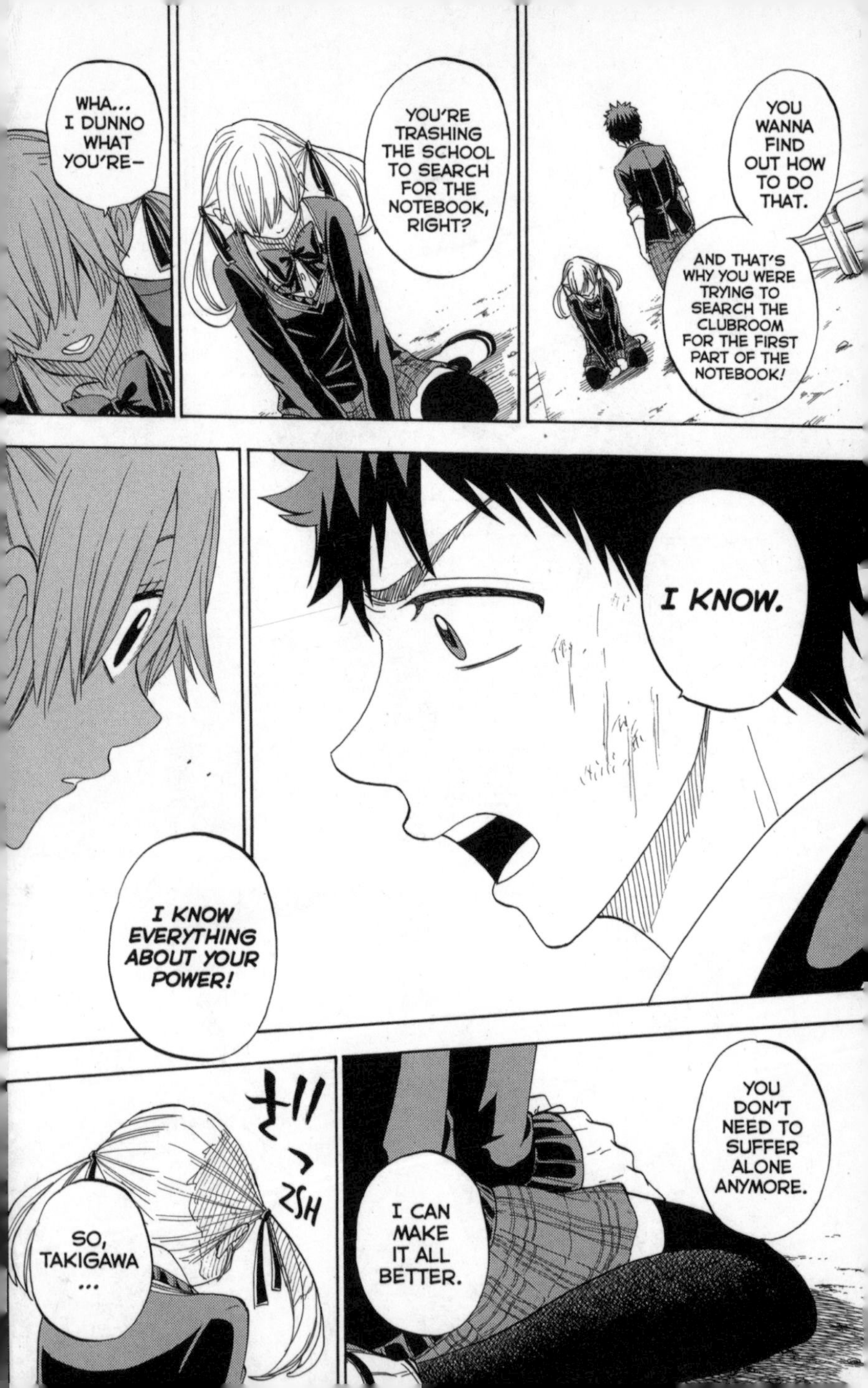
YOU WANNA FIND OUT HOW TO DO THAT.
AND THAT'S WHY YOU WERE TRYING TO SEARCH THE CLUBROOM FOR THE FIRST PART OF THE NOTEBOOK!
YOU'RE TRASHING THE SCHOOL TO SEARCH FOR THE NOTEBOOK, RIGHT?
WHA... I DUNNO WHAT YOU'RE–
I KNOW.
I KNOW EVERYTHING ABOUT YOUR POWER!
YOU DON'T NEED TO SUFFER ALONE ANYMORE.
I CAN MAKE IT ALL BETTER.
ZSH
SO, TAKIGAWA ...

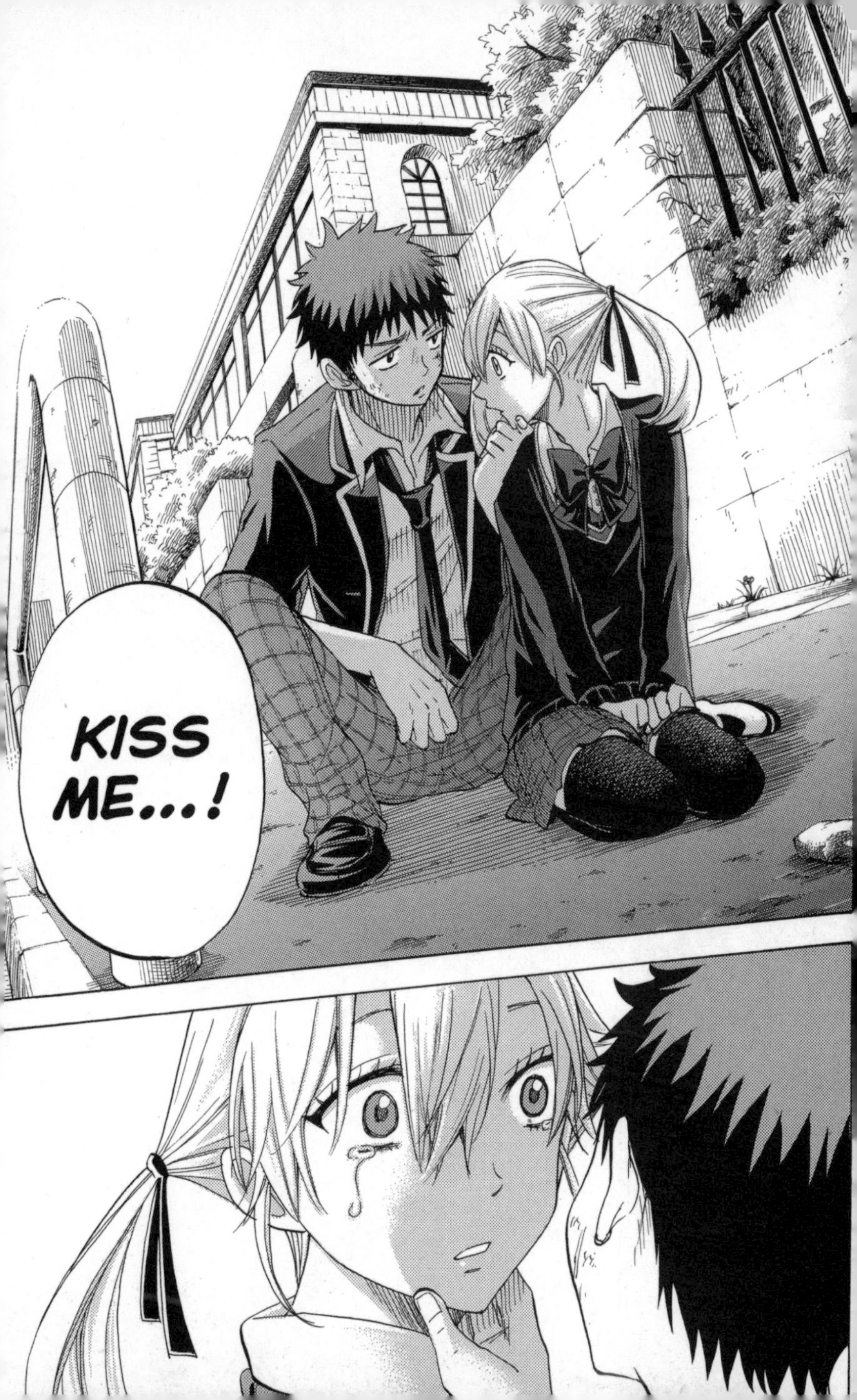
KISS ME...!

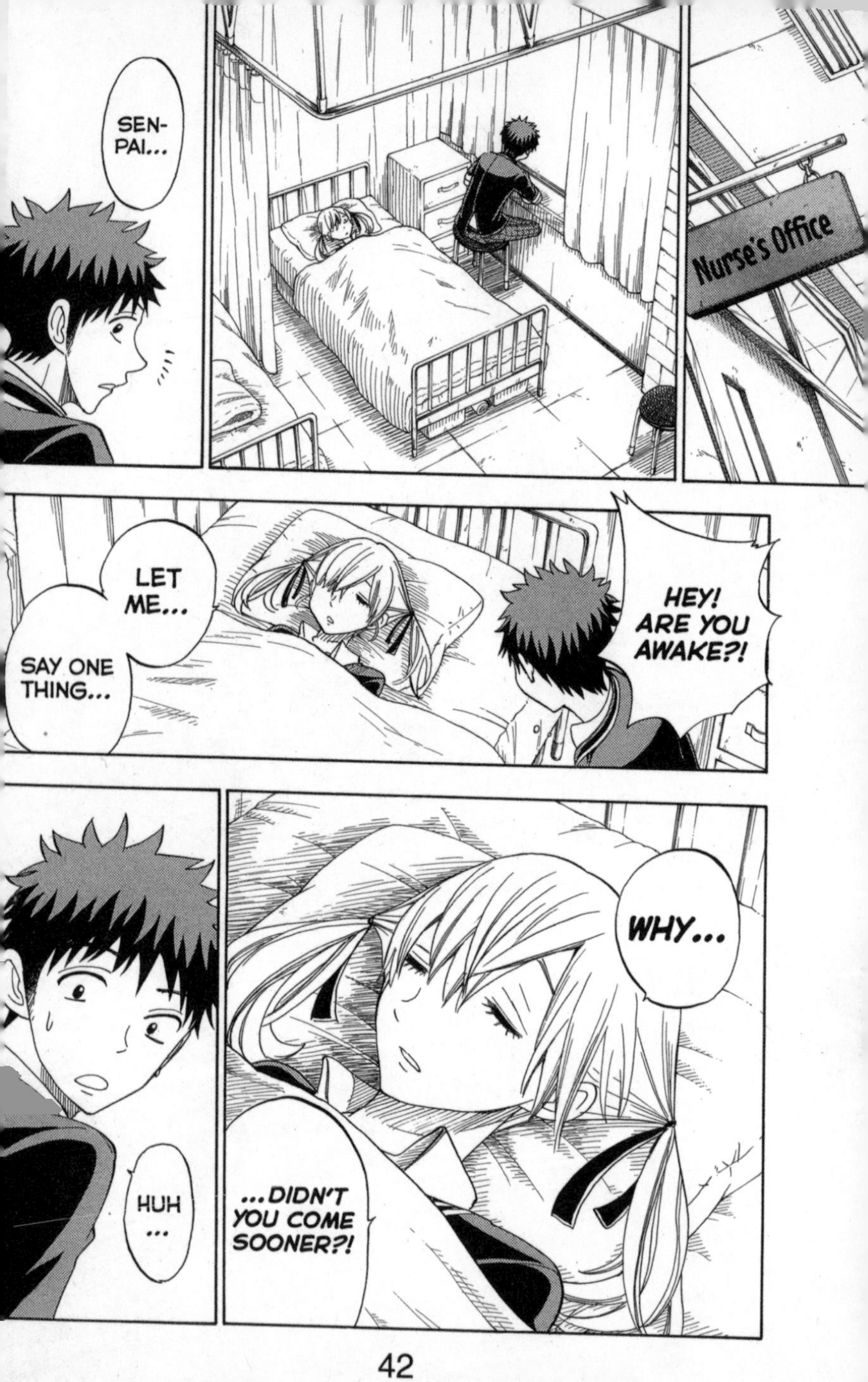
Nurse's Office
SEN-PAI...
HEY! ARE YOU AWAKE?!
LET ME...
SAY ONE THING...
WHY...
...DIDN'T YOU COME SOONER?!
HUH...

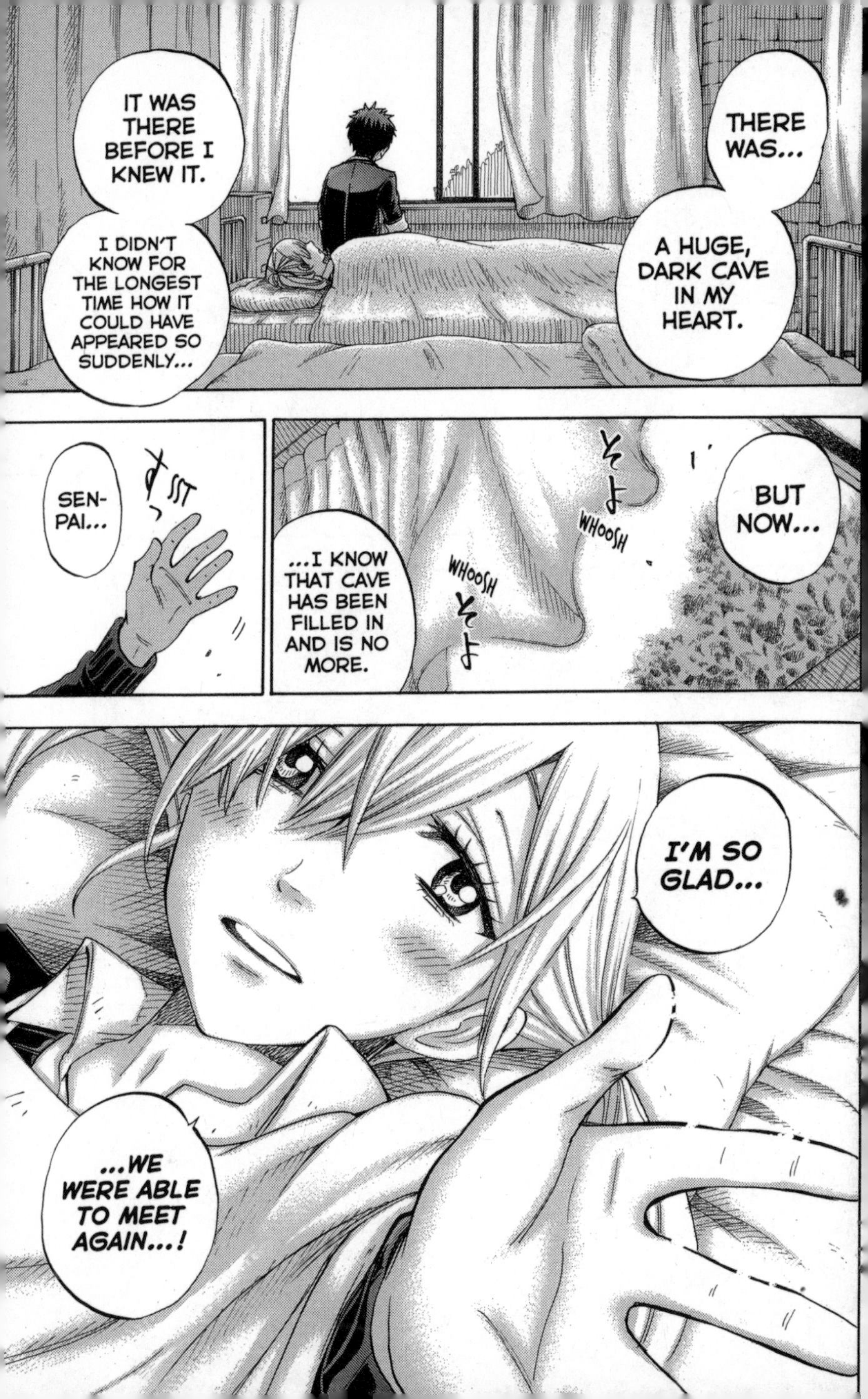
THERE WAS...
A HUGE, DARK CAVE IN MY HEART.
IT WAS THERE BEFORE I KNEW IT.
I DIDN'T KNOW FOR THE LONGEST TIME HOW IT COULD HAVE APPEARED SO SUDDENLY...
BUT NOW...
WHOOSH
WHOOSH
...I KNOW THAT CAVE HAS BEEN FILLED IN AND IS NO MORE.
SST
SEN-PAI...
I'M SO GLAD...
...WE WERE ABLE TO MEET AGAIN...!

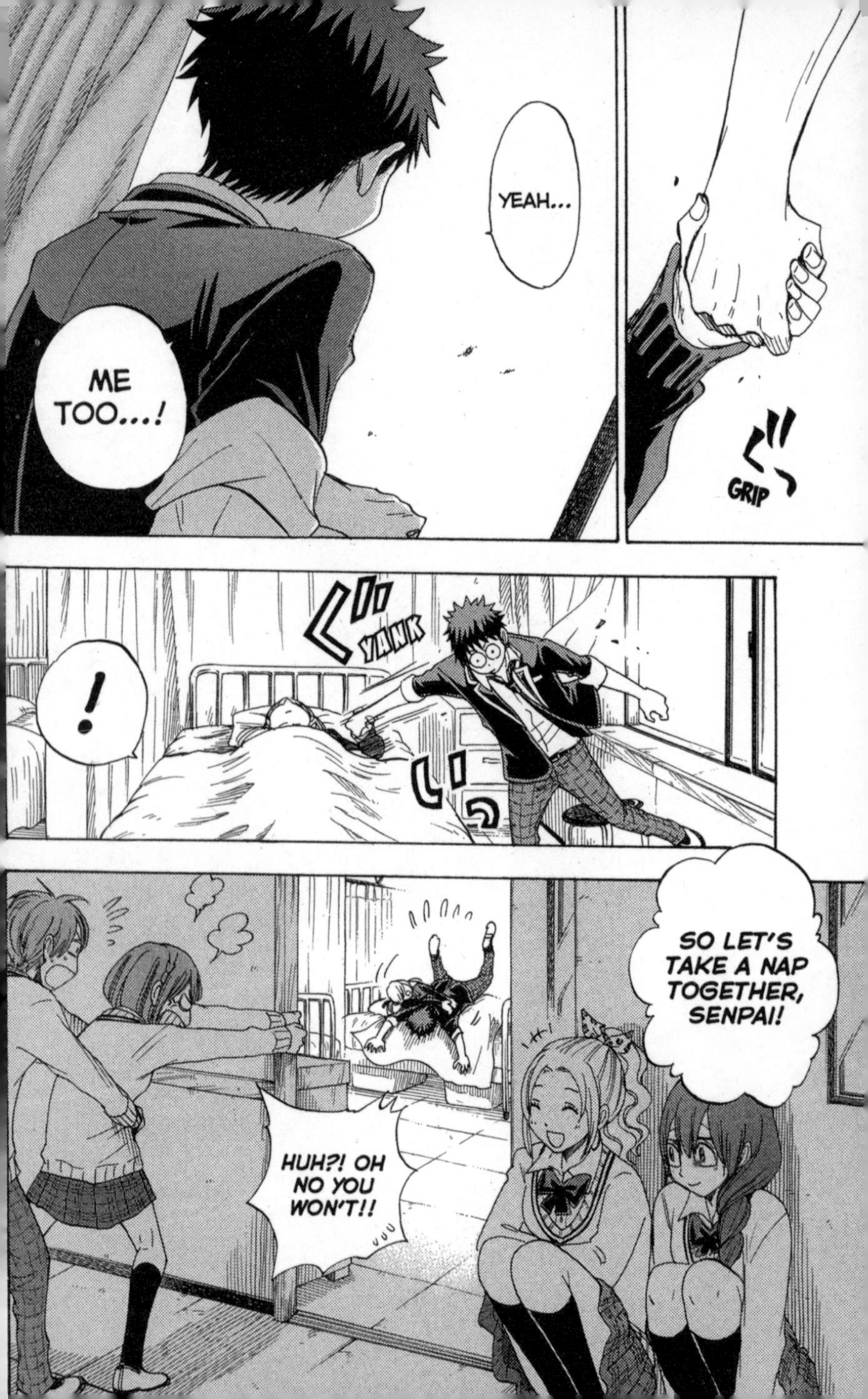
GRIP
YEAH...
ME TOO...!
YANK
!
SO LET'S TAKE A NAP TOGETHER, SENPAI!
HUH?! OH NO YOU WON'T!!

CHAPTER 79: I'm a hottie, aren't I?

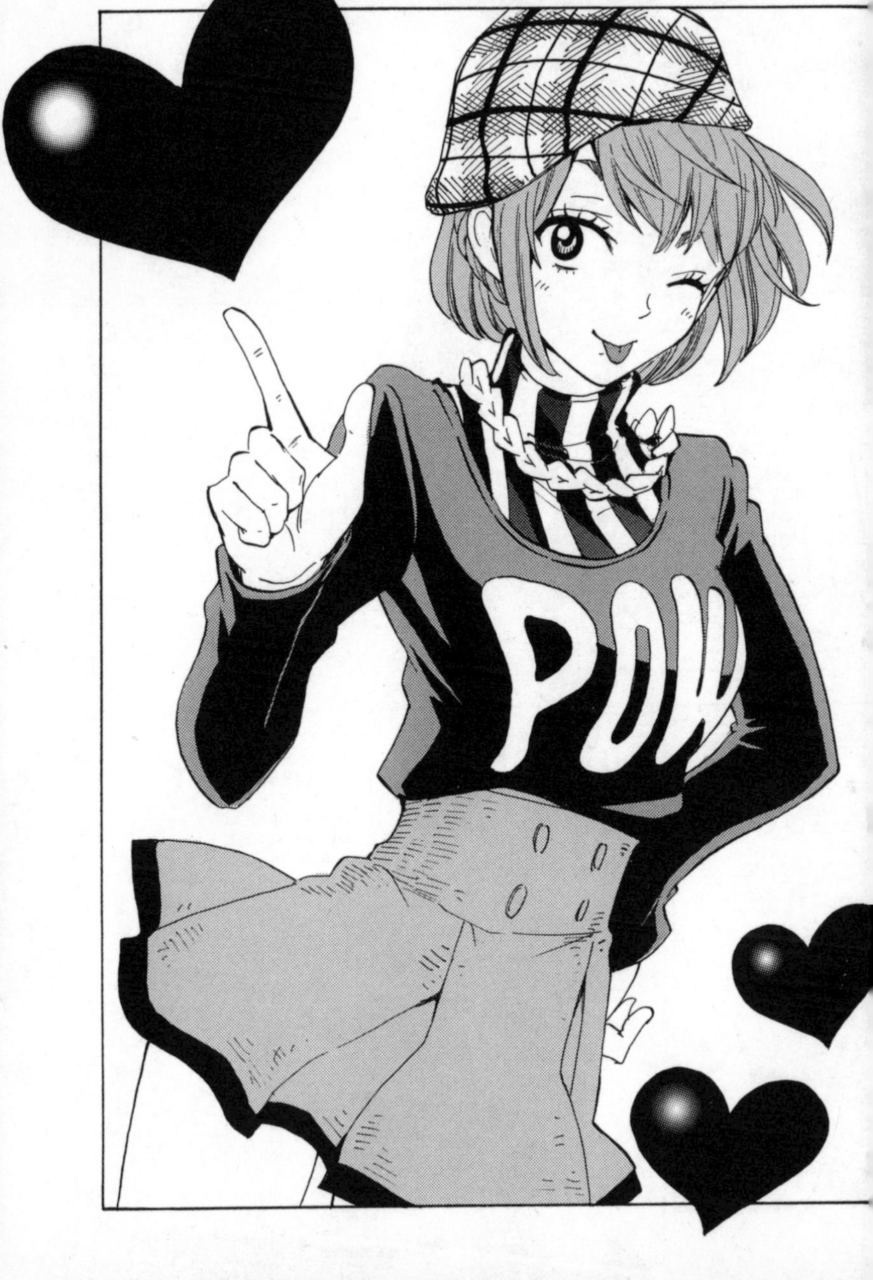
POW

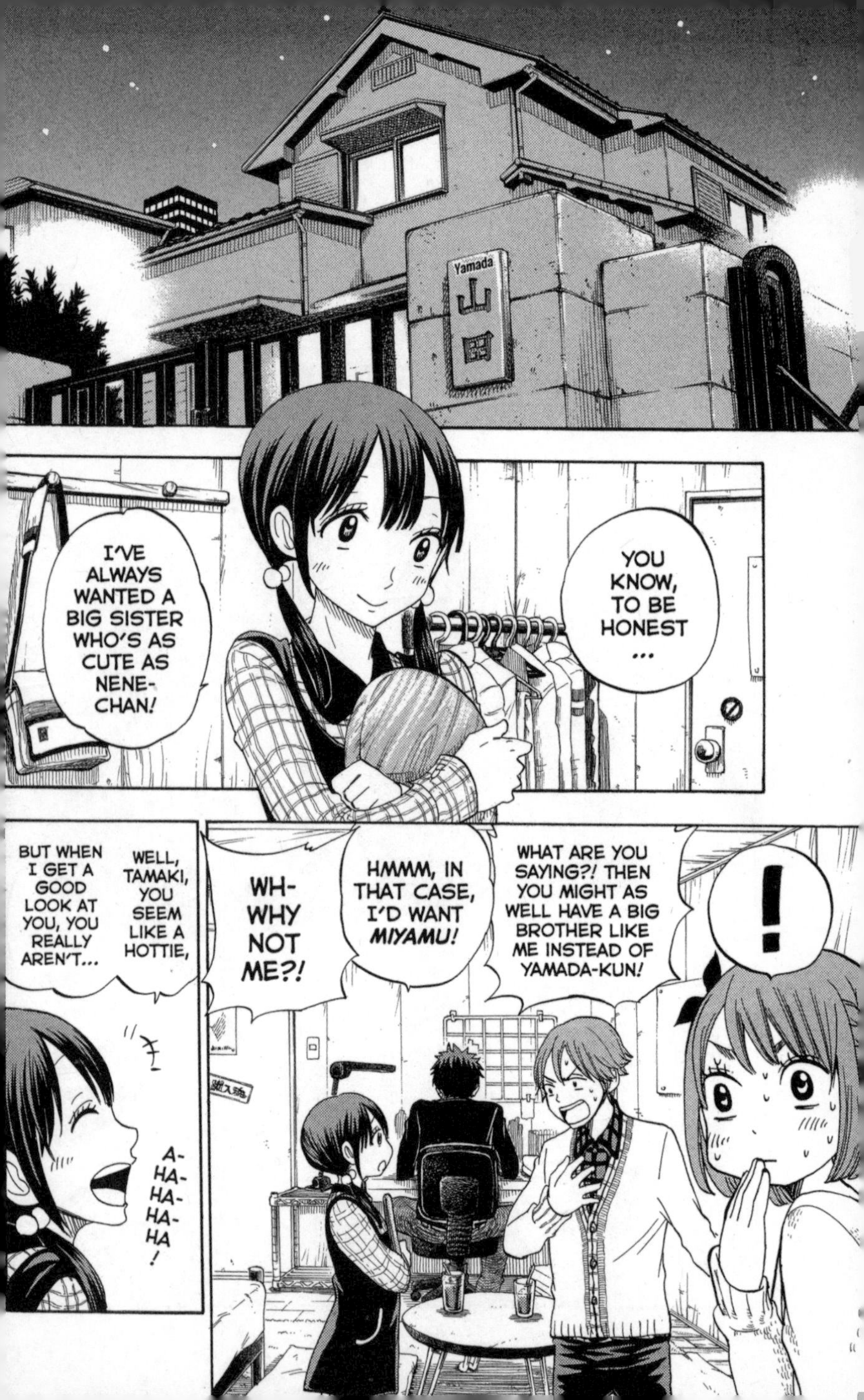
Yamada
YOU KNOW, TO BE HONEST...
I'VE ALWAYS WANTED A BIG SISTER WHO'S AS CUTE AS NENE-CHAN!
!
WHAT ARE YOU SAYING?! THEN YOU MIGHT AS WELL HAVE A BIG BROTHER LIKE ME INSTEAD OF YAMADA-KUN!
HMMM, IN THAT CASE, I'D WANT *MIYAMU*!
WH-WHY NOT ME?!
WELL, TAMAKI, YOU SEEM LIKE A HOTTIE,
BUT WHEN I GET A GOOD LOOK AT YOU, YOU REALLY AREN'T...
A-HA-HA-HA-HA!

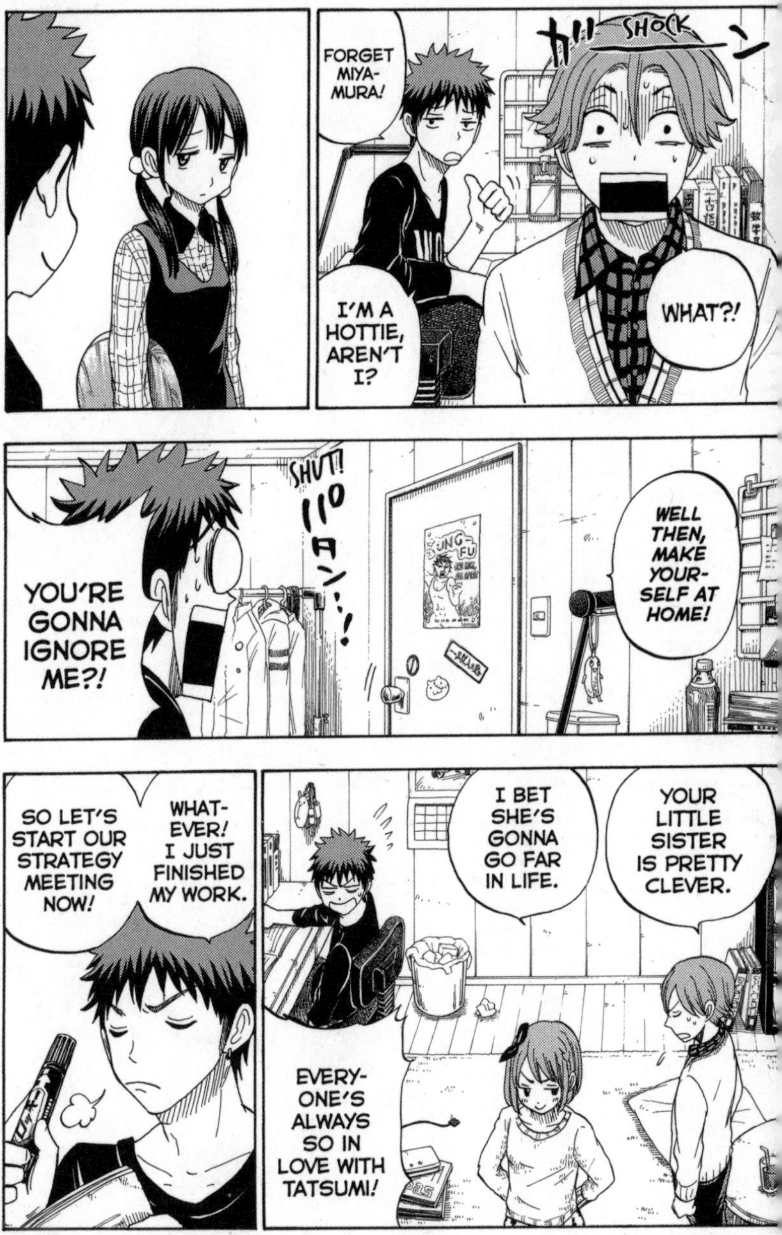
SHOCK
FORGET MIYA-MURA!
I'M A HOTTIE, AREN'T I?
WHAT?!
WELL THEN, MAKE YOUR-SELF AT HOME!
SHUT!
パタン
YOU'RE GONNA IGNORE ME?!
YOUR LITTLE SISTER IS PRETTY CLEVER.
I BET SHE'S GONNA GO FAR IN LIFE.
EVERY-ONE'S ALWAYS SO IN LOVE WITH TATSUMI!
WHAT-EVER! I JUST FINISHED MY WORK.
SO LET'S START OUR STRATEGY MEETING NOW!

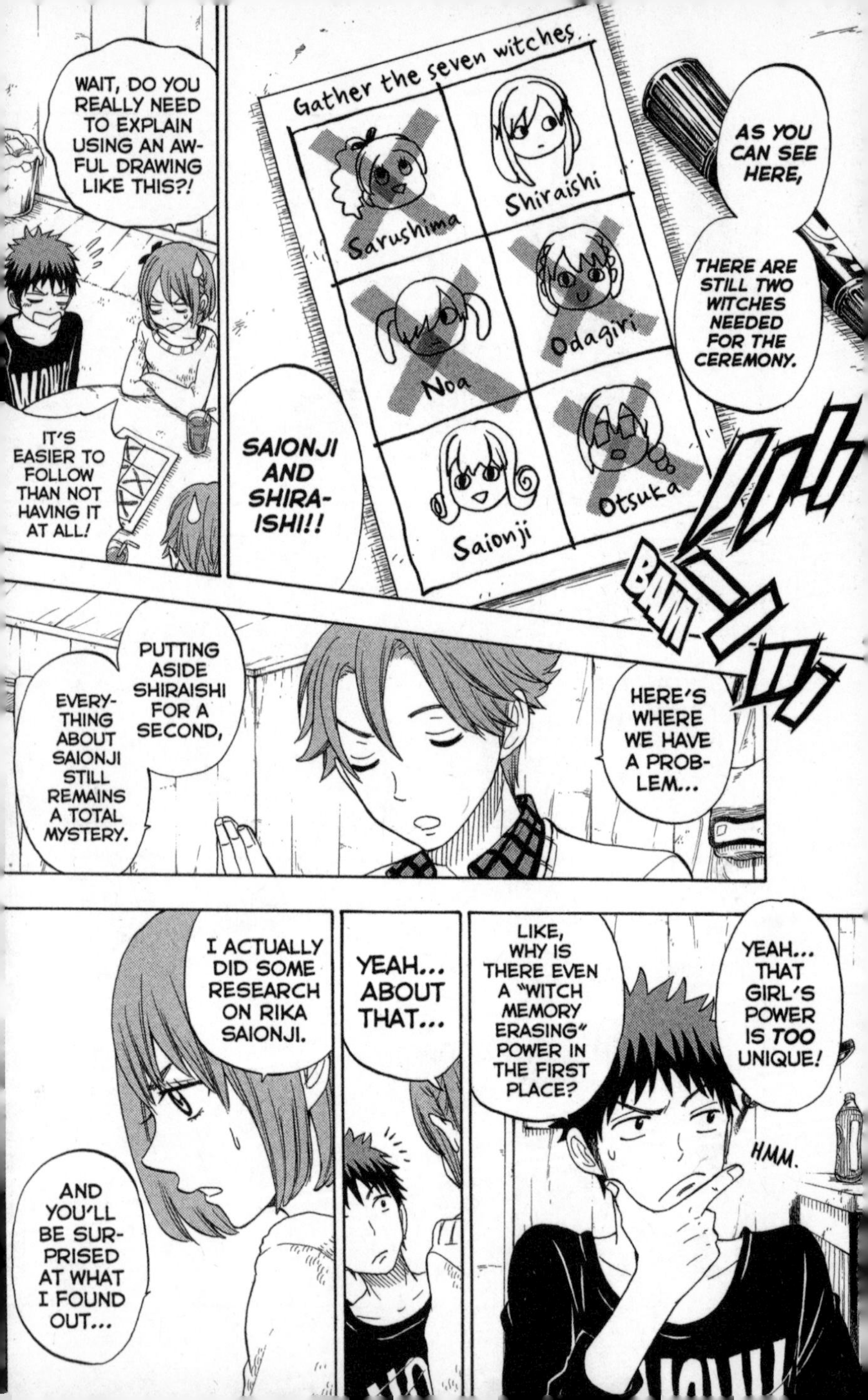
AS YOU CAN SEE HERE,
THERE ARE STILL TWO WITCHES NEEDED FOR THE CEREMONY.
Gather the seven witches
Shiraishi
Sarushima
Odagiri
Noa
Otsuka
Saionji
SAIONJI AND SHIRA-ISHI!!
BAM
WAIT, DO YOU REALLY NEED TO EXPLAIN USING AN AW-FUL DRAWING LIKE THIS?!
IT'S EASIER TO FOLLOW THAN NOT HAVING IT AT ALL!
HERE'S WHERE WE HAVE A PROB-LEM...
PUTTING ASIDE SHIRAISHI FOR A SECOND,
EVERY-THING ABOUT SAIONJI STILL REMAINS A TOTAL MYSTERY.
YEAH... THAT GIRL'S POWER IS TOO UNIQUE!
HMM.
LIKE, WHY IS THERE EVEN A "WITCH MEMORY ERASING" POWER IN THE FIRST PLACE?
YEAH... ABOUT THAT...
I ACTUALLY DID SOME RESEARCH ON RIKA SAIONJI.
AND YOU'LL BE SUR-PRISED AT WHAT I FOUND OUT...

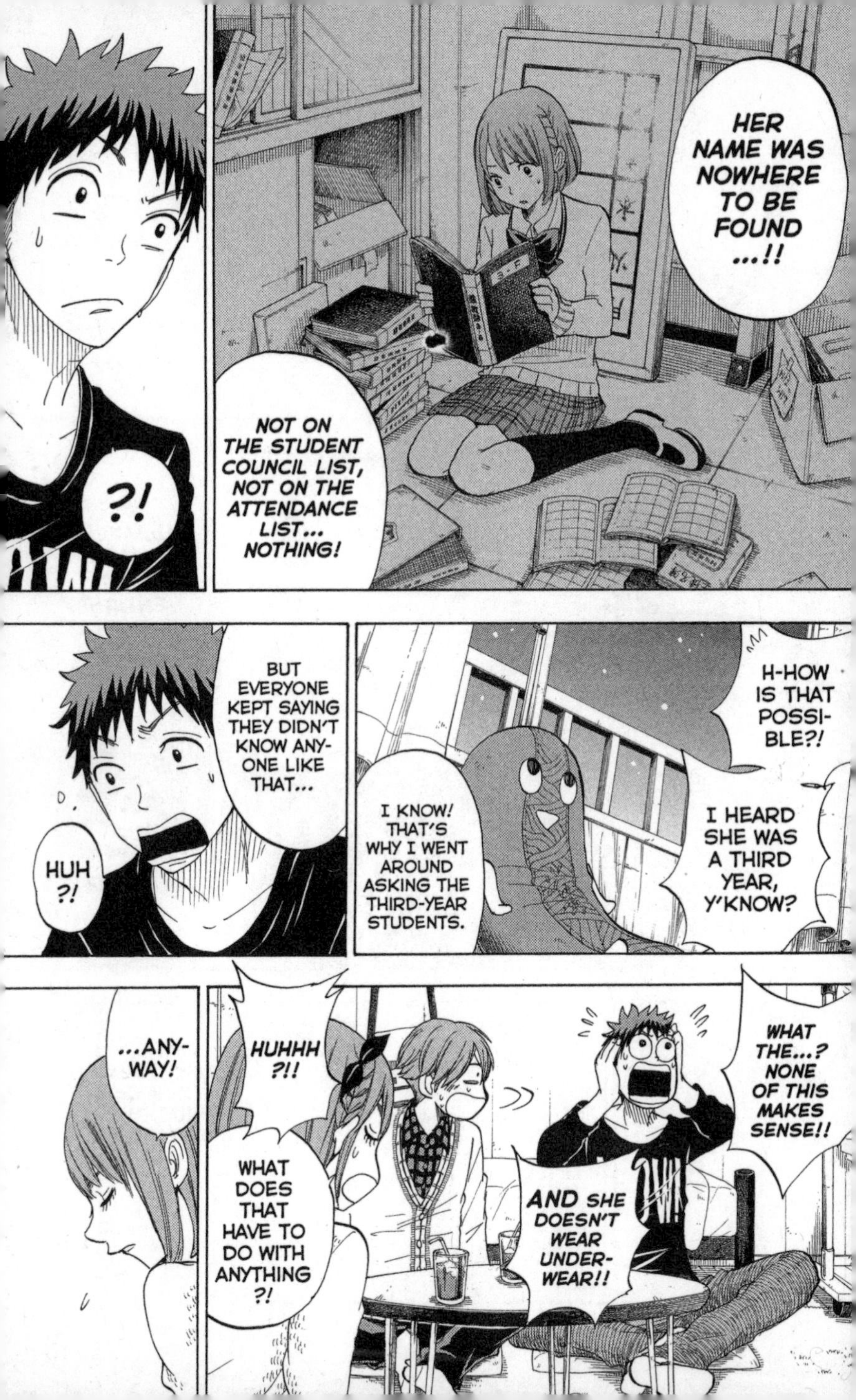
HER NAME WAS NOWHERE TO BE FOUND ...!!
NOT ON THE STUDENT COUNCIL LIST, NOT ON THE ATTENDANCE LIST... NOTHING!
?!
H-HOW IS THAT POSSI-BLE?!
I HEARD SHE WAS A THIRD YEAR, Y'KNOW?
I KNOW! THAT'S WHY I WENT AROUND ASKING THE THIRD-YEAR STUDENTS.
BUT EVERYONE KEPT SAYING THEY DIDN'T KNOW ANY-ONE LIKE THAT...
HUH ?!
WHAT THE...? NONE OF THIS MAKES SENSE!!
AND SHE DOESN'T WEAR UNDER-WEAR!!
HUHHH ?!!
WHAT DOES THAT HAVE TO DO WITH ANYTHING ?!
...ANY-WAY!

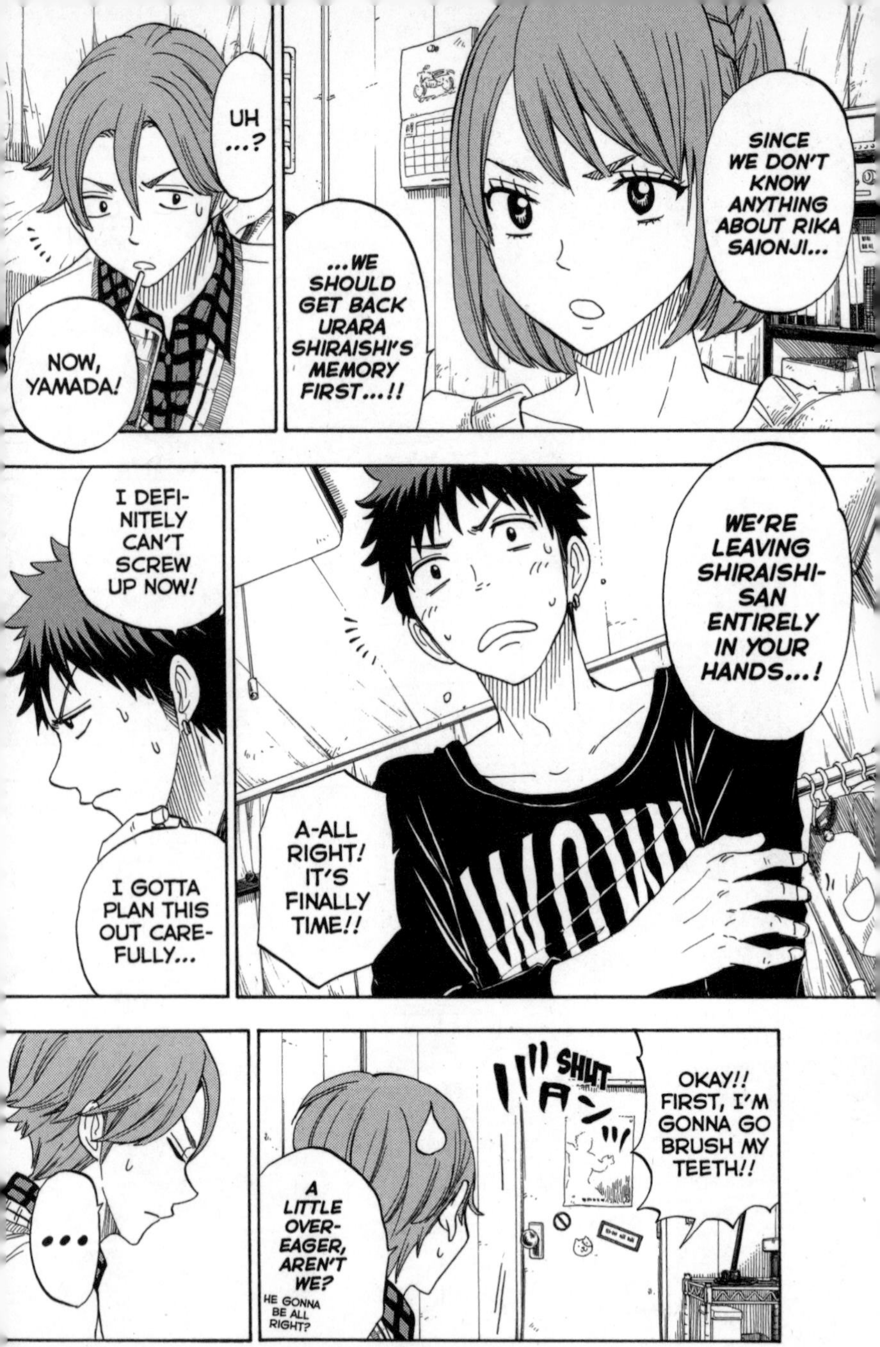
SINCE WE DON'T KNOW ANYTHING ABOUT RIKA SAIONJI...
...WE SHOULD GET BACK URARA SHIRAISHI'S MEMORY FIRST...!!
UH ...?
NOW, YAMADA!
WE'RE LEAVING SHIRAISHI-SAN ENTIRELY IN YOUR HANDS...!
A-ALL RIGHT! IT'S FINALLY TIME!!
I DEFINITELY CAN'T SCREW UP NOW!
I GOTTA PLAN THIS OUT CAREFULLY...
SHUT
OKAY!! FIRST, I'M GONNA GO BRUSH MY TEETH!!
A LITTLE OVER-EAGER, AREN'T WE?
HE GONNA BE ALL RIGHT?
...

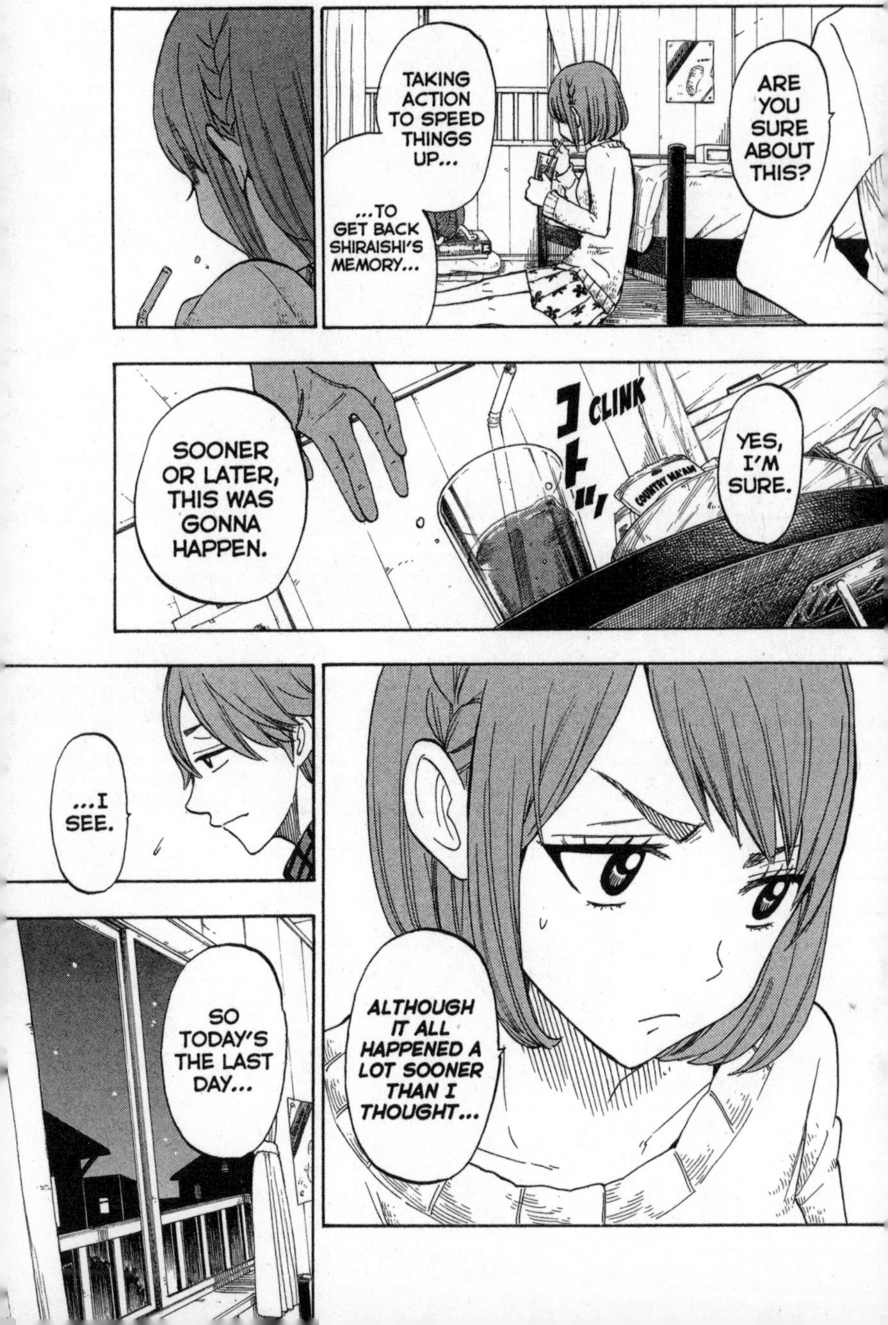
ARE YOU SURE ABOUT THIS?
TAKING ACTION TO SPEED THINGS UP...
...TO GET BACK SHIRAISHI'S MEMORY...
YES, I'M SURE.
CLINK
SOONER OR LATER, THIS WAS GONNA HAPPEN.
ALTHOUGH IT ALL HAPPENED A LOT SOONER THAN I THOUGHT...
...I SEE.
SO TODAY'S THE LAST DAY...

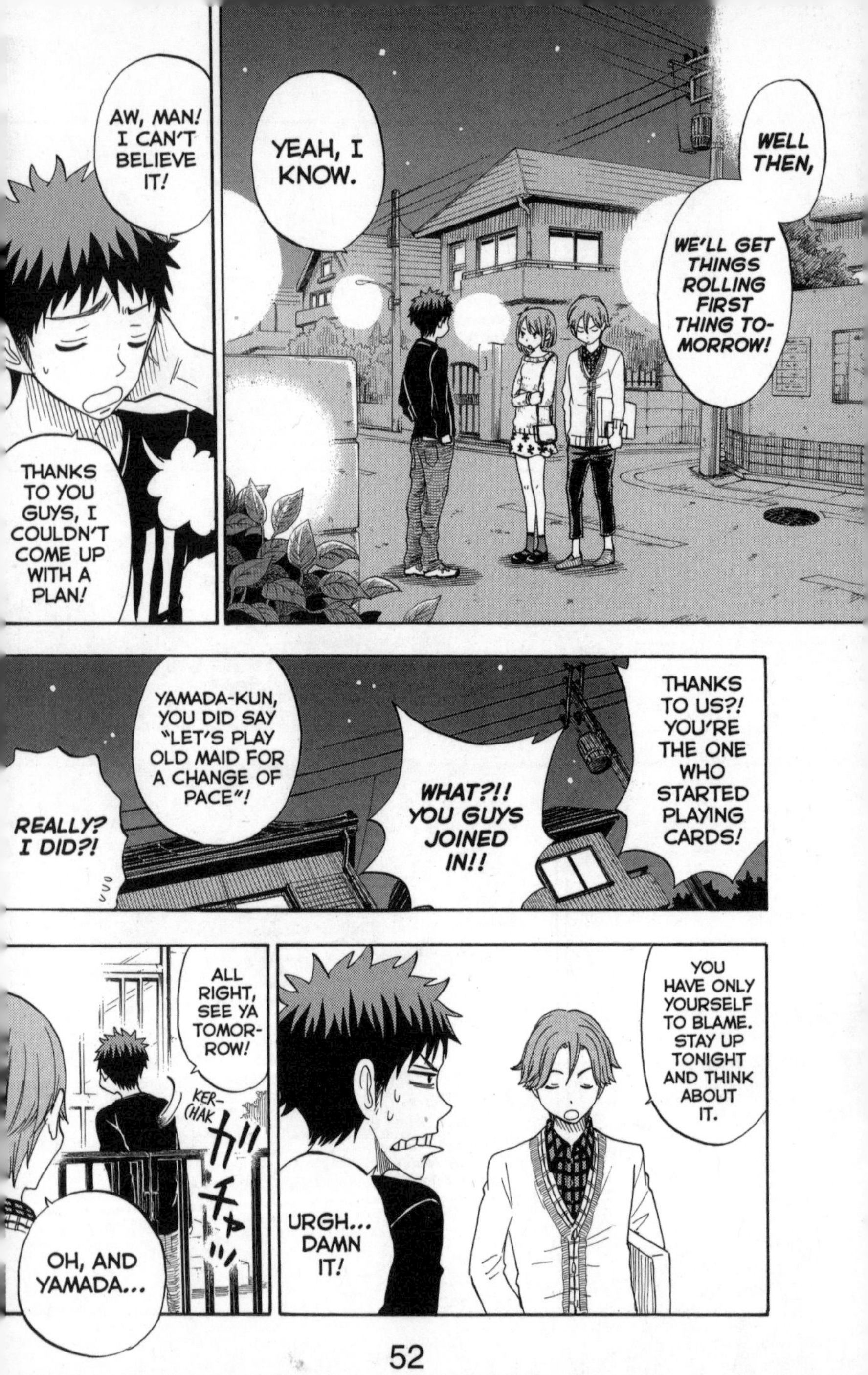
WELL THEN,
WE'LL GET THINGS ROLLING FIRST THING TO-MORROW!
YEAH, I KNOW.
AW, MAN! I CAN'T BELIEVE IT!
THANKS TO YOU GUYS, I COULDN'T COME UP WITH A PLAN!
THANKS TO US?! YOU'RE THE ONE WHO STARTED PLAYING CARDS!
WHAT?!! YOU GUYS JOINED IN!!
YAMADA-KUN, YOU DID SAY "LET'S PLAY OLD MAID FOR A CHANGE OF PACE"!
REALLY? I DID?!
YOU HAVE ONLY YOURSELF TO BLAME. STAY UP TONIGHT AND THINK ABOUT IT.
URGH... DAMN IT!
ALL RIGHT, SEE YA TOMOR-ROW!
KER-CHAK
ガチャッ
OH, AND YAMADA...

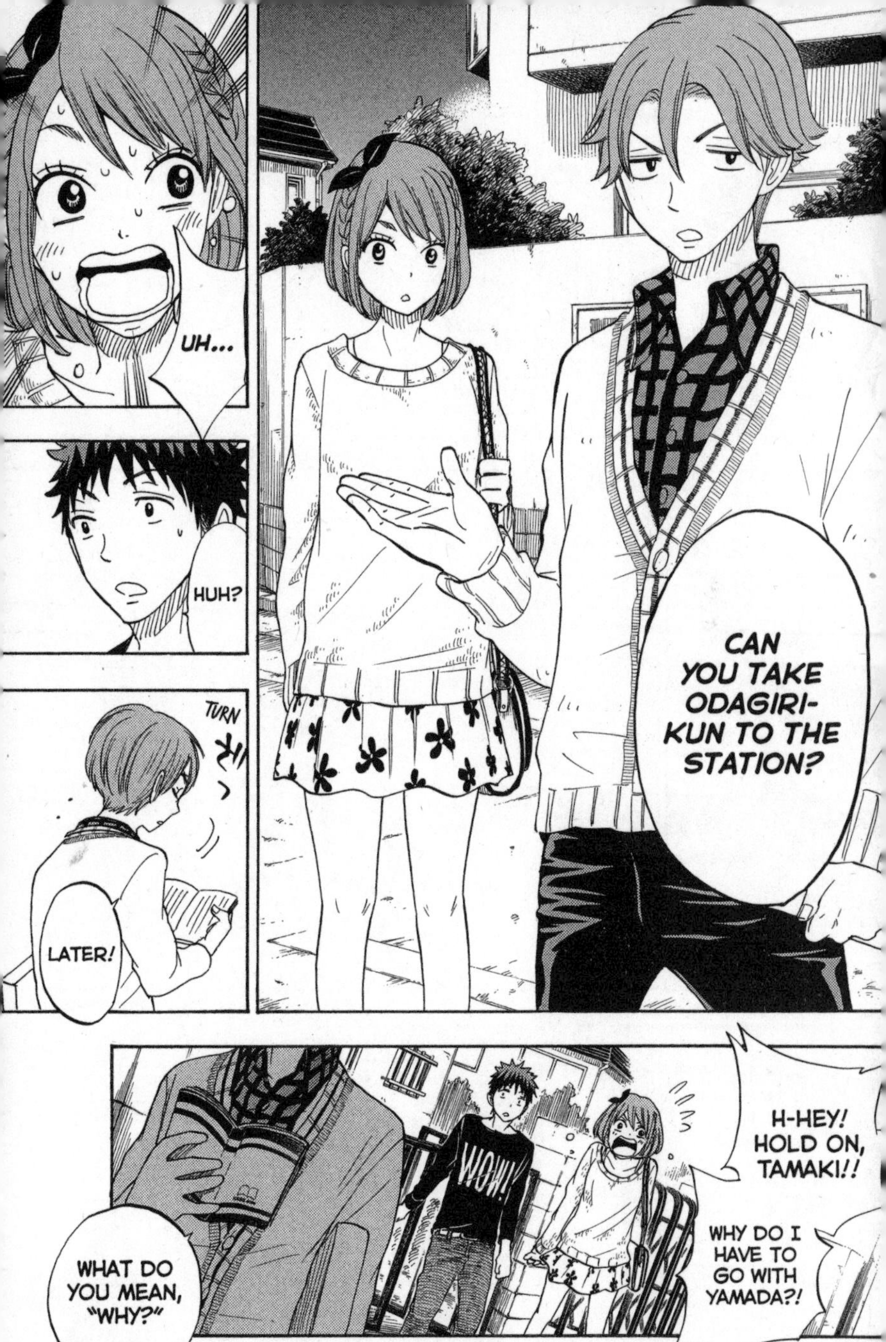
CAN YOU TAKE ODAGIRI-KUN TO THE STATION?
UH...
HUH?
TURN
LATER!
H-HEY! HOLD ON, TAMAKI!!
WHY DO I HAVE TO GO WITH YAMADA?!
WHAT DO YOU MEAN, "WHY?"

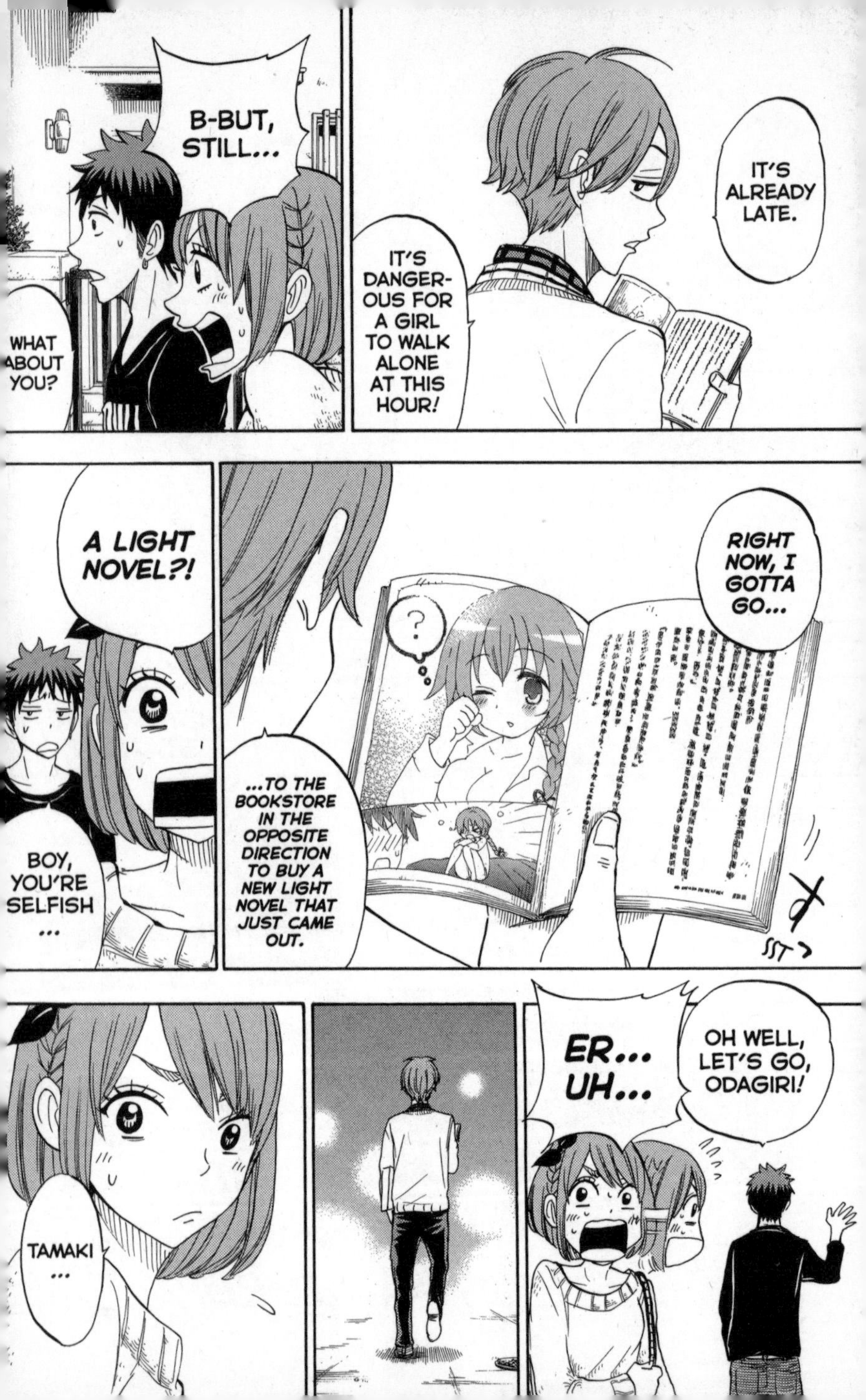

IT'S ALREADY LATE.
IT'S DANGEROUS FOR A GIRL TO WALK ALONE AT THIS HOUR!
B-BUT, STILL...
WHAT ABOUT YOU?
RIGHT NOW, I GOTTA GO...
...TO THE BOOKSTORE IN THE OPPOSITE DIRECTION TO BUY A NEW LIGHT NOVEL THAT JUST CAME OUT.
SST
A LIGHT NOVEL?!
BOY, YOU'RE SELFISH...
OH WELL, LET'S GO, ODAGIRI!
ER... UH...
TAMAKI...

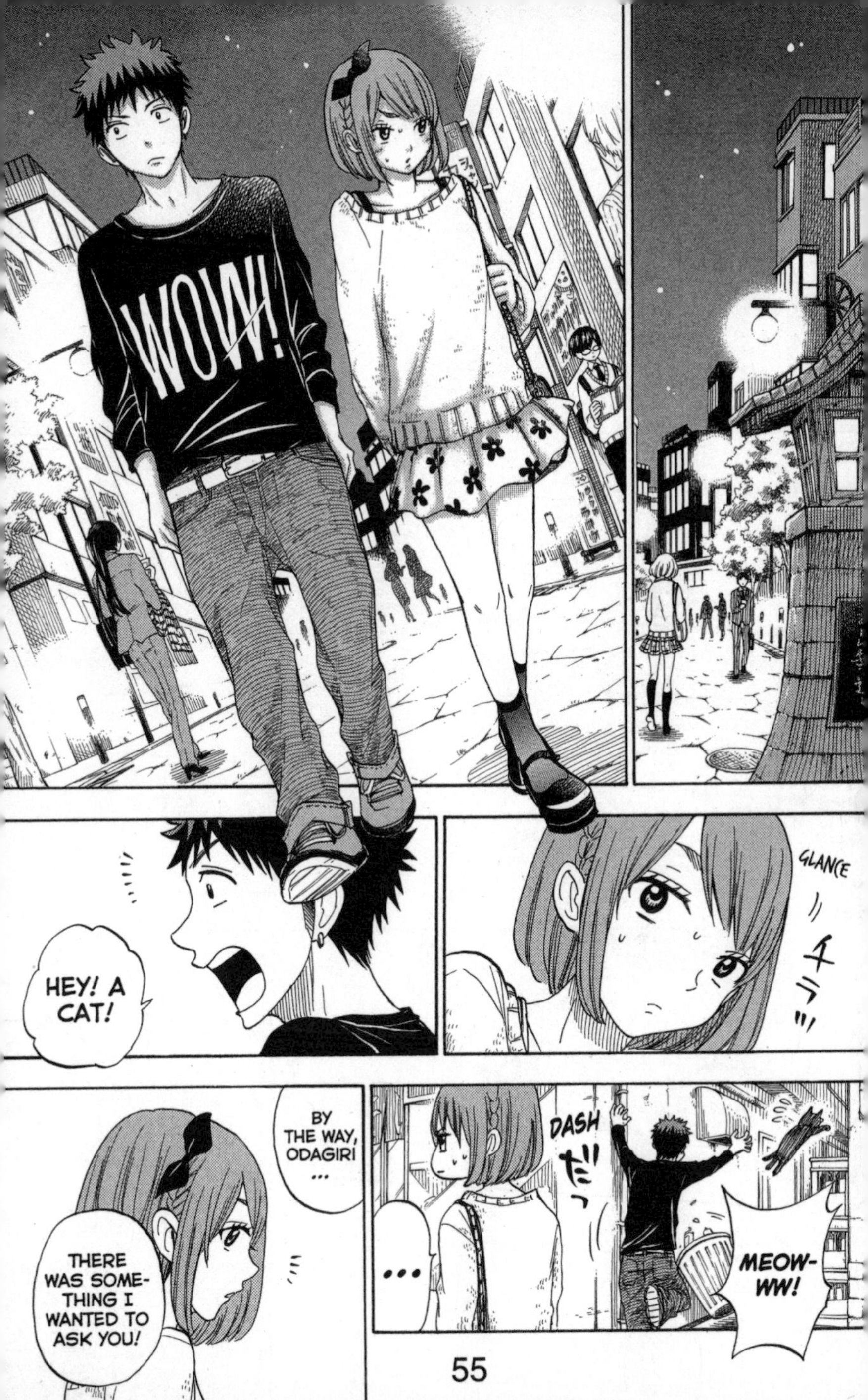
GLANCE
HEY! A CAT!
DASH
MEOW-WW!
...
BY THE WAY, ODAGIRI ...
THERE WAS SOMETHING I WANTED TO ASK YOU!

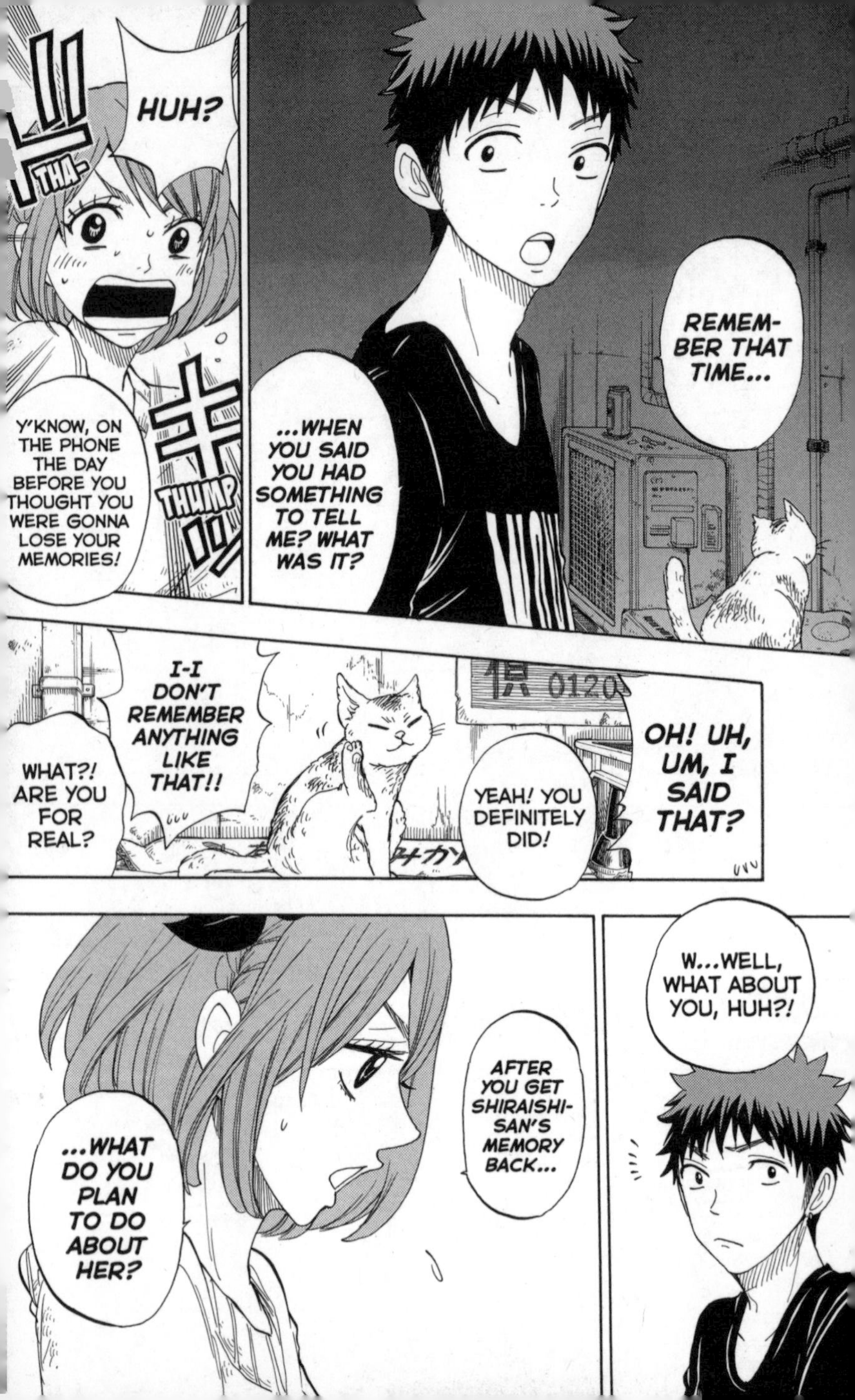
REMEMBER THAT TIME...
...WHEN YOU SAID YOU HAD SOMETHING TO TELL ME? WHAT WAS IT?
HUH?
THA-
Y'KNOW, ON THE PHONE THE DAY BEFORE YOU THOUGHT YOU WERE GONNA LOSE YOUR MEMORIES!
THUMP
OH! UH, UM, I SAID THAT?
YEAH! YOU DEFINITELY DID!
I-I DON'T REMEMBER ANYTHING LIKE THAT!!
WHAT?! ARE YOU FOR REAL?
W...WELL, WHAT ABOUT YOU, HUH?!
AFTER YOU GET SHIRAISHI-SAN'S MEMORY BACK...
...WHAT DO YOU PLAN TO DO ABOUT HER?

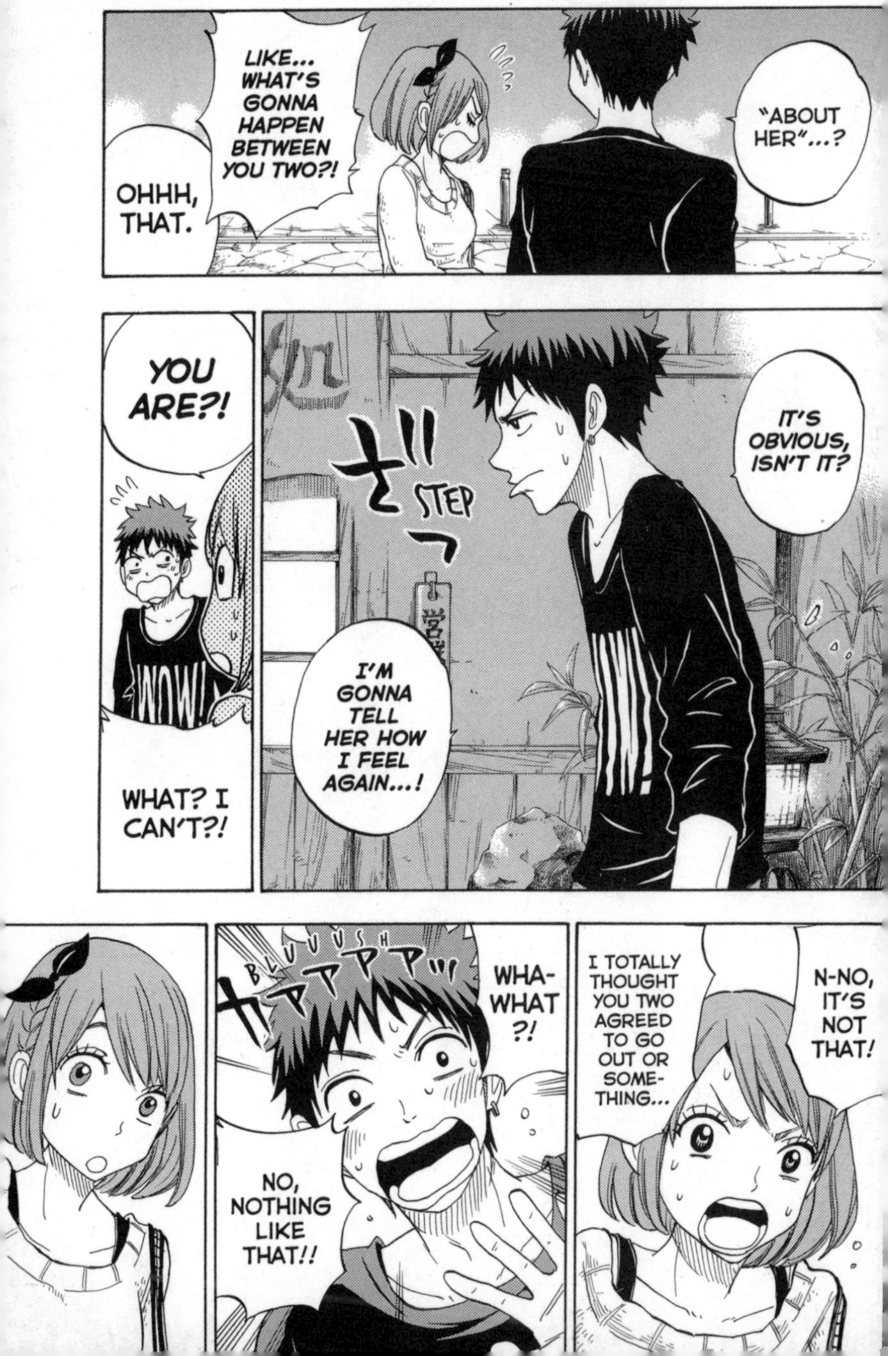
"ABOUT HER"...?
LIKE... WHAT'S GONNA HAPPEN BETWEEN YOU TWO?!
OHHH, THAT.
IT'S OBVIOUS, ISN'T IT?
STEP
I'M GONNA TELL HER HOW I FEEL AGAIN...!
YOU ARE?!
WHAT? I CAN'T?!
N-NO, IT'S NOT THAT!
I TOTALLY THOUGHT YOU TWO AGREED TO GO OUT OR SOME-THING...
WHA-WHAT?!
BLUUUSH
NO, NOTHING LIKE THAT!!

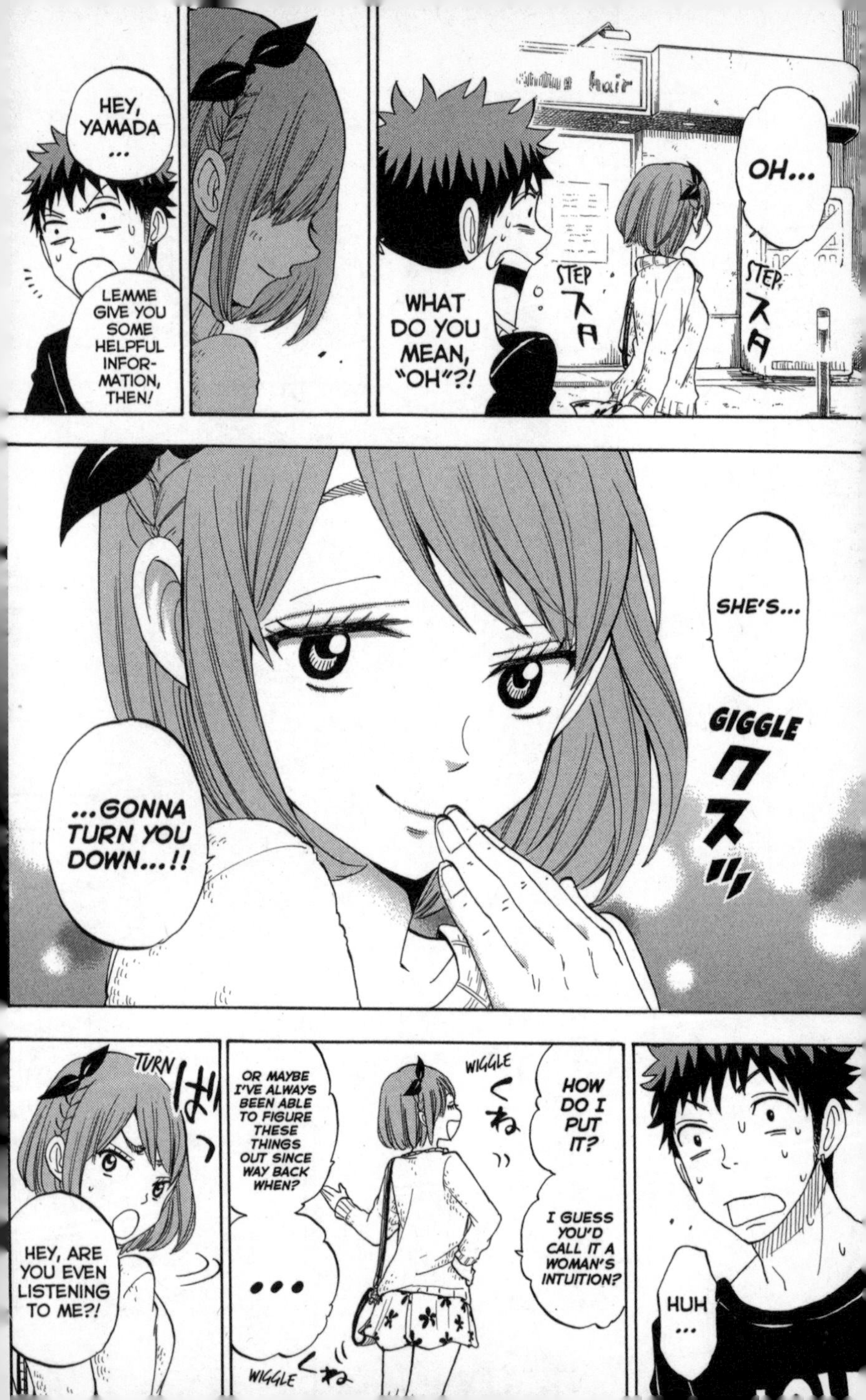
OH...
STEP スタ
STEP スタ
WHAT DO YOU MEAN, "OH"?!
HEY, YAMADA ...
LEMME GIVE YOU SOME HELPFUL INFORMATION, THEN!
SHE'S...
GIGGLE クスッ
...GONNA TURN YOU DOWN...!!
HUH ...
HOW DO I PUT IT?
I GUESS YOU'D CALL IT A WOMAN'S INTUITION?
WIGGLE くね
OR MAYBE I'VE ALWAYS BEEN ABLE TO FIGURE THESE THINGS OUT SINCE WAY BACK WHEN?
...
WIGGLE くね
TURN ぱっ
HEY, ARE YOU EVEN LISTENING TO ME?!

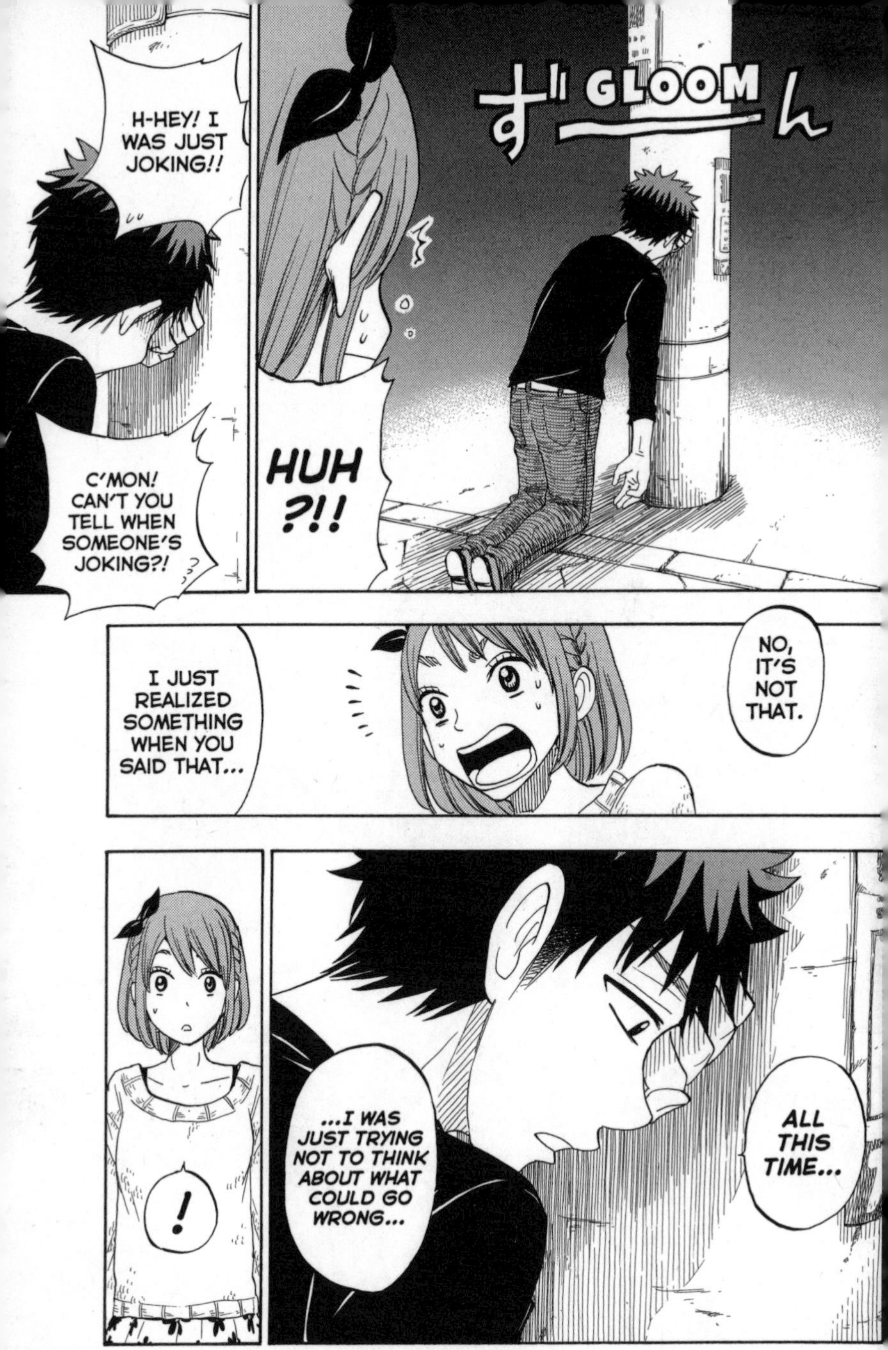
GLOOM
HUH ?!!
H-HEY! I WAS JUST JOKING!!
C'MON! CAN'T YOU TELL WHEN SOMEONE'S JOKING?!
NO, IT'S NOT THAT.
I JUST REALIZED SOMETHING WHEN YOU SAID THAT...
ALL THIS TIME...
...I WAS JUST TRYING NOT TO THINK ABOUT WHAT COULD GO WRONG...
!

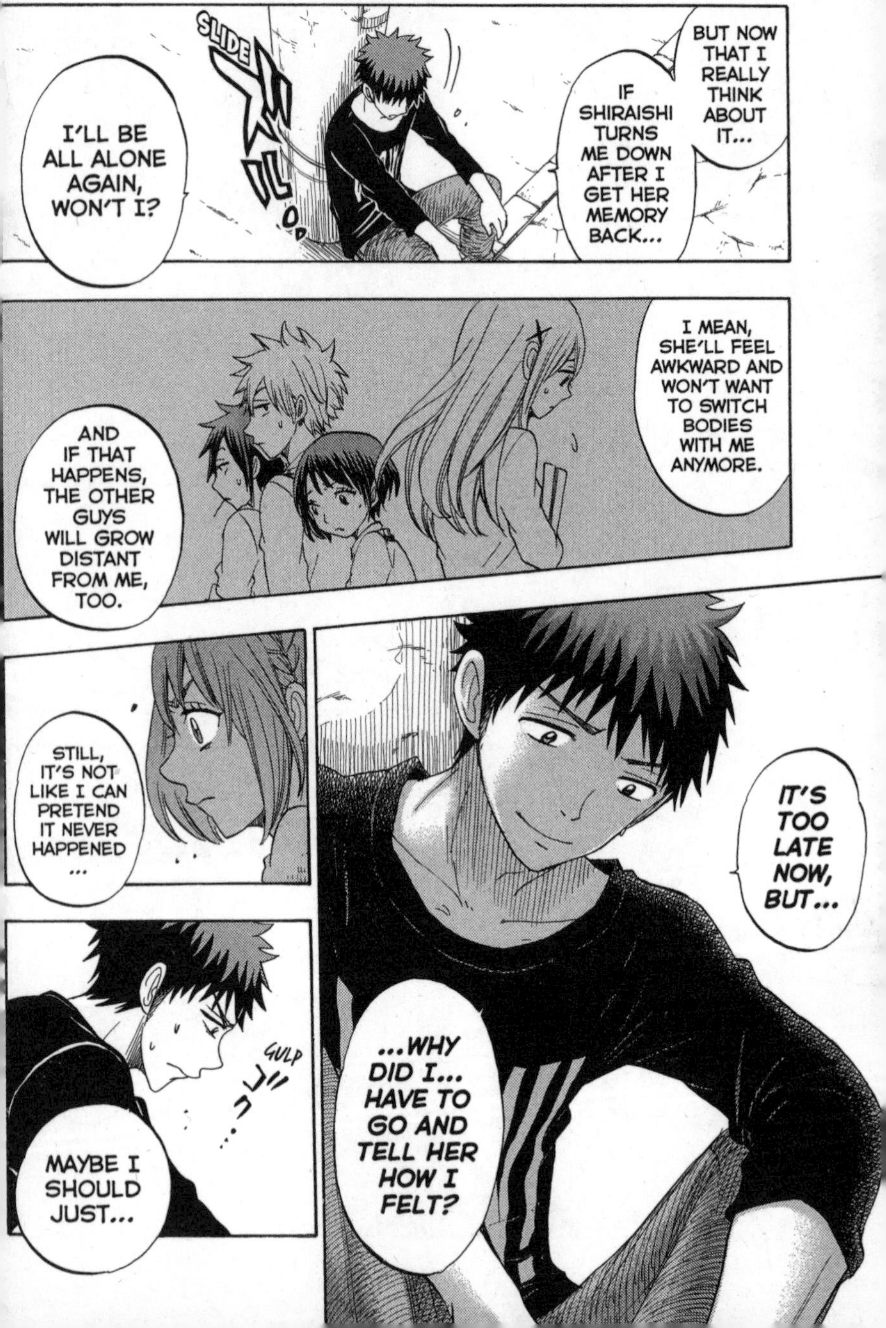

BUT NOW THAT I REALLY THINK ABOUT IT...
IF SHIRAISHI TURNS ME DOWN AFTER I GET HER MEMORY BACK...
SLIDE
I'LL BE ALL ALONE AGAIN, WON'T I?
I MEAN, SHE'LL FEEL AWKWARD AND WON'T WANT TO SWITCH BODIES WITH ME ANYMORE.
AND IF THAT HAPPENS, THE OTHER GUYS WILL GROW DISTANT FROM ME, TOO.
IT'S TOO LATE NOW, BUT...
...WHY DID I... HAVE TO GO AND TELL HER HOW I FELT?
STILL, IT'S NOT LIKE I CAN PRETEND IT NEVER HAPPENED ...
GULP
MAYBE I SHOULD JUST...

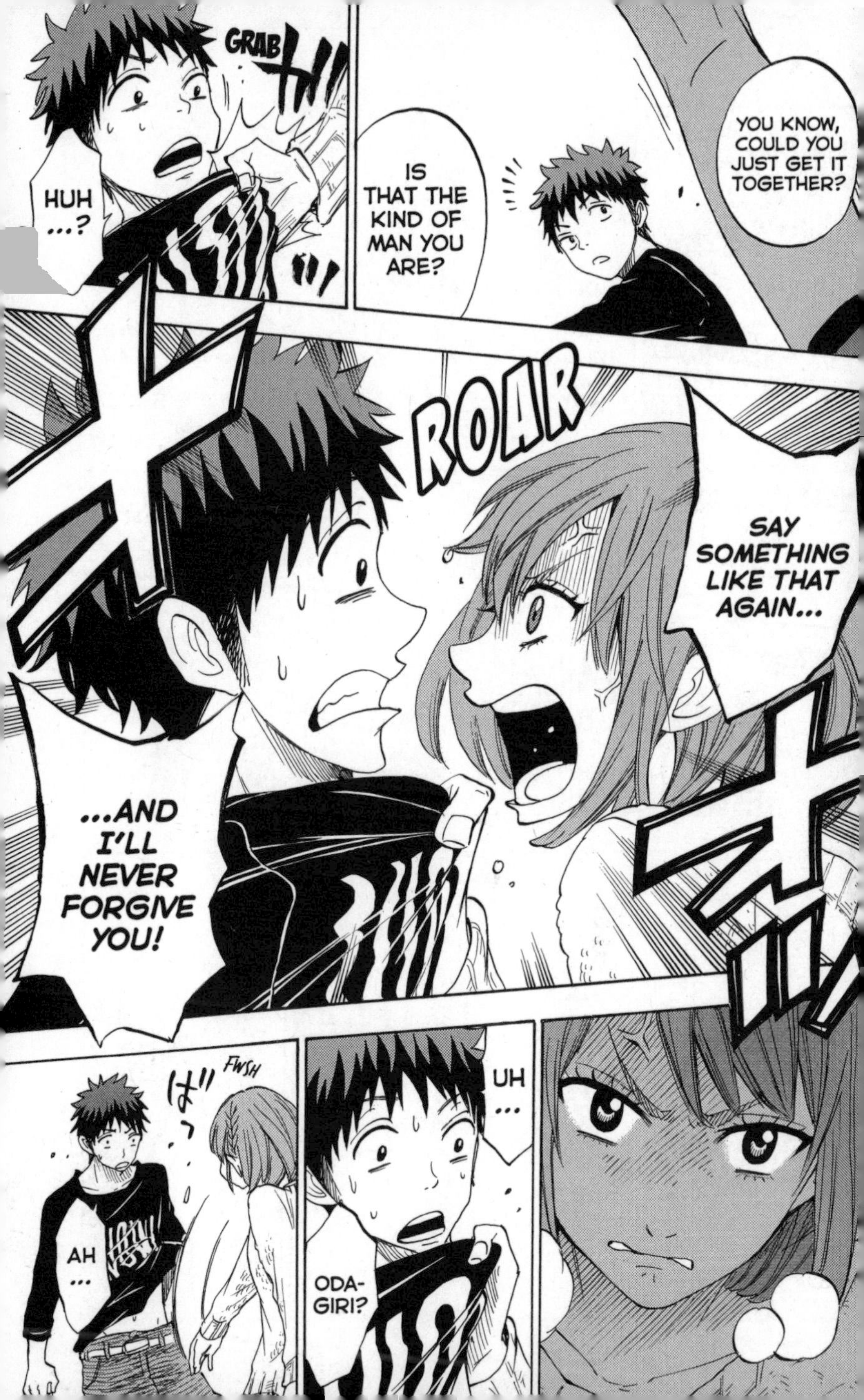
YOU KNOW, COULD YOU JUST GET IT TOGETHER?
IS THAT THE KIND OF MAN YOU ARE?
GRAB
HUH ...?
ROAR
SAY SOMETHING LIKE THAT AGAIN...
...AND I'LL NEVER FORGIVE YOU!
UH ...
ODA-GIRI?
FWSH
ばっ
AH ...

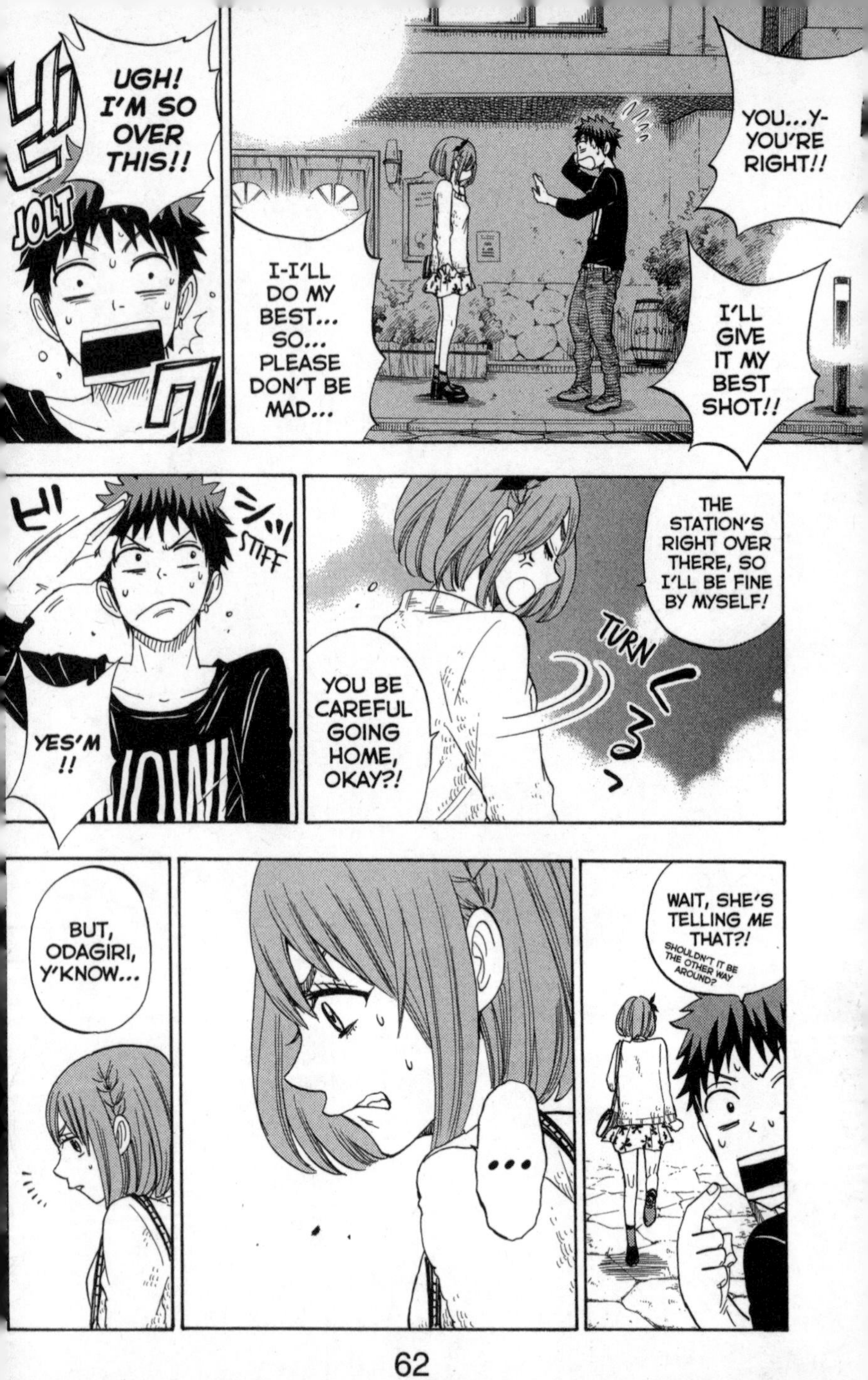
YOU...Y-YOU'RE RIGHT!!
I'LL GIVE IT MY BEST SHOT!!
I-I'LL DO MY BEST... SO... PLEASE DON'T BE MAD...
UGH! I'M SO OVER THIS!!
JOLT
THE STATION'S RIGHT OVER THERE, SO I'LL BE FINE BY MYSELF!
TURN
YOU BE CAREFUL GOING HOME, OKAY?!
STIFF
YES'M!!
WAIT, SHE'S TELLING ME THAT?!
SHOULDN'T IT BE THE OTHER WAY AROUND?
...
BUT, ODAGIRI, Y'KNOW...

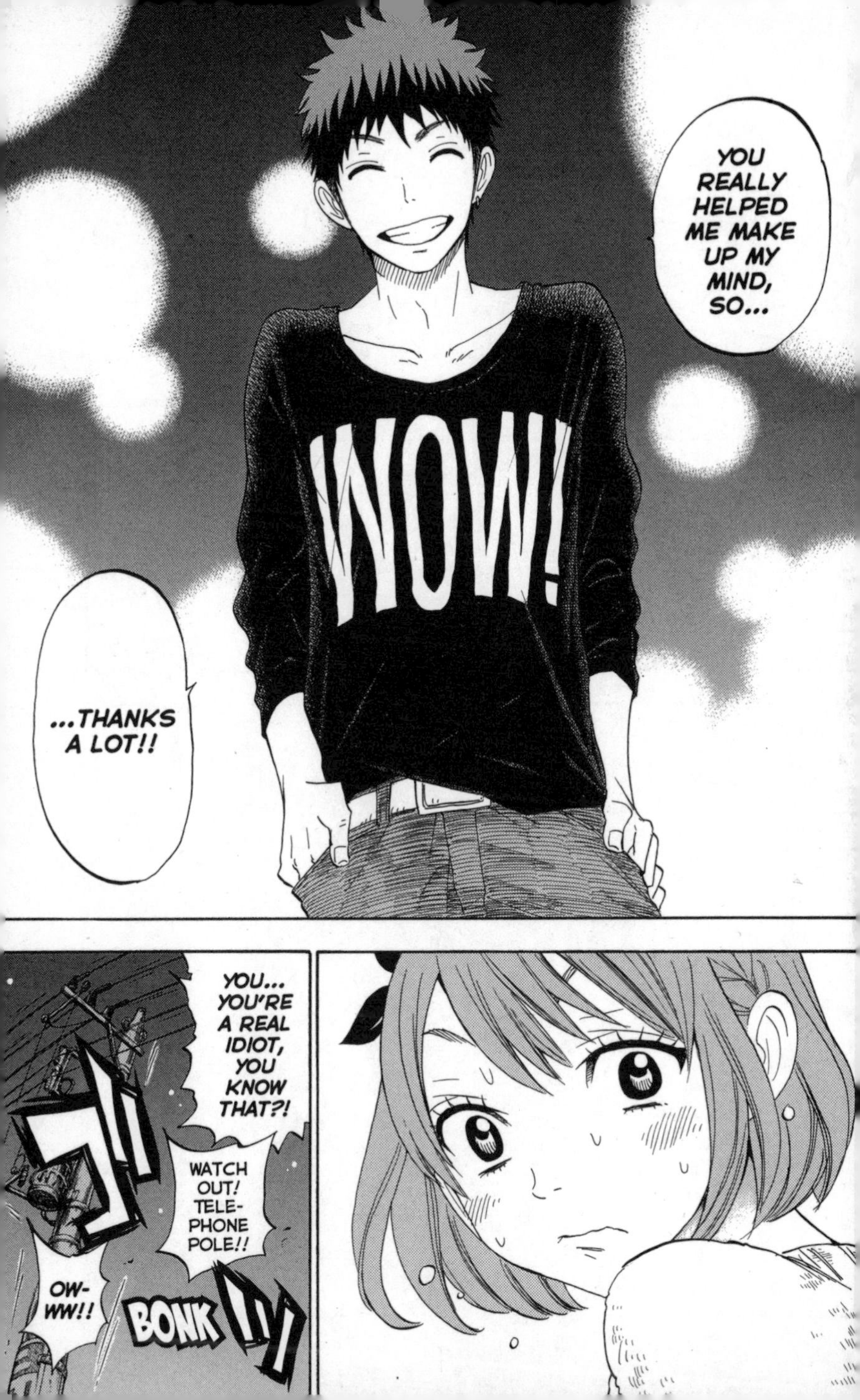
YOU REALLY HELPED ME MAKE UP MY MIND, SO...
WOW!
...THANKS A LOT!!
YOU... YOU'RE A REAL IDIOT, YOU KNOW THAT?!
WATCH OUT! TELE-PHONE POLE!!
BONK
OW-WW!!

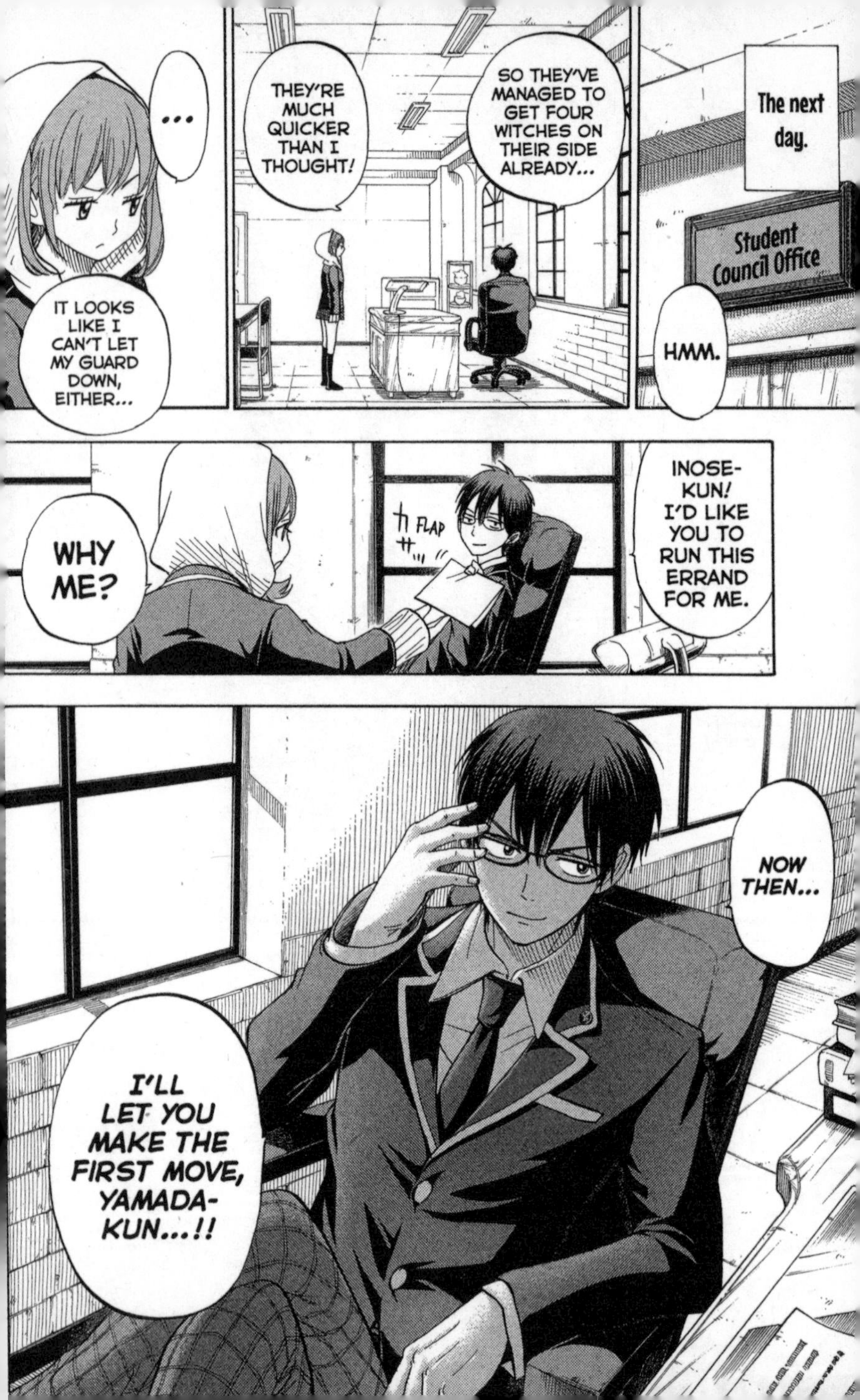
The next day.
Student Council Office
HMM.
SO THEY'VE MANAGED TO GET FOUR WITCHES ON THEIR SIDE ALREADY...
THEY'RE MUCH QUICKER THAN I THOUGHT!
...
IT LOOKS LIKE I CAN'T LET MY GUARD DOWN, EITHER...
INOSE-KUN! I'D LIKE YOU TO RUN THIS ERRAND FOR ME.
FLAP
WHY ME?
NOW THEN...
I'LL LET YOU MAKE THE FIRST MOVE, YAMADA-KUN...!!

CHAPTER 80: Perverted, just perverted!

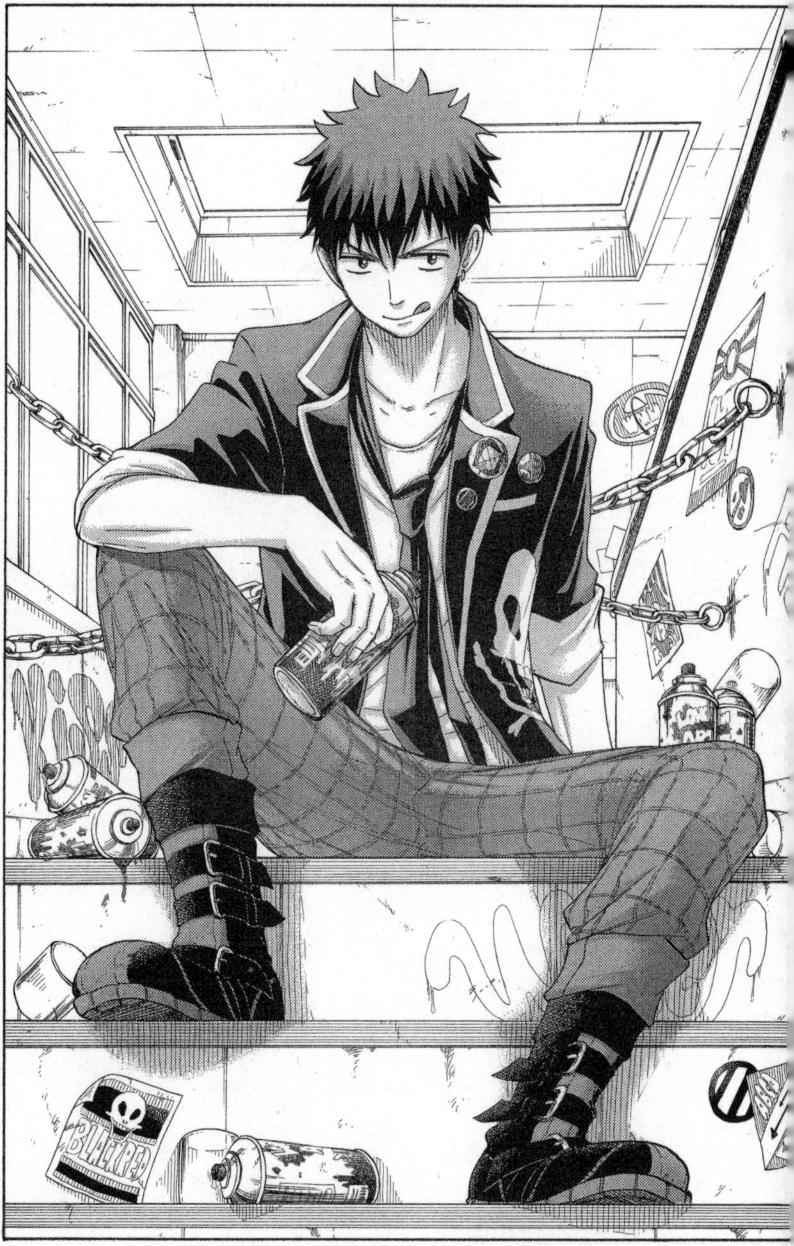
BLACKRED

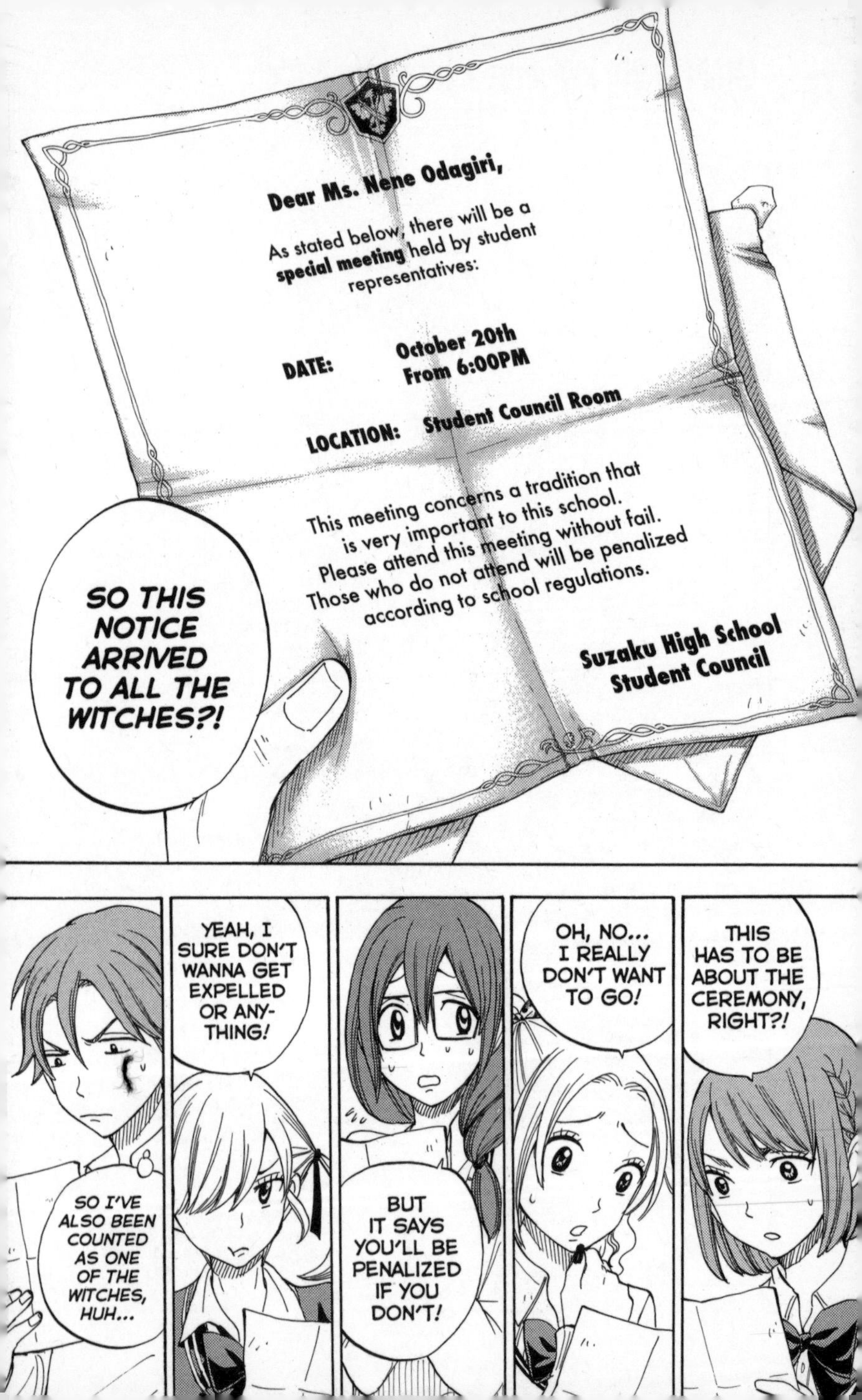
Dear Ms. Nene Odagiri,
As stated below, there will be a special meeting held by student representatives:
DATE: October 20th From 6:00PM
LOCATION: Student Council Room
This meeting concerns a tradition that is very important to this school. Please attend this meeting without fail. Those who do not attend will be penalized according to school regulations.
Suzaku High School Student Council
SO THIS NOTICE ARRIVED TO ALL THE WITCHES?!
THIS HAS TO BE ABOUT THE CEREMONY, RIGHT?!
OH, NO... I REALLY DON'T WANT TO GO!
BUT IT SAYS YOU'LL BE PENALIZED IF YOU DON'T!
YEAH, I SURE DON'T WANNA GET EXPELLED OR ANY-THING!
SO I'VE ALSO BEEN COUNTED AS ONE OF THE WITCHES, HUH...

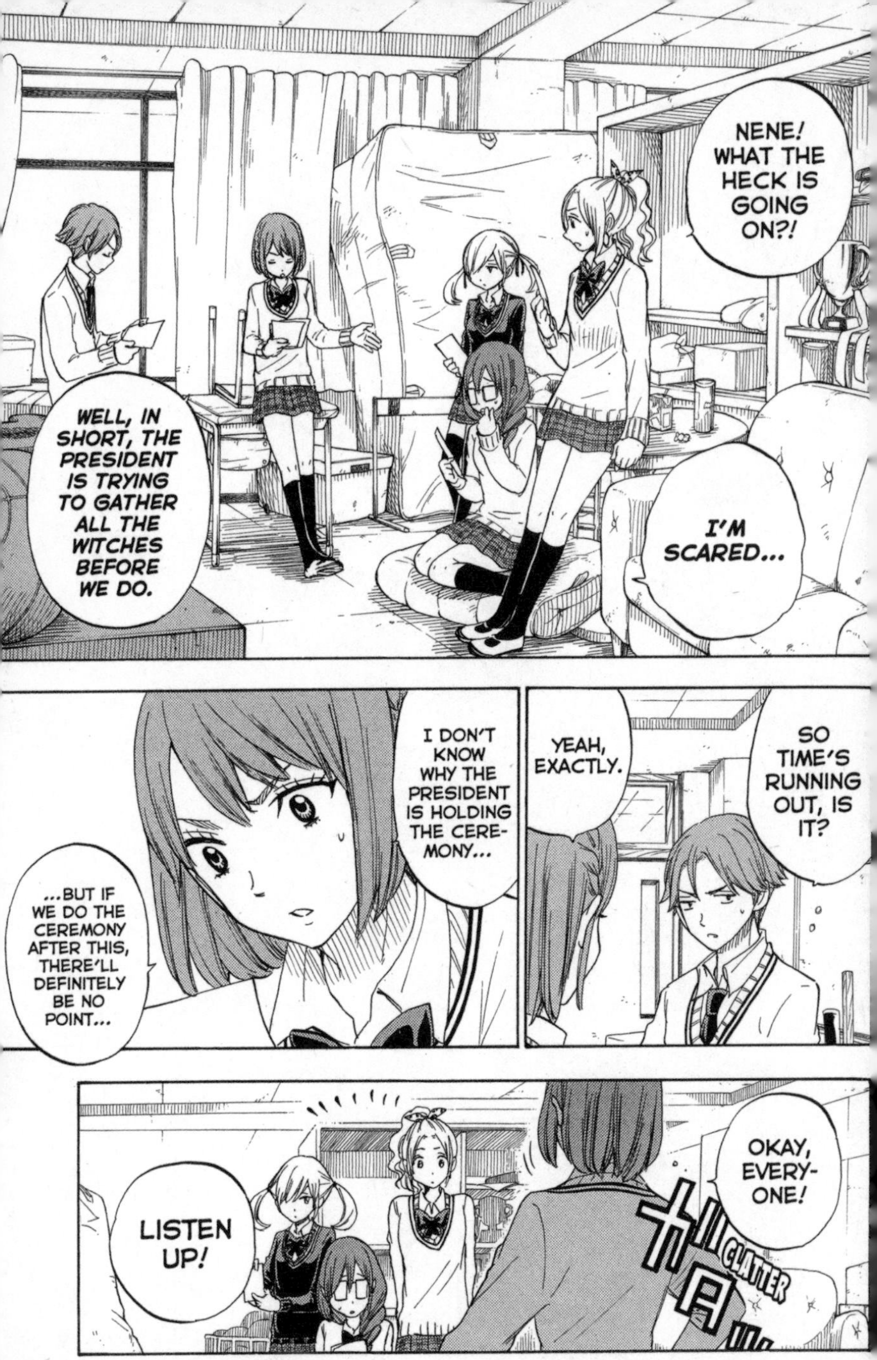
NENE! WHAT THE HECK IS GOING ON?!
WELL, IN SHORT, THE PRESIDENT IS TRYING TO GATHER ALL THE WITCHES BEFORE WE DO.
I'M SCARED...
SO TIME'S RUNNING OUT, IS IT?
YEAH, EXACTLY.
I DON'T KNOW WHY THE PRESIDENT IS HOLDING THE CERE-MONY...
...BUT IF WE DO THE CEREMONY AFTER THIS, THERE'LL DEFINITELY BE NO POINT...
OKAY, EVERY-ONE!
CLATTER
LISTEN UP!

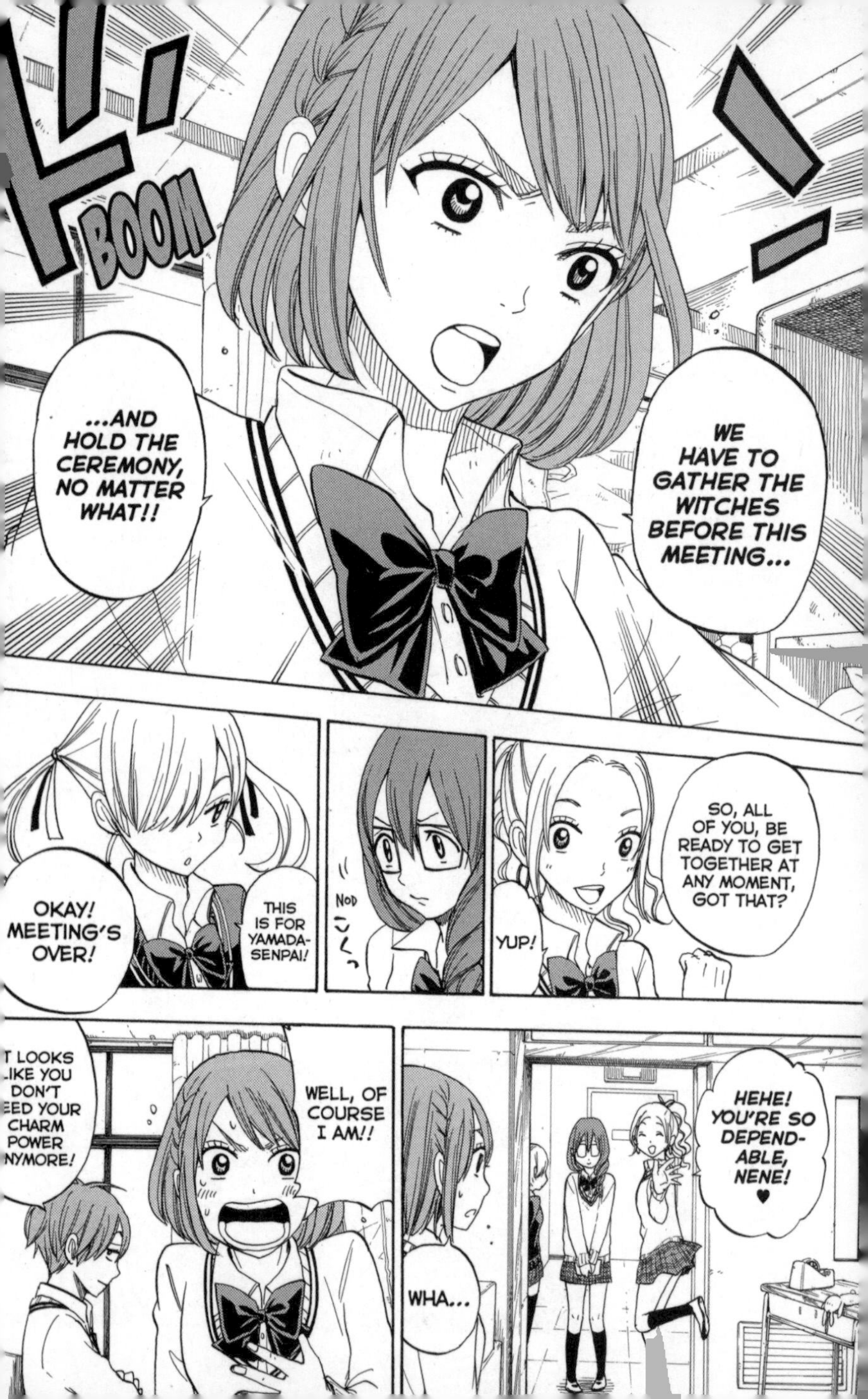
BOOM
WE HAVE TO GATHER THE WITCHES BEFORE THIS MEETING...
...AND HOLD THE CEREMONY, NO MATTER WHAT!!
SO, ALL OF YOU, BE READY TO GET TOGETHER AT ANY MOMENT, GOT THAT?
YUP!
NOD
THIS IS FOR YAMADA-SENPAI!
OKAY! MEETING'S OVER!
HEHE! YOU'RE SO DEPENDABLE, NENE! ♥
WHA...
WELL, OF COURSE I AM!!
T LOOKS LIKE YOU DON'T EED YOUR CHARM POWER NYMORE!

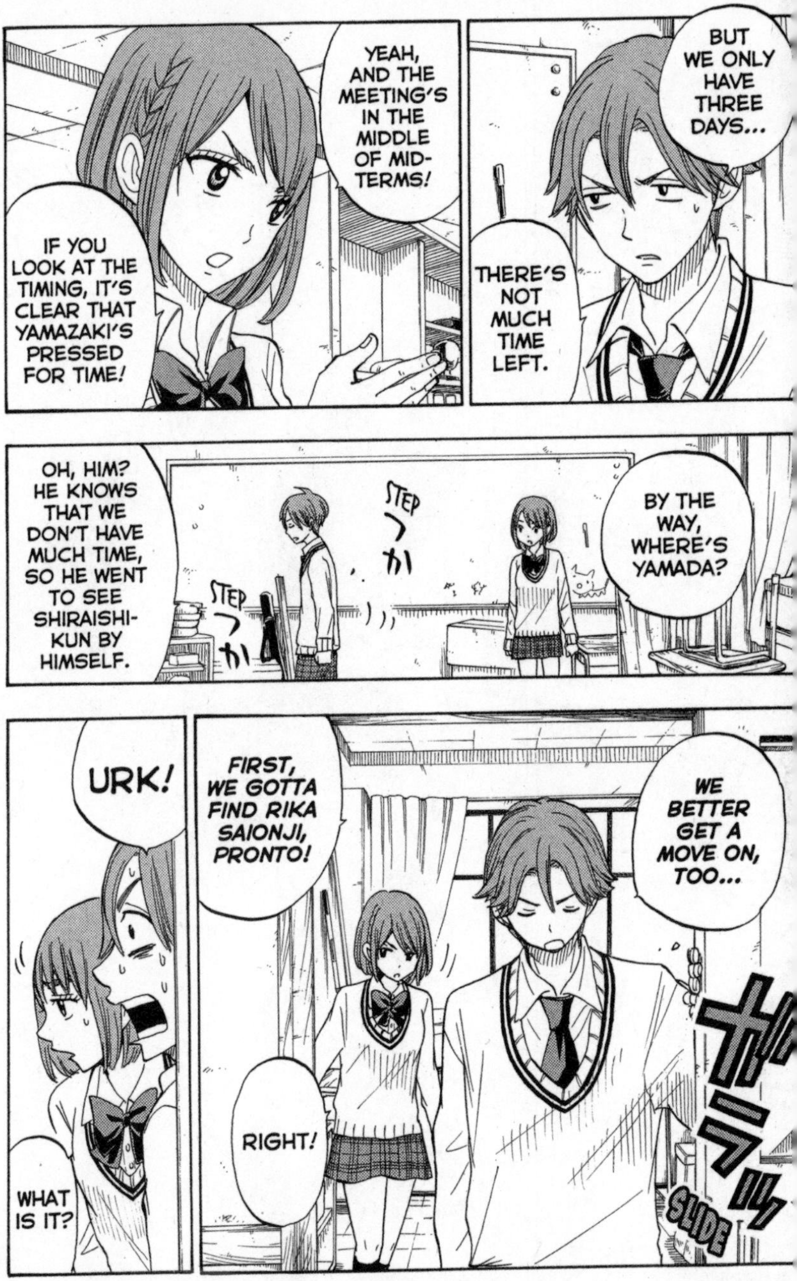
BUT WE ONLY HAVE THREE DAYS...
THERE'S NOT MUCH TIME LEFT.
YEAH, AND THE MEETING'S IN THE MIDDLE OF MID-TERMS!
IF YOU LOOK AT THE TIMING, IT'S CLEAR THAT YAMAZAKI'S PRESSED FOR TIME!
BY THE WAY, WHERE'S YAMADA?
STEP
つか
STEP
つか
OH, HIM? HE KNOWS THAT WE DON'T HAVE MUCH TIME, SO HE WENT TO SEE SHIRAISHI-KUN BY HIMSELF.
WE BETTER GET A MOVE ON, TOO...
ガラッ
SLIDE
FIRST, WE GOTTA FIND RIKA SAIONJI, PRONTO!
RIGHT!
URK!
WHAT IS IT?

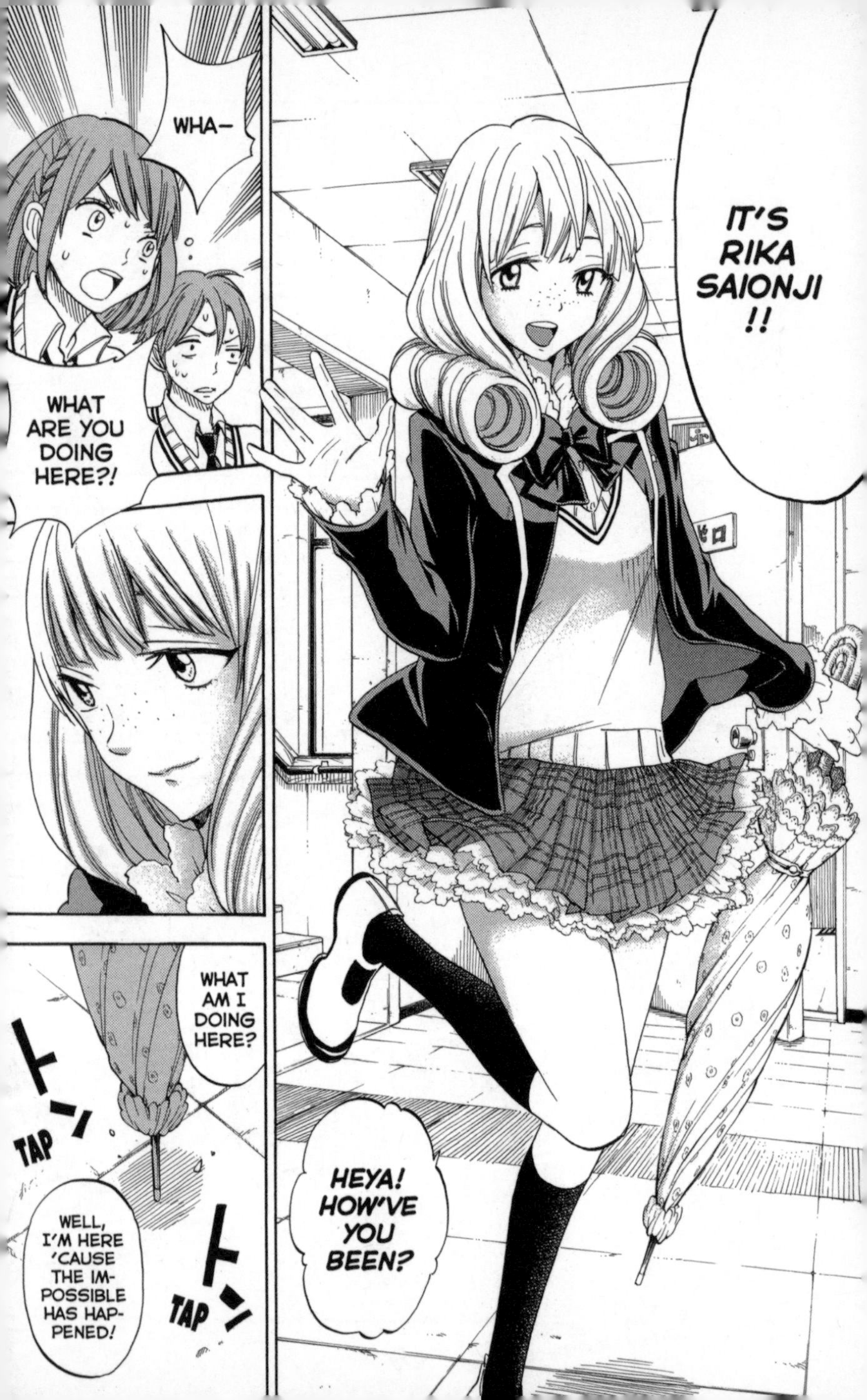
IT'S RIKA SAIONJI !!
HEYA! HOW'VE YOU BEEN?
WHA–
WHAT ARE YOU DOING HERE?!
WHAT AM I DOING HERE?
TAP
TAP
WELL, I'M HERE 'CAUSE THE IMPOSSIBLE HAS HAPPENED!

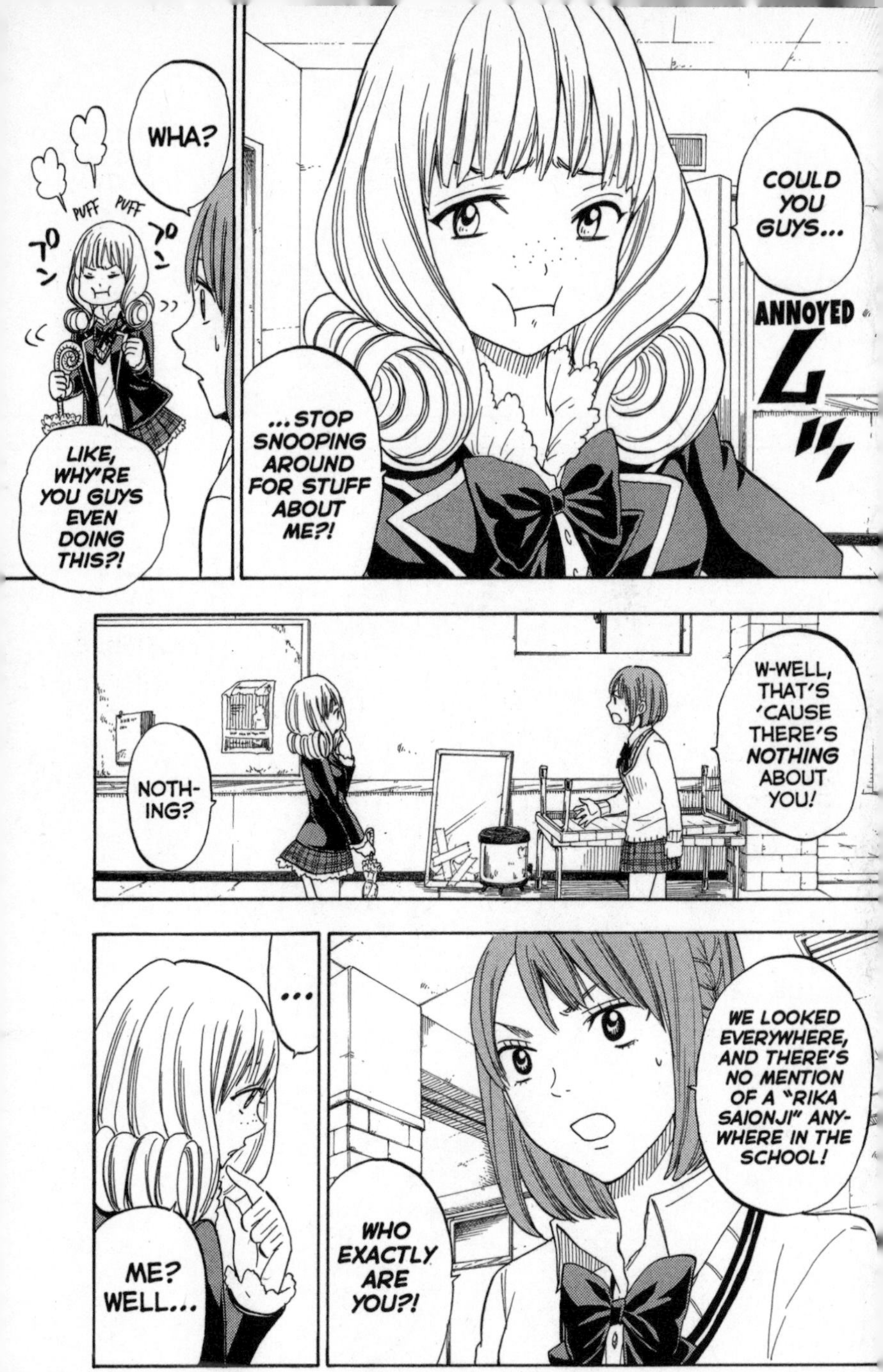
COULD YOU GUYS...
ANNOYED
...STOP SNOOPING AROUND FOR STUFF ABOUT ME?!
WHA?
PUFF PUFF
LIKE, WHY'RE YOU GUYS EVEN DOING THIS?!
W-WELL, THAT'S 'CAUSE THERE'S NOTHING ABOUT YOU!
NOTH-ING?
WE LOOKED EVERYWHERE, AND THERE'S NO MENTION OF A "RIKA SAIONJI" ANY-WHERE IN THE SCHOOL!
WHO EXACTLY ARE YOU?!
...
ME? WELL...

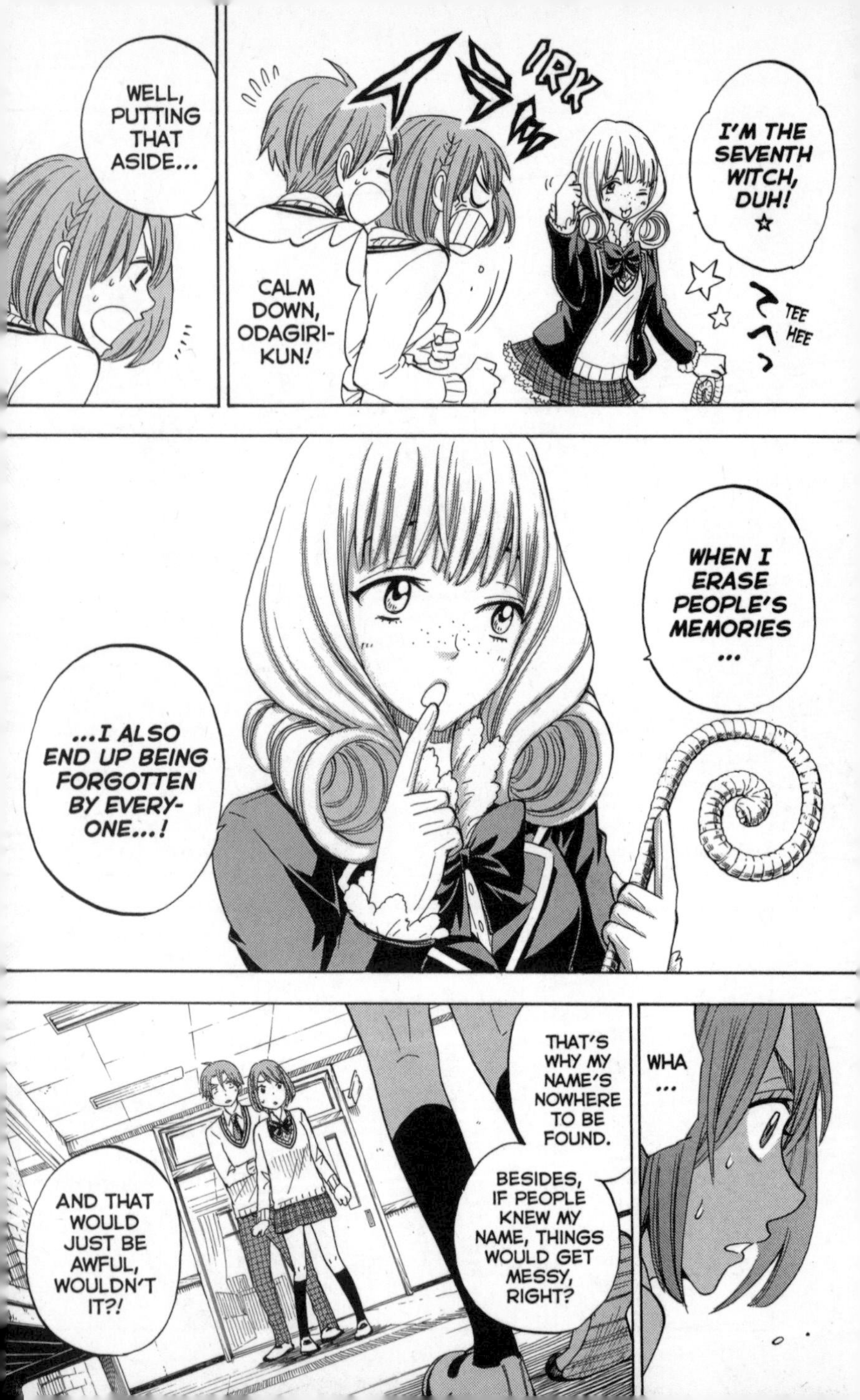
I'M THE SEVENTH WITCH, DUH! ☆
TEE HEE
IRK
CALM DOWN, ODAGIRI-KUN!
WELL, PUTTING THAT ASIDE...
WHEN I ERASE PEOPLE'S MEMORIES ...
...I ALSO END UP BEING FORGOTTEN BY EVERY-ONE...!
WHA ...
THAT'S WHY MY NAME'S NOWHERE TO BE FOUND.
BESIDES, IF PEOPLE KNEW MY NAME, THINGS WOULD GET MESSY, RIGHT?
AND THAT WOULD JUST BE AWFUL, WOULDN'T IT?!

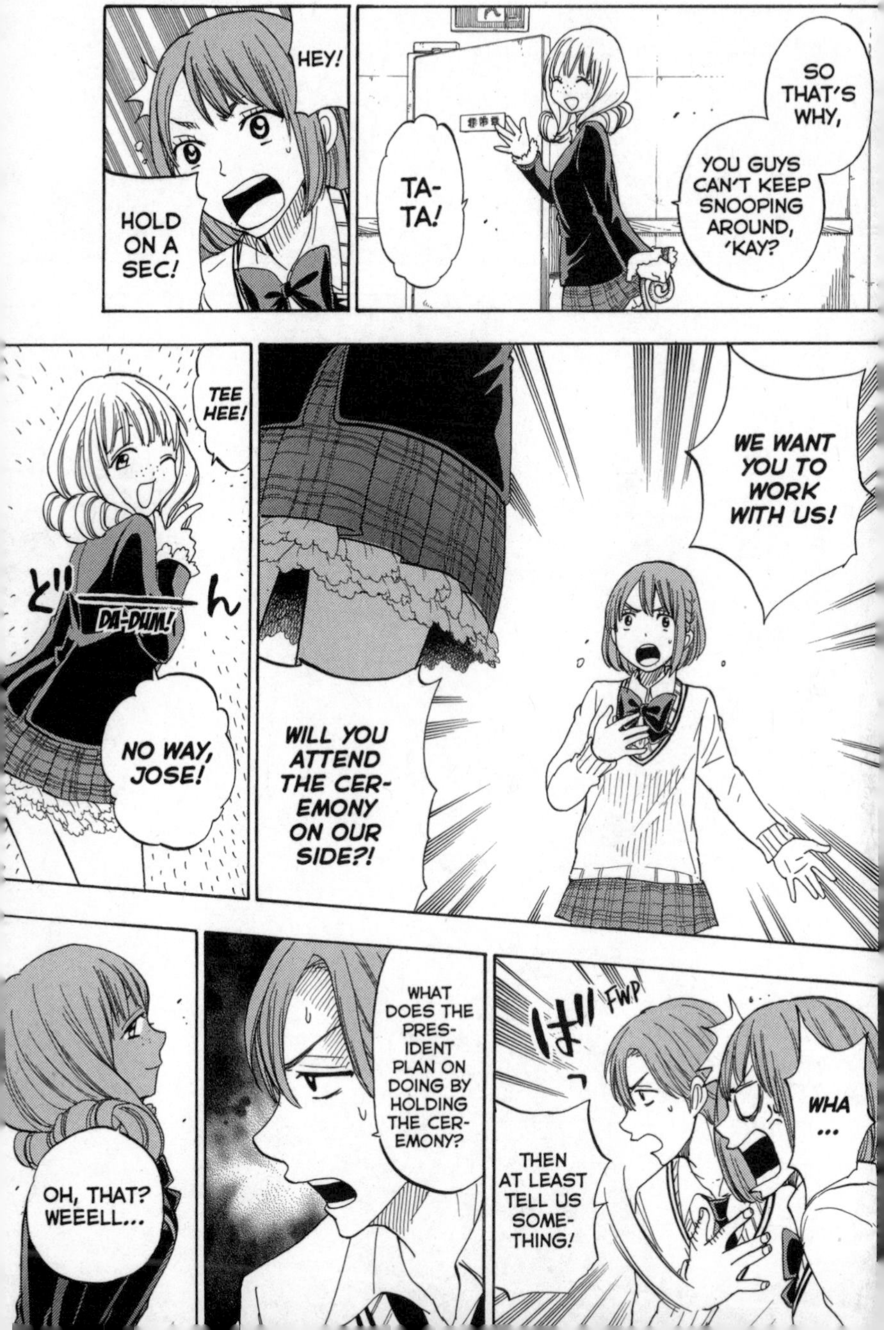
SO THAT'S WHY,
YOU GUYS CAN'T KEEP SNOOPING AROUND, 'KAY?
TA-TA!
HEY!
HOLD ON A SEC!
WE WANT YOU TO WORK WITH US!
WILL YOU ATTEND THE CER-EMONY ON OUR SIDE?!
TEE HEE!
どーん
DA-DUM!
NO WAY, JOSE!
ぱっ
FWP
WHA ...
THEN AT LEAST TELL US SOME-THING!
WHAT DOES THE PRES-IDENT PLAN ON DOING BY HOLDING THE CER-EMONY?
OH, THAT? WEEELL...

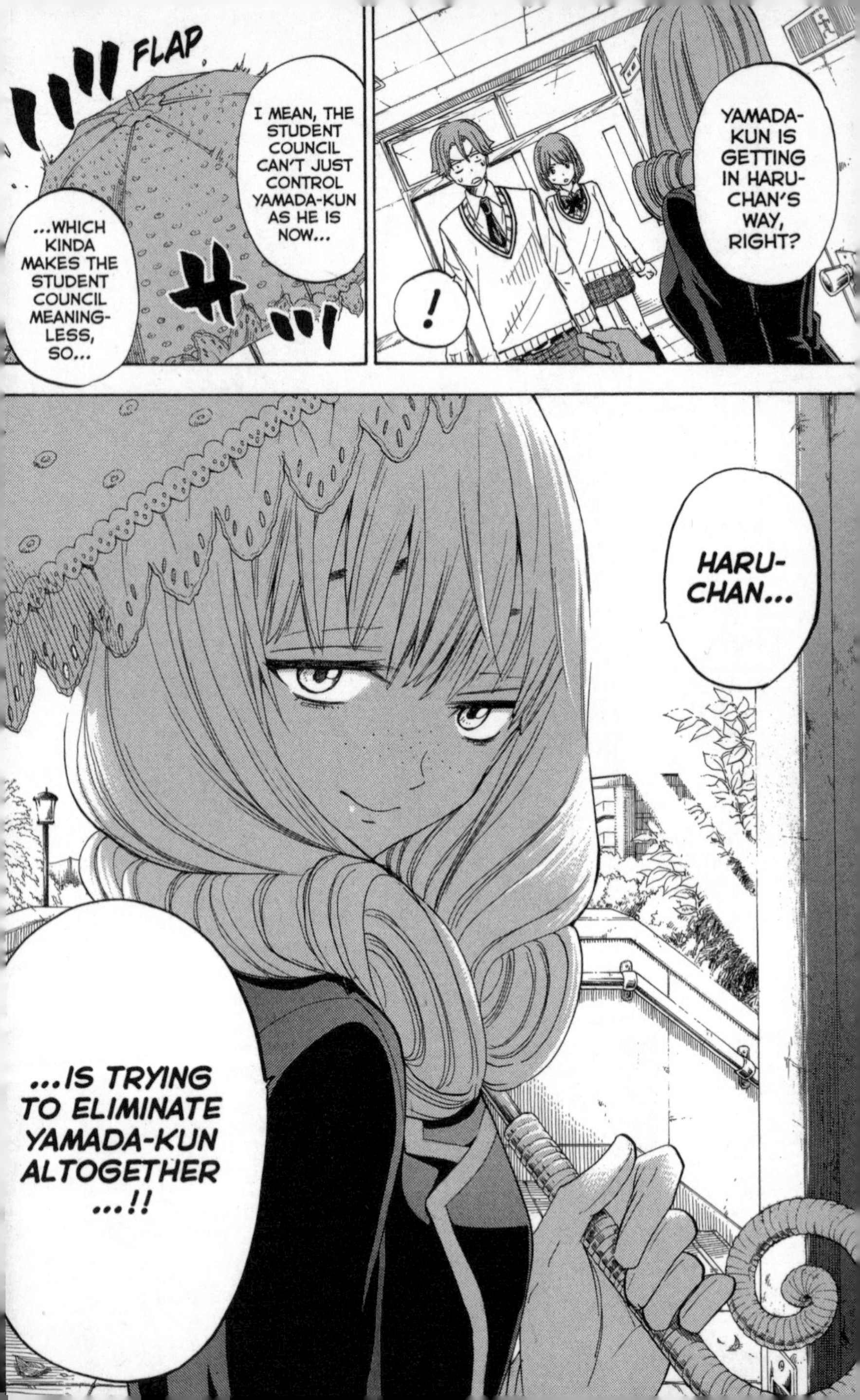
YAMADA-KUN IS GETTING IN HARU-CHAN'S WAY, RIGHT?
!
FLAP
I MEAN, THE STUDENT COUNCIL CAN'T JUST CONTROL YAMADA-KUN AS HE IS NOW...
...WHICH KINDA MAKES THE STUDENT COUNCIL MEANING-LESS, SO...
HARU-CHAN...
...IS TRYING TO ELIMINATE YAMADA-KUN ALTOGETHER ...!!

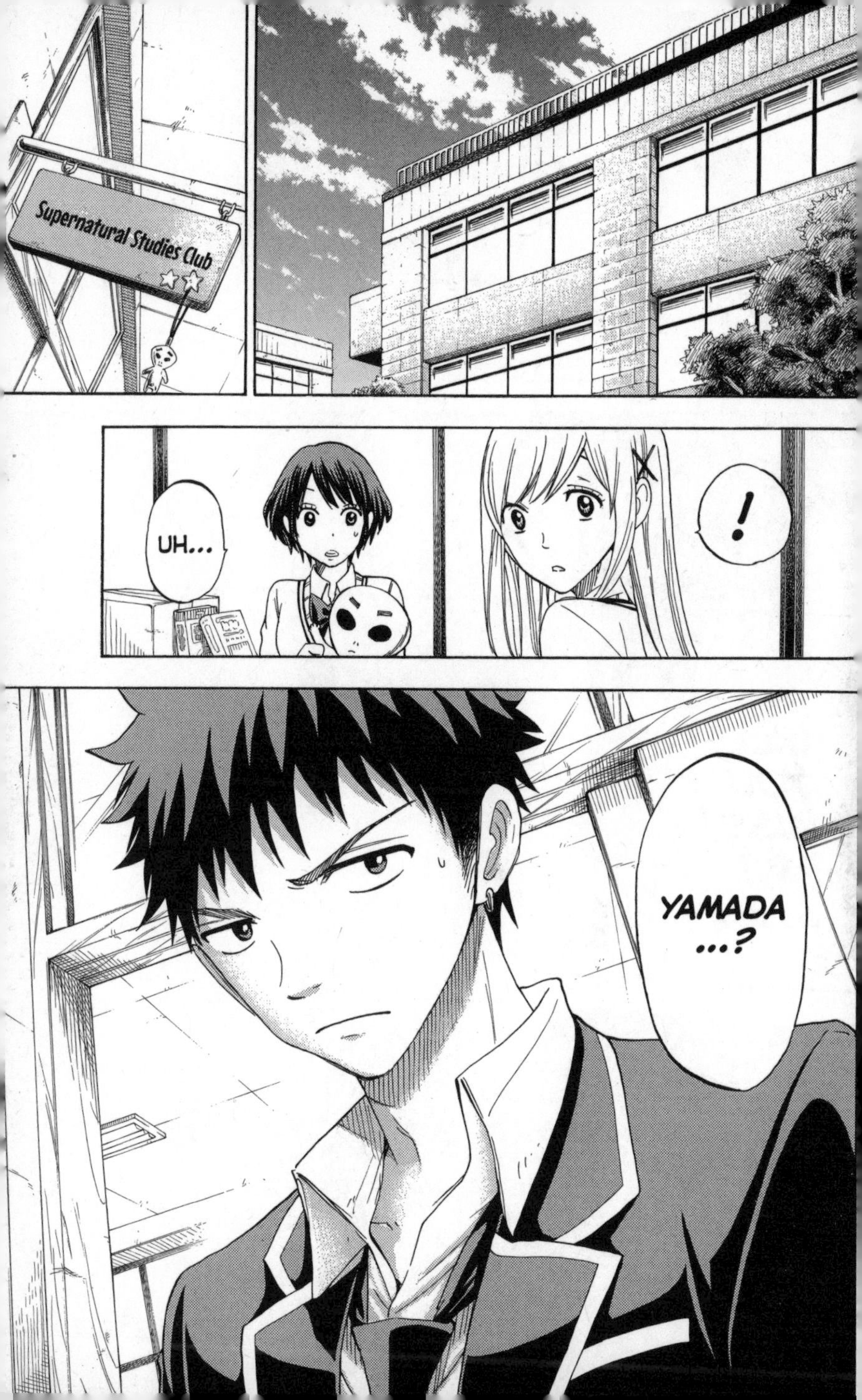
Supernatural Studies Club
!
UH...
YAMADA ...?

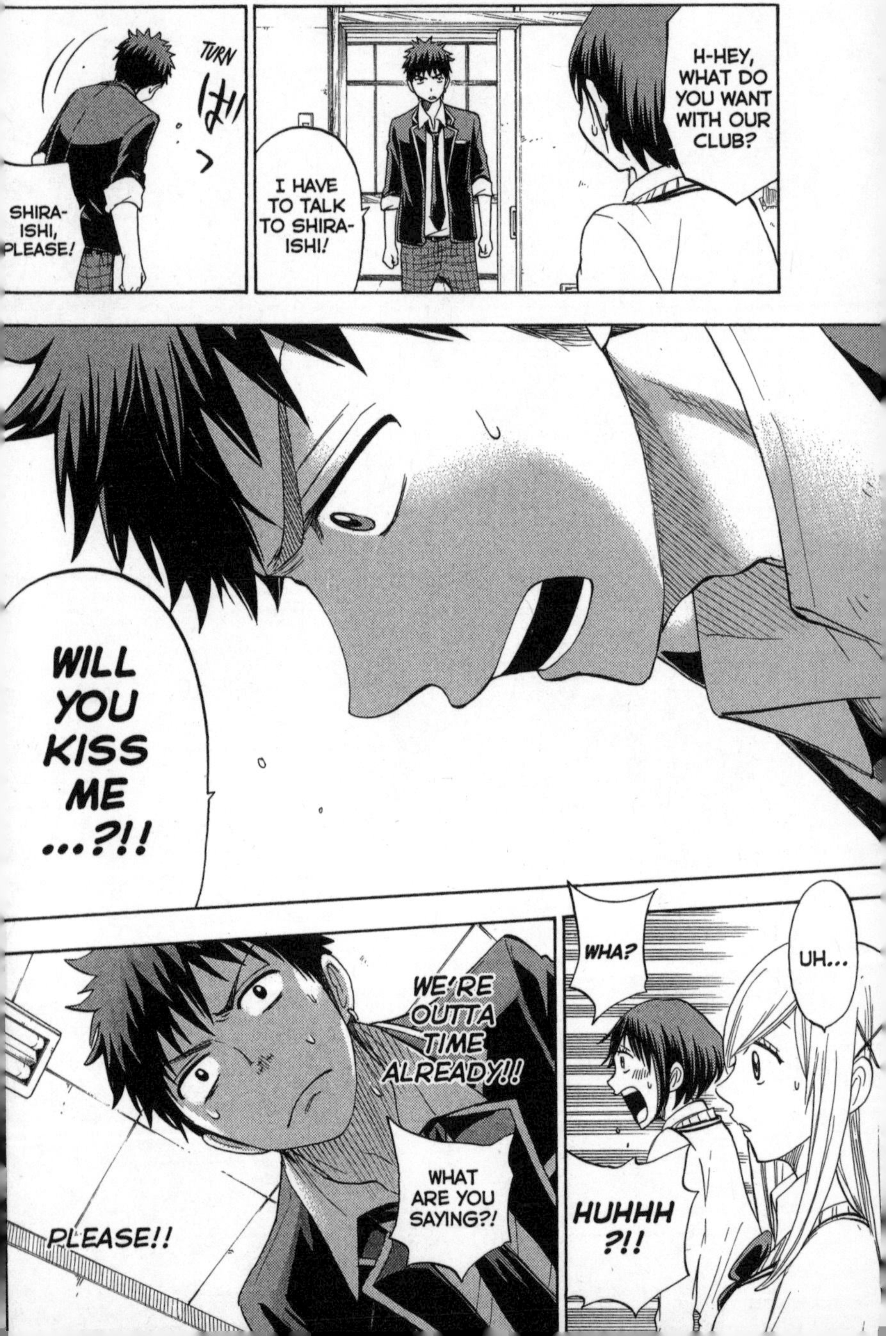
H-HEY, WHAT DO YOU WANT WITH OUR CLUB?
I HAVE TO TALK TO SHIRA-ISHI!
TURN
はっ
SHIRA-ISHI, PLEASE!
WILL YOU KISS ME ...?!!
UH...
WHA?
HUHHH ?!!
WE'RE OUTTA TIME ALREADY!!
WHAT ARE YOU SAYING?!
PLEASE!!

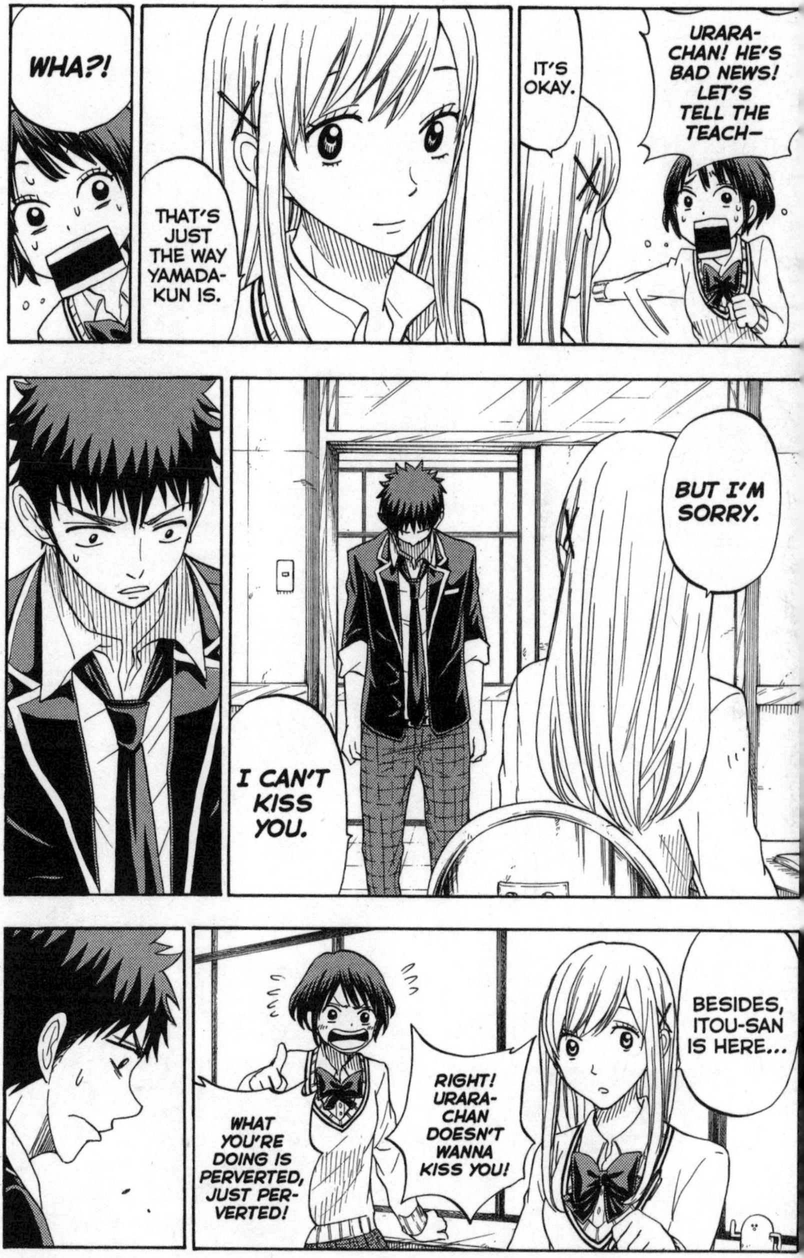
URARA-CHAN! HE'S BAD NEWS! LET'S TELL THE TEACH—
IT'S OKAY.
THAT'S JUST THE WAY YAMADA-KUN IS.
WHA?!
BUT I'M SORRY.
I CAN'T KISS YOU.
BESIDES, ITOU-SAN IS HERE...
RIGHT! URARA-CHAN DOESN'T WANNA KISS YOU!
WHAT YOU'RE DOING IS PERVERTED, JUST PERVERTED!

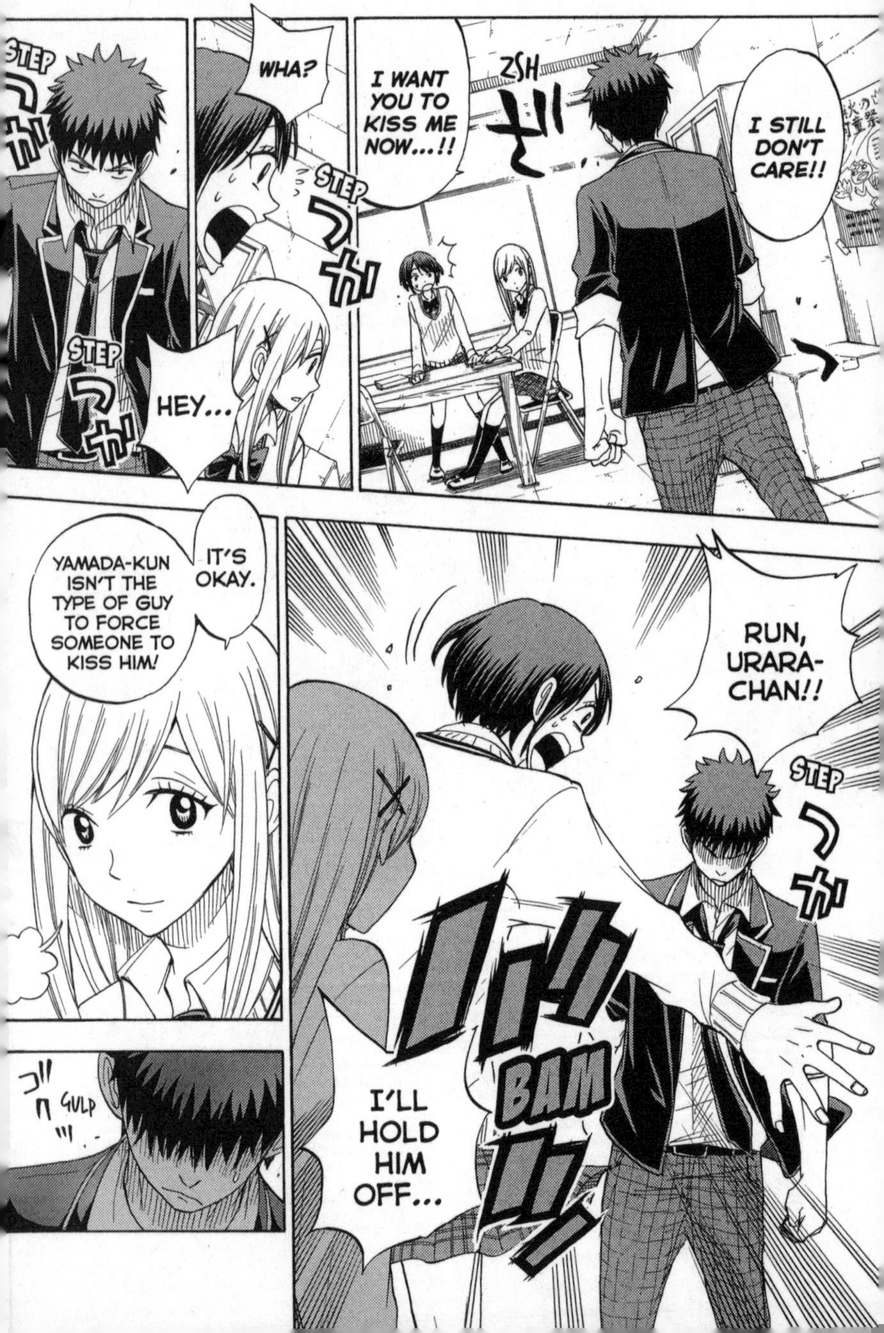

I STILL DON'T CARE!!
ZSH
I WANT YOU TO KISS ME NOW...!!
WHA?
STEP
HEY...
STEP
STEP
RUN, URARA-CHAN!!
STEP
I'LL HOLD HIM OFF...
BAM
IT'S OKAY.
YAMADA-KUN ISN'T THE TYPE OF GUY TO FORCE SOMEONE TO KISS HIM!
GULP

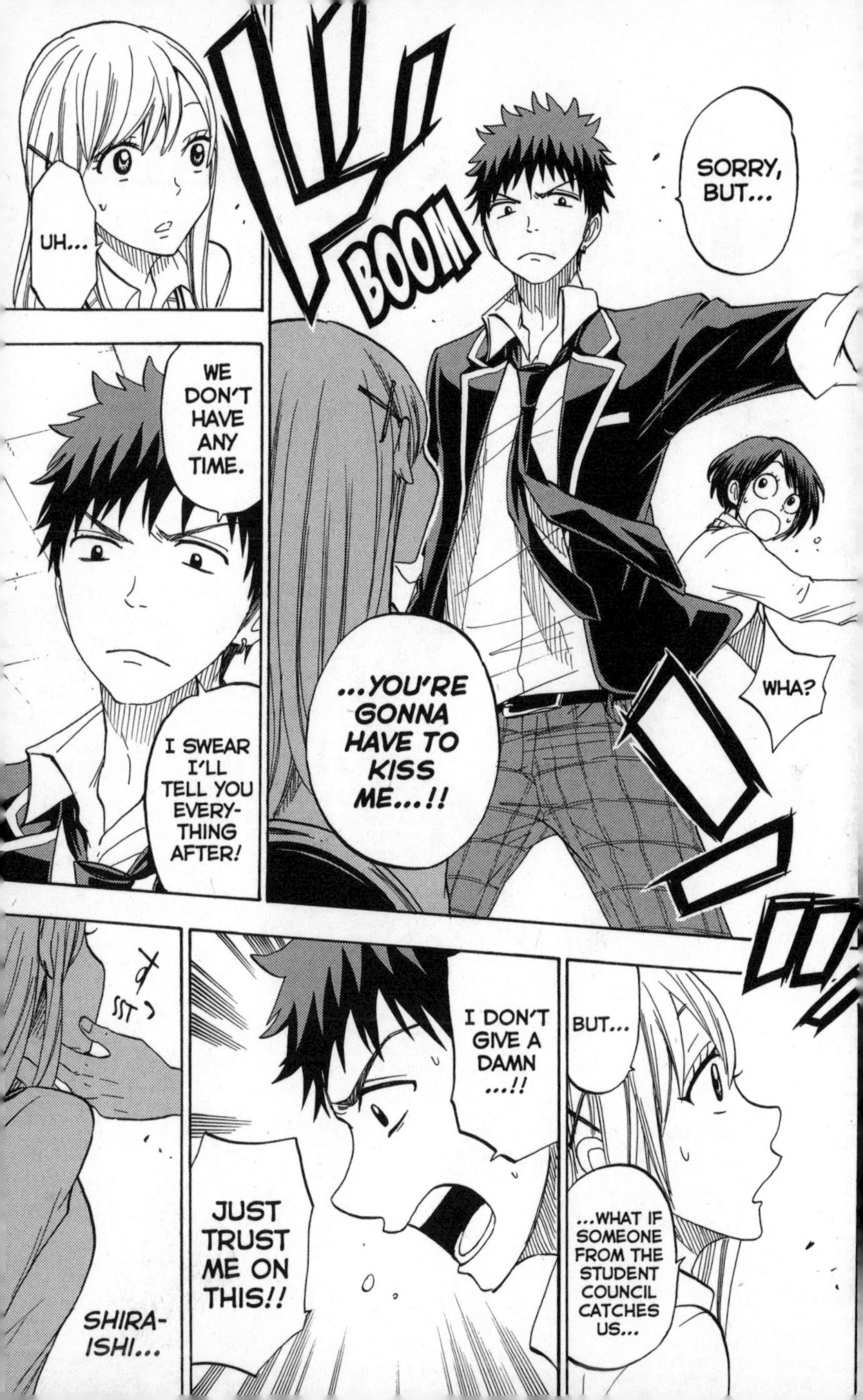
SORRY, BUT...
BOOM
WHA?
...YOU'RE GONNA HAVE TO KISS ME...!!
UH...
WE DON'T HAVE ANY TIME.
I SWEAR I'LL TELL YOU EVERY-THING AFTER!
BUT...
...WHAT IF SOMEONE FROM THE STUDENT COUNCIL CATCHES US...
I DON'T GIVE A DAMN ...!!
JUST TRUST ME ON THIS!!
SST
SHIRA-ISHI...

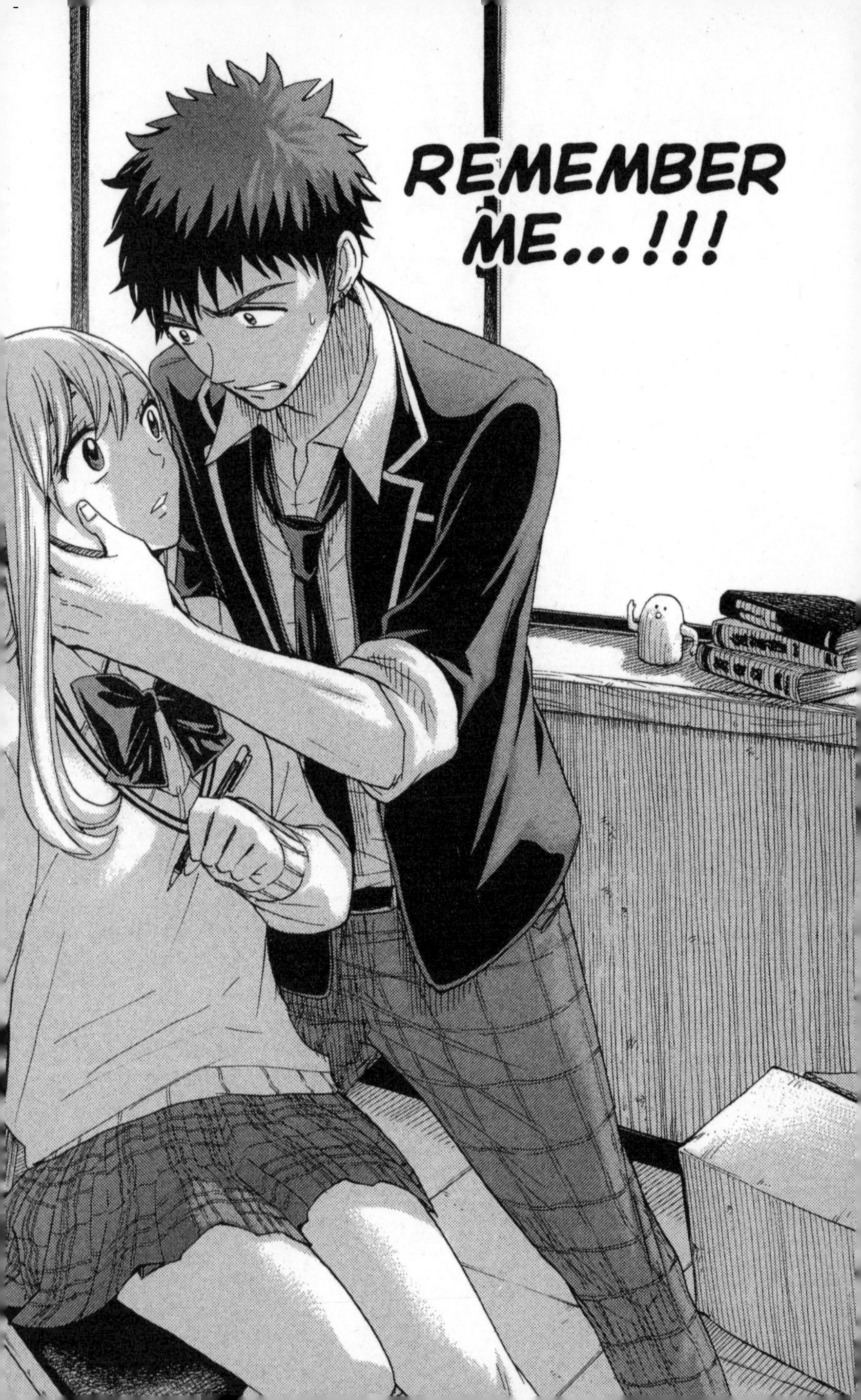
REMEMBER ME...!!!

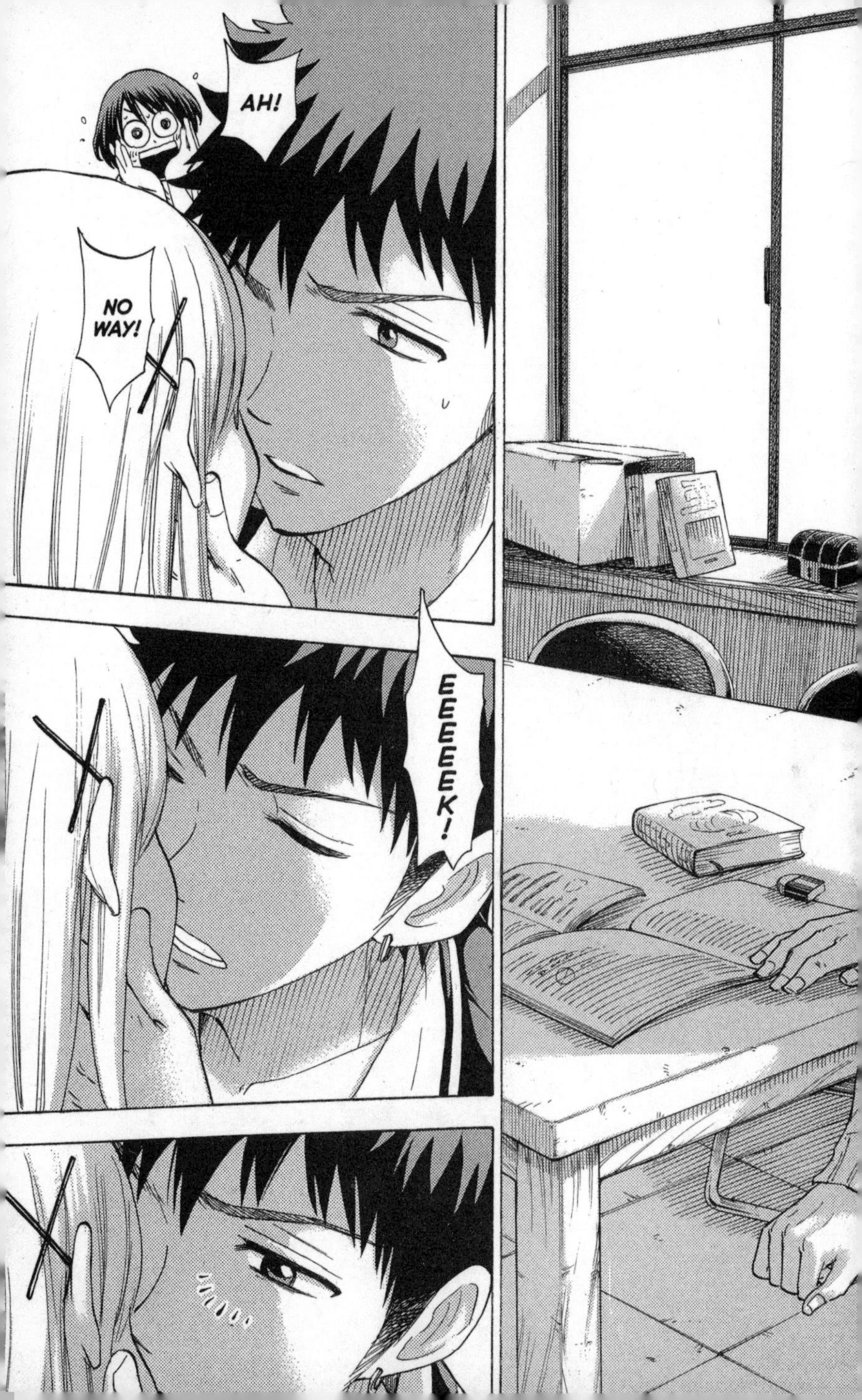
AH!
NO WAY!
EEEEEEK!

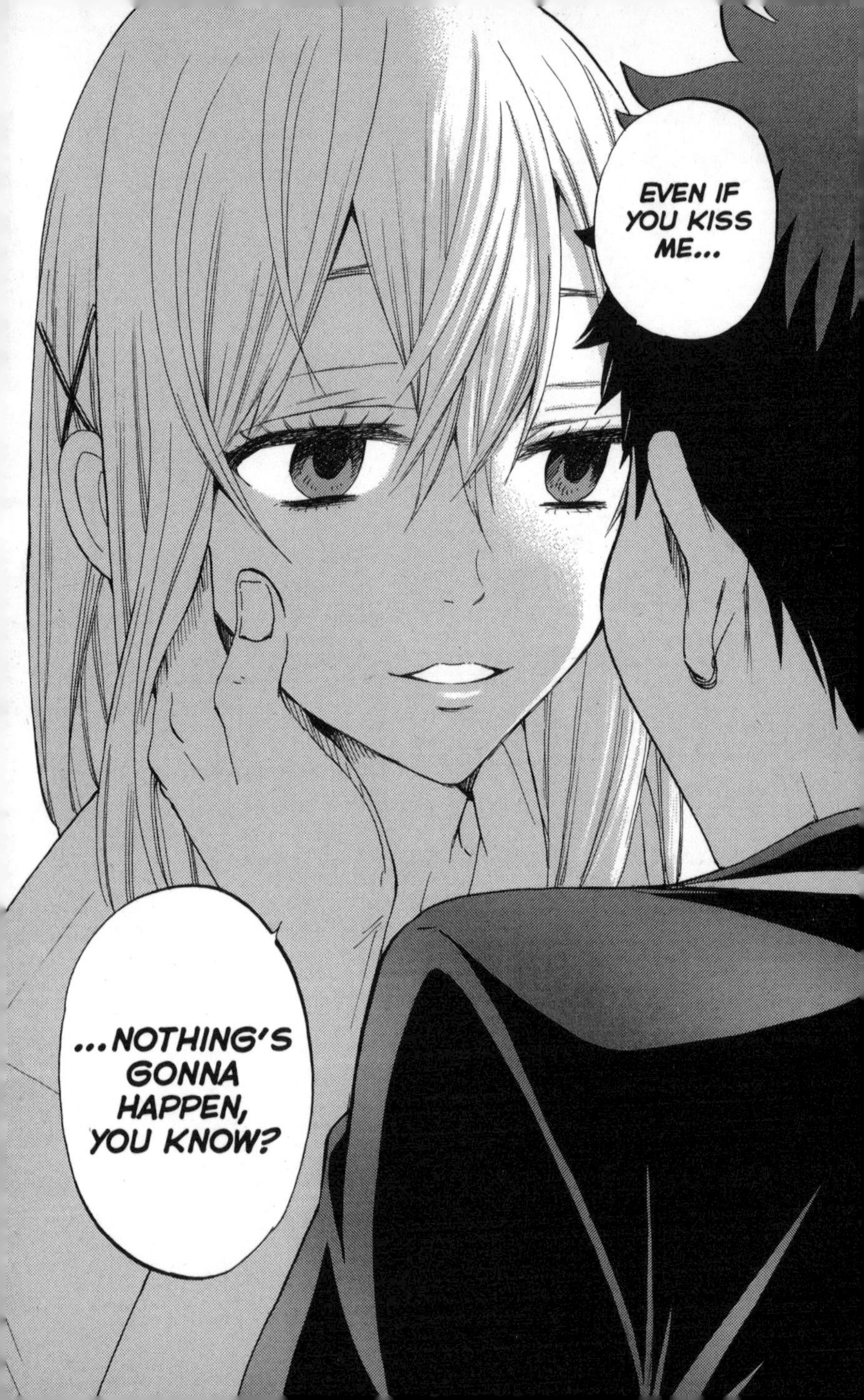
EVEN IF YOU KISS ME...
...NOTHING'S GONNA HAPPEN, YOU KNOW?

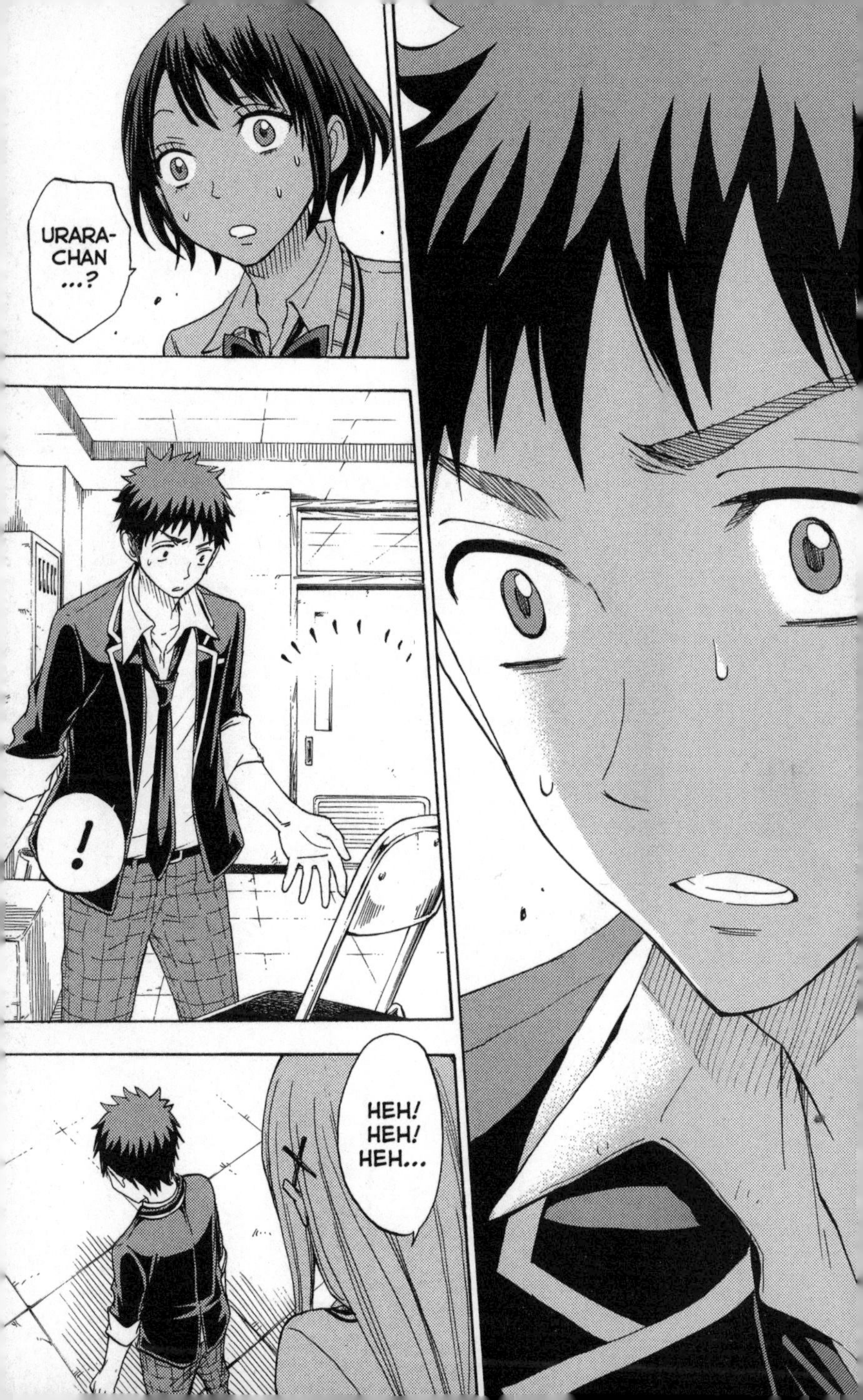
URARA-CHAN ...?
!
HEH! HEH! HEH...

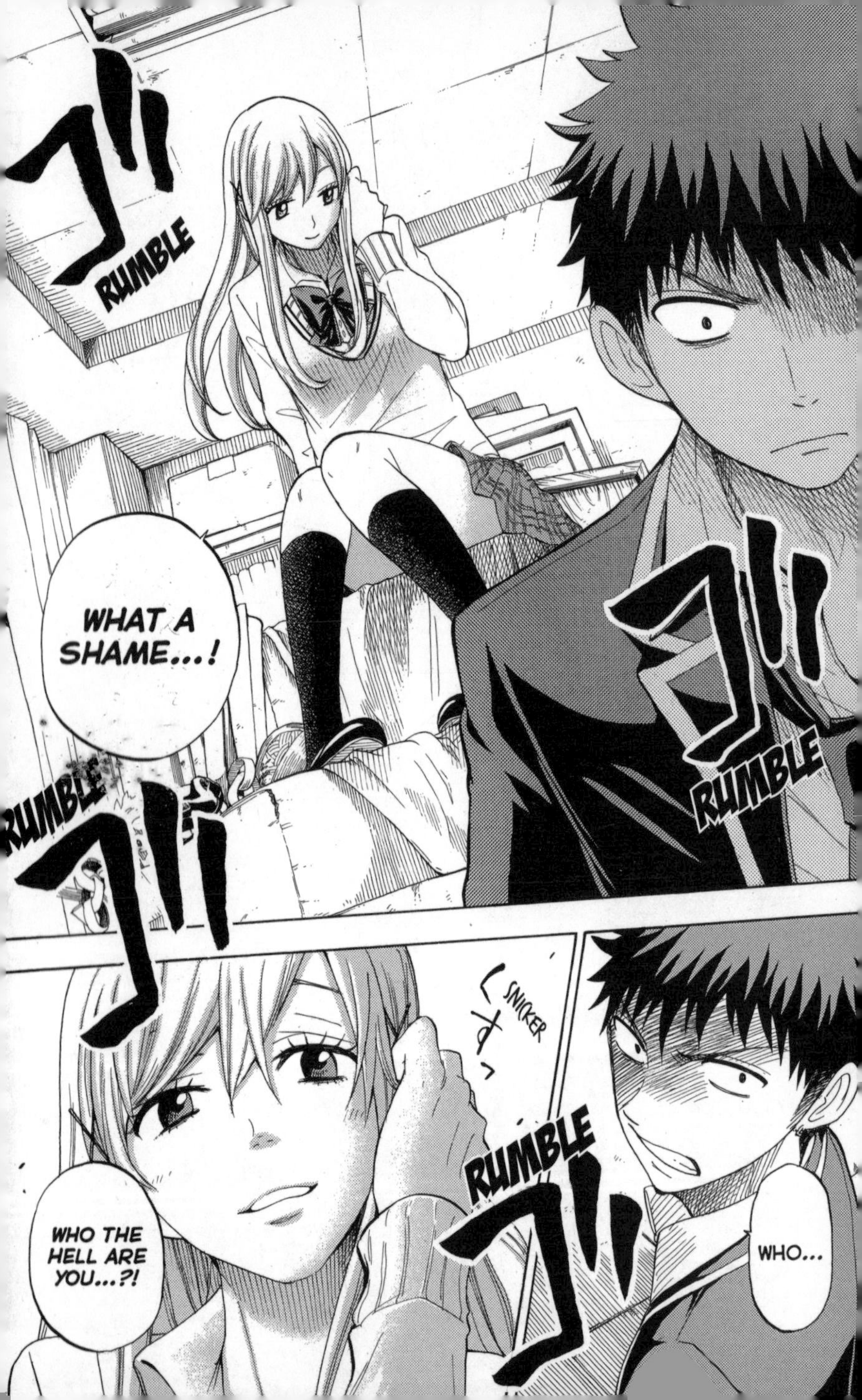
RUMBLE
RUMBLE
WHAT A SHAME...!
RUMBLE
RUMBLE
WHO...
SNICKER
WHO THE HELL ARE YOU...?!

CHAPTER 81: I'm watching a movie!

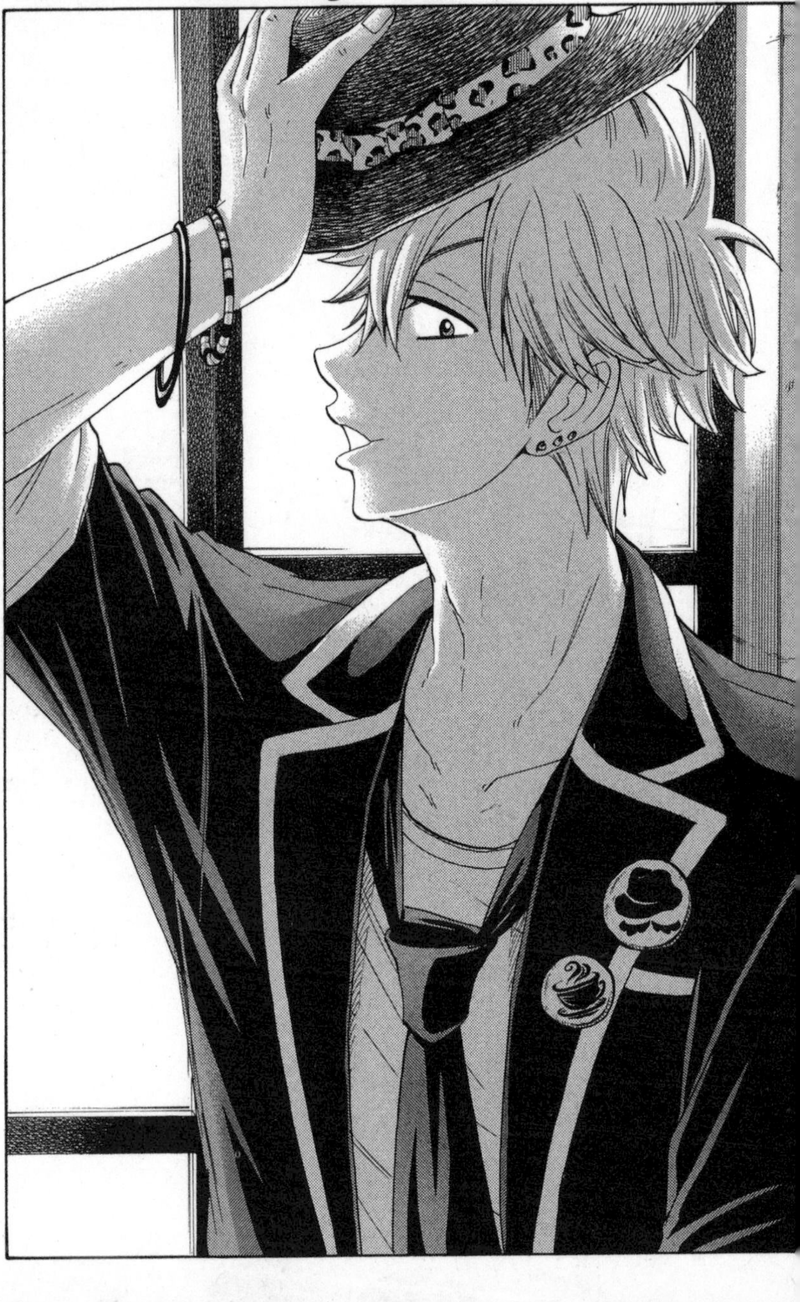

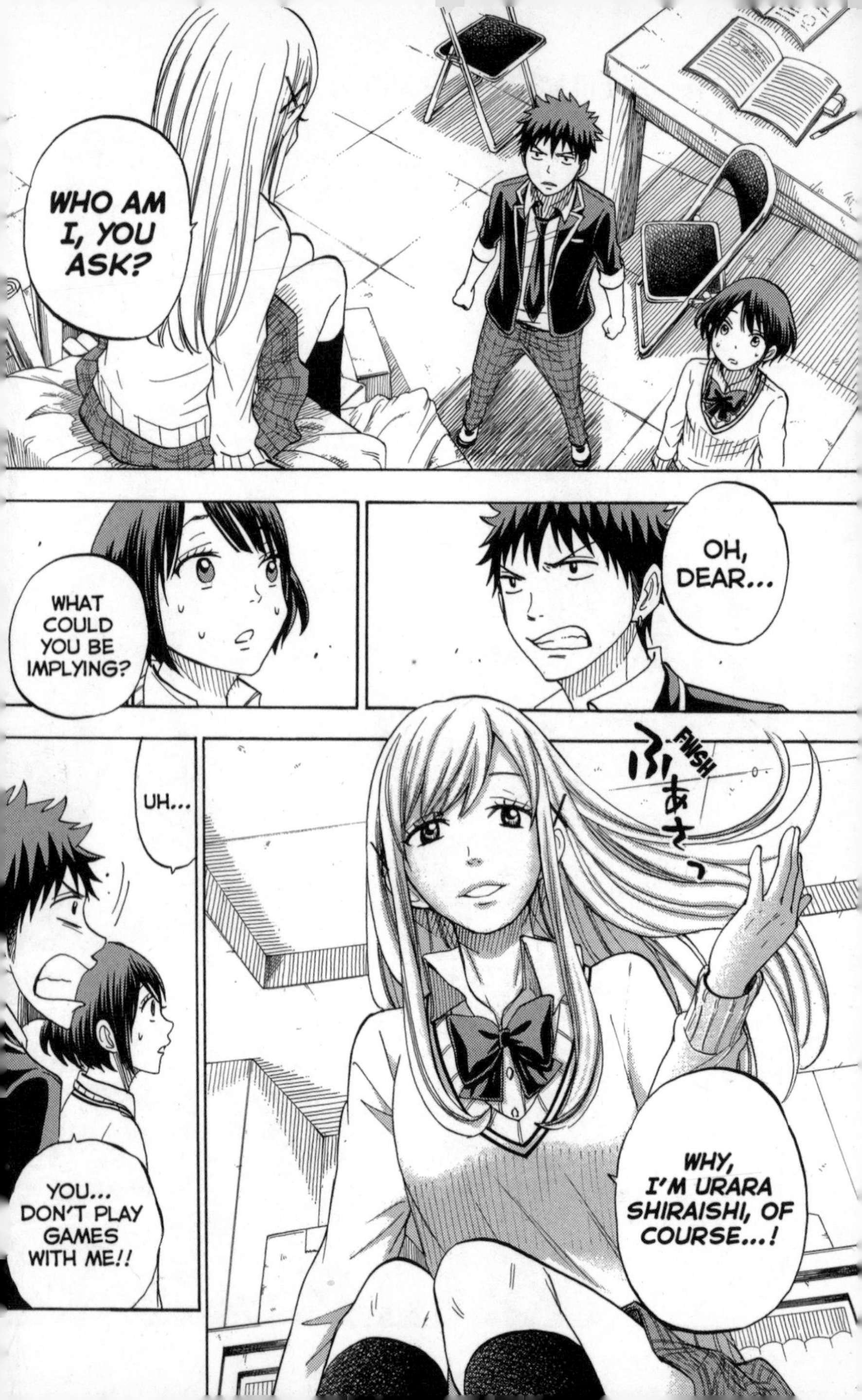
WHO AM I, YOU ASK?
OH, DEAR...
WHAT COULD YOU BE IMPLYING?
ふぁさっ
FWSH
WHY, I'M URARA SHIRAISHI, OF COURSE...!
UH...
YOU... DON'T PLAY GAMES WITH ME!!

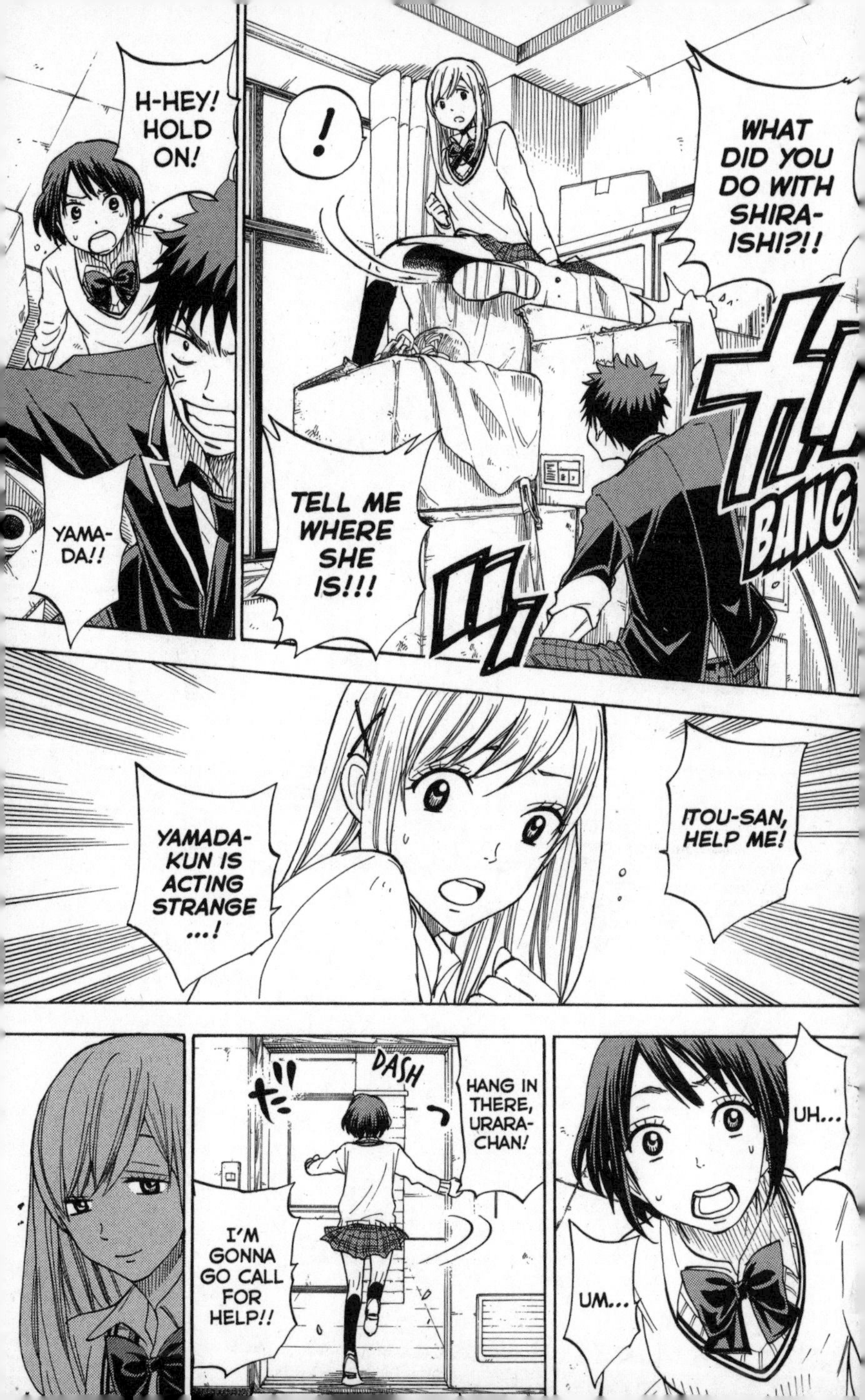
WHAT DID YOU DO WITH SHIRA-ISHI?!!
!
TELL ME WHERE SHE IS!!!
BANG
H-HEY! HOLD ON!
YAMA-DA!!
ITOU-SAN, HELP ME!
YAMADA-KUN IS ACTING STRANGE ...!
UH...
UM...
DASH
HANG IN THERE, URARA-CHAN!
I'M GONNA GO CALL FOR HELP!!

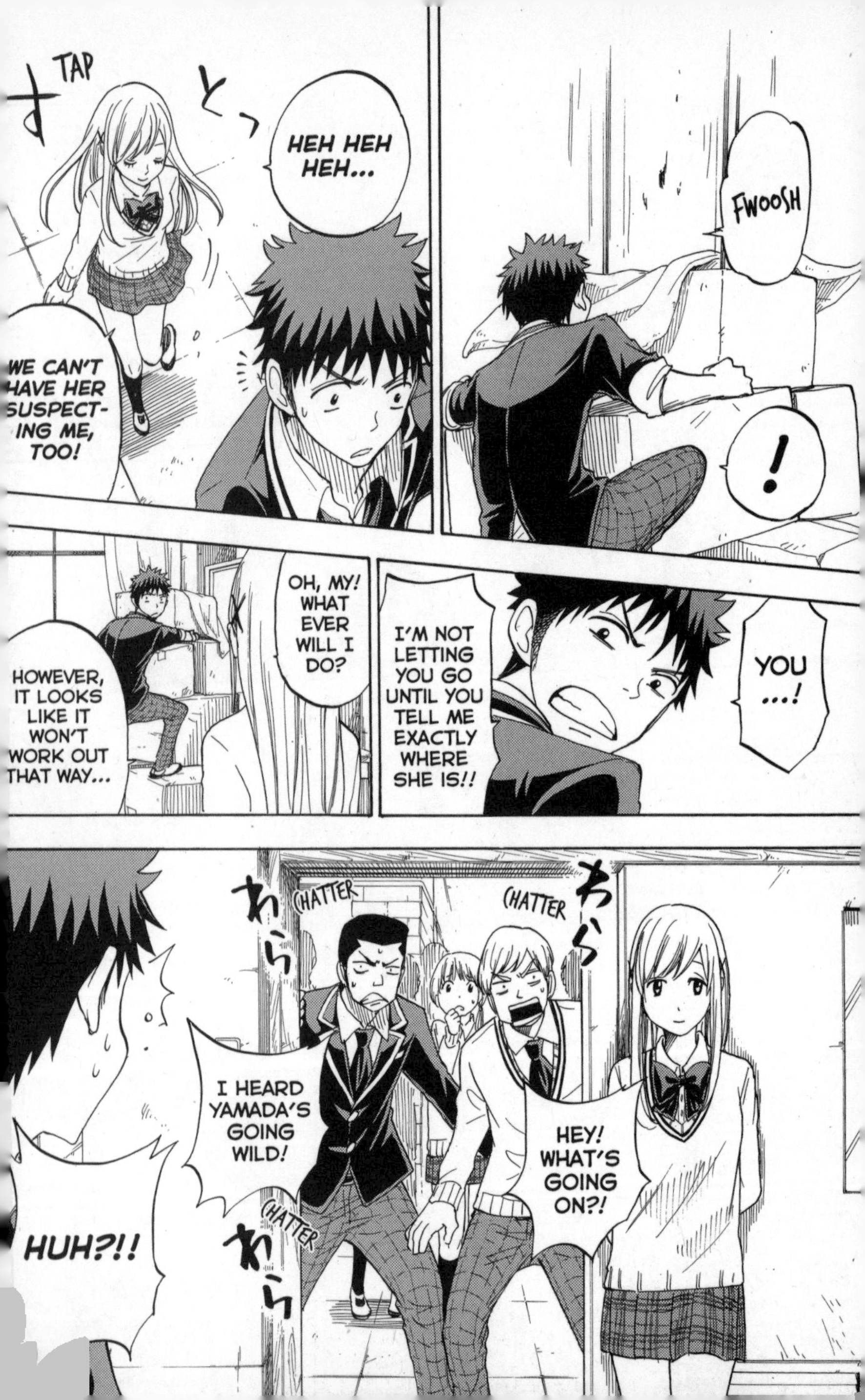
FWOOSH
!
とっ
HEH HEH HEH...
TAP
す
WE CAN'T HAVE HER SUSPECT-ING ME, TOO!
YOU ...!
I'M NOT LETTING YOU GO UNTIL YOU TELL ME EXACTLY WHERE SHE IS!!
OH, MY! WHAT EVER WILL I DO?
HOWEVER, IT LOOKS LIKE IT WON'T WORK OUT THAT WAY...
わら
CHATTER
HEY! WHAT'S GOING ON?!
CHATTER
わら
I HEARD YAMADA'S GOING WILD!
CHATTER
わら
HUH?!!

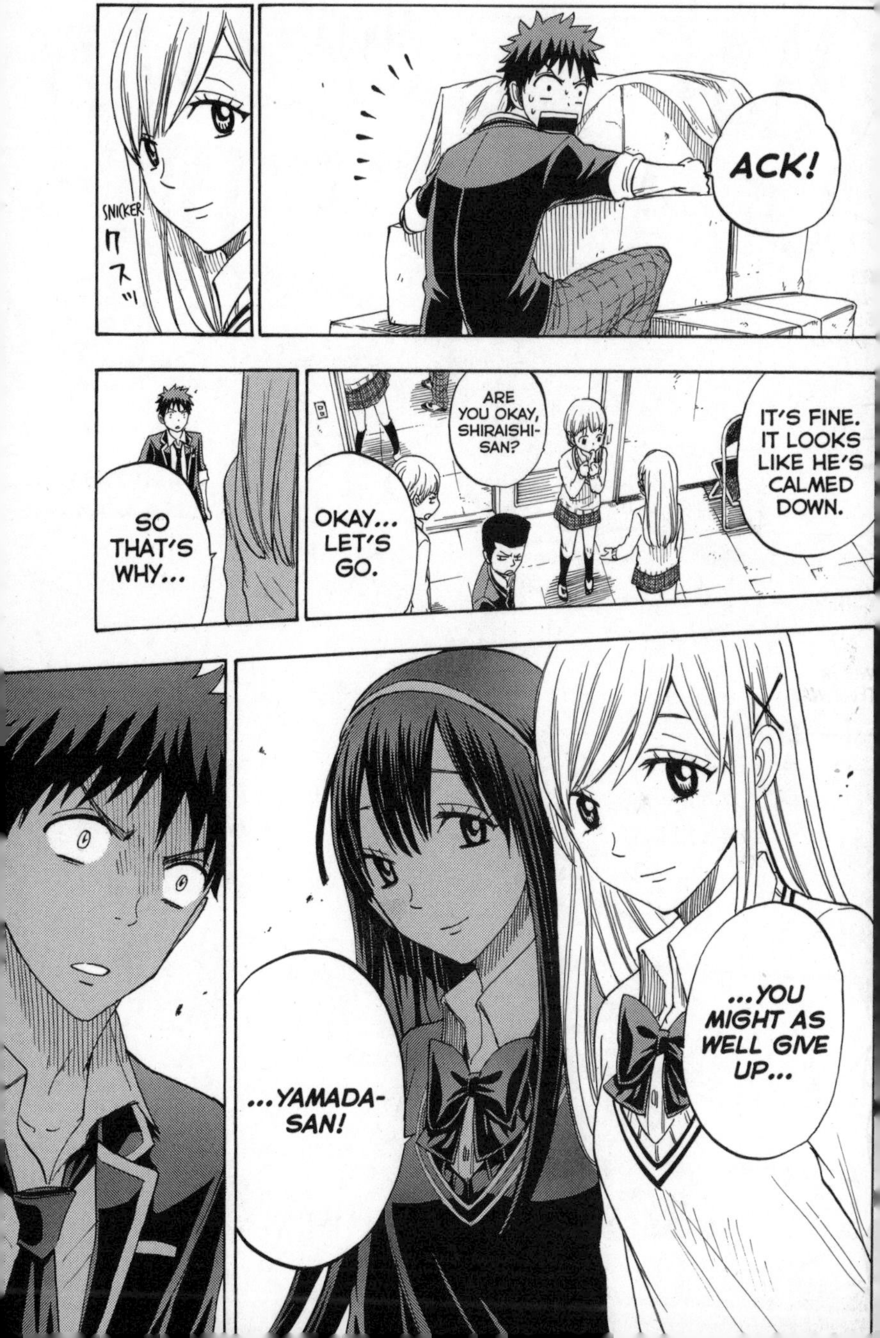
ACK!
SNICKER
クスッ
ARE YOU OKAY, SHIRAISHI-SAN?
IT'S FINE. IT LOOKS LIKE HE'S CALMED DOWN.
OKAY... LET'S GO.
SO THAT'S WHY...
...YOU MIGHT AS WELL GIVE UP...
...YAMADA-SAN!

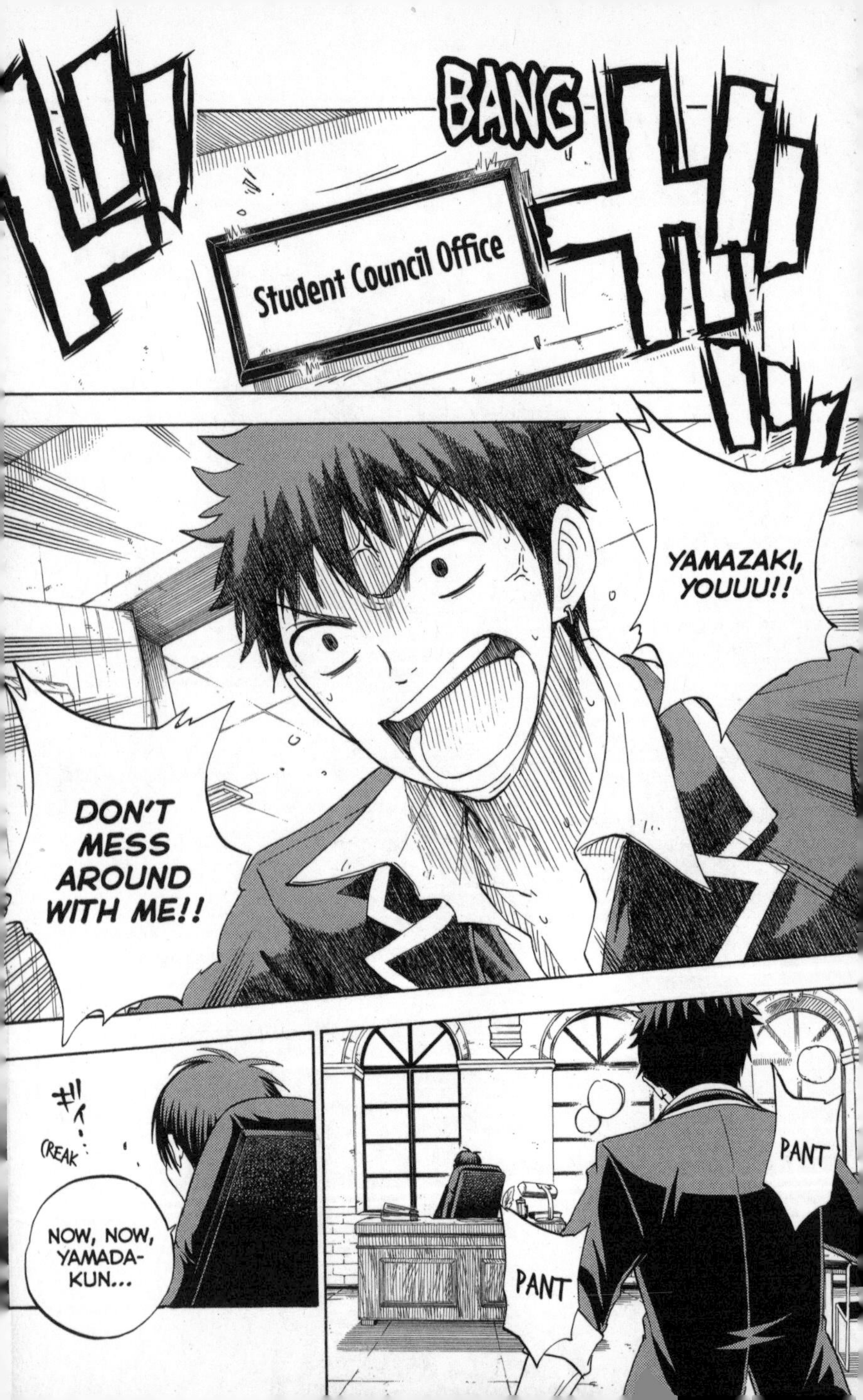
BANG
Student Council Office
YAMAZAKI, YOUUU!!
DON'T MESS AROUND WITH ME!!
PANT
PANT
CREAK
NOW, NOW, YAMADA-KUN...

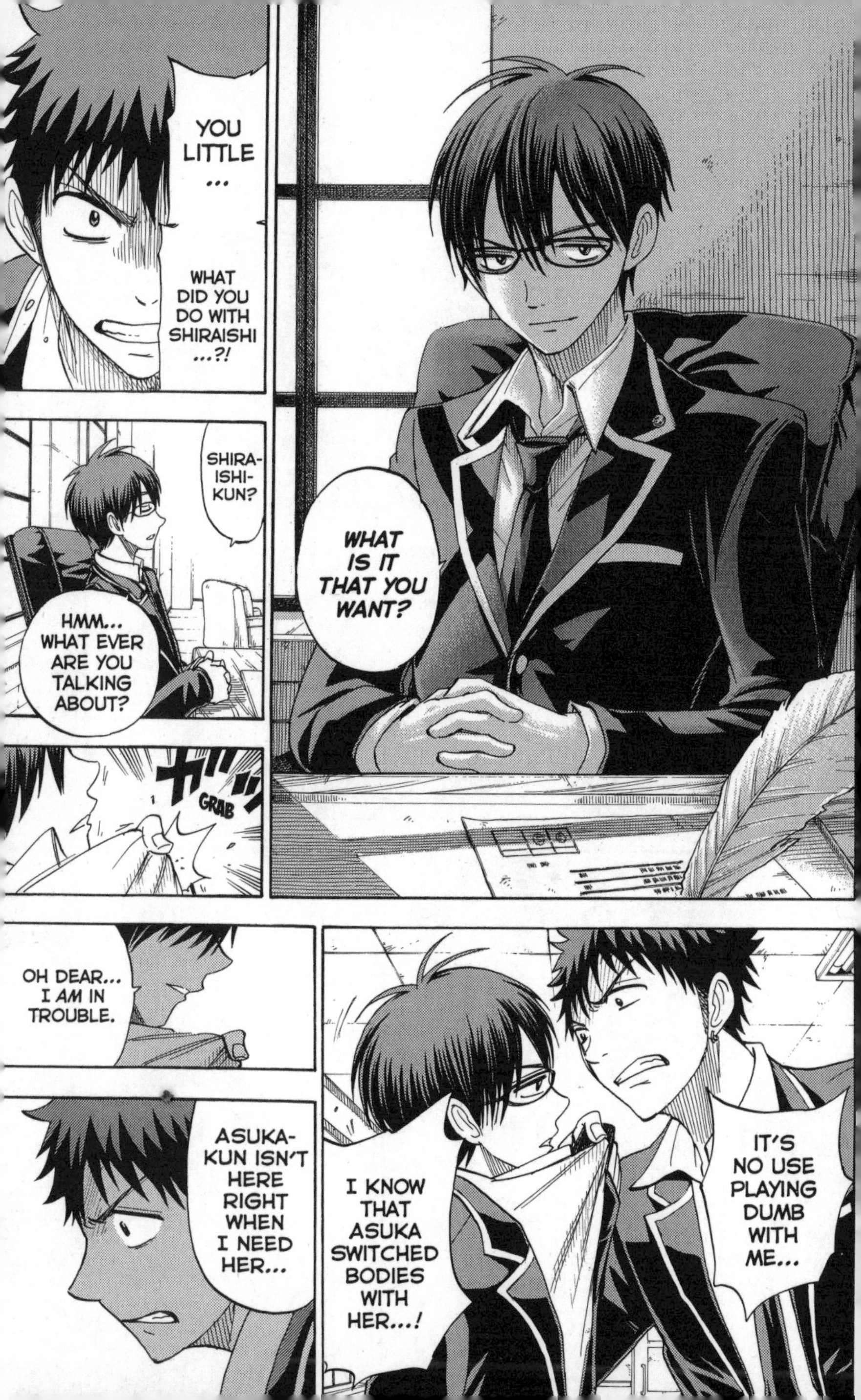
WHAT IS IT THAT YOU WANT?
YOU LITTLE ...
WHAT DID YOU DO WITH SHIRAISHI ...?!
SHIRA-ISHI-KUN?
HMM... WHAT EVER ARE YOU TALKING ABOUT?
GRAB
IT'S NO USE PLAYING DUMB WITH ME...
I KNOW THAT ASUKA SWITCHED BODIES WITH HER...!
OH DEAR... I *AM* IN TROUBLE.
ASUKA-KUN ISN'T HERE RIGHT WHEN I NEED HER...

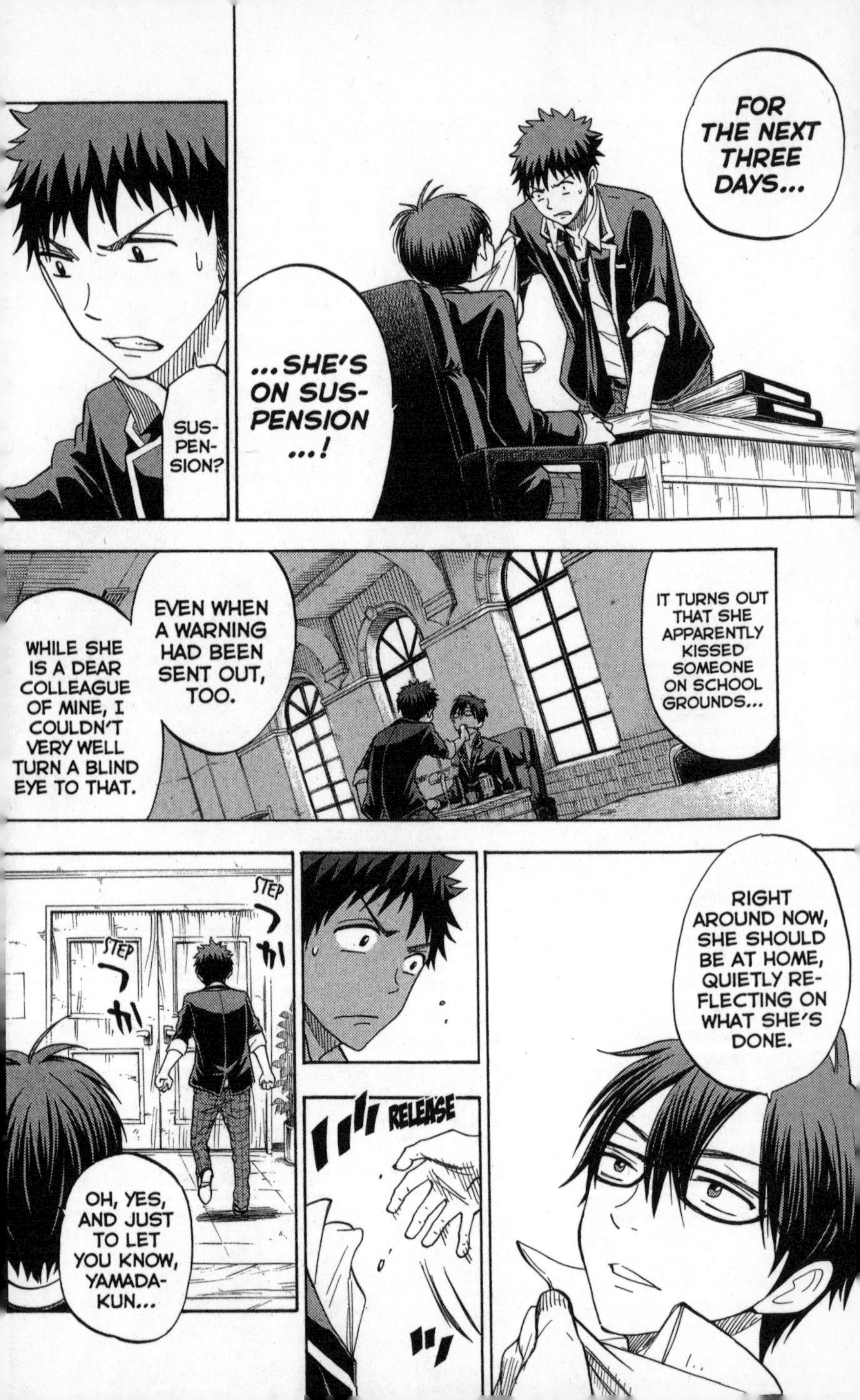
FOR THE NEXT THREE DAYS...
...SHE'S ON SUS-PENSION ...!
SUS-PEN-SION?
IT TURNS OUT THAT SHE APPARENTLY KISSED SOMEONE ON SCHOOL GROUNDS...
EVEN WHEN A WARNING HAD BEEN SENT OUT, TOO.
WHILE SHE IS A DEAR COLLEAGUE OF MINE, I COULDN'T VERY WELL TURN A BLIND EYE TO THAT.
RIGHT AROUND NOW, SHE SHOULD BE AT HOME, QUIETLY RE-FLECTING ON WHAT SHE'S DONE.
RELEASE
STEP
STEP
OH, YES, AND JUST TO LET YOU KNOW, YAMADA-KUN...

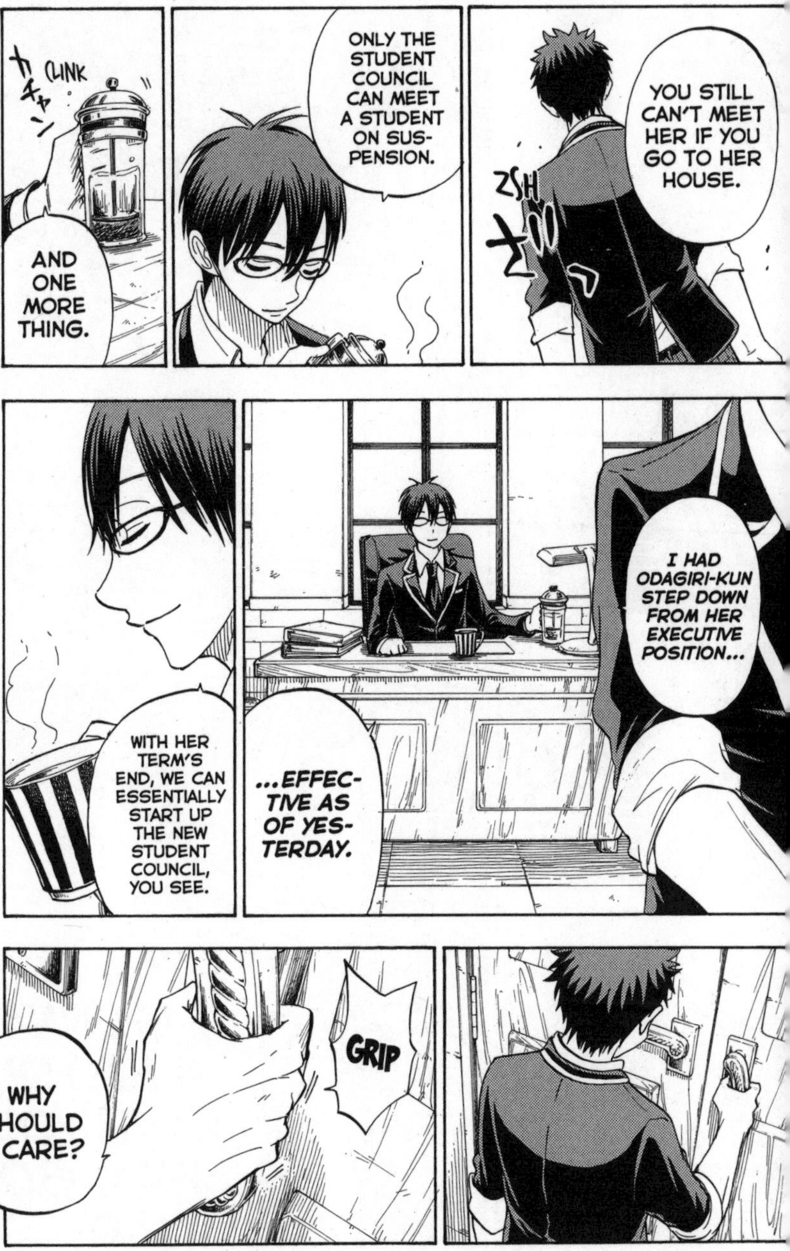
YOU STILL CAN'T MEET HER IF YOU GO TO HER HOUSE.
ZSH
ONLY THE STUDENT COUNCIL CAN MEET A STUDENT ON SUS-PENSION.
CLINK
AND ONE MORE THING.
I HAD ODAGIRI-KUN STEP DOWN FROM HER EXECUTIVE POSITION...
...EFFEC-TIVE AS OF YES-TERDAY.
WITH HER TERM'S END, WE CAN ESSENTIALLY START UP THE NEW STUDENT COUNCIL, YOU SEE.
GRIP
WHY SHOULD I CARE?

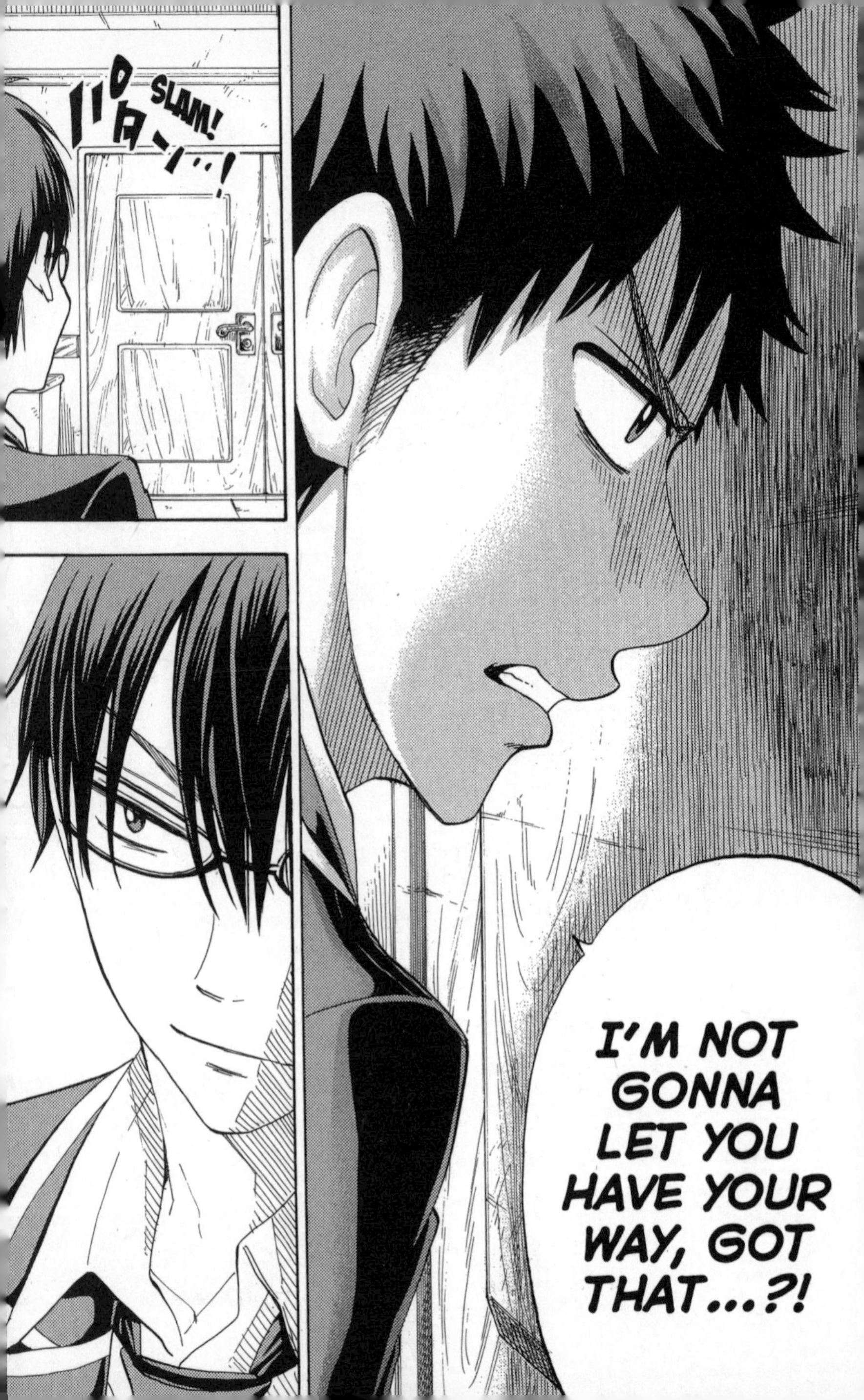
I'M NOT GONNA LET YOU HAVE YOUR WAY, GOT THAT...?!
バタン…!
SLAM!

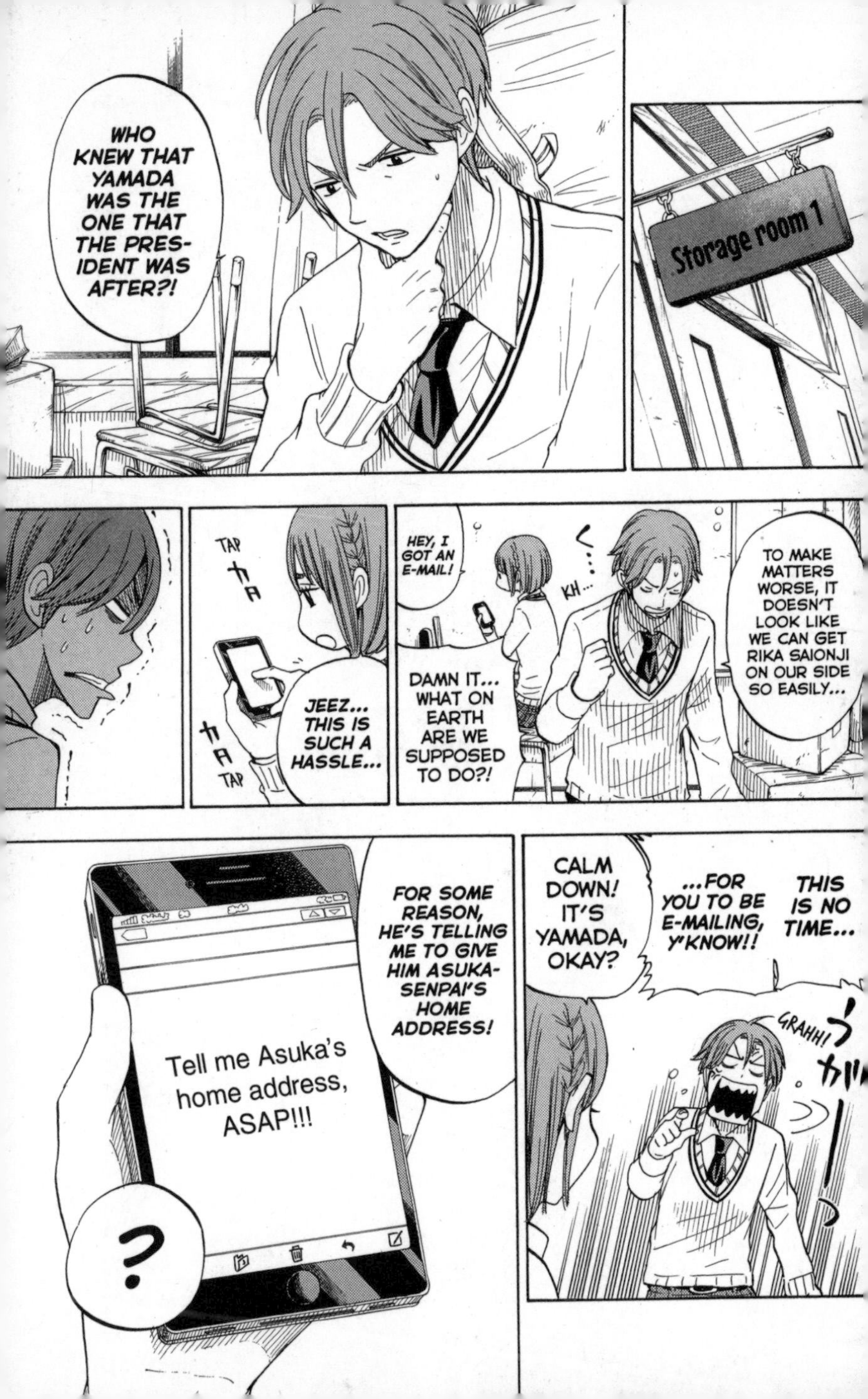
Storage room 1
WHO KNEW THAT YAMADA WAS THE ONE THAT THE PRES-IDENT WAS AFTER?!
TO MAKE MATTERS WORSE, IT DOESN'T LOOK LIKE WE CAN GET RIKA SAIONJI ON OUR SIDE SO EASILY...
KH...
HEY, I GOT AN E-MAIL!
DAMN IT... WHAT ON EARTH ARE WE SUPPOSED TO DO?!
TAP
TAP
JEEZ... THIS IS SUCH A HASSLE...
THIS IS NO TIME...
...FOR YOU TO BE E-MAILING, Y'KNOW!!
GRAHH!
CALM DOWN! IT'S YAMADA, OKAY?
FOR SOME REASON, HE'S TELLING ME TO GIVE HIM ASUKA-SENPAI'S HOME ADDRESS!
Tell me Asuka's home address, ASAP!!!
?

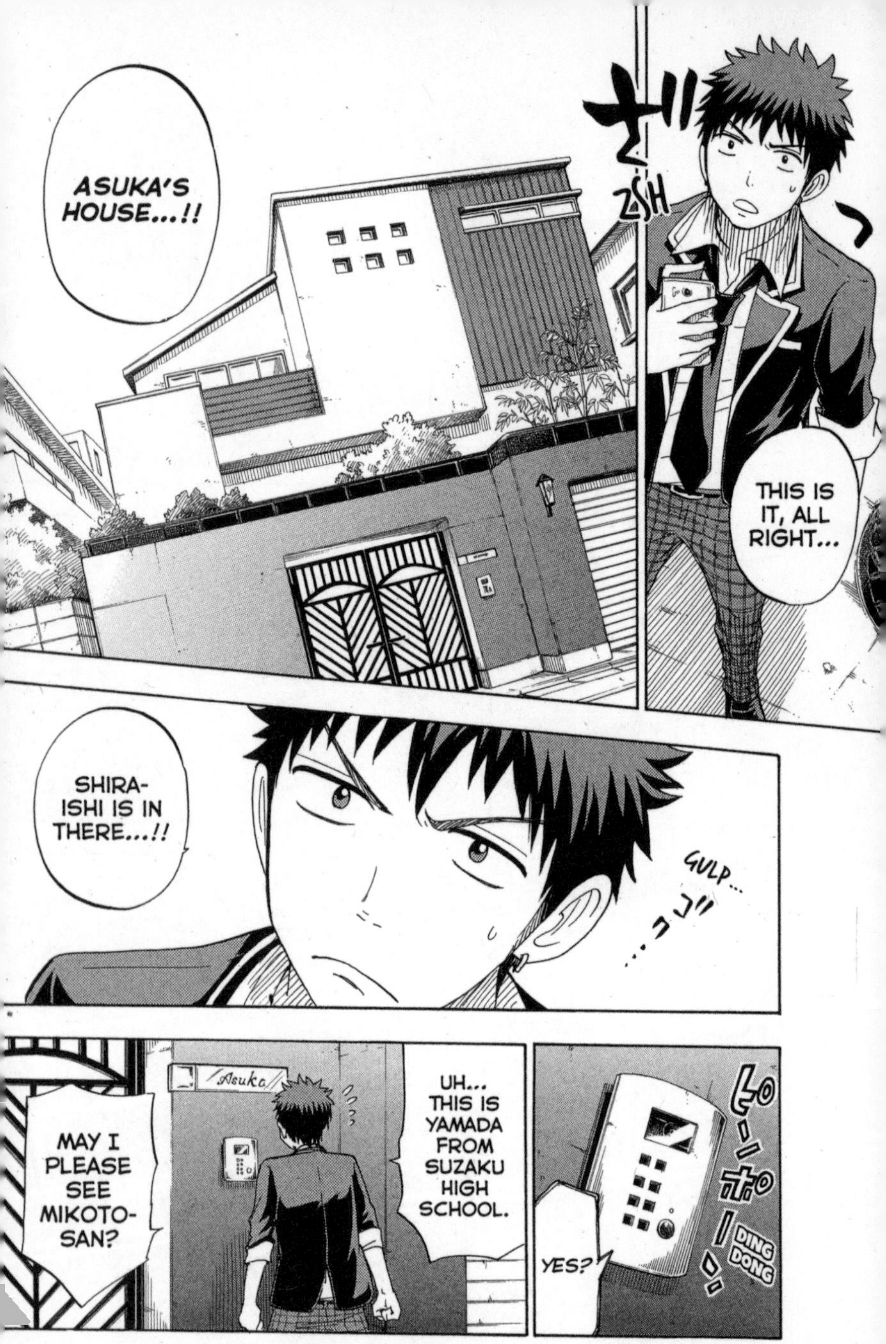
ZSH
THIS IS IT, ALL RIGHT...
ASUKA'S HOUSE...!!
SHIRA-ISHI IS IN THERE...!!
GULP...
DING DONG
YES?
Asuka
UH... THIS IS YAMADA FROM SUZAKU HIGH SCHOOL.
MAY I PLEASE SEE MIKOTO-SAN?

BLIP

HUH?

I'M SORRY, BUT ONLY SOMEONE FROM THE STUDENT COUNCIL IS ALLOWED TO SEE HER.

B-BUT... CAN'T YOU—

DING DOONG

I REALLY NEED TO TALK TO ASUKA!!

CLICK CLICK CLICK

H-HOLD ON... W-WAIT!!

DING DONG DING DONG

...DAMN.

I GUESS I CAN'T CONFRONT THIS HEAD-ON, AFTER ALL.

HEY!!

97

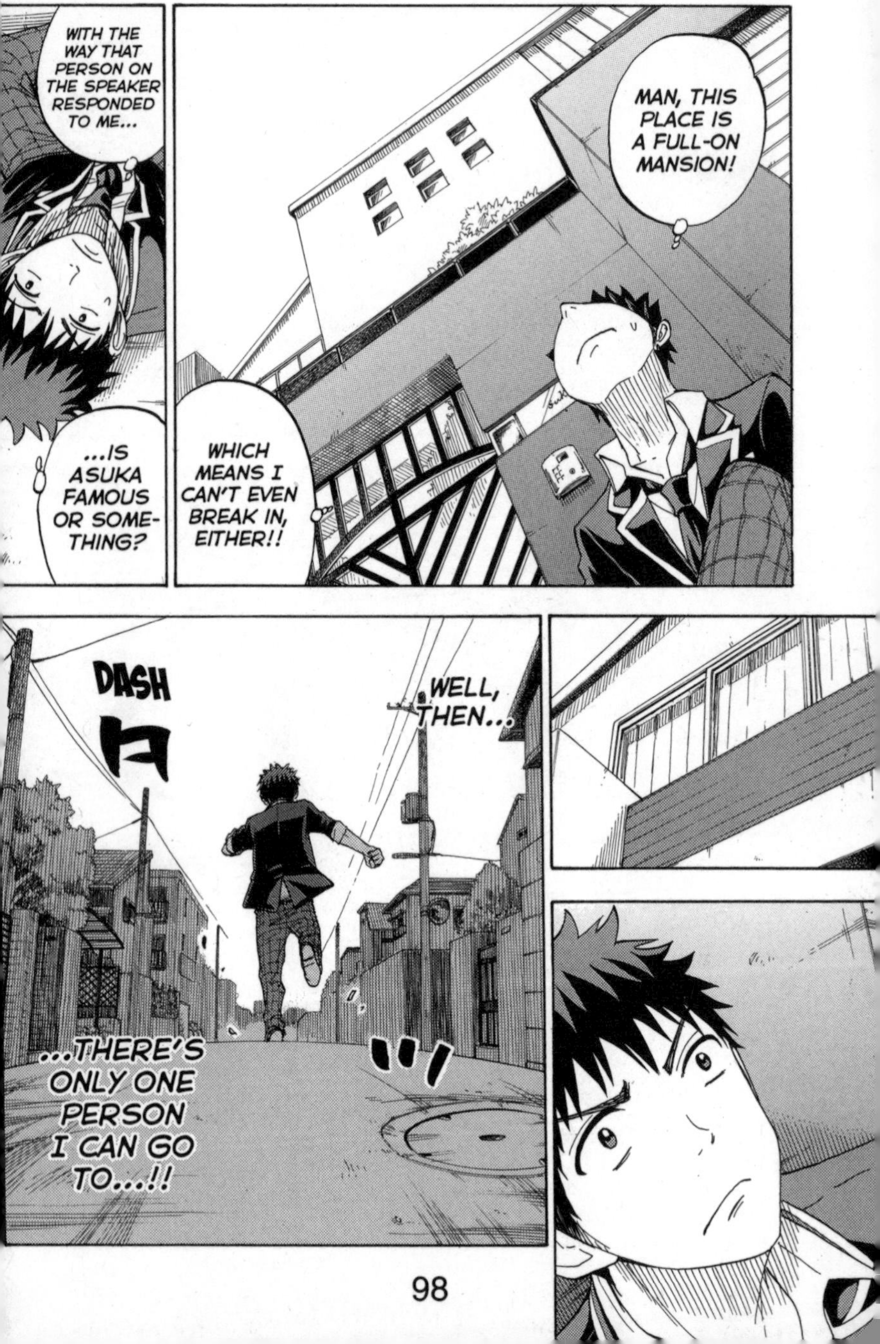
MAN, THIS PLACE IS A FULL-ON MANSION!
WHICH MEANS I CAN'T EVEN BREAK IN, EITHER!!
WITH THE WAY THAT PERSON ON THE SPEAKER RESPONDED TO ME...
...IS ASUKA FAMOUS OR SOME-THING?
WELL, THEN...
DASH
...THERE'S ONLY ONE PERSON I CAN GO TO...!!

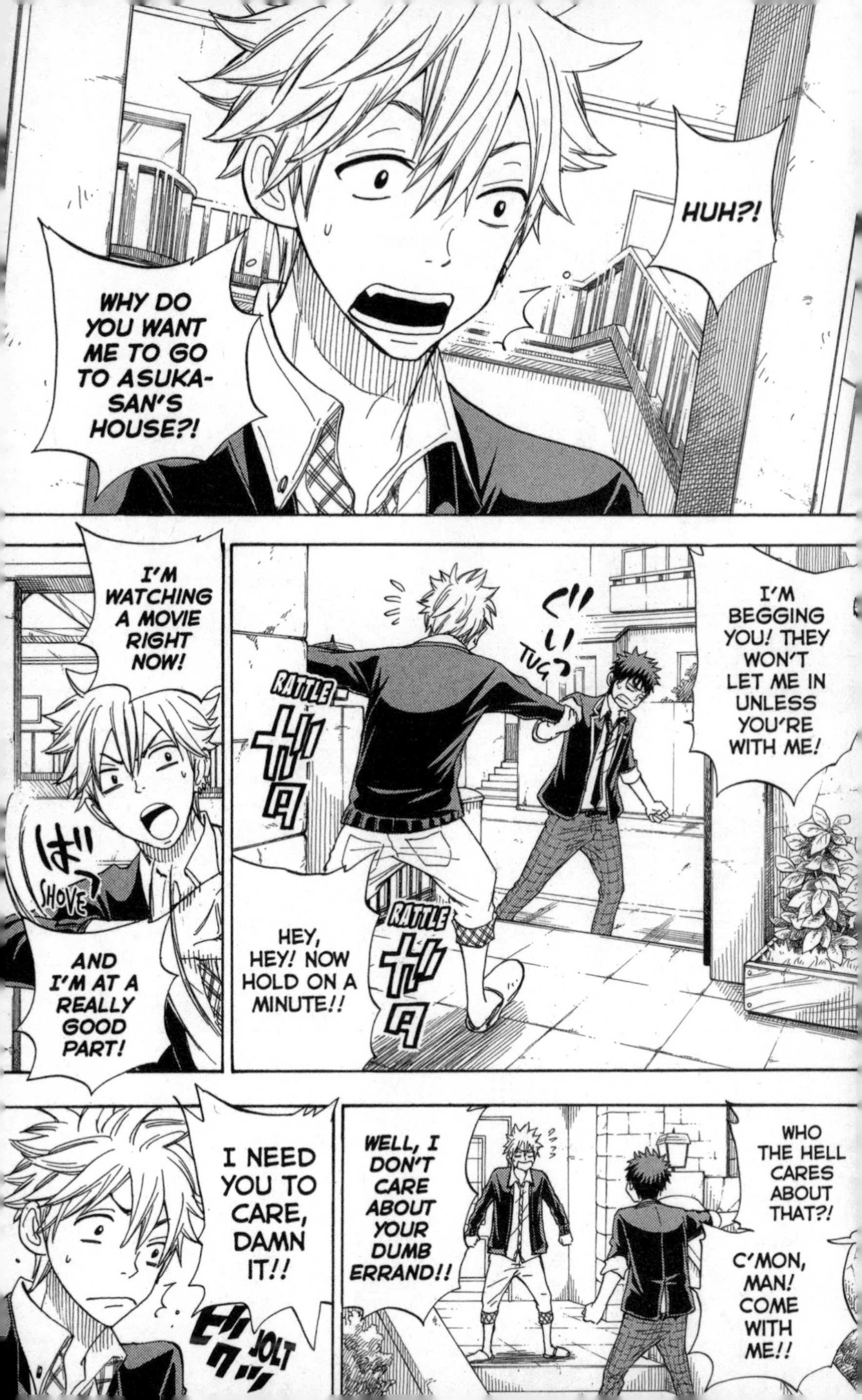
HUH?!
WHY DO YOU WANT ME TO GO TO ASUKA-SAN'S HOUSE?!
I'M BEGGING YOU! THEY WON'T LET ME IN UNLESS YOU'RE WITH ME!
ぐいっ
TUG
ガタ
RATTLE
ガタ
RATTLE
HEY, HEY! NOW HOLD ON A MINUTE!!
I'M WATCHING A MOVIE RIGHT NOW!
ばっ
SHOVE
AND I'M AT A REALLY GOOD PART!
WHO THE HELL CARES ABOUT THAT?!
C'MON, MAN! COME WITH ME!!
WELL, I DON'T CARE ABOUT YOUR DUMB ERRAND!!
I NEED YOU TO CARE, DAMN IT!!
ビクッ
JOLT

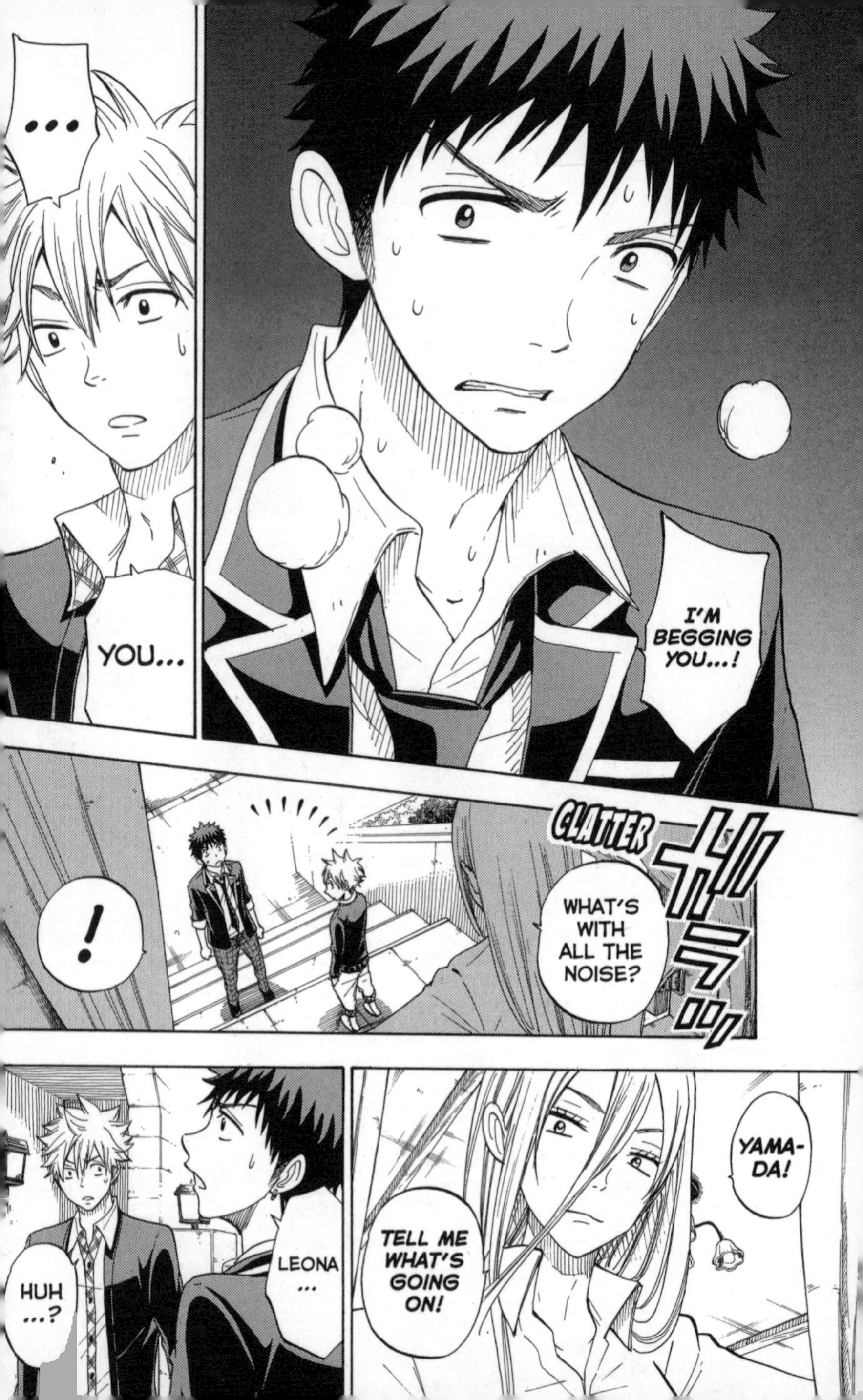
I'M BEGGING YOU...!
...
YOU...
CLATTER
WHAT'S WITH ALL THE NOISE?
!
YAMA-DA!
TELL ME WHAT'S GOING ON!
LEONA...
HUH...?

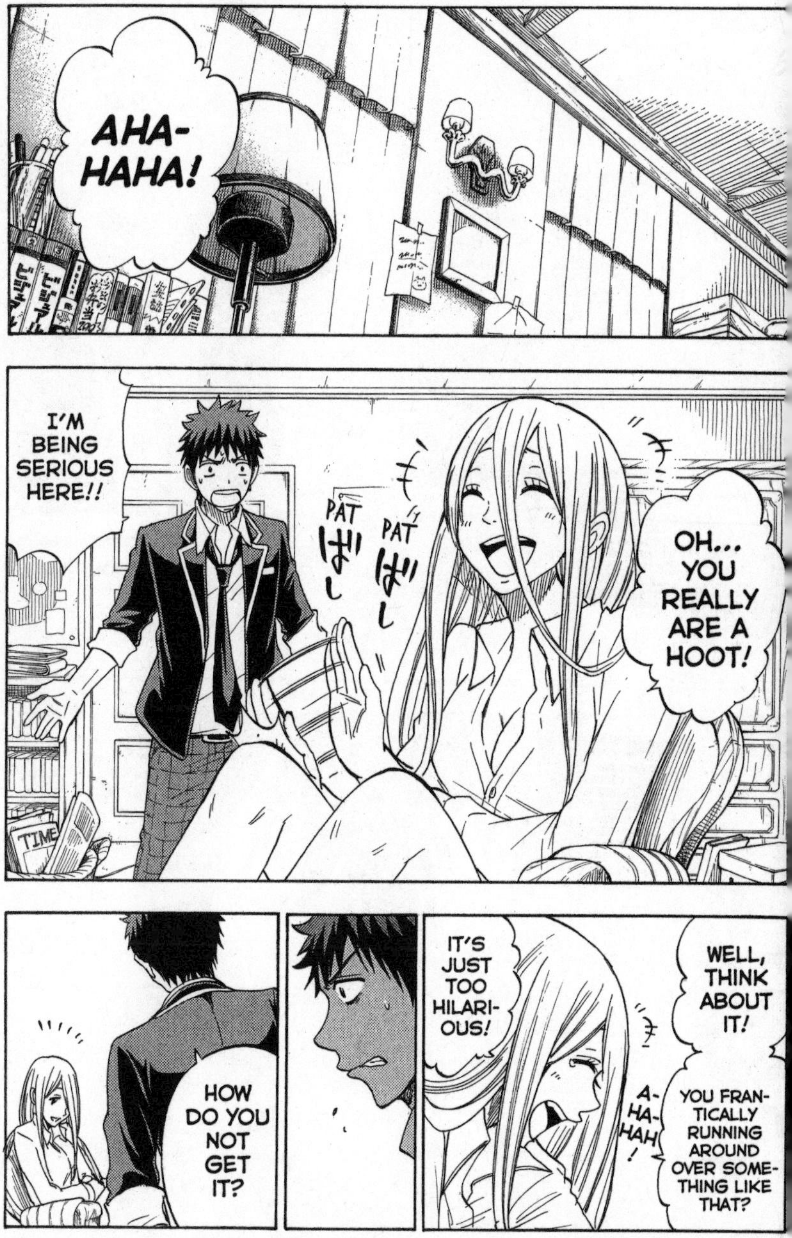
AHA-HAHA!
OH... YOU REALLY ARE A HOOT!
PAT ぱし
PAT ぱし
I'M BEING SERIOUS HERE!!
WELL, THINK ABOUT IT!
YOU FRANTICALLY RUNNING AROUND OVER SOMETHING LIKE THAT?
A-HA-HAH!
IT'S JUST TOO HILARIOUS!
HOW DO YOU NOT GET IT?

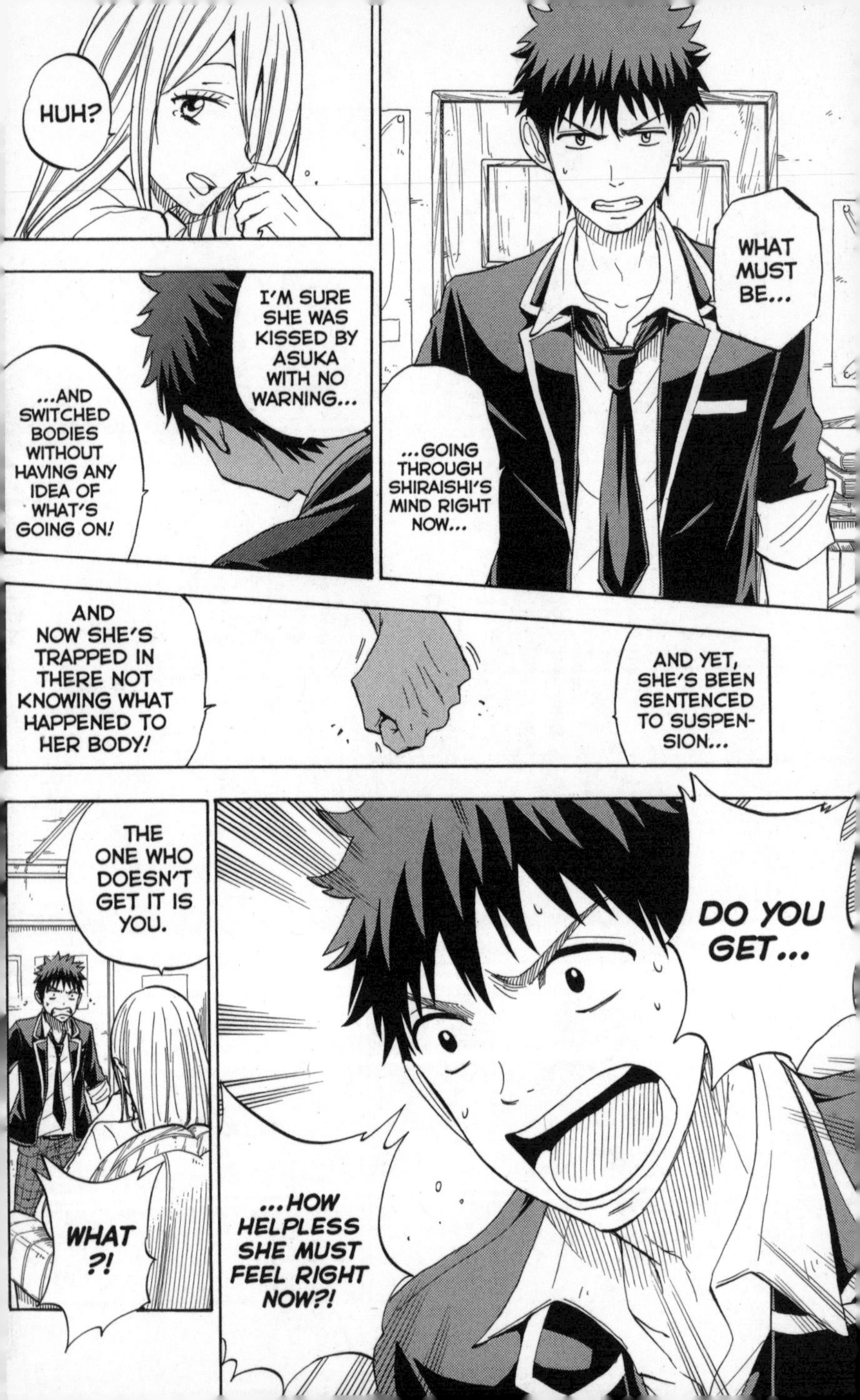
WHAT MUST BE...
...GOING THROUGH SHIRAISHI'S MIND RIGHT NOW...
HUH?
I'M SURE SHE WAS KISSED BY ASUKA WITH NO WARNING...
...AND SWITCHED BODIES WITHOUT HAVING ANY IDEA OF WHAT'S GOING ON!
AND YET, SHE'S BEEN SENTENCED TO SUSPENSION...
AND NOW SHE'S TRAPPED IN THERE NOT KNOWING WHAT HAPPENED TO HER BODY!
DO YOU GET...
...HOW HELPLESS SHE MUST FEEL RIGHT NOW?!
THE ONE WHO DOESN'T GET IT IS YOU.
WHAT?!

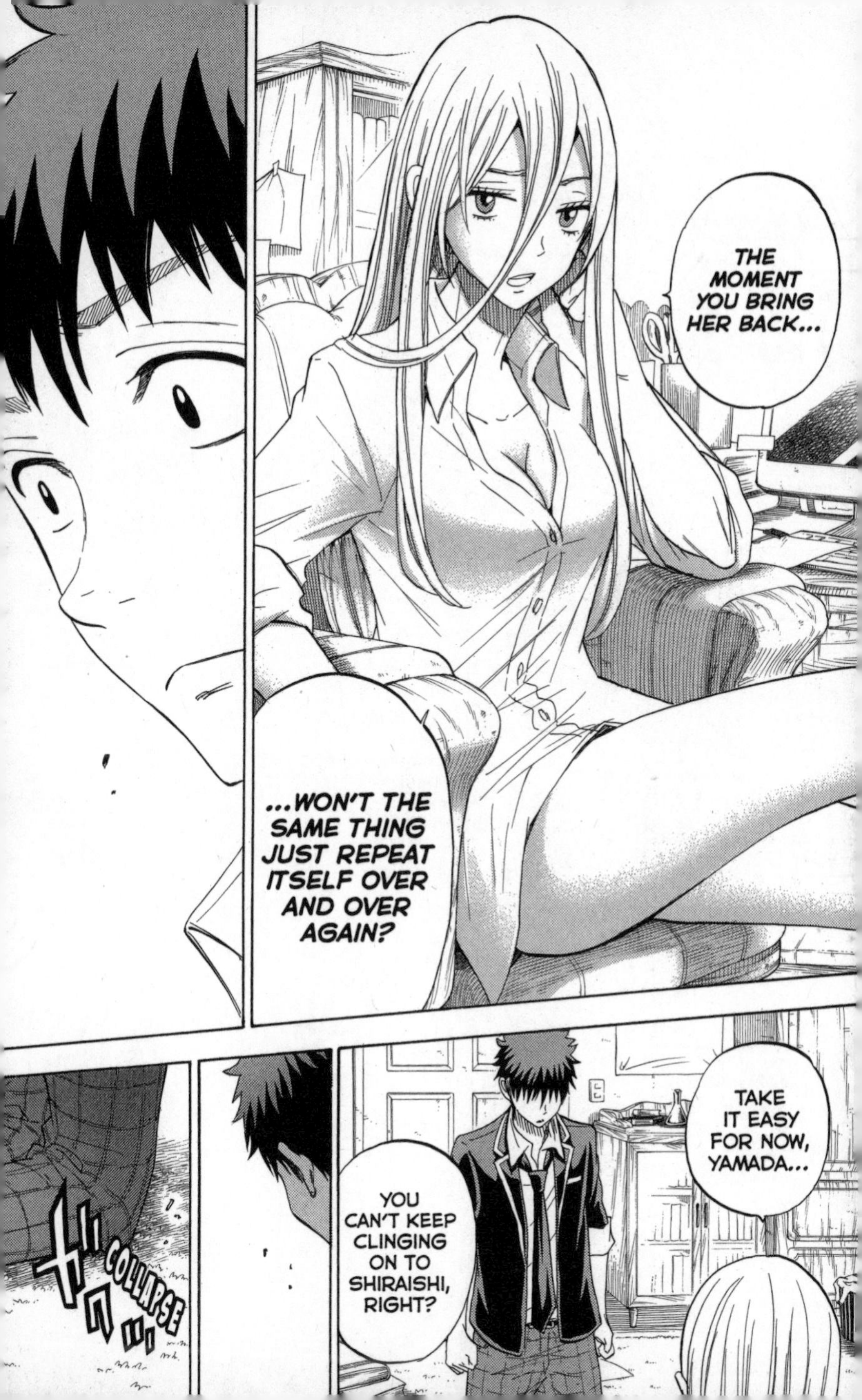
THE MOMENT YOU BRING HER BACK...
...WON'T THE SAME THING JUST REPEAT ITSELF OVER AND OVER AGAIN?
TAKE IT EASY FOR NOW, YAMADA...
YOU CAN'T KEEP CLINGING ON TO SHIRAISHI, RIGHT?
COLLAPSE

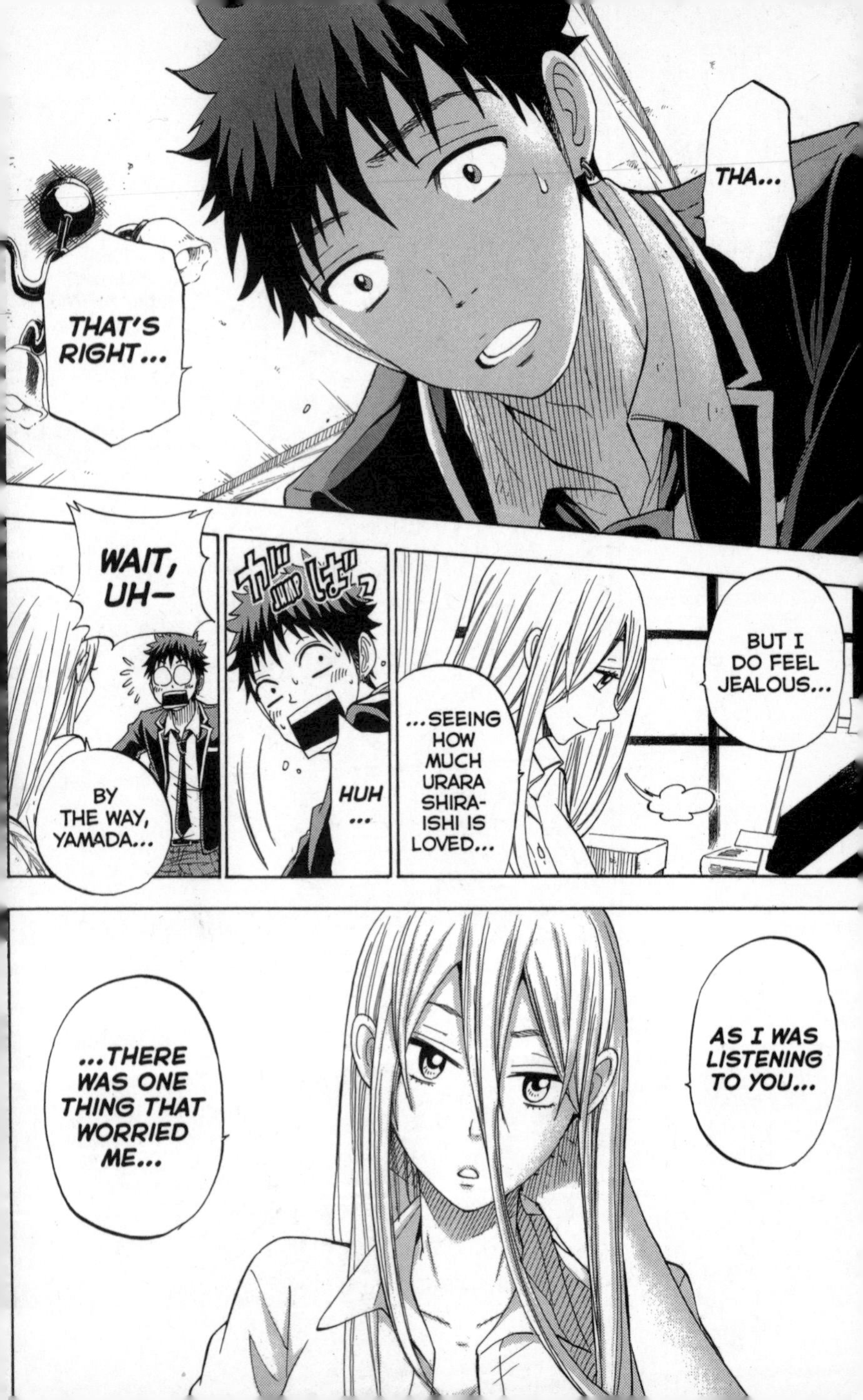
THA...
THAT'S RIGHT...
BUT I DO FEEL JEALOUS...
...SEEING HOW MUCH URARA SHIRAISHI IS LOVED...
JUMP
HUH...
WAIT, UH—
BY THE WAY, YAMADA...
AS I WAS LISTENING TO YOU...
...THERE WAS ONE THING THAT WORRIED ME...

CHAPTER 82: Rika SAIONJI is into SCIENCE ONLY!

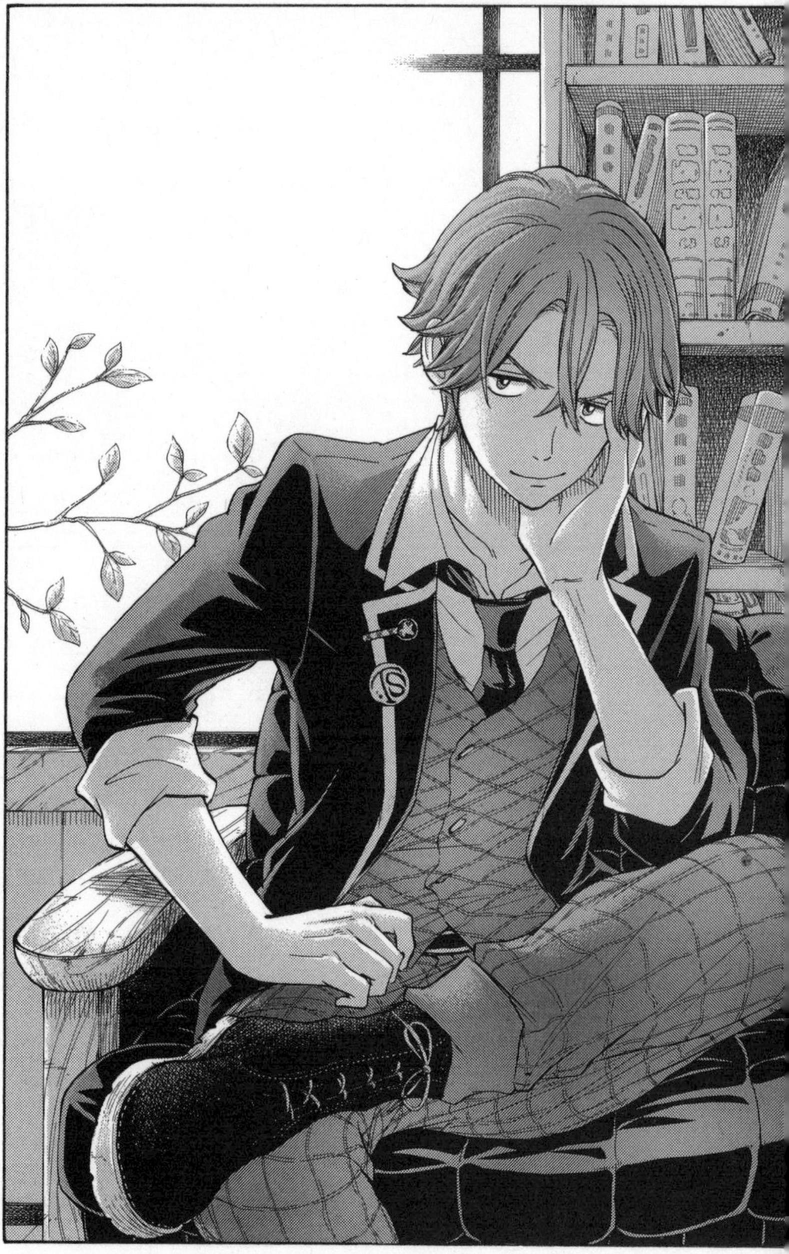

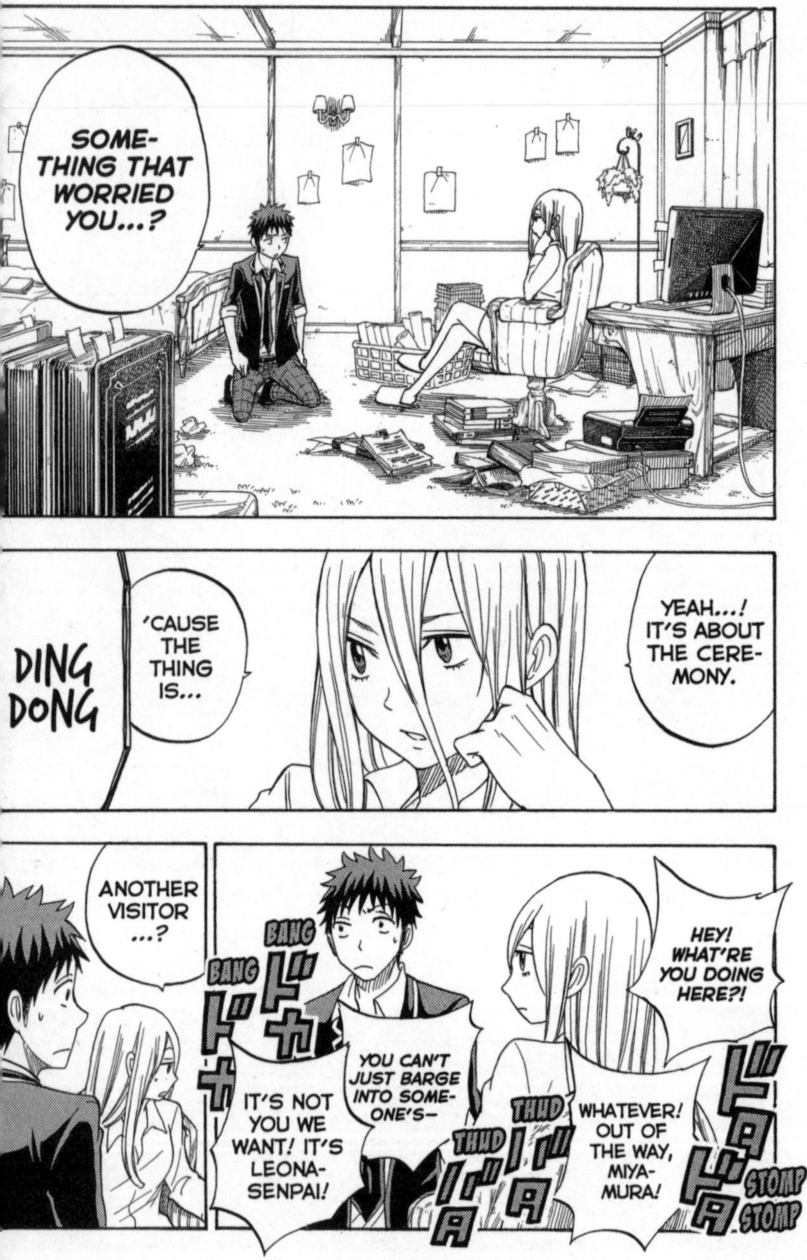
SOME-THING THAT WORRIED YOU...?
YEAH...! IT'S ABOUT THE CERE-MONY.
'CAUSE THE THING IS...
DING DONG
HEY! WHAT'RE YOU DOING HERE?!
STOMP STOMP
WHATEVER! OUT OF THE WAY, MIYA-MURA!
THUD THUD
YOU CAN'T JUST BARGE INTO SOME-ONE'S—
IT'S NOT YOU WE WANT! IT'S LEONA-SENPAI!
BANG BANG
ANOTHER VISITOR ...?

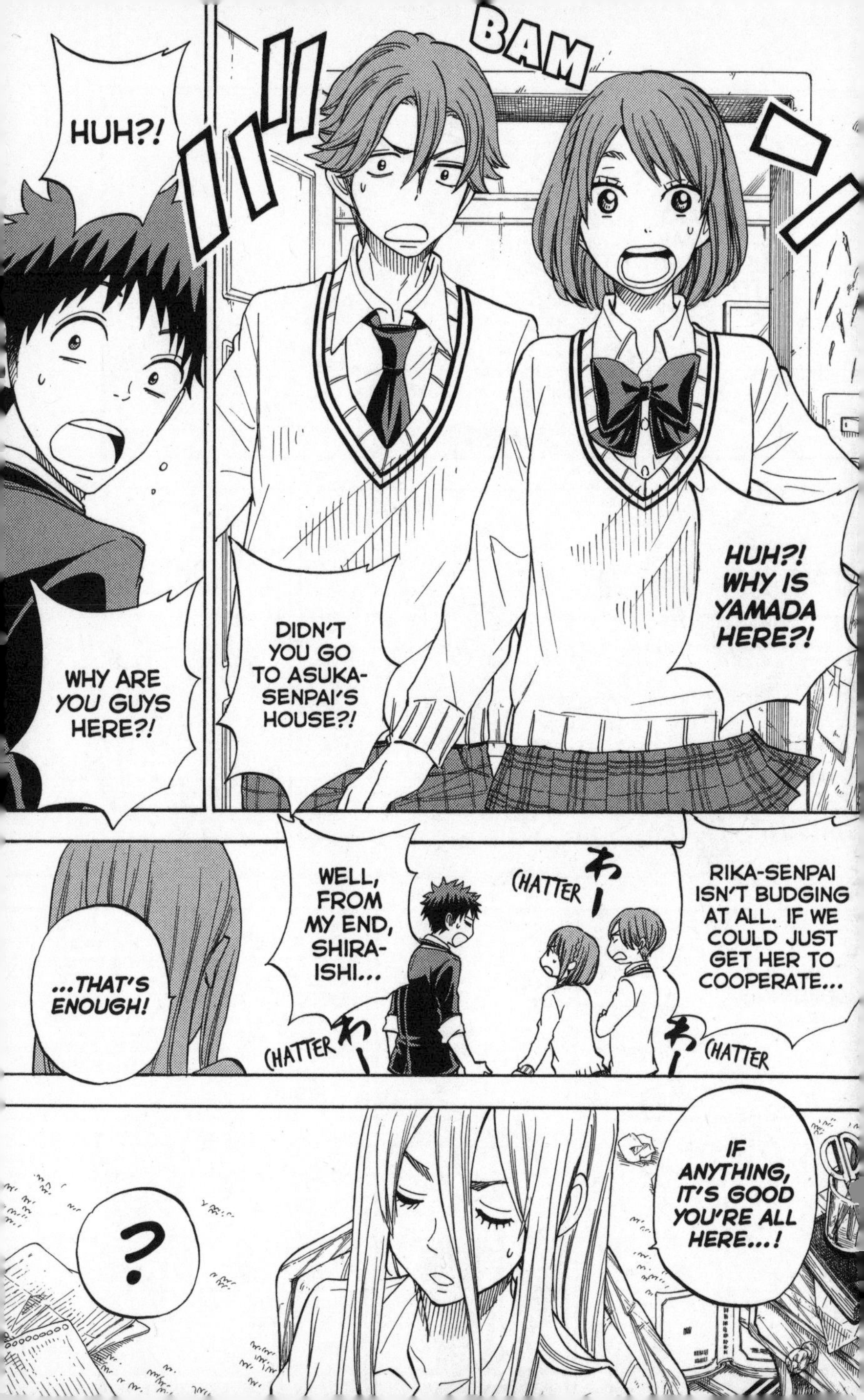
BAM
HUH?! WHY IS YAMADA HERE?!
DIDN'T YOU GO TO ASUKA-SENPAI'S HOUSE?!
HUH?!
WHY ARE YOU GUYS HERE?!
RIKA-SENPAI ISN'T BUDGING AT ALL. IF WE COULD JUST GET HER TO COOPERATE...
CHATTER
CHATTER
WELL, FROM MY END, SHIRA-ISHI...
CHATTER
...THAT'S ENOUGH!
IF ANYTHING, IT'S GOOD YOU'RE ALL HERE...!
?

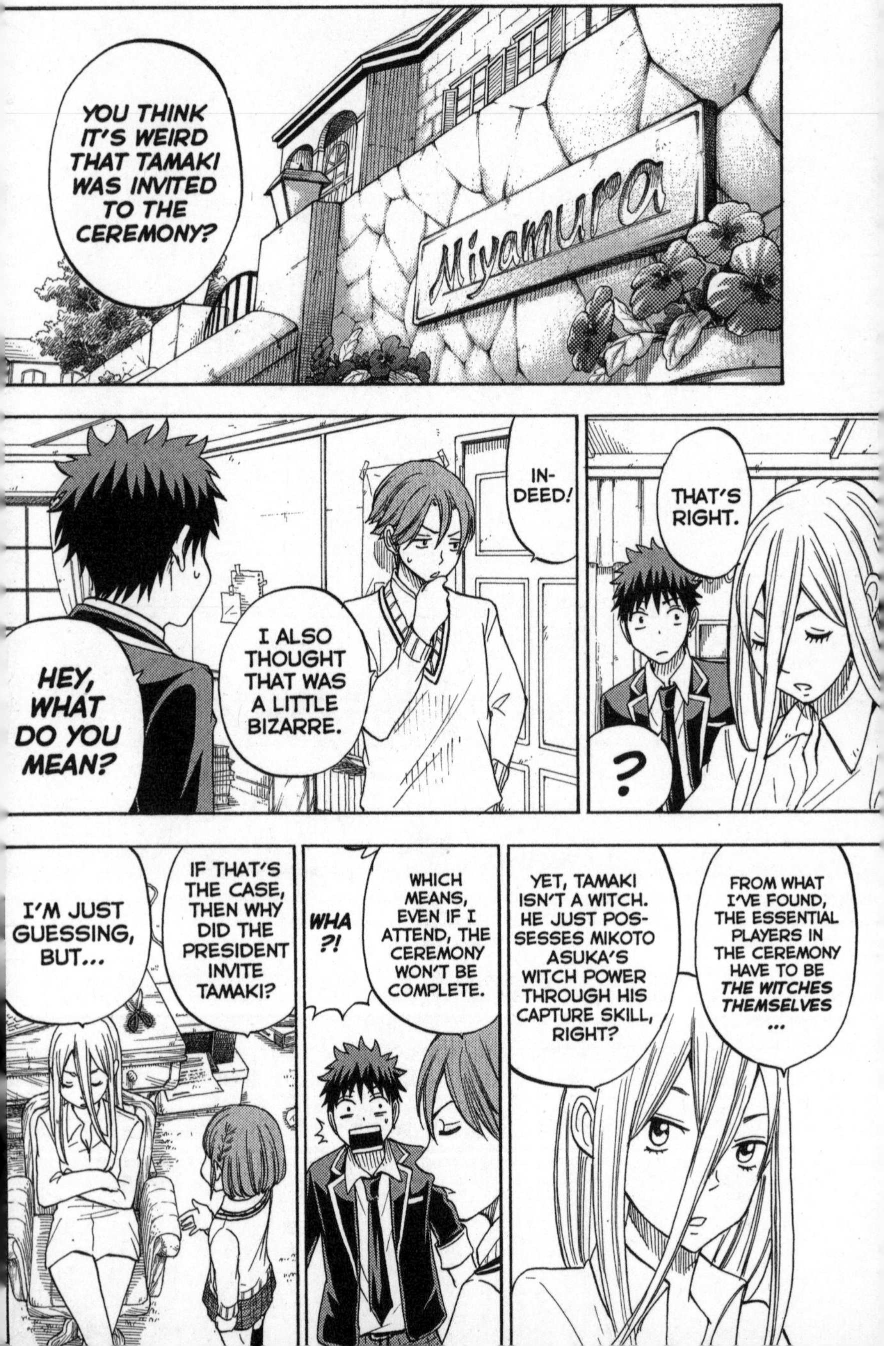
Miyamura
YOU THINK IT'S WEIRD THAT TAMAKI WAS INVITED TO THE CEREMONY?
THAT'S RIGHT.
?
IN-DEED!
I ALSO THOUGHT THAT WAS A LITTLE BIZARRE.
HEY, WHAT DO YOU MEAN?
FROM WHAT I'VE FOUND, THE ESSENTIAL PLAYERS IN THE CEREMONY HAVE TO BE *THE WITCHES THEMSELVES* ...
YET, TAMAKI ISN'T A WITCH. HE JUST POS-SESSES MIKOTO ASUKA'S WITCH POWER THROUGH HIS CAPTURE SKILL, RIGHT?
WHICH MEANS, EVEN IF I ATTEND, THE CEREMONY WON'T BE COMPLETE.
WHA ?!
IF THAT'S THE CASE, THEN WHY DID THE PRESIDENT INVITE TAMAKI?
I'M JUST GUESSING, BUT...

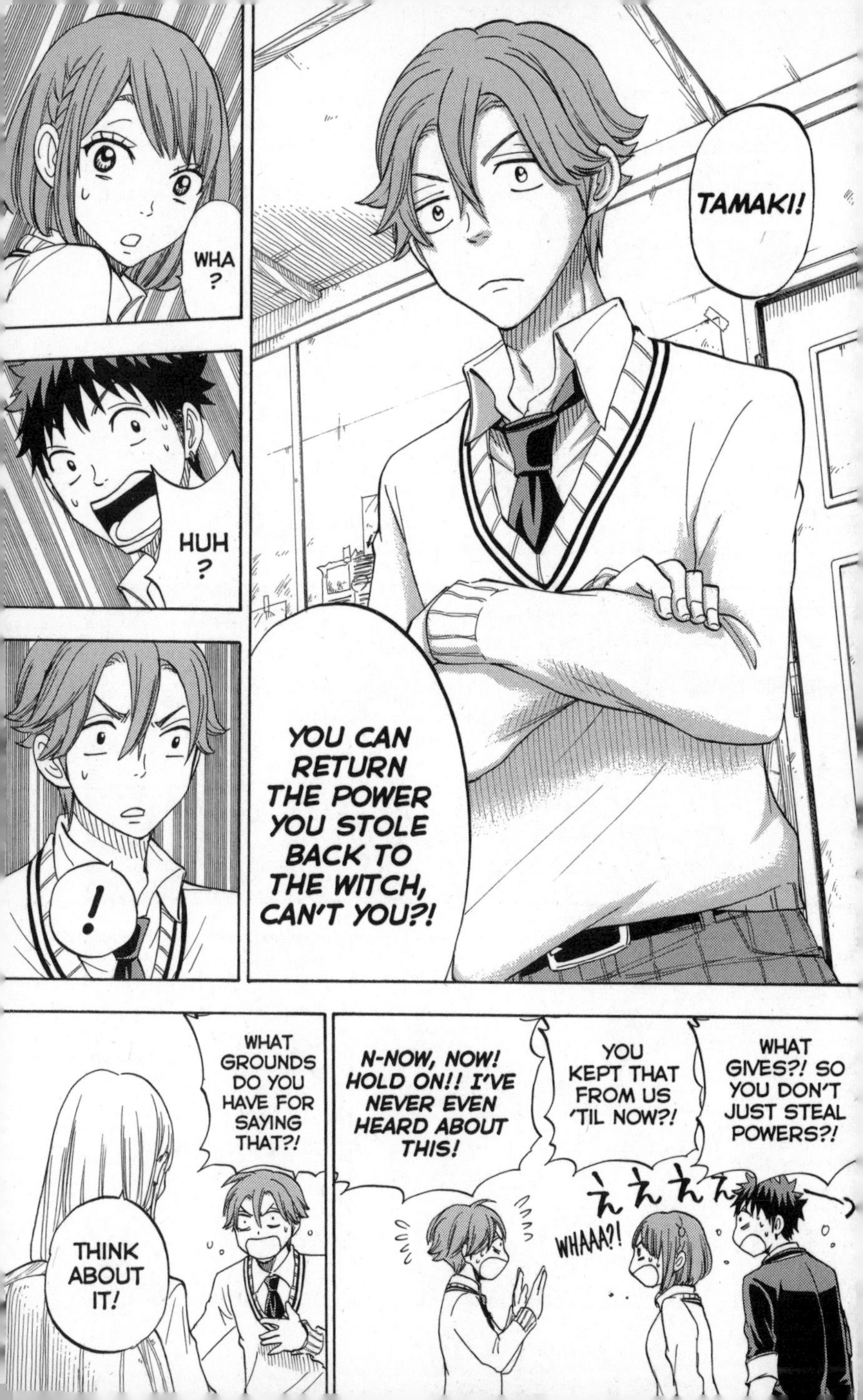
TAMAKI!
YOU CAN RETURN THE POWER YOU STOLE BACK TO THE WITCH, CAN'T YOU?!
WHA?
HUH?
!
WHAT GIVES?! SO YOU DON'T JUST STEAL POWERS?!
YOU KEPT THAT FROM US 'TIL NOW?!
N-NOW, NOW! HOLD ON!! I'VE NEVER EVEN HEARD ABOUT THIS!
ええええ
WHAAA?!
WHAT GROUNDS DO YOU HAVE FOR SAYING THAT?!
THINK ABOUT IT!

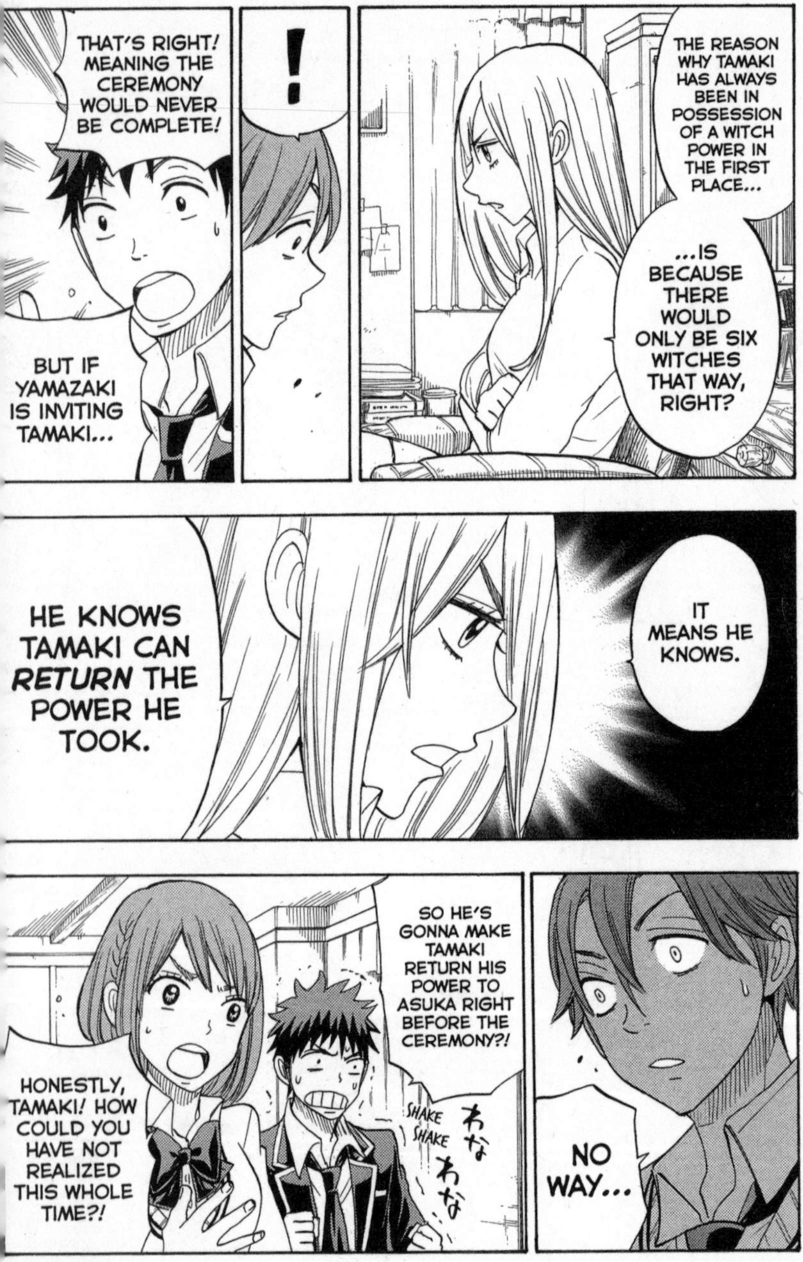
THE REASON WHY TAMAKI HAS ALWAYS BEEN IN POSSESSION OF A WITCH POWER IN THE FIRST PLACE...
...IS BECAUSE THERE WOULD ONLY BE SIX WITCHES THAT WAY, RIGHT?
!
THAT'S RIGHT! MEANING THE CEREMONY WOULD NEVER BE COMPLETE!
BUT IF YAMAZAKI IS INVITING TAMAKI...
IT MEANS HE KNOWS.
HE KNOWS TAMAKI CAN *RETURN* THE POWER HE TOOK.
NO WAY...
SO HE'S GONNA MAKE TAMAKI RETURN HIS POWER TO ASUKA RIGHT BEFORE THE CEREMONY?!
HONESTLY, TAMAKI! HOW COULD YOU HAVE NOT REALIZED THIS WHOLE TIME?!
SHAKE SHAKE
わな わな

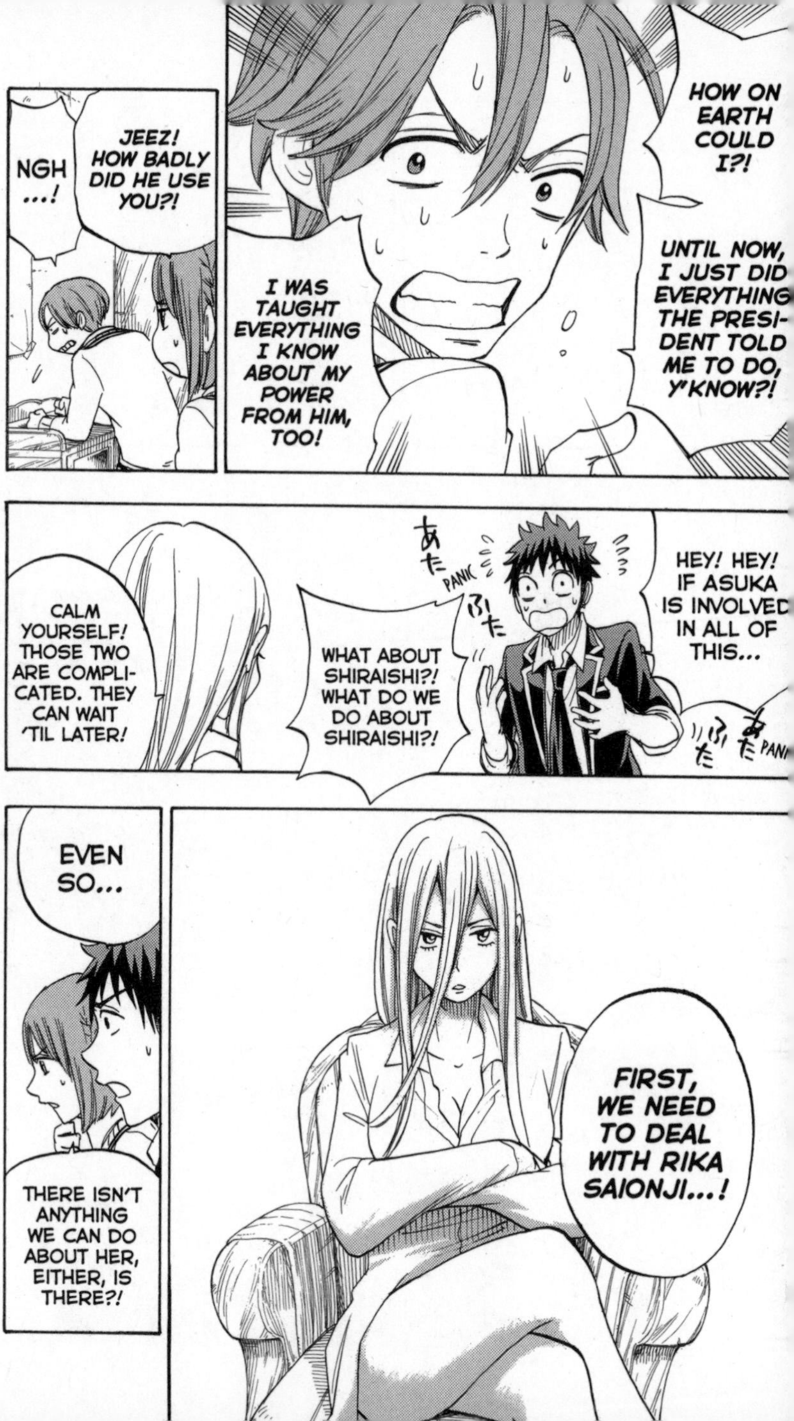
HOW ON EARTH COULD I?!
UNTIL NOW, I JUST DID EVERYTHING THE PRESIDENT TOLD ME TO DO, Y'KNOW?!
I WAS TAUGHT EVERYTHING I KNOW ABOUT MY POWER FROM HIM, TOO!
JEEZ! HOW BADLY DID HE USE YOU?!
NGH ...!
HEY! HEY! IF ASUKA IS INVOLVED IN ALL OF THIS...
あたふた
PANIC
あたふた
PANIC
WHAT ABOUT SHIRAISHI?! WHAT DO WE DO ABOUT SHIRAISHI?!
CALM YOURSELF! THOSE TWO ARE COMPLICATED. THEY CAN WAIT 'TIL LATER!
FIRST, WE NEED TO DEAL WITH RIKA SAIONJI...!
EVEN SO...
THERE ISN'T ANYTHING WE CAN DO ABOUT HER, EITHER, IS THERE?!

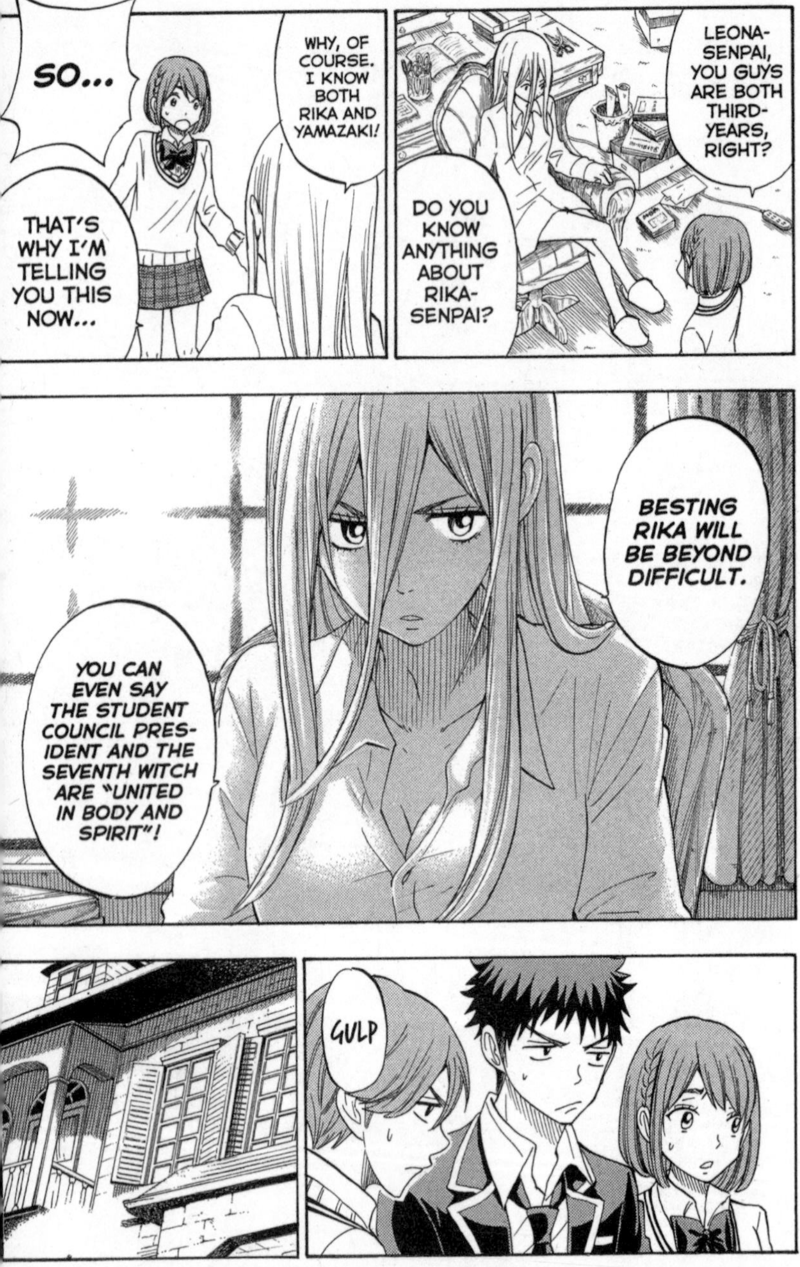
LEONA-SENPAI, YOU GUYS ARE BOTH THIRD-YEARS, RIGHT?
DO YOU KNOW ANYTHING ABOUT RIKA-SENPAI?
WHY, OF COURSE. I KNOW BOTH RIKA AND YAMAZAKI!
SO...
THAT'S WHY I'M TELLING YOU THIS NOW...
BESTING RIKA WILL BE BEYOND DIFFICULT.
YOU CAN EVEN SAY THE STUDENT COUNCIL PRES-IDENT AND THE SEVENTH WITCH ARE "UNITED IN BODY AND SPIRIT"!
GULP

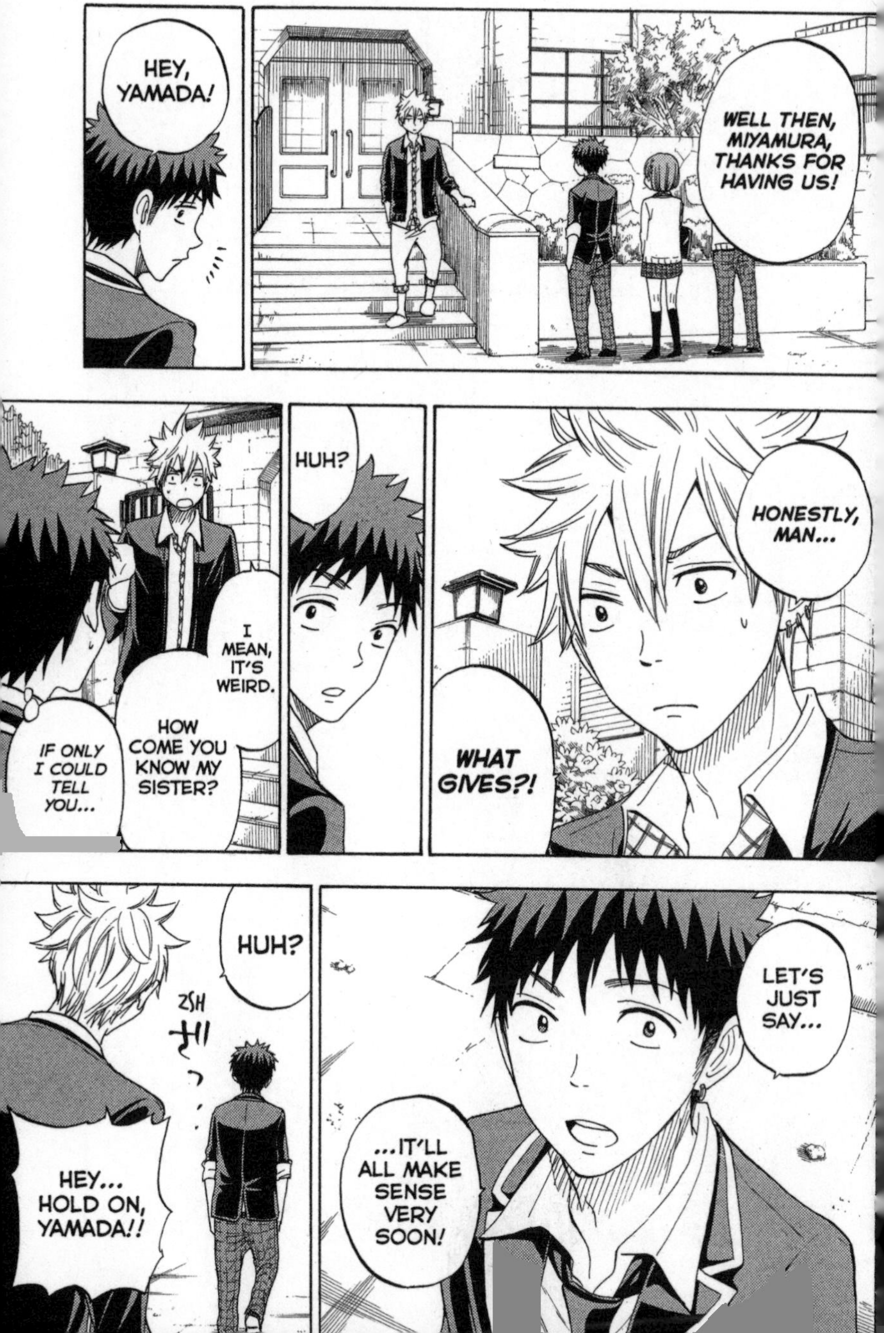
WELL THEN, MIYAMURA, THANKS FOR HAVING US!
HEY, YAMADA!
HONESTLY, MAN...
WHAT GIVES?!
HUH?
I MEAN, IT'S WEIRD.
HOW COME YOU KNOW MY SISTER?
IF ONLY I COULD TELL YOU...
LET'S JUST SAY...
...IT'LL ALL MAKE SENSE VERY SOON!
HUH?
ZSH
HEY... HOLD ON, YAMADA!!

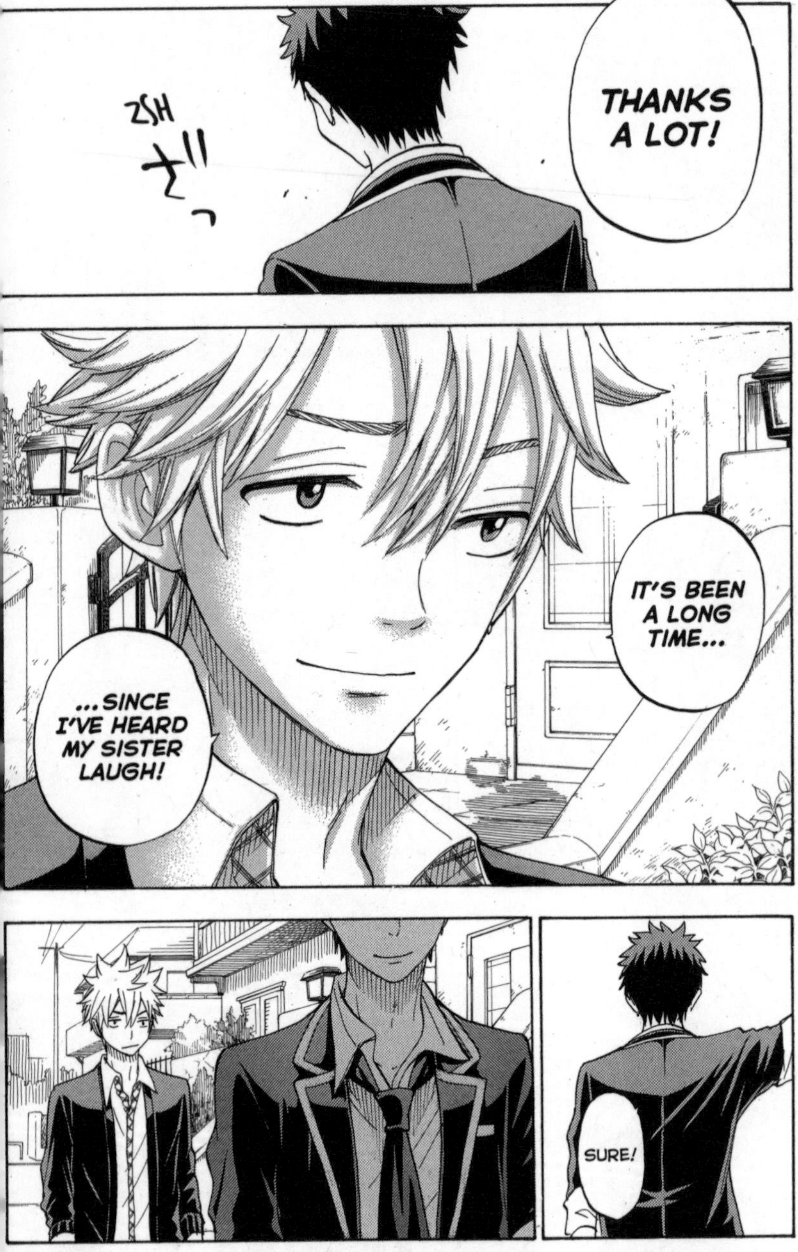
THANKS A LOT!
ZSH
IT'S BEEN A LONG TIME...
...SINCE I'VE HEARD MY SISTER LAUGH!
SURE!

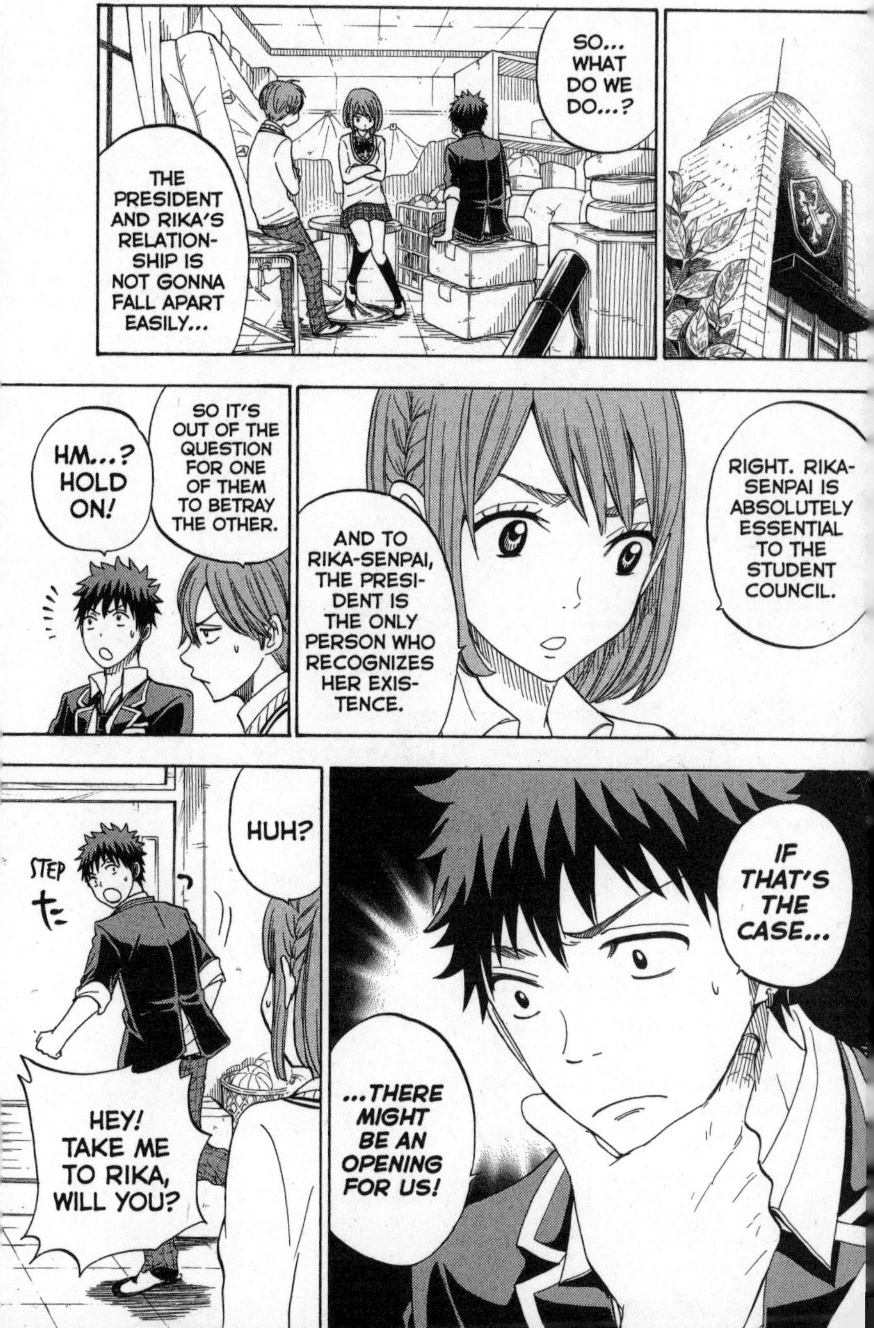
SO... WHAT DO WE DO...?
THE PRESIDENT AND RIKA'S RELATION-SHIP IS NOT GONNA FALL APART EASILY...
RIGHT. RIKA-SENPAI IS ABSOLUTELY ESSENTIAL TO THE STUDENT COUNCIL.
AND TO RIKA-SENPAI, THE PRESI-DENT IS THE ONLY PERSON WHO RECOGNIZES HER EXIS-TENCE.
SO IT'S OUT OF THE QUESTION FOR ONE OF THEM TO BETRAY THE OTHER.
HM...? HOLD ON!
IF THAT'S THE CASE...
...THERE MIGHT BE AN OPENING FOR US!
HUH?
STEP
HEY! TAKE ME TO RIKA, WILL YOU?

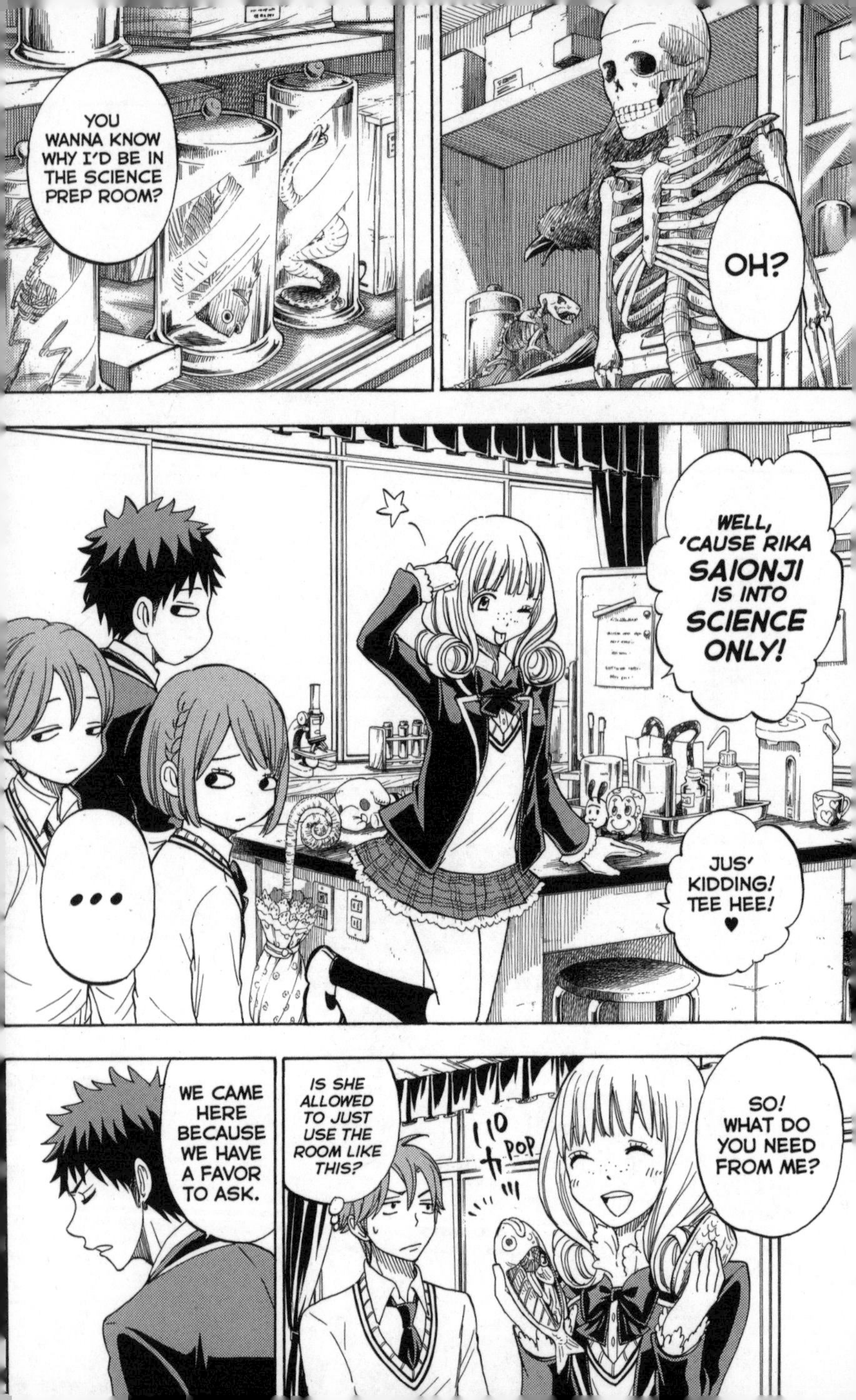
OH?
YOU WANNA KNOW WHY I'D BE IN THE SCIENCE PREP ROOM?
WELL, 'CAUSE RIKA SAIONJI IS INTO SCIENCE ONLY!
JUS' KIDDING! TEE HEE! ♥
...
SO! WHAT DO YOU NEED FROM ME?
POP
IS SHE ALLOWED TO JUST USE THE ROOM LIKE THIS?
WE CAME HERE BECAUSE WE HAVE A FAVOR TO ASK.

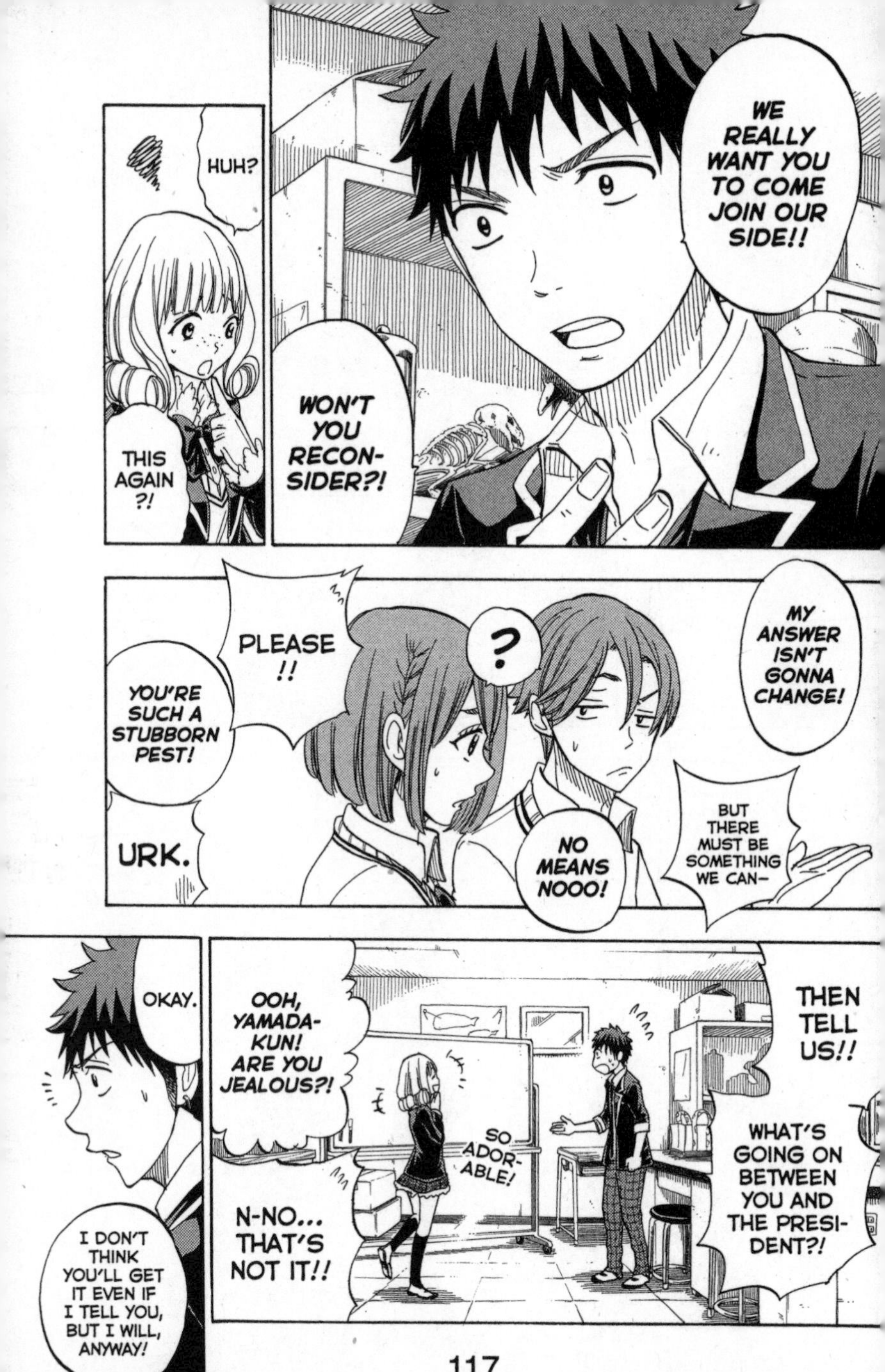
WE REALLY WANT YOU TO COME JOIN OUR SIDE!!
WON'T YOU RECONSIDER?!
HUH?
THIS AGAIN ?!
MY ANSWER ISN'T GONNA CHANGE!
?
PLEASE !!
BUT THERE MUST BE SOMETHING WE CAN–
NO MEANS NOOO!
YOU'RE SUCH A STUBBORN PEST!
URK.
THEN TELL US!!
WHAT'S GOING ON BETWEEN YOU AND THE PRESIDENT?!
OOH, YAMADA-KUN! ARE YOU JEALOUS?!
SO ADORABLE!
N-NO... THAT'S NOT IT!!
OKAY.
I DON'T THINK YOU'LL GET IT EVEN IF I TELL YOU, BUT I WILL, ANYWAY!

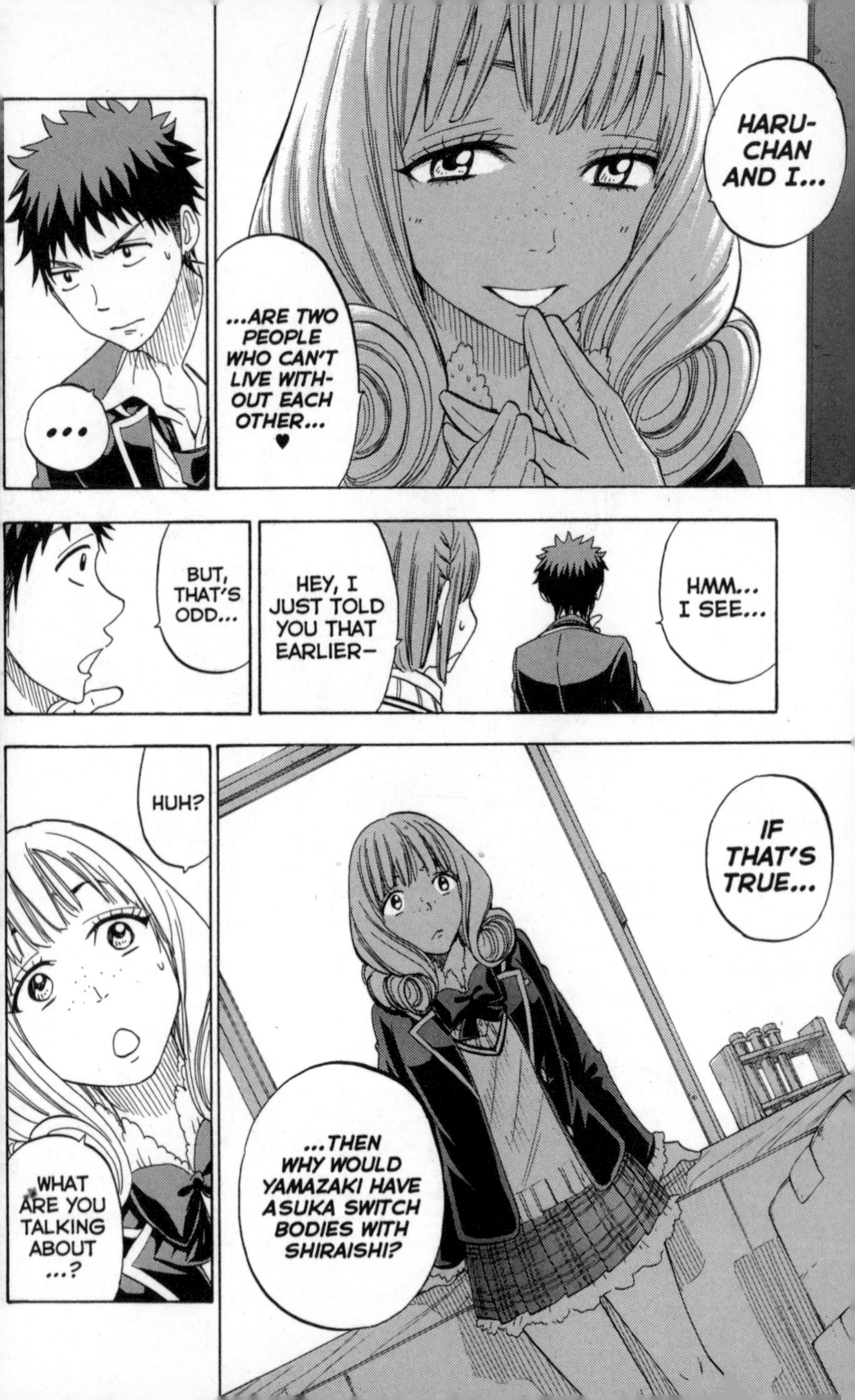
HARU-CHAN AND I...
...ARE TWO PEOPLE WHO CAN'T LIVE WITH-OUT EACH OTHER... ♥
...
HMM... I SEE...
HEY, I JUST TOLD YOU THAT EARLIER–
BUT, THAT'S ODD...
IF THAT'S TRUE...
...THEN WHY WOULD YAMAZAKI HAVE ASUKA SWITCH BODIES WITH SHIRAISHI?
HUH?
WHAT ARE YOU TALKING ABOUT ...?

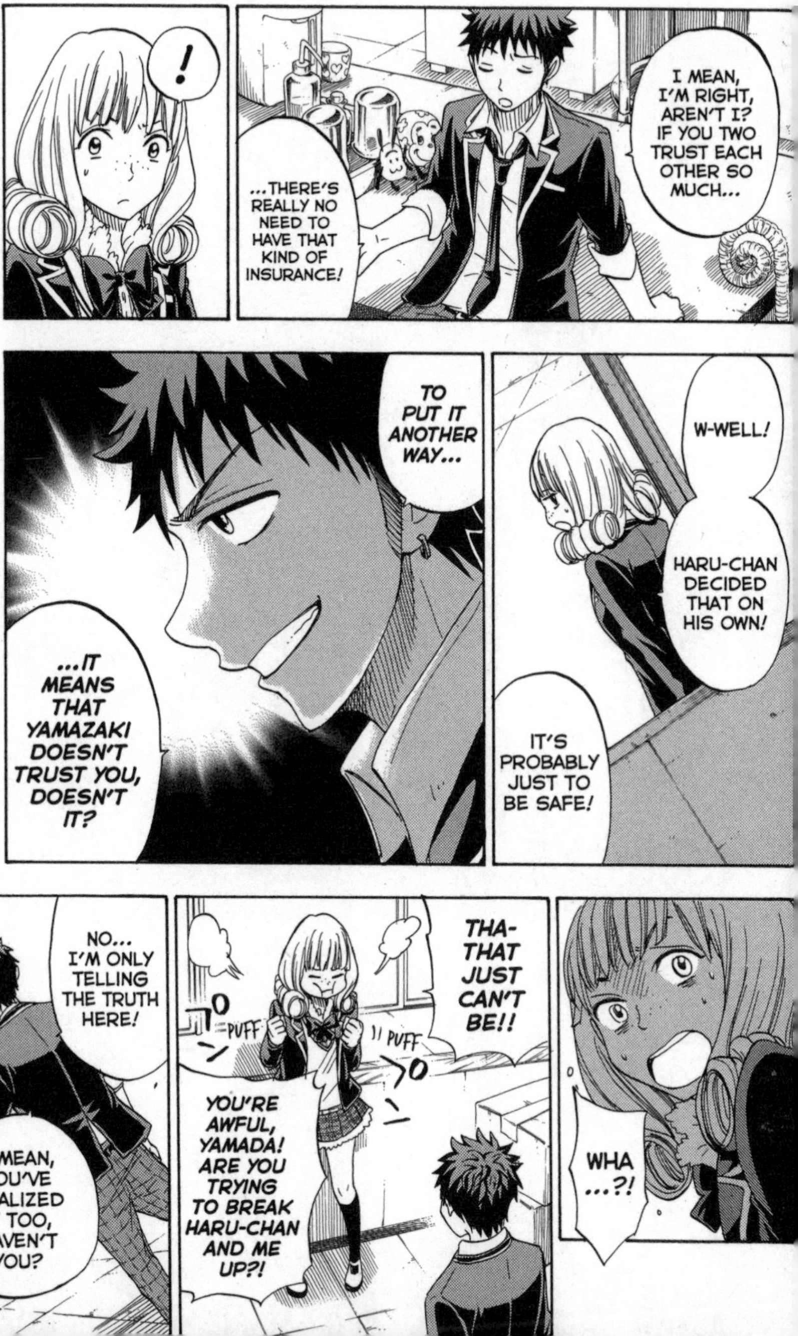
I MEAN, I'M RIGHT, AREN'T I? IF YOU TWO TRUST EACH OTHER SO MUCH...
...THERE'S REALLY NO NEED TO HAVE THAT KIND OF INSURANCE!
!
W-WELL!
HARU-CHAN DECIDED THAT ON HIS OWN!
IT'S PROBABLY JUST TO BE SAFE!
TO PUT IT ANOTHER WAY...
...IT MEANS THAT YAMAZAKI DOESN'T TRUST YOU, DOESN'T IT?
WHA ...?!
THA-THAT JUST CAN'T BE!!
PUFF
PUFF
YOU'RE AWFUL, YAMADA! ARE YOU TRYING TO BREAK HARU-CHAN AND ME UP?!
NO... I'M ONLY TELLING THE TRUTH HERE!
I MEAN, YOU'VE REALIZED IT TOO, HAVEN'T YOU?

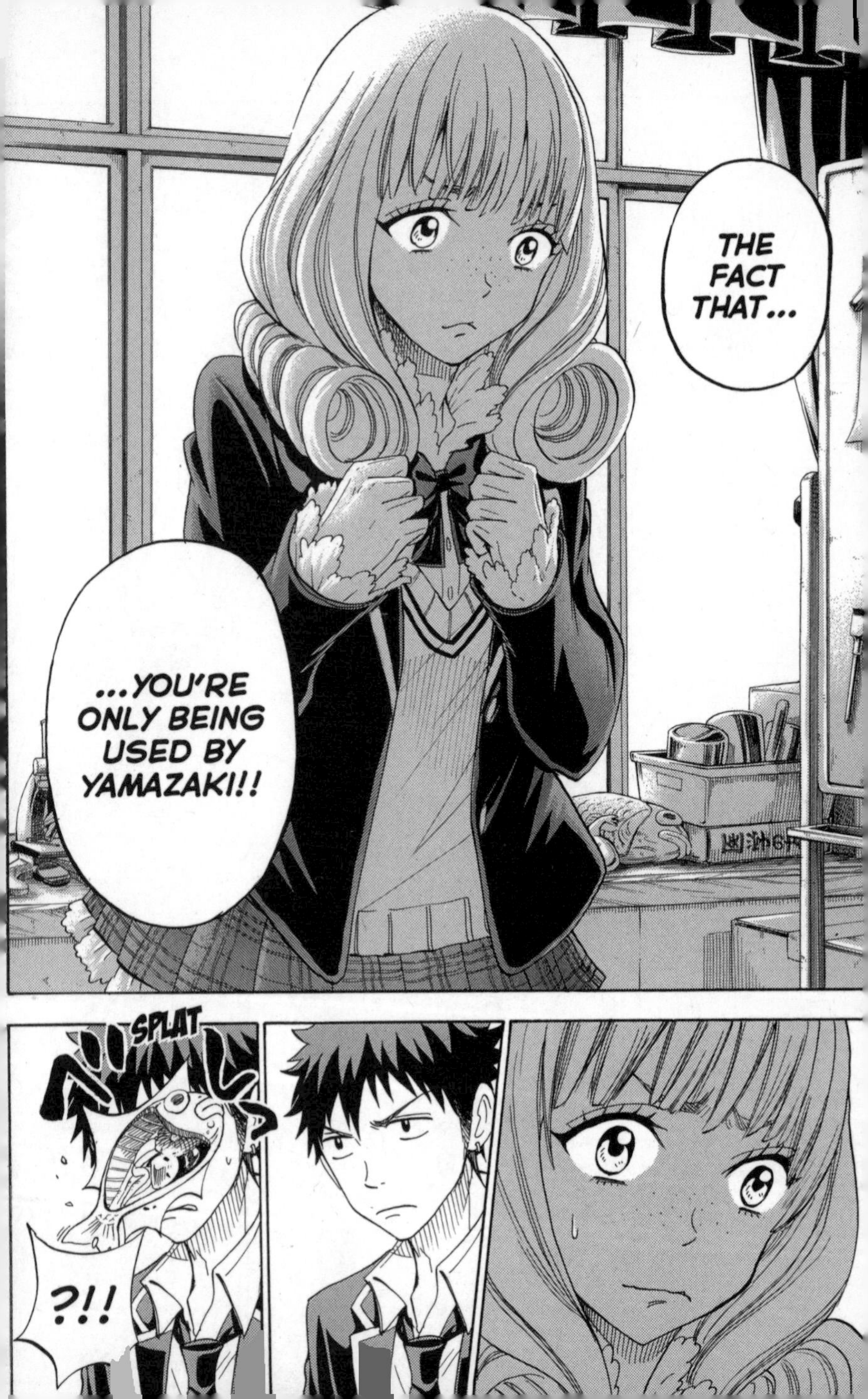
THE FACT THAT...
...YOU'RE ONLY BEING USED BY YAMAZAKI!!
SPLAT
?!!

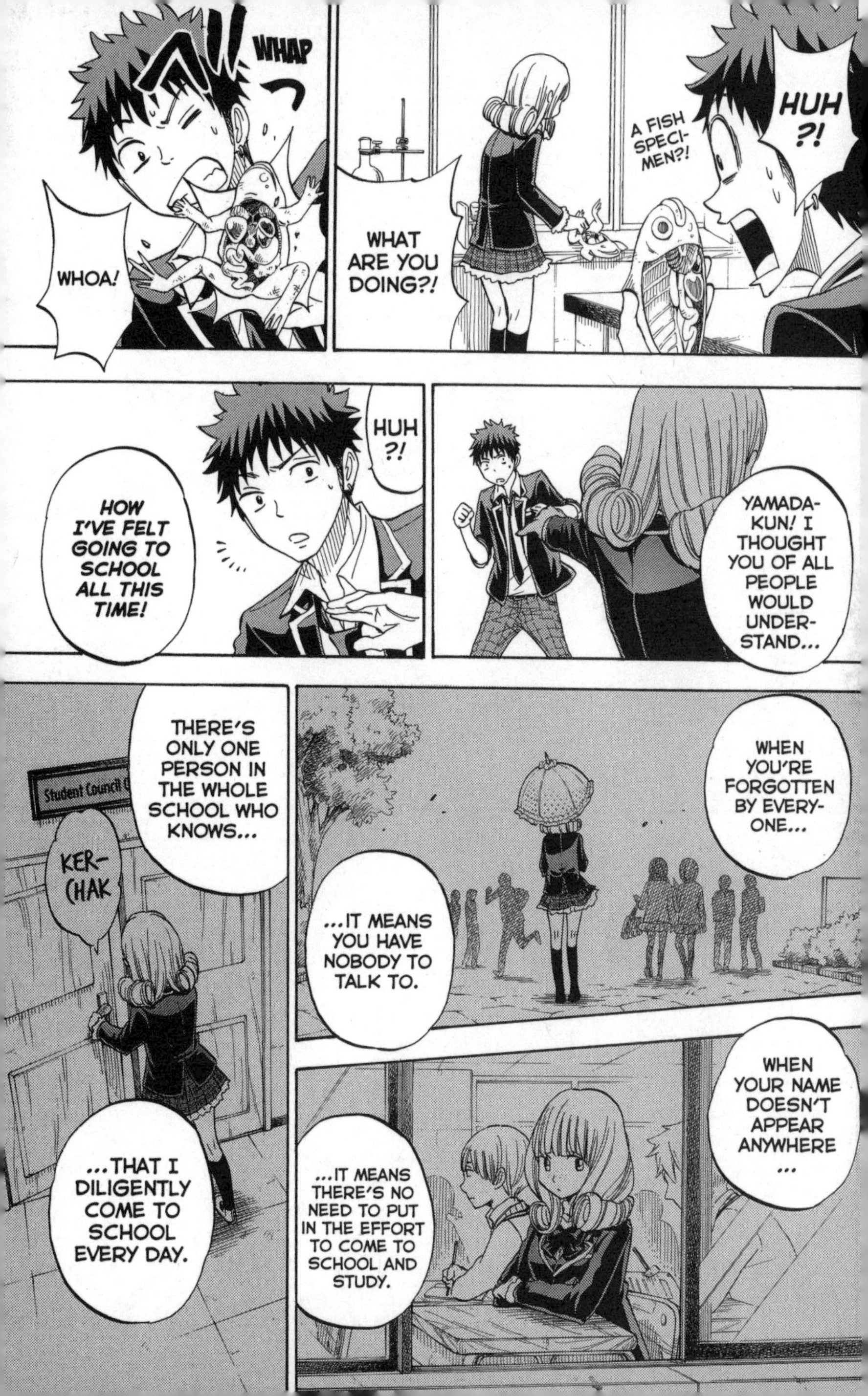
HUH ?!
A FISH SPECI-MEN?!
WHAT ARE YOU DOING?!
WHAP
WHOA!
YAMADA-KUN! I THOUGHT YOU OF ALL PEOPLE WOULD UNDER-STAND...
HUH ?!
HOW I'VE FELT GOING TO SCHOOL ALL THIS TIME!
WHEN YOU'RE FORGOTTEN BY EVERY-ONE...
...IT MEANS YOU HAVE NOBODY TO TALK TO.
WHEN YOUR NAME DOESN'T APPEAR ANYWHERE ...
...IT MEANS THERE'S NO NEED TO PUT IN THE EFFORT TO COME TO SCHOOL AND STUDY.
THERE'S ONLY ONE PERSON IN THE WHOLE SCHOOL WHO KNOWS...
Student Council
KER-CHAK
...THAT I DILIGENTLY COME TO SCHOOL EVERY DAY.

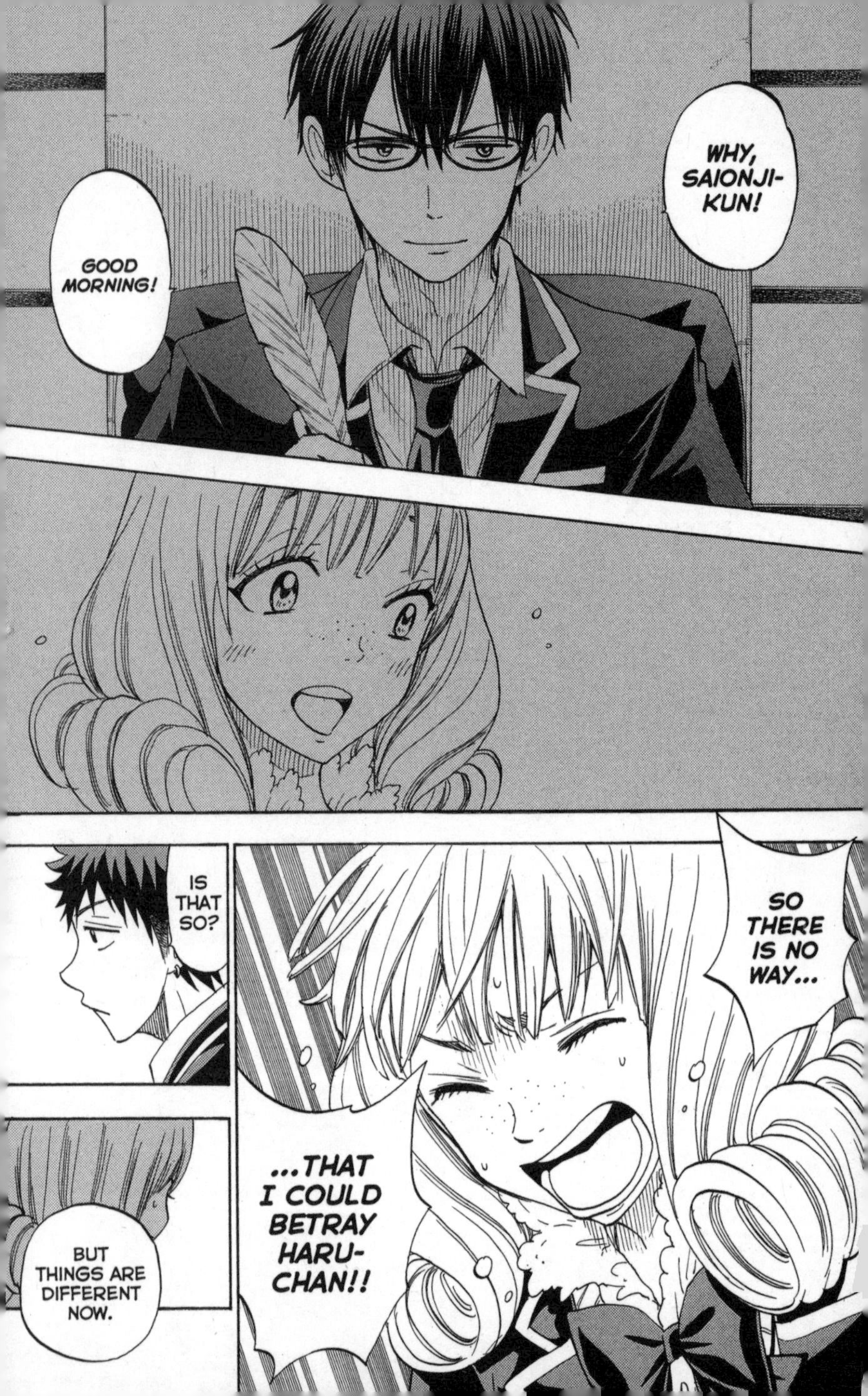
WHY, SAIONJI-KUN!
GOOD MORNING!
SO THERE IS NO WAY...
...THAT I COULD BETRAY HARU-CHAN!!
IS THAT SO?
BUT THINGS ARE DIFFERENT NOW.

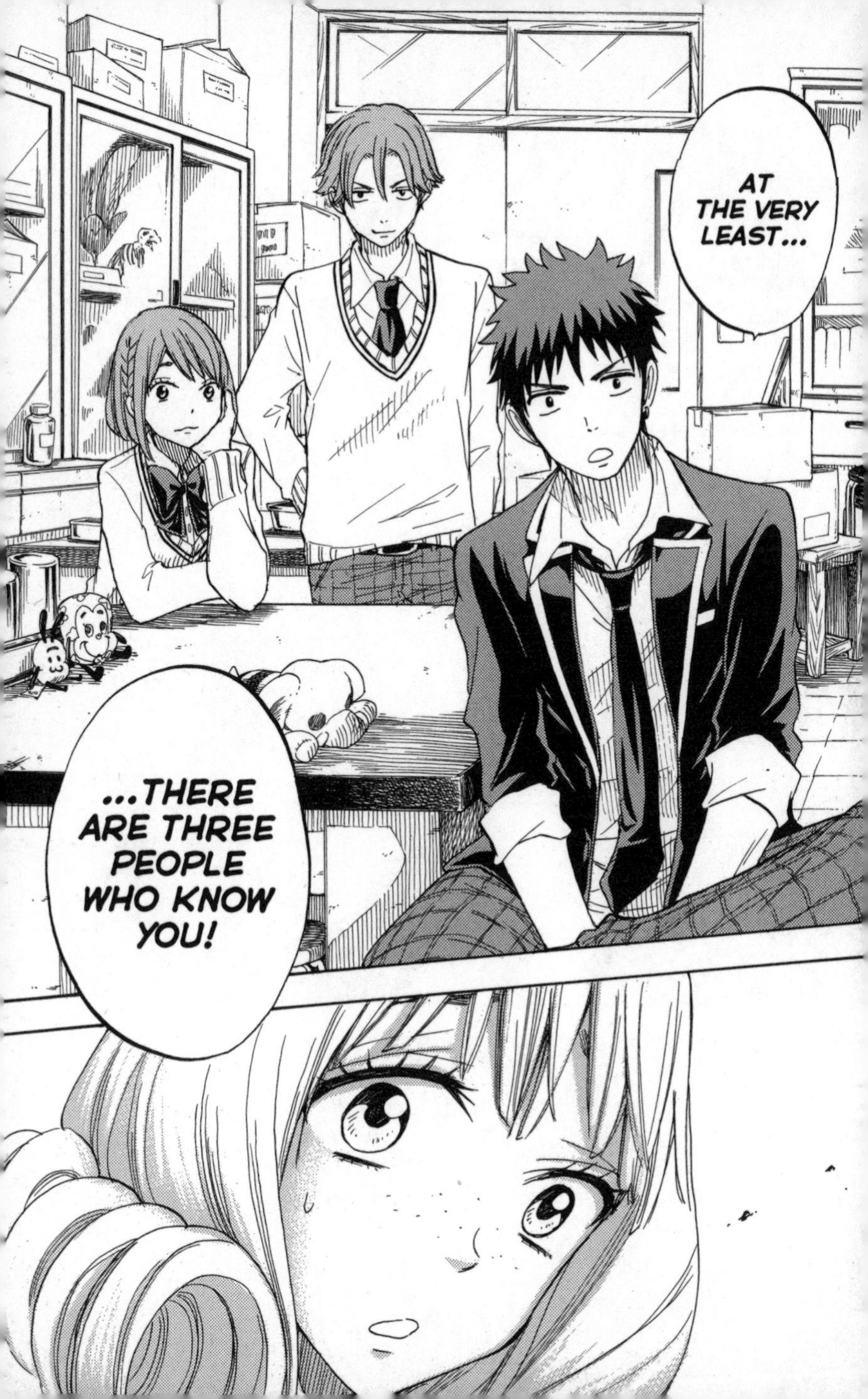
AT THE VERY LEAST...
...THERE ARE THREE PEOPLE WHO KNOW YOU!

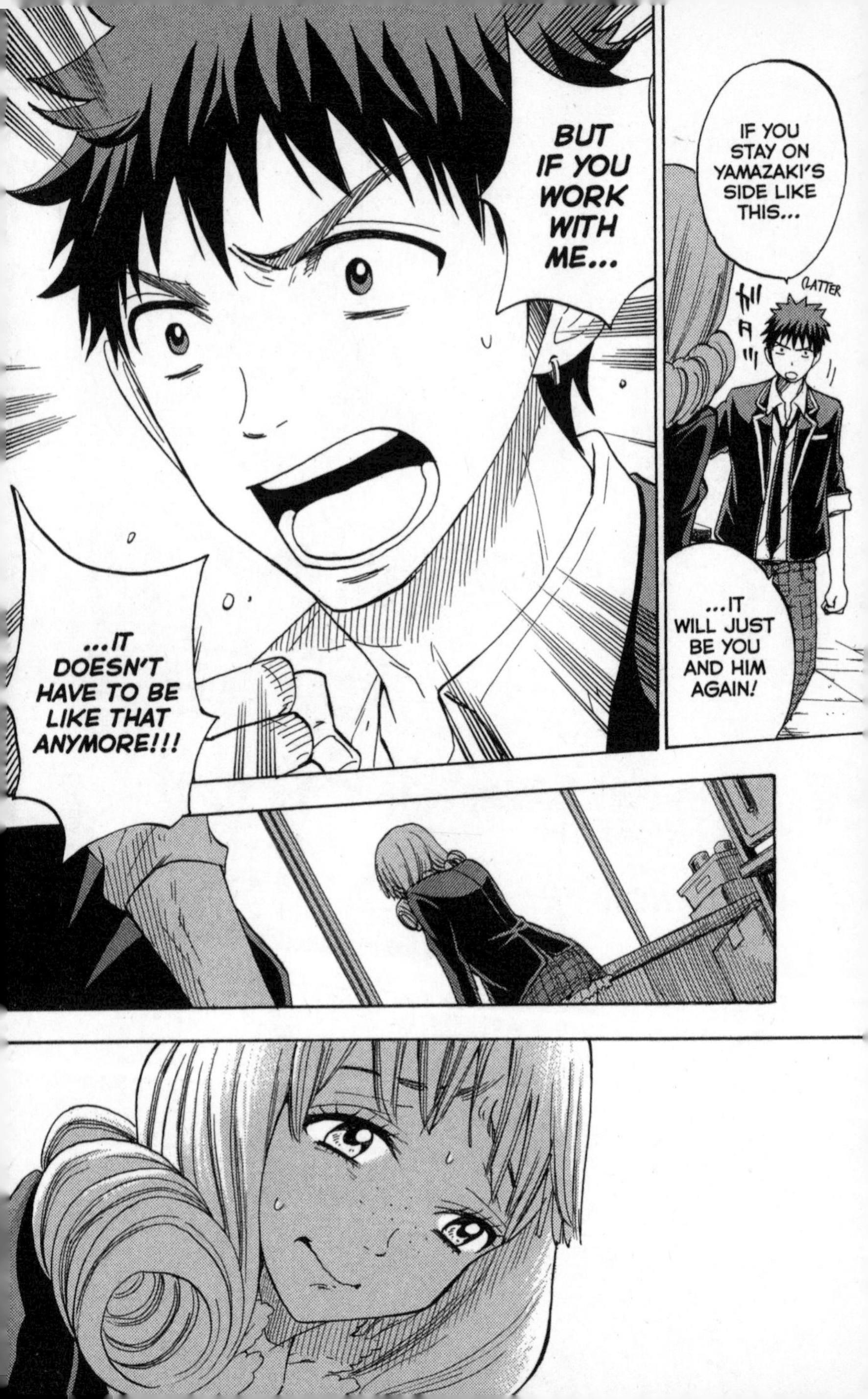
IF YOU STAY ON YAMAZAKI'S SIDE LIKE THIS...
CLATTER
...IT WILL JUST BE YOU AND HIM AGAIN!
BUT IF YOU WORK WITH ME...
...IT DOESN'T HAVE TO BE LIKE THAT ANYMORE!!!

CHAPTER 83: I have underwear already!

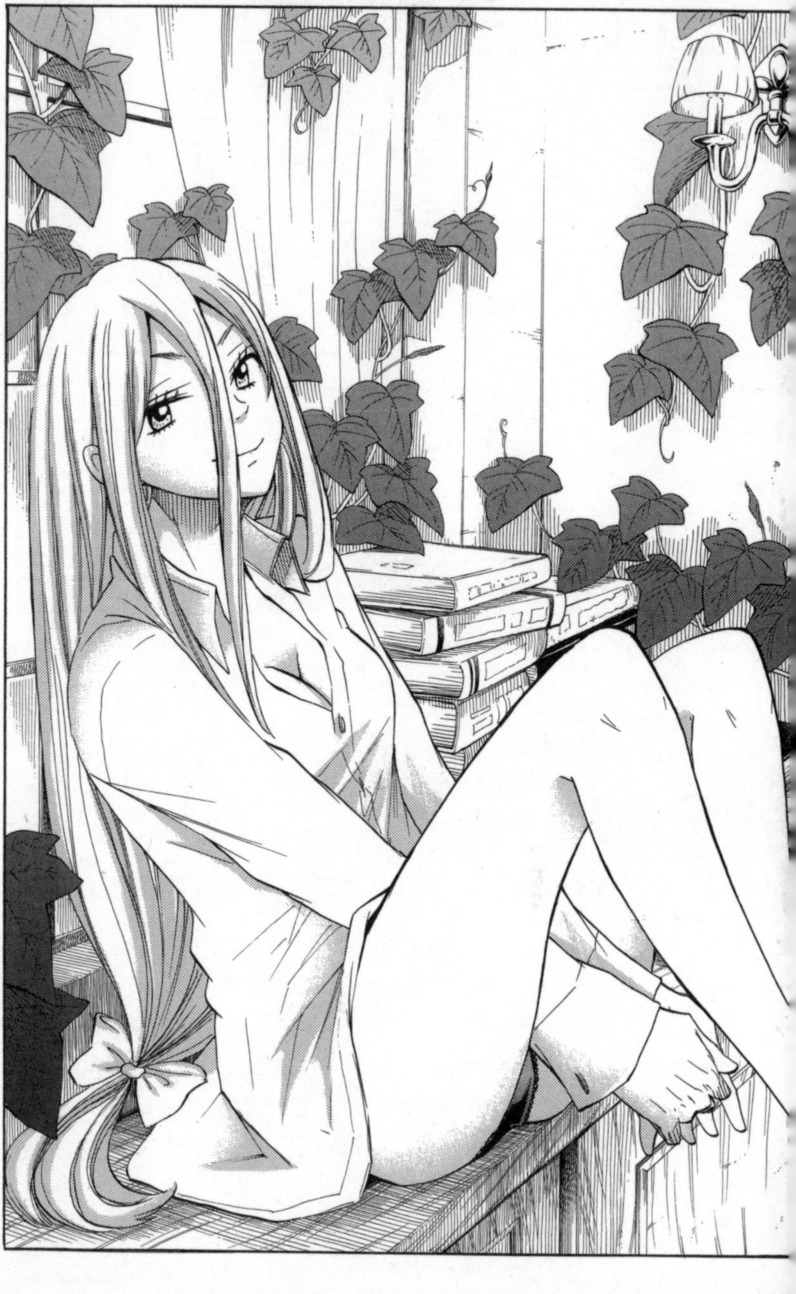

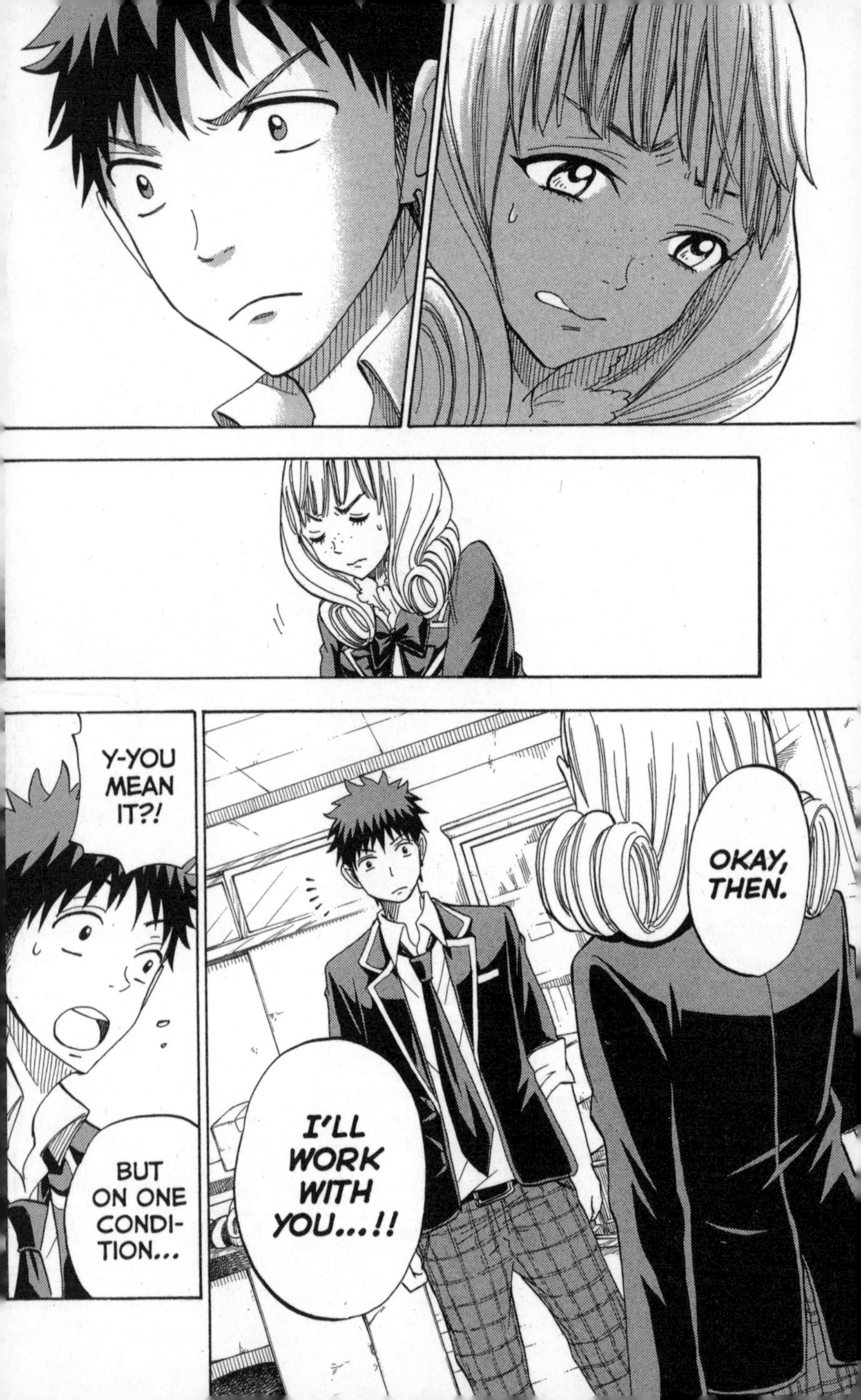
OKAY, THEN.
I'LL WORK WITH YOU...!!
Y-YOU MEAN IT?!
BUT ON ONE CONDITION...

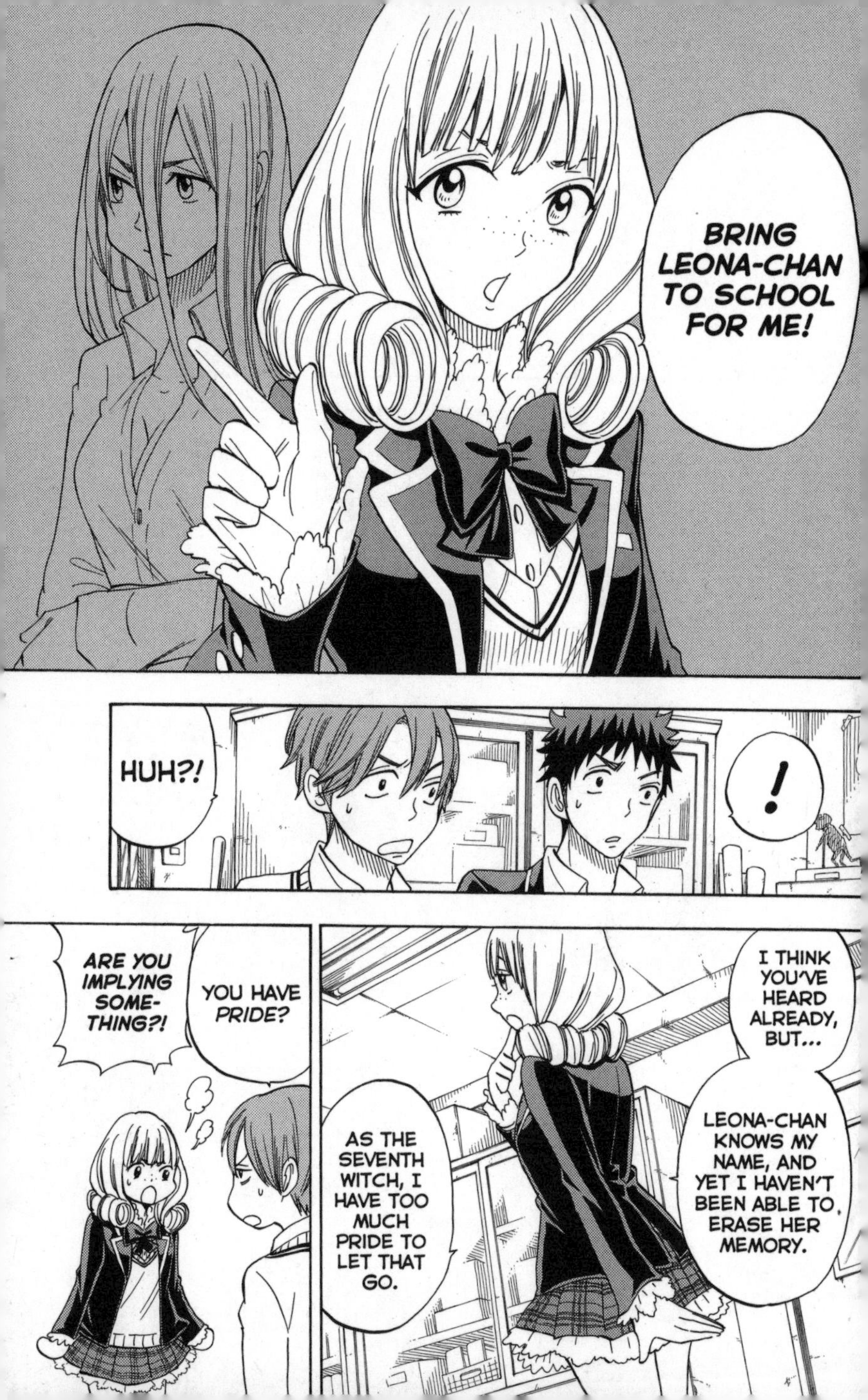
BRING LEONA-CHAN TO SCHOOL FOR ME!
!
HUH?!
I THINK YOU'VE HEARD ALREADY, BUT...
LEONA-CHAN KNOWS MY NAME, AND YET I HAVEN'T BEEN ABLE TO ERASE HER MEMORY.
AS THE SEVENTH WITCH, I HAVE TOO MUCH PRIDE TO LET THAT GO.
YOU HAVE PRIDE?
ARE YOU IMPLYING SOMETHING?!

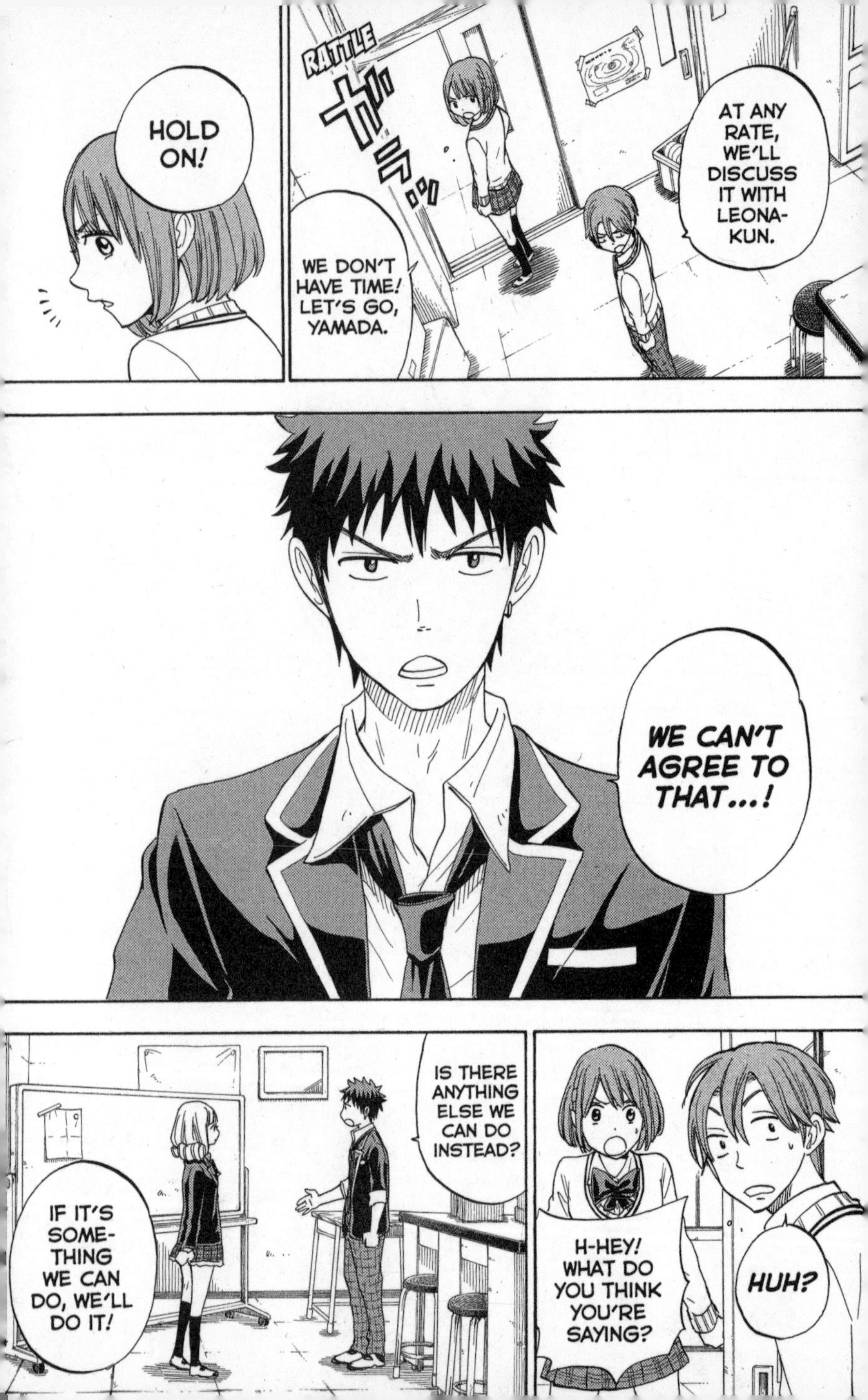

AT ANY RATE, WE'LL DISCUSS IT WITH LEONA-KUN.
RATTLE
WE DON'T HAVE TIME! LET'S GO, YAMADA.
HOLD ON!
WE CAN'T AGREE TO THAT...!
HUH?
H-HEY! WHAT DO YOU THINK YOU'RE SAYING?
IS THERE ANYTHING ELSE WE CAN DO INSTEAD?
IF IT'S SOMETHING WE CAN DO, WE'LL DO IT!

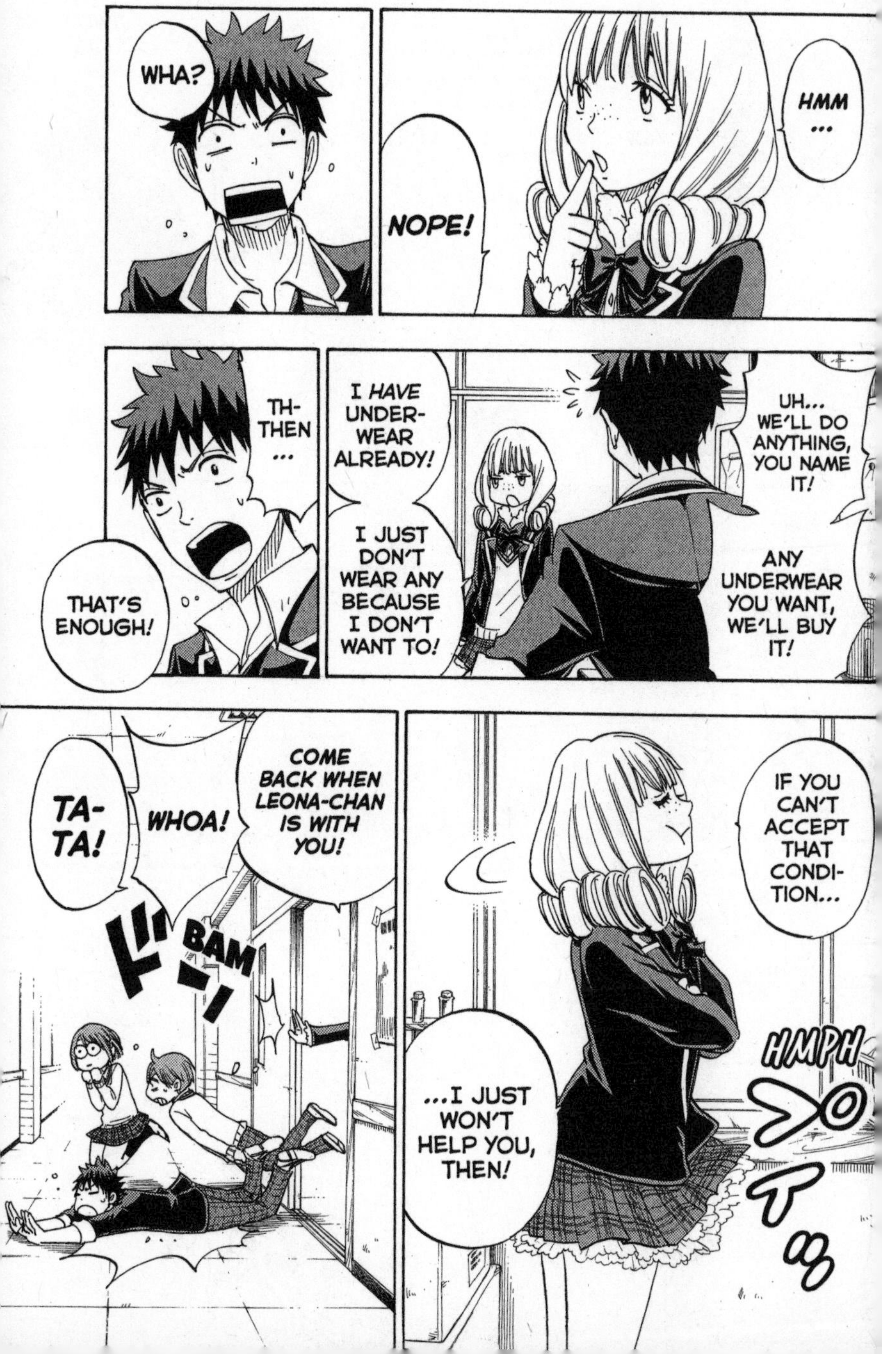
HMM ...
NOPE!
WHA?
UH... WE'LL DO ANYTHING, YOU NAME IT!
ANY UNDERWEAR YOU WANT, WE'LL BUY IT!
I HAVE UNDERWEAR ALREADY!
I JUST DON'T WEAR ANY BECAUSE I DON'T WANT TO!
TH-THEN ...
THAT'S ENOUGH!
IF YOU CAN'T ACCEPT THAT CONDITION...
HMPH
...I JUST WON'T HELP YOU, THEN!
COME BACK WHEN LEONA-CHAN IS WITH YOU!
WHOA!
TA-TA!
BAM

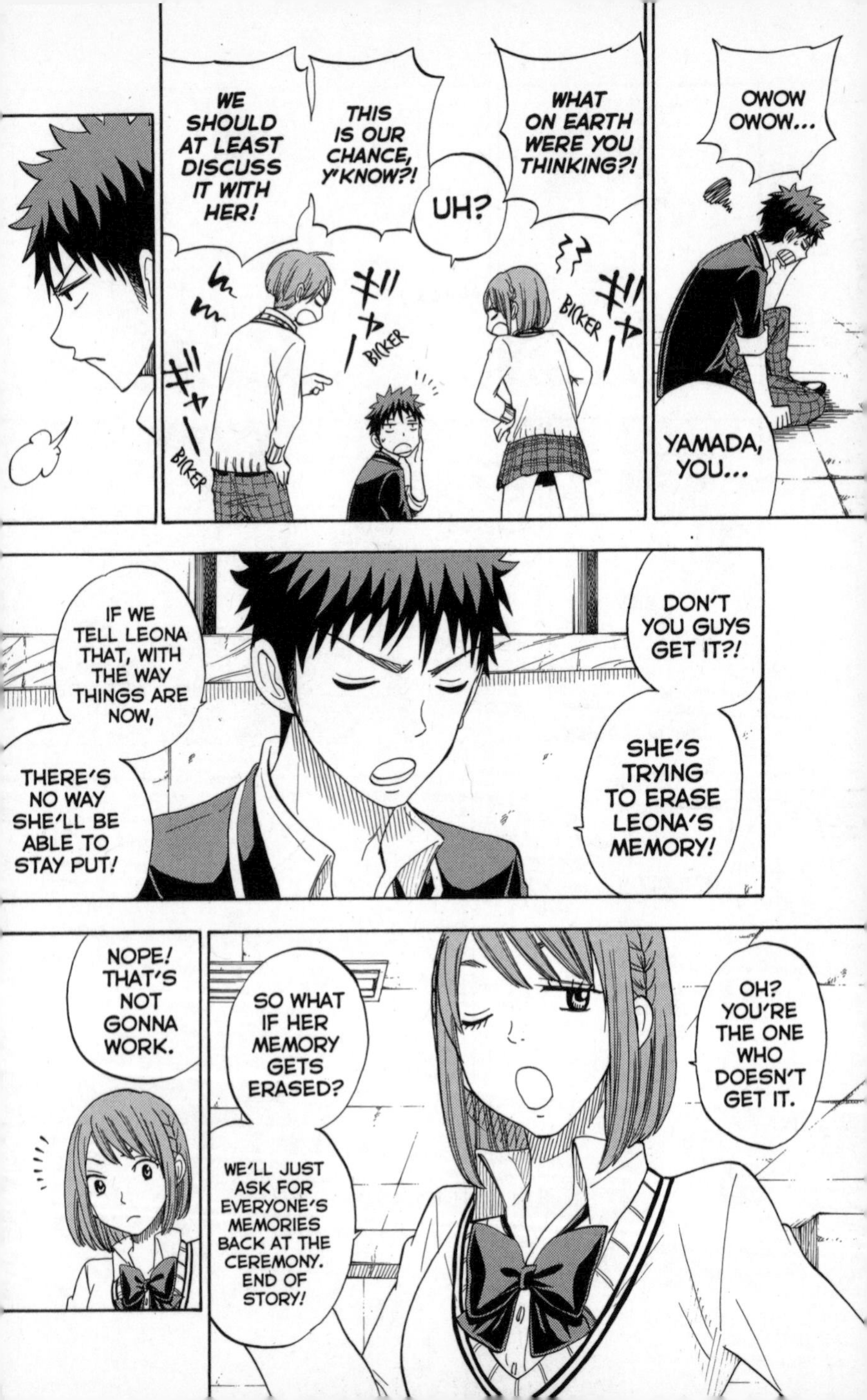
OWOW OWOW...
YAMADA, YOU...
WHAT ON EARTH WERE YOU THINKING?!
BICKER
UH?
THIS IS OUR CHANCE, Y'KNOW?!
WE SHOULD AT LEAST DISCUSS IT WITH HER!
BICKER
BICKER
DON'T YOU GUYS GET IT?!
SHE'S TRYING TO ERASE LEONA'S MEMORY!
IF WE TELL LEONA THAT, WITH THE WAY THINGS ARE NOW,
THERE'S NO WAY SHE'LL BE ABLE TO STAY PUT!
OH? YOU'RE THE ONE WHO DOESN'T GET IT.
SO WHAT IF HER MEMORY GETS ERASED?
WE'LL JUST ASK FOR EVERYONE'S MEMORIES BACK AT THE CEREMONY. END OF STORY!
NOPE! THAT'S NOT GONNA WORK.

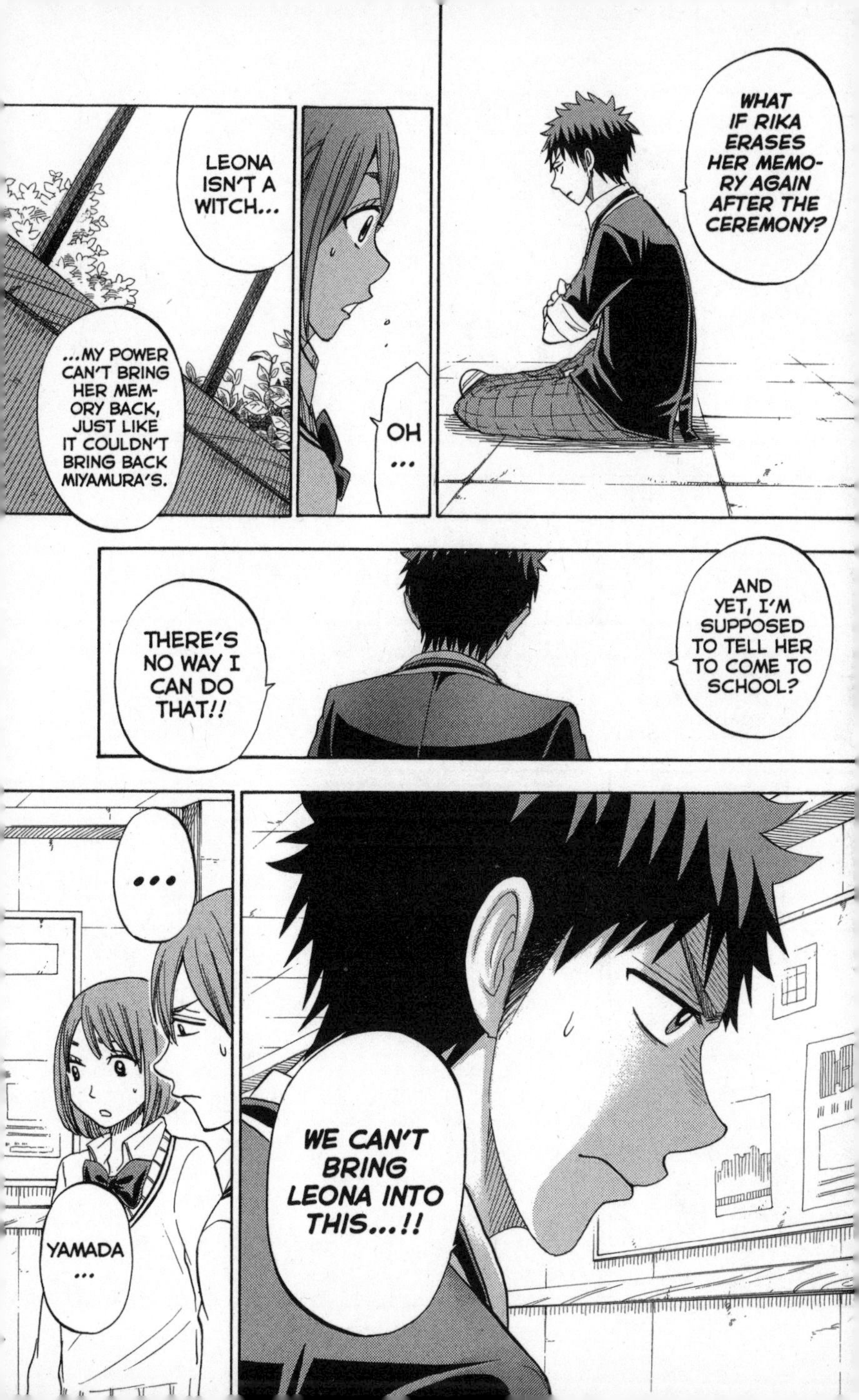
WHAT IF RIKA ERASES HER MEMORY AGAIN AFTER THE CEREMONY?
OH ...
LEONA ISN'T A WITCH...
...MY POWER CAN'T BRING HER MEMORY BACK, JUST LIKE IT COULDN'T BRING BACK MIYAMURA'S.
AND YET, I'M SUPPOSED TO TELL HER TO COME TO SCHOOL?
THERE'S NO WAY I CAN DO THAT!!
WE CAN'T BRING LEONA INTO THIS...!!
...
YAMADA ...

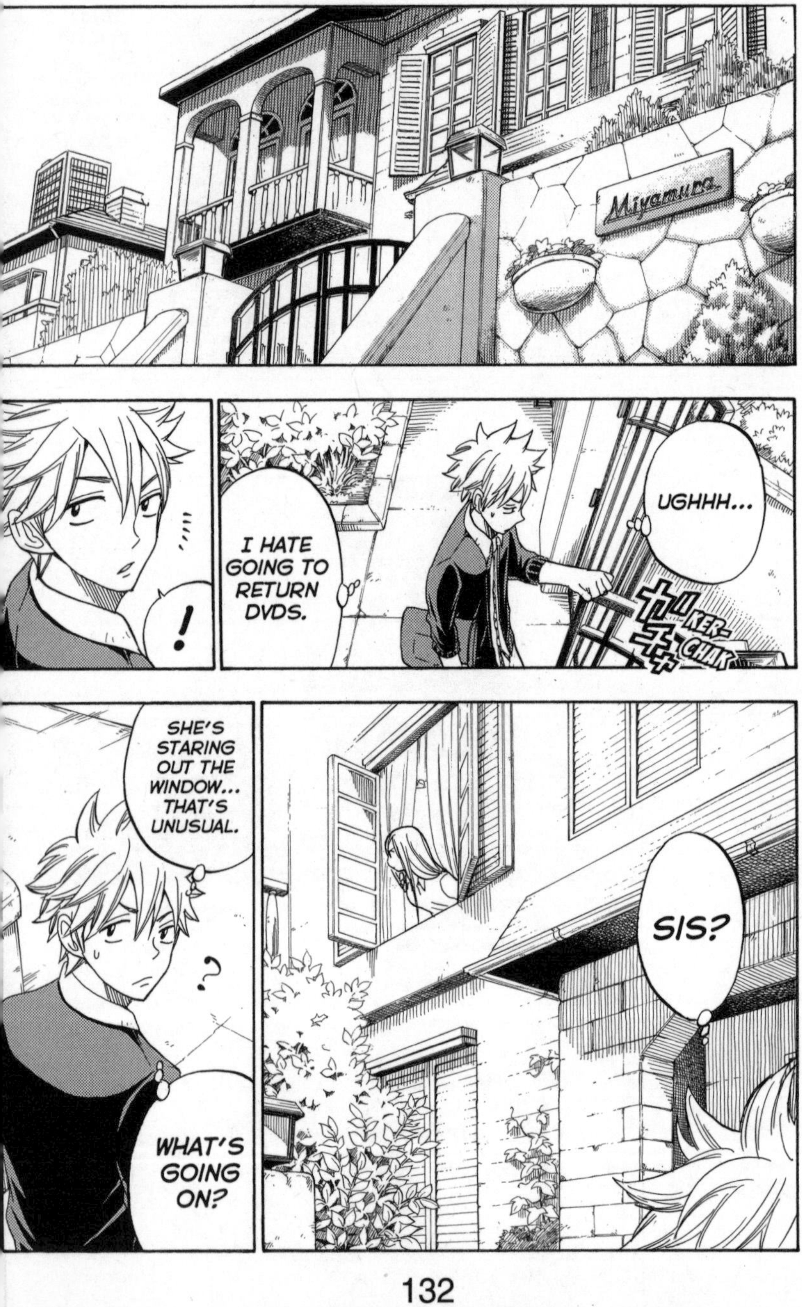
Miyamura
UGHHH...
カチャ
KER-CHAK
I HATE GOING TO RETURN DVDS.
!
SIS?
SHE'S STARING OUT THE WINDOW... THAT'S UNUSUAL.
?
WHAT'S GOING ON?

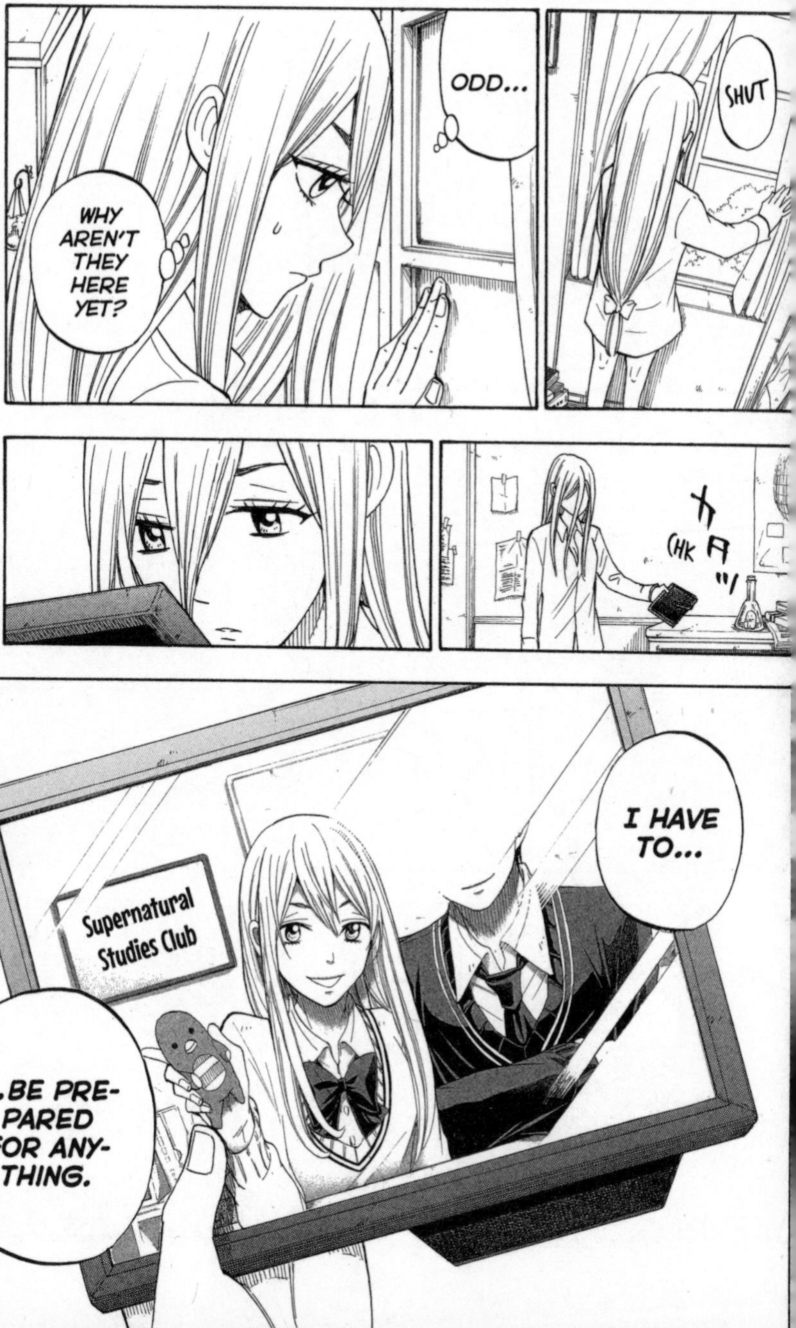
SHUT
ODD...
WHY AREN'T THEY HERE YET?
CHK
I HAVE TO...
Supernatural Studies Club
...BE PRE-PARED FOR ANY-THING.

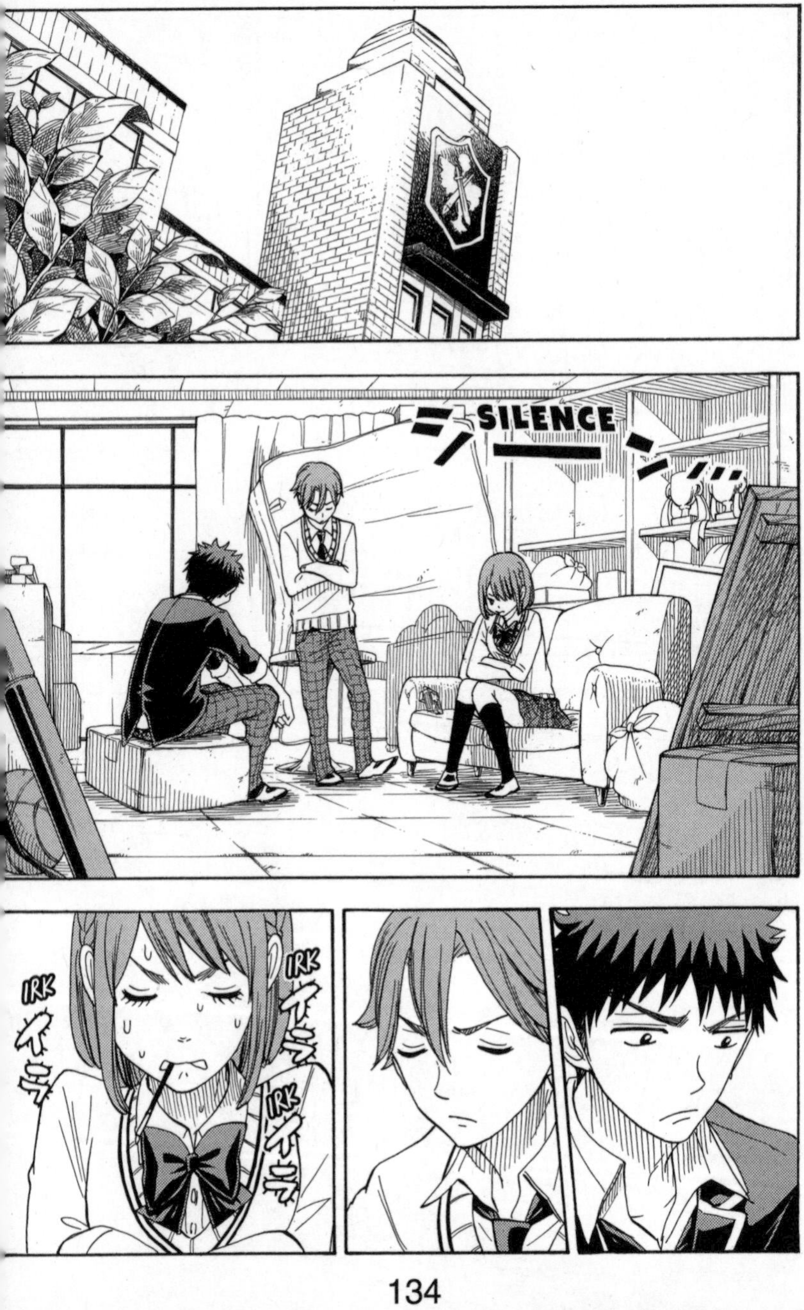
SILENCE
IRK
IRK
IRK

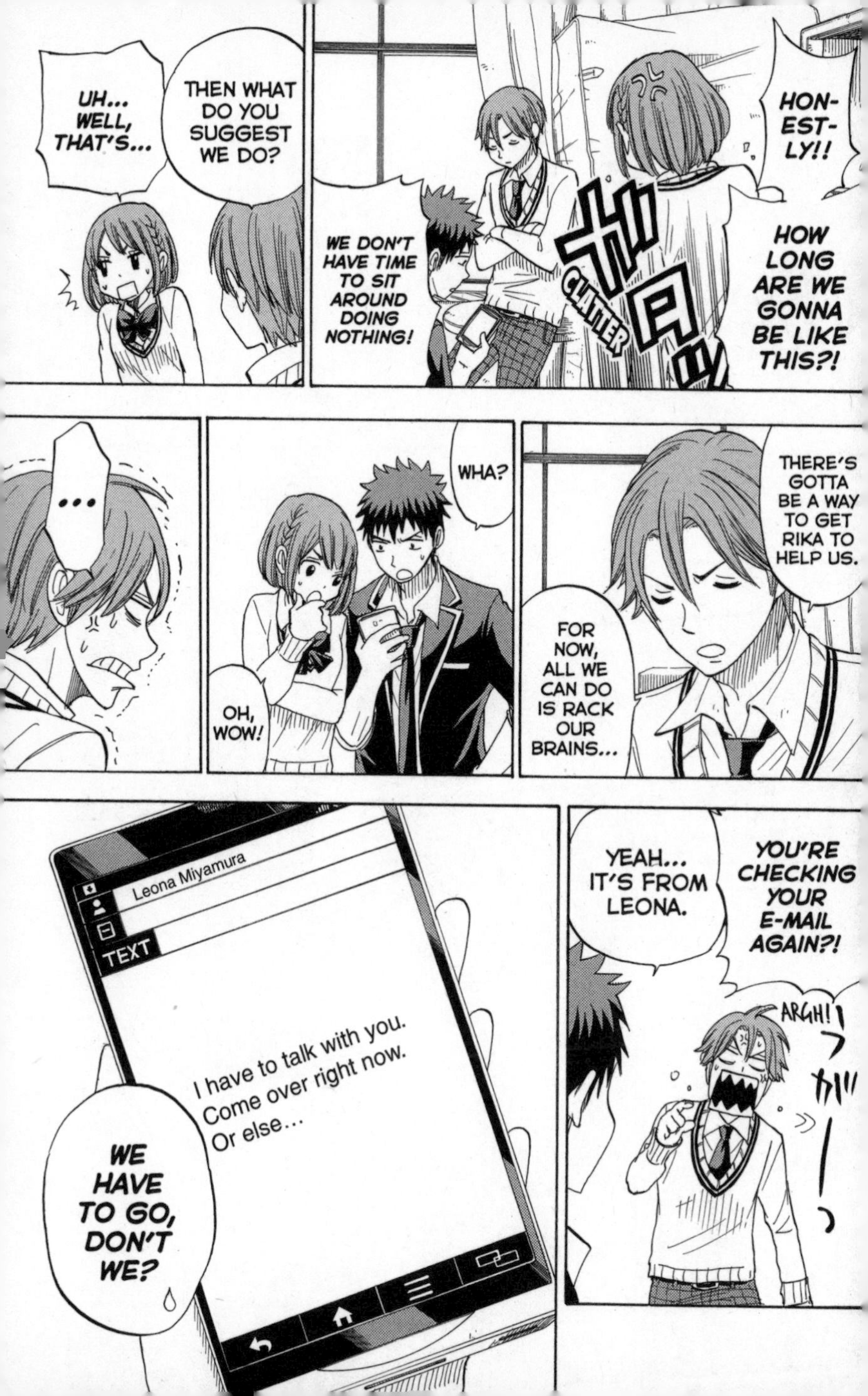
HON-EST-LY!!
HOW LONG ARE WE GONNA BE LIKE THIS?!
CLATTER
WE DON'T HAVE TIME TO SIT AROUND DOING NOTHING!
THEN WHAT DO YOU SUGGEST WE DO?
UH... WELL, THAT'S...
THERE'S GOTTA BE A WAY TO GET RIKA TO HELP US.
FOR NOW, ALL WE CAN DO IS RACK OUR BRAINS...
WHA?
OH, WOW!
...
YOU'RE CHECKING YOUR E-MAIL AGAIN?!
YEAH... IT'S FROM LEONA.
ARGH!
Leona Miyamura
TEXT
I have to talk with you.
Come over right now.
Or else...
WE HAVE TO GO, DON'T WE?

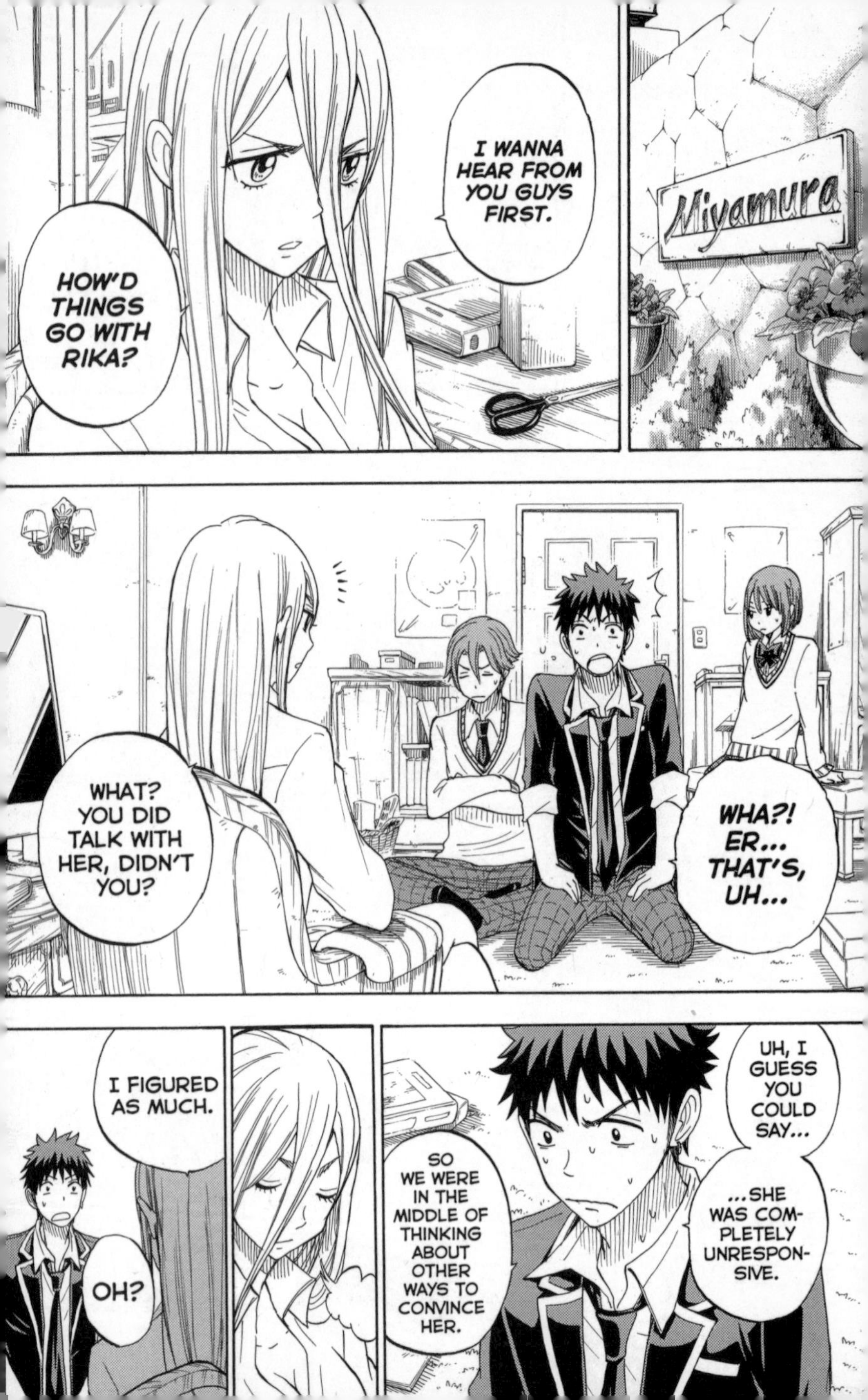
Miyamura
I WANNA HEAR FROM YOU GUYS FIRST.
HOW'D THINGS GO WITH RIKA?
WHAT? YOU DID TALK WITH HER, DIDN'T YOU?
WHA?! ER... THAT'S, UH...
UH, I GUESS YOU COULD SAY...
...SHE WAS COM-PLETELY UNRESPON-SIVE.
SO WE WERE IN THE MIDDLE OF THINKING ABOUT OTHER WAYS TO CONVINCE HER.
I FIGURED AS MUCH.
OH?

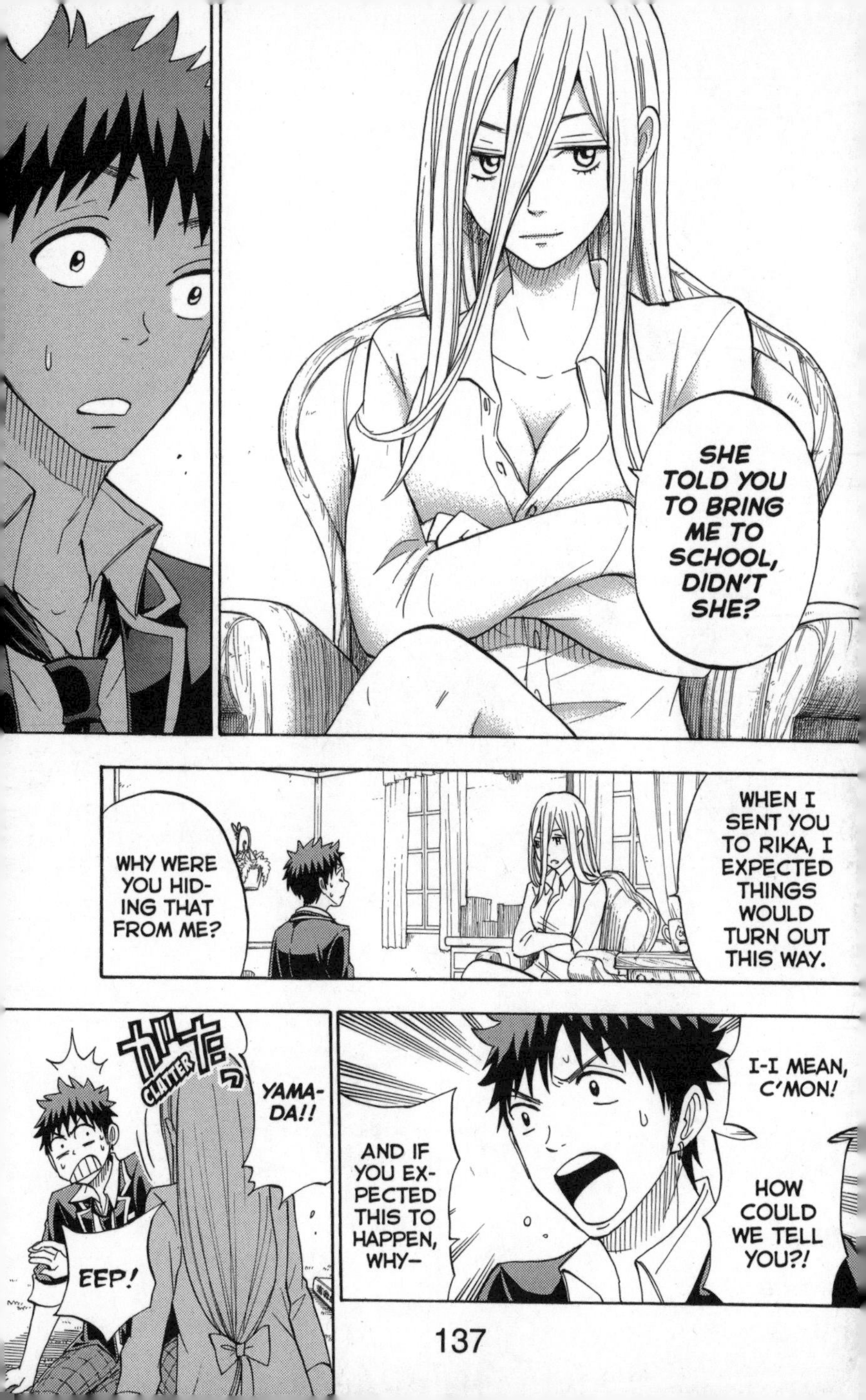
SHE TOLD YOU TO BRING ME TO SCHOOL, DIDN'T SHE?
WHEN I SENT YOU TO RIKA, I EXPECTED THINGS WOULD TURN OUT THIS WAY.
WHY WERE YOU HID-ING THAT FROM ME?
I-I MEAN, C'MON!
HOW COULD WE TELL YOU?!
AND IF YOU EX-PECTED THIS TO HAPPEN, WHY–
YAMA-DA!!
CLATTER
EEP!

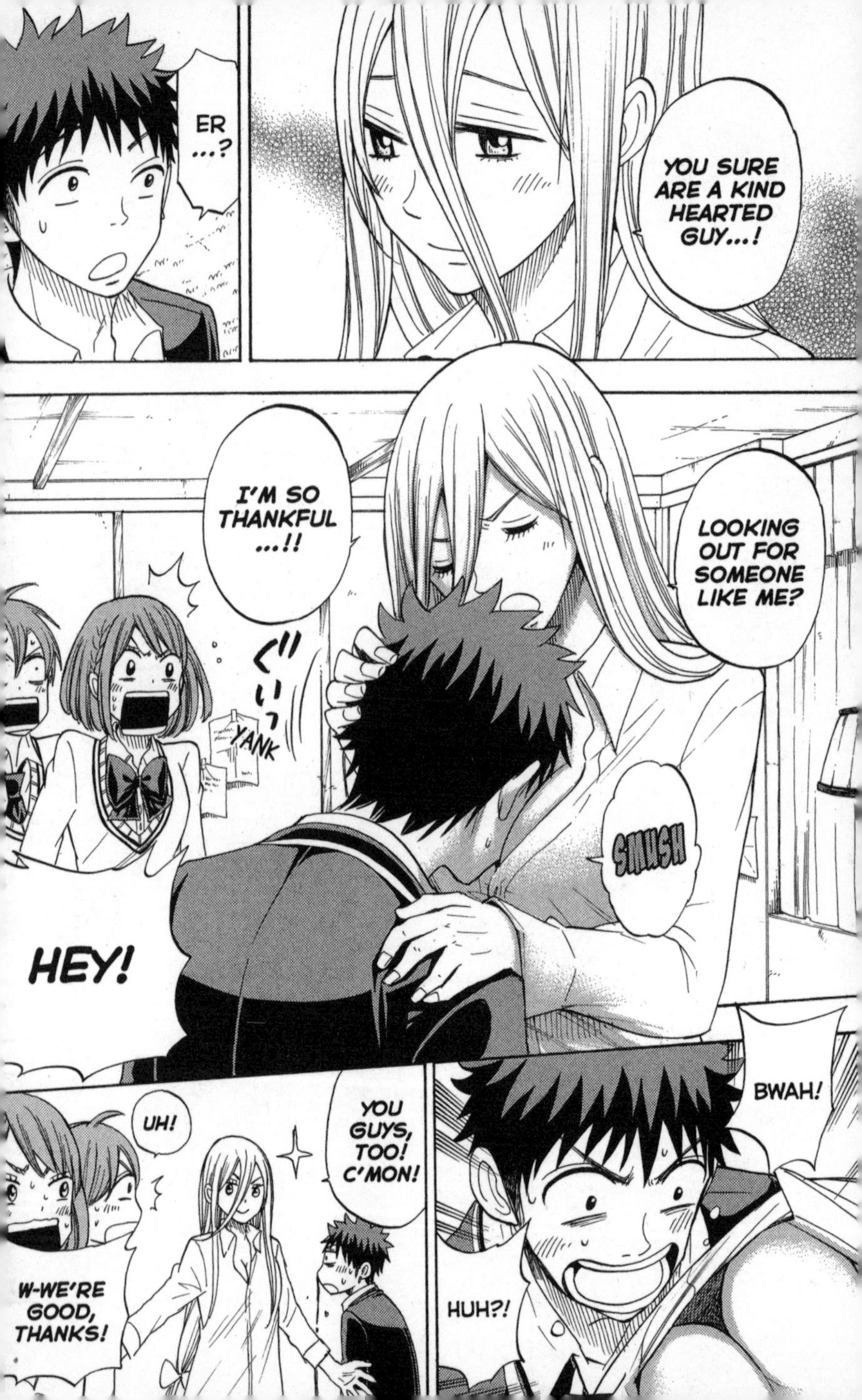
YOU SURE ARE A KIND HEARTED GUY...!
ER ...?
LOOKING OUT FOR SOMEONE LIKE ME?
I'M SO THANKFUL ...!!
ぐいっ
YANK
SMUSH
HEY!
BWAH!
HUH?!
YOU GUYS, TOO! C'MON!
UH!
W-WE'RE GOOD, THANKS!

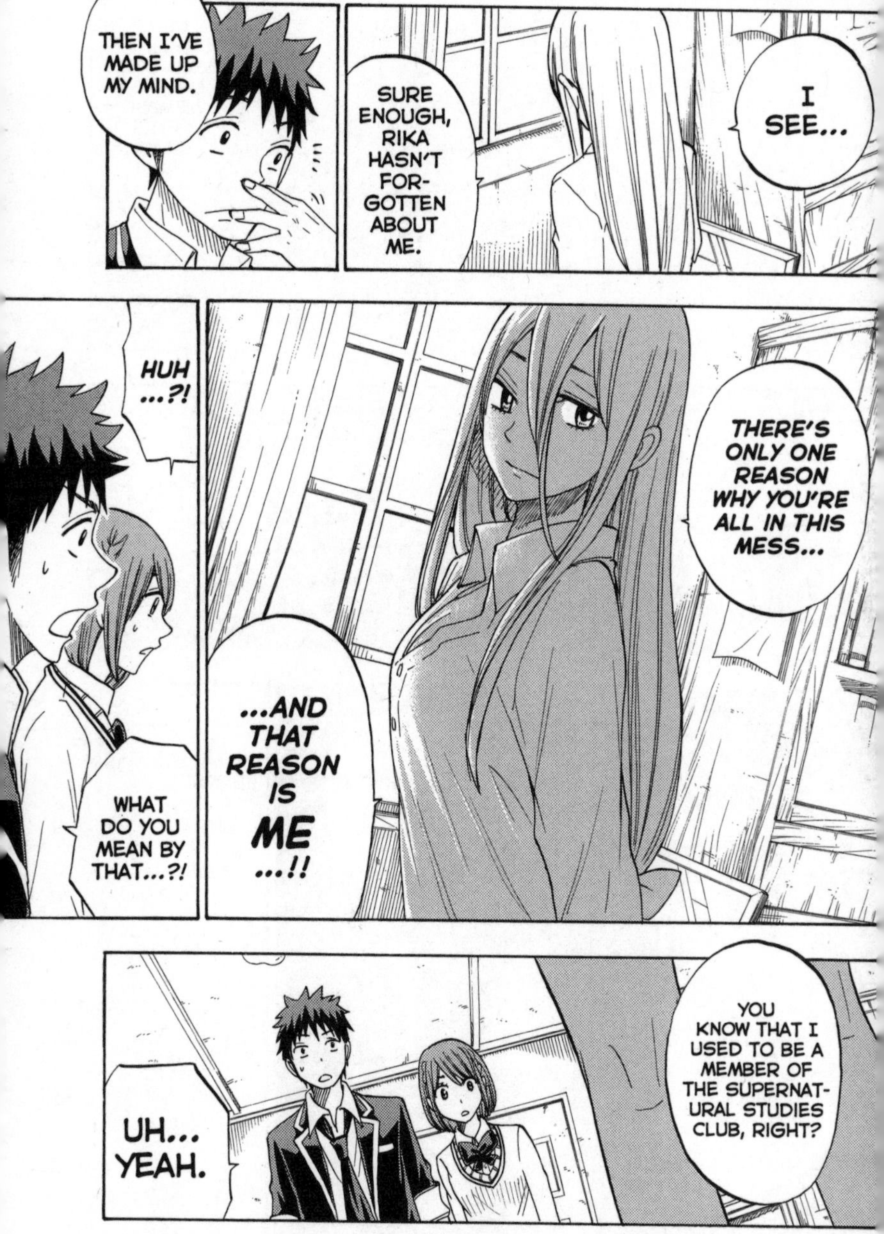
I SEE...
SURE ENOUGH, RIKA HASN'T FOR-GOTTEN ABOUT ME.
THEN I'VE MADE UP MY MIND.
THERE'S ONLY ONE REASON WHY YOU'RE ALL IN THIS MESS...
...AND THAT REASON IS ME ...!!
HUH ...?!
WHAT DO YOU MEAN BY THAT...?!
YOU KNOW THAT I USED TO BE A MEMBER OF THE SUPERNAT-URAL STUDIES CLUB, RIGHT?
UH... YEAH.

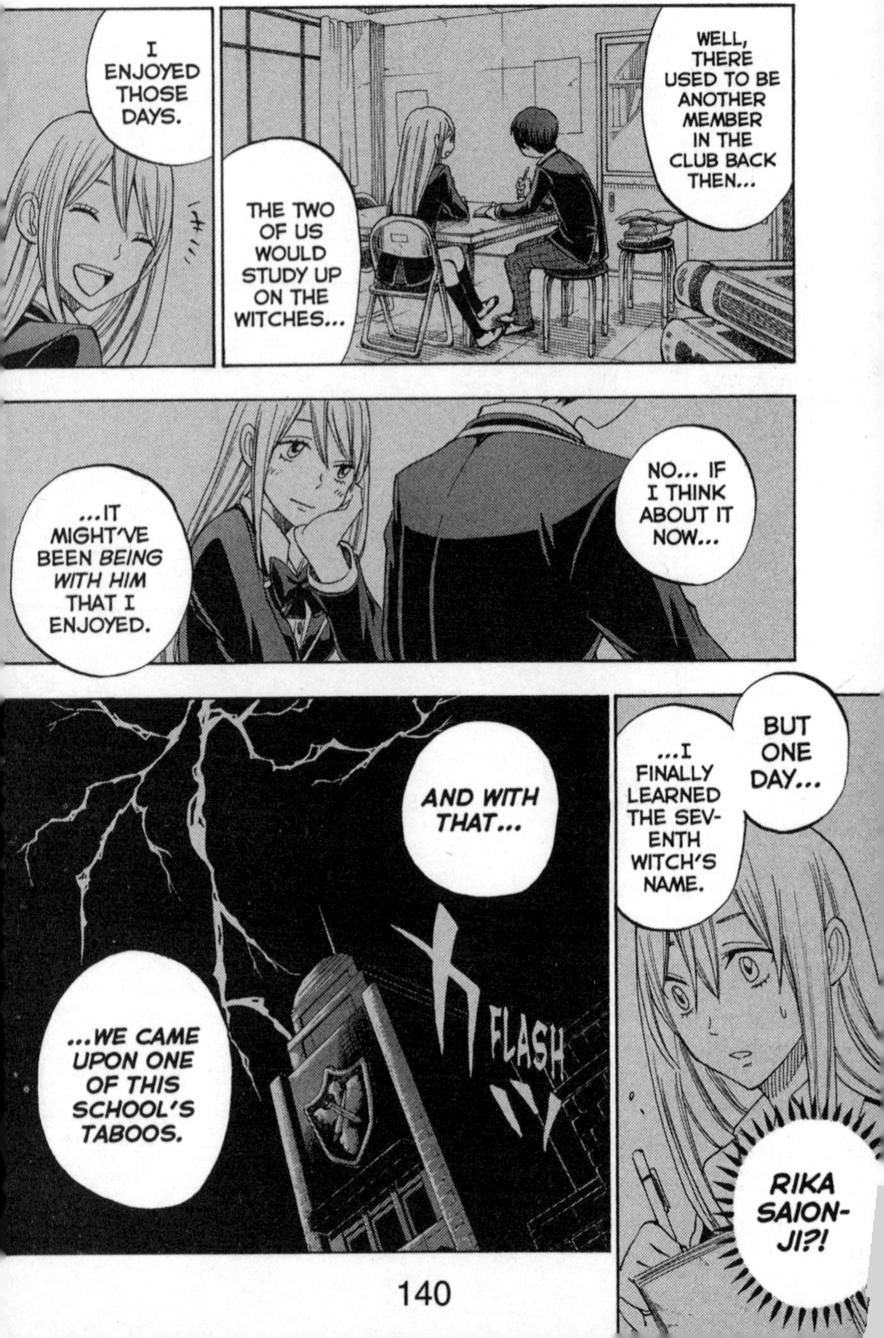
WELL, THERE USED TO BE ANOTHER MEMBER IN THE CLUB BACK THEN...
THE TWO OF US WOULD STUDY UP ON THE WITCHES...
I ENJOYED THOSE DAYS.
NO... IF I THINK ABOUT IT NOW...
...IT MIGHT'VE BEEN *BEING WITH HIM* THAT I ENJOYED.
BUT ONE DAY...
...I FINALLY LEARNED THE SEV- ENTH WITCH'S NAME.
RIKA SAIONJI?!
AND WITH THAT...
FLASH
...WE CAME UPON ONE OF THIS SCHOOL'S TABOOS.

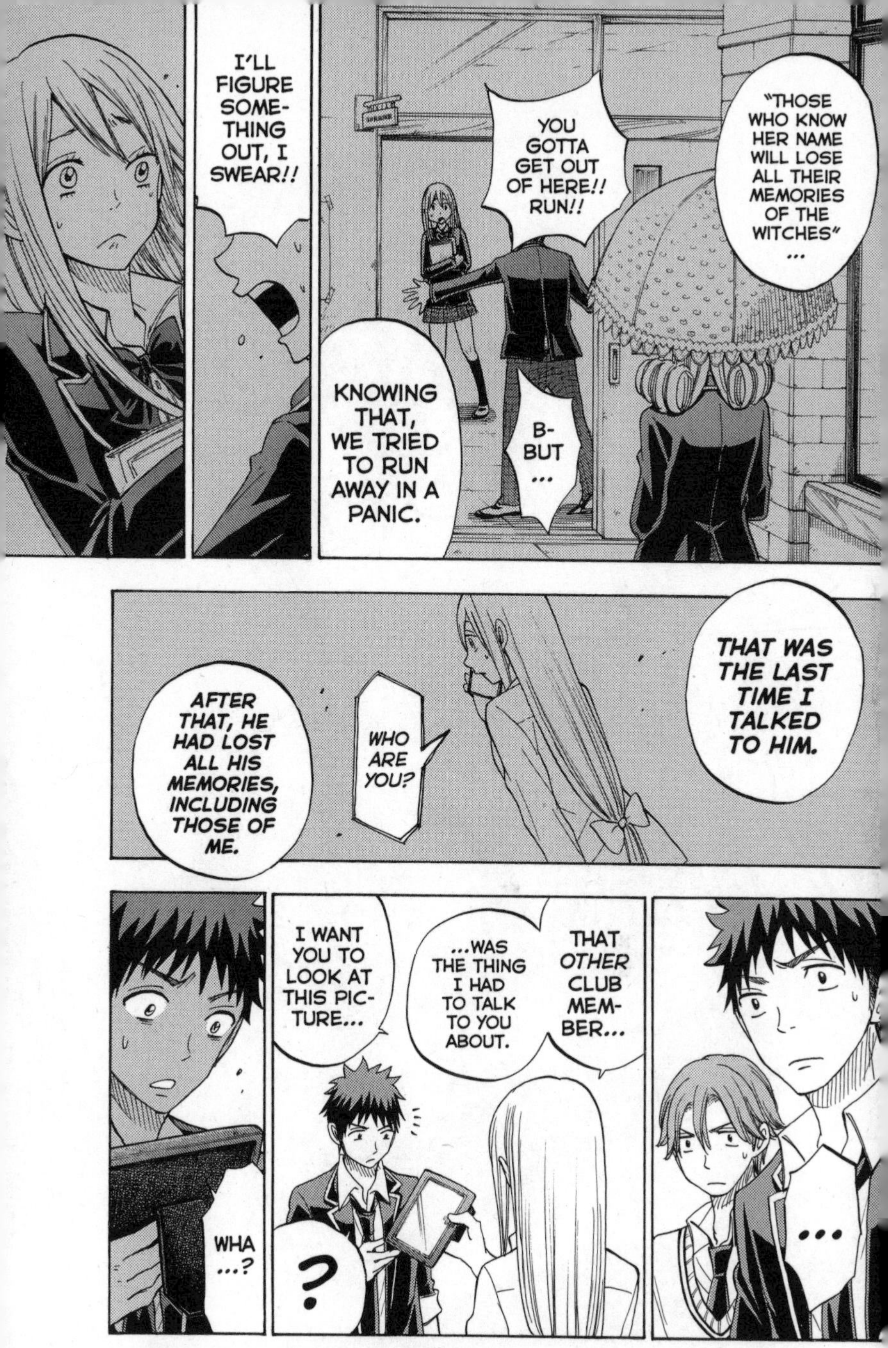
"THOSE WHO KNOW HER NAME WILL LOSE ALL THEIR MEMORIES OF THE WITCHES" ...
YOU GOTTA GET OUT OF HERE!! RUN!!
B-BUT ...
KNOWING THAT, WE TRIED TO RUN AWAY IN A PANIC.
I'LL FIGURE SOME-THING OUT, I SWEAR!!
THAT WAS THE LAST TIME I TALKED TO HIM.
WHO ARE YOU?
AFTER THAT, HE HAD LOST ALL HIS MEMORIES, INCLUDING THOSE OF ME.
...
THAT OTHER CLUB MEM-BER...
...WAS THE THING I HAD TO TALK TO YOU ABOUT.
I WANT YOU TO LOOK AT THIS PIC-TURE...
?
WHA ...?

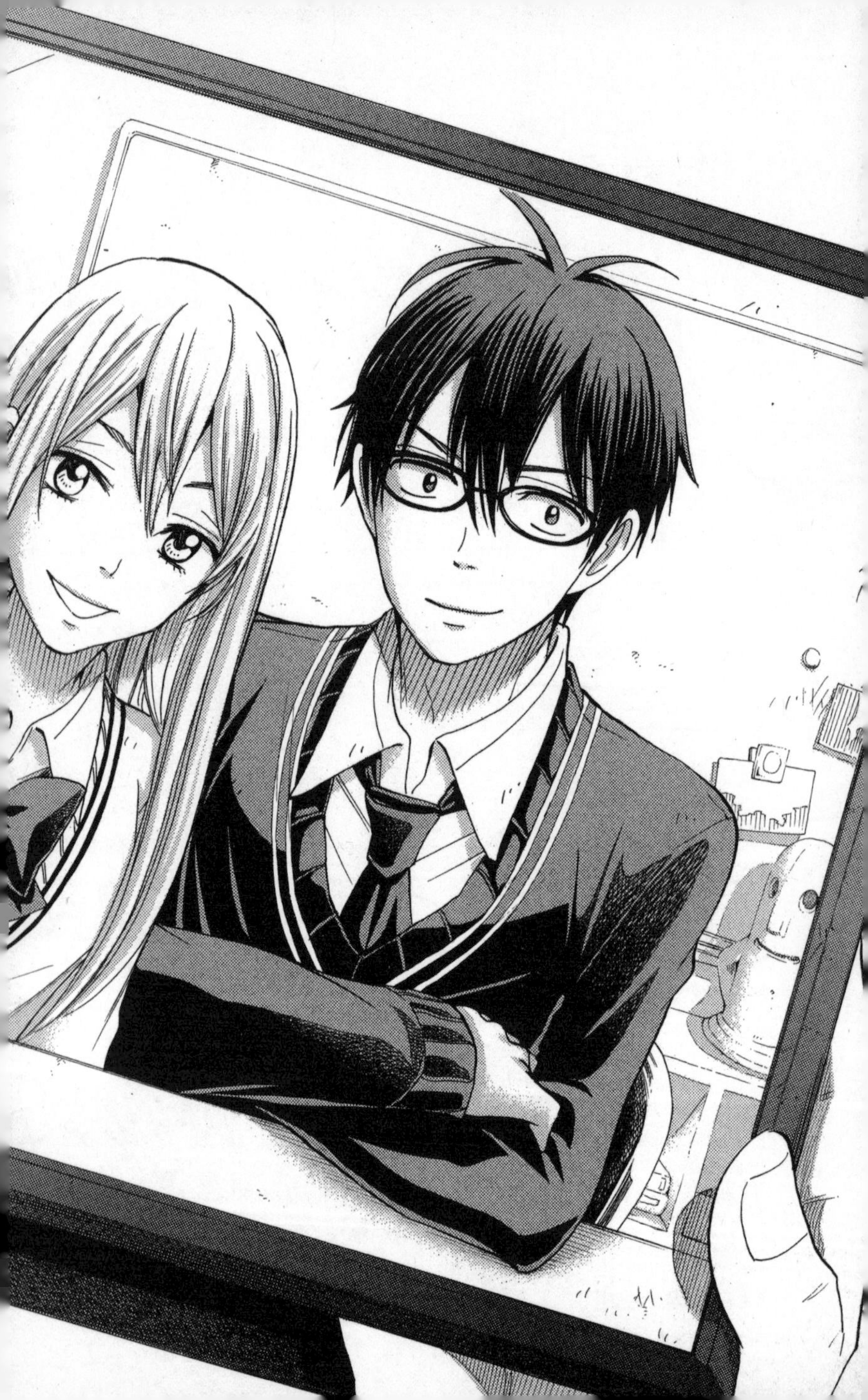

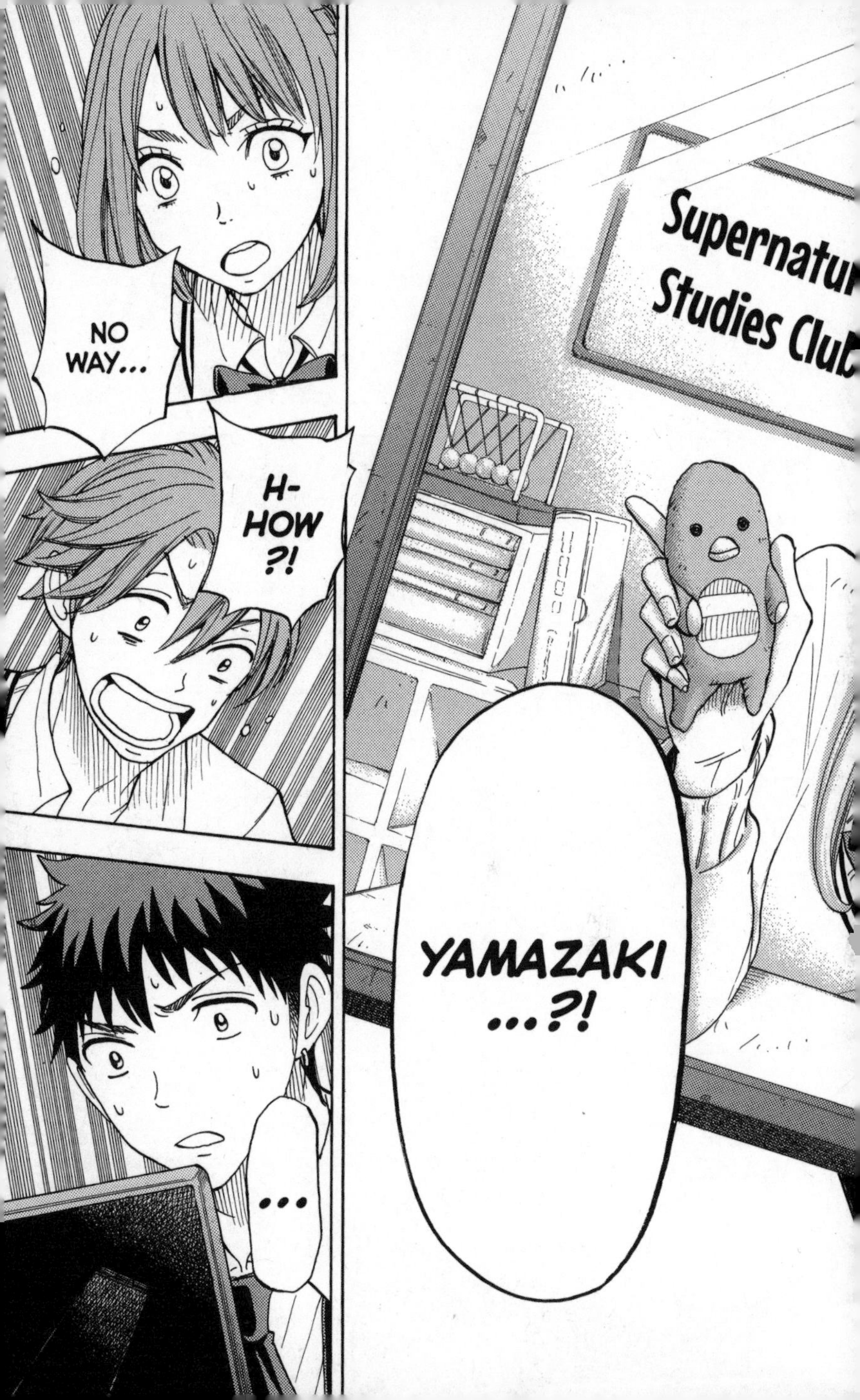
Supernatur
Studies Club
YAMAZAKI ...?!
NO WAY...
H-HOW?!
...

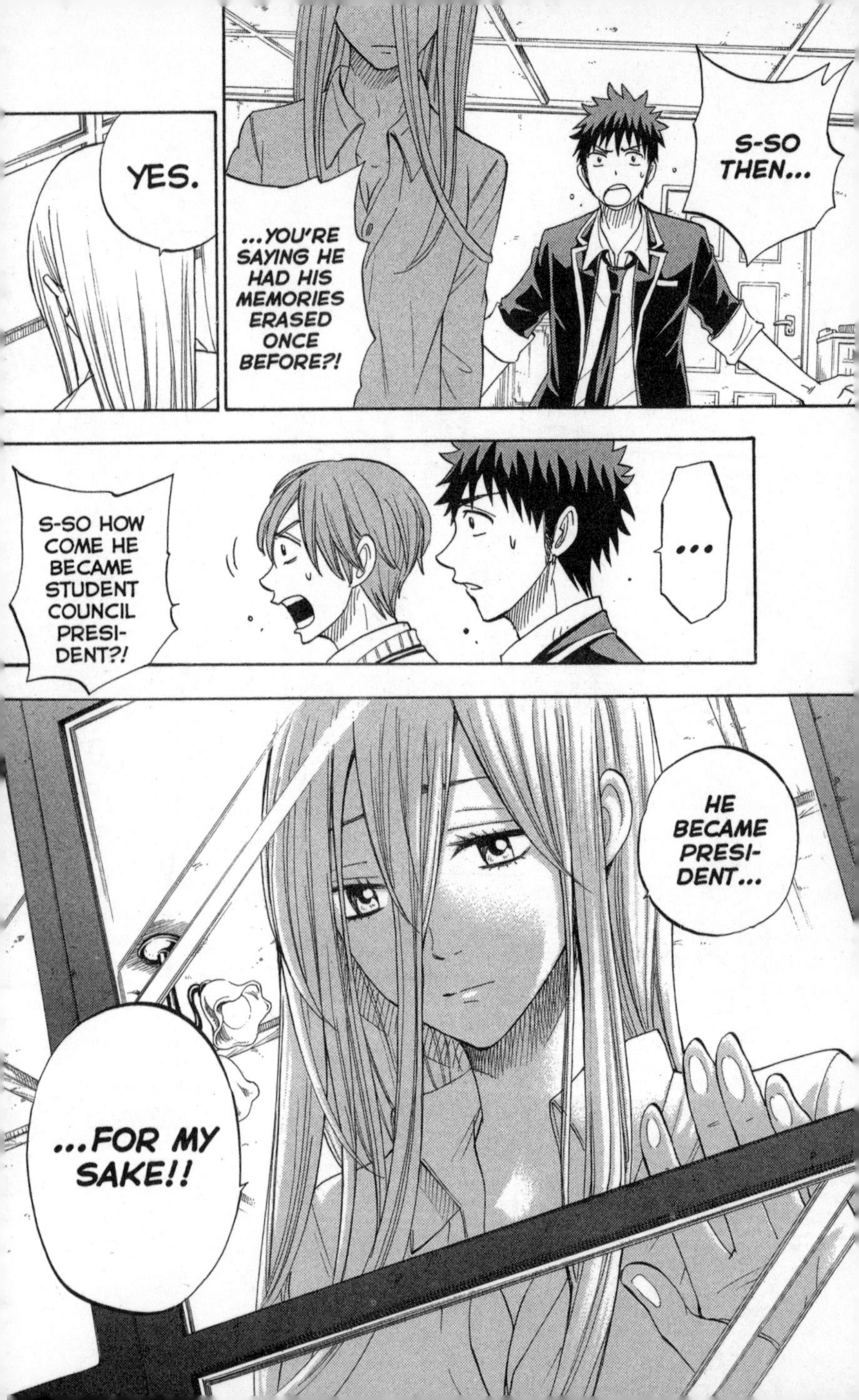
S-SO THEN...
...YOU'RE SAYING HE HAD HIS MEMORIES ERASED ONCE BEFORE?!
YES.
...
S-SO HOW COME HE BECAME STUDENT COUNCIL PRESI-DENT?!
HE BECAME PRESI-DENT...
...FOR MY SAKE!!

CHAPTER 84: That's the end of the club!!

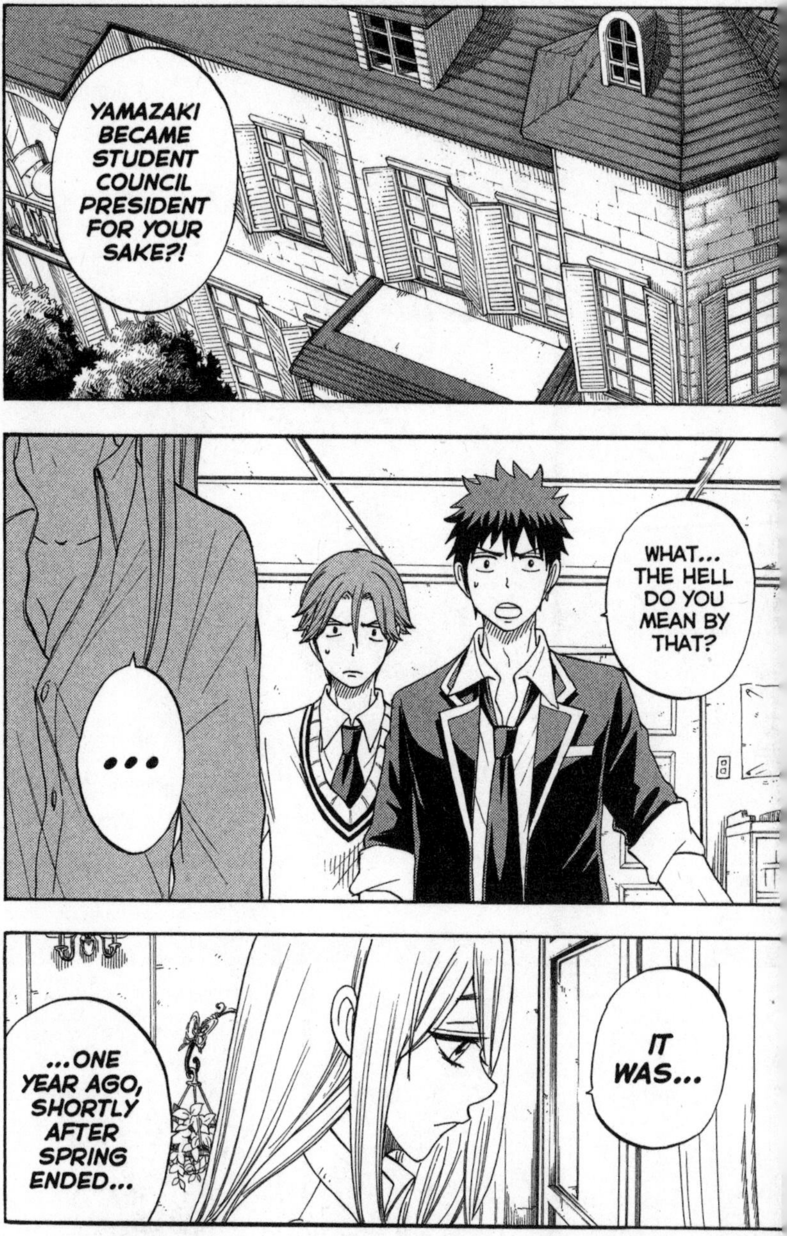
YAMAZAKI BECAME STUDENT COUNCIL PRESIDENT FOR YOUR SAKE?!
WHAT... THE HELL DO YOU MEAN BY THAT?
...
IT WAS...
...ONE YEAR AGO, SHORTLY AFTER SPRING ENDED...

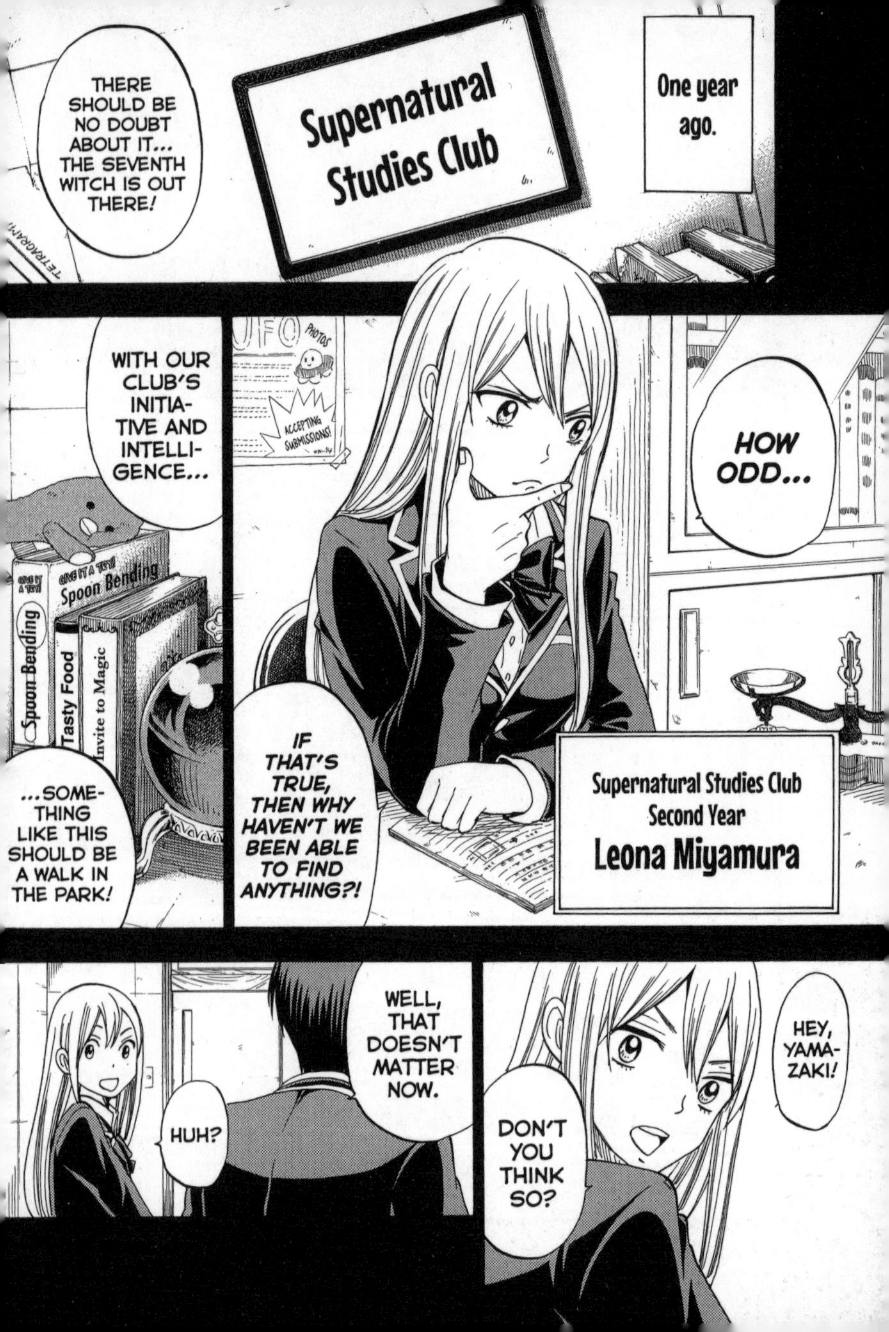
One year ago.
Supernatural Studies Club
THERE SHOULD BE NO DOUBT ABOUT IT... THE SEVENTH WITCH IS OUT THERE!
HOW ODD...
UFO PHOTOS
ACCEPTING SUBMISSIONS!
Supernatural Studies Club
Second Year
Leona Miyamura
IF THAT'S TRUE, THEN WHY HAVEN'T WE BEEN ABLE TO FIND ANYTHING?!
WITH OUR CLUB'S INITIATIVE AND INTELLIGENCE...
GIVE IT A TRY! Spoon Bending
Spoon Bending
Tasty Food
Invite to Magic
...SOMETHING LIKE THIS SHOULD BE A WALK IN THE PARK!
HEY, YAMAZAKI!
DON'T YOU THINK SO?
WELL, THAT DOESN'T MATTER NOW.
HUH?

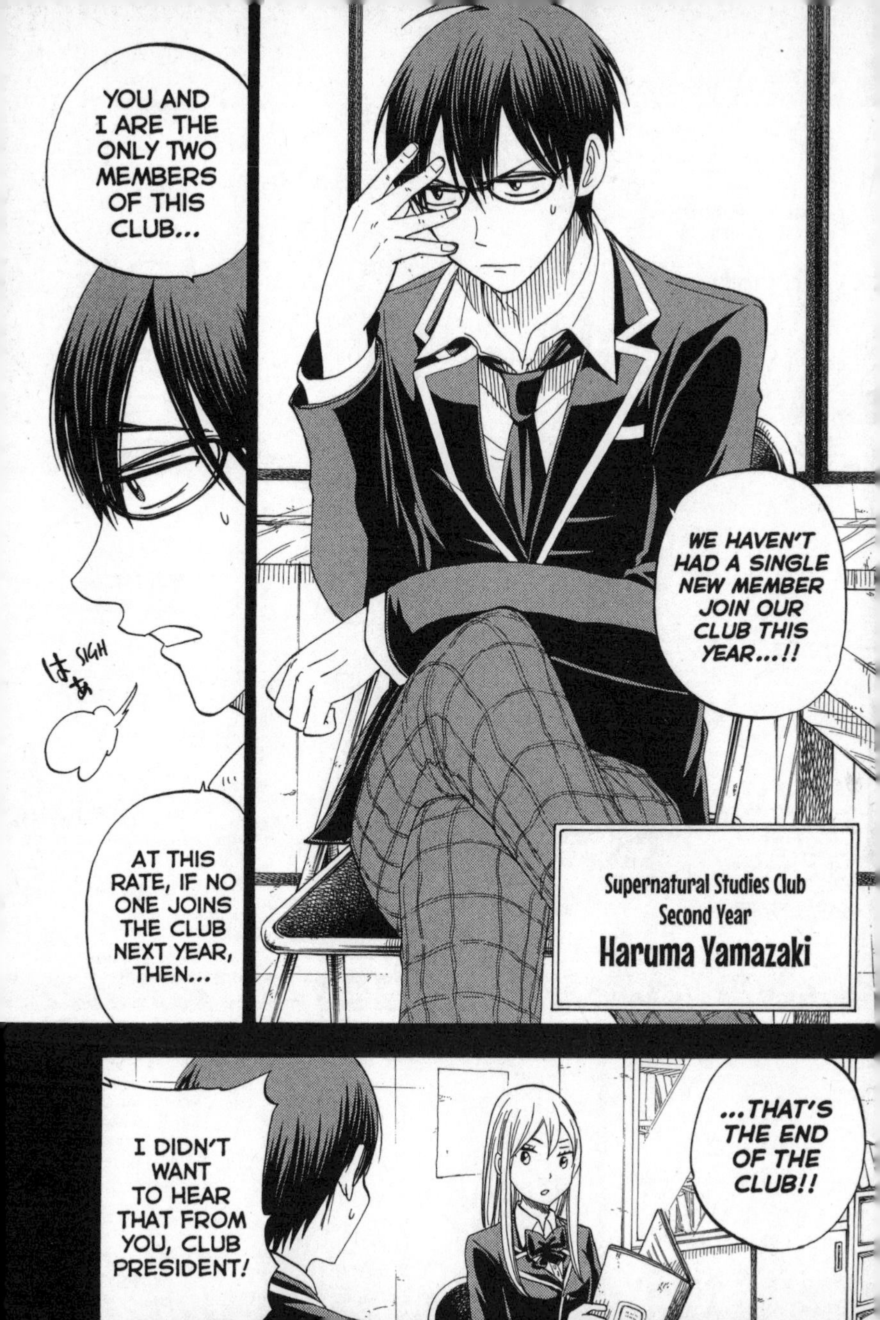
WE HAVEN'T HAD A SINGLE NEW MEMBER JOIN OUR CLUB THIS YEAR...!!
Supernatural Studies Club
Second Year
Haruma Yamazaki
YOU AND I ARE THE ONLY TWO MEMBERS OF THIS CLUB...
はあ SIGH
AT THIS RATE, IF NO ONE JOINS THE CLUB NEXT YEAR, THEN...
...THAT'S THE END OF THE CLUB!!
I DIDN'T WANT TO HEAR THAT FROM YOU, CLUB PRESIDENT!

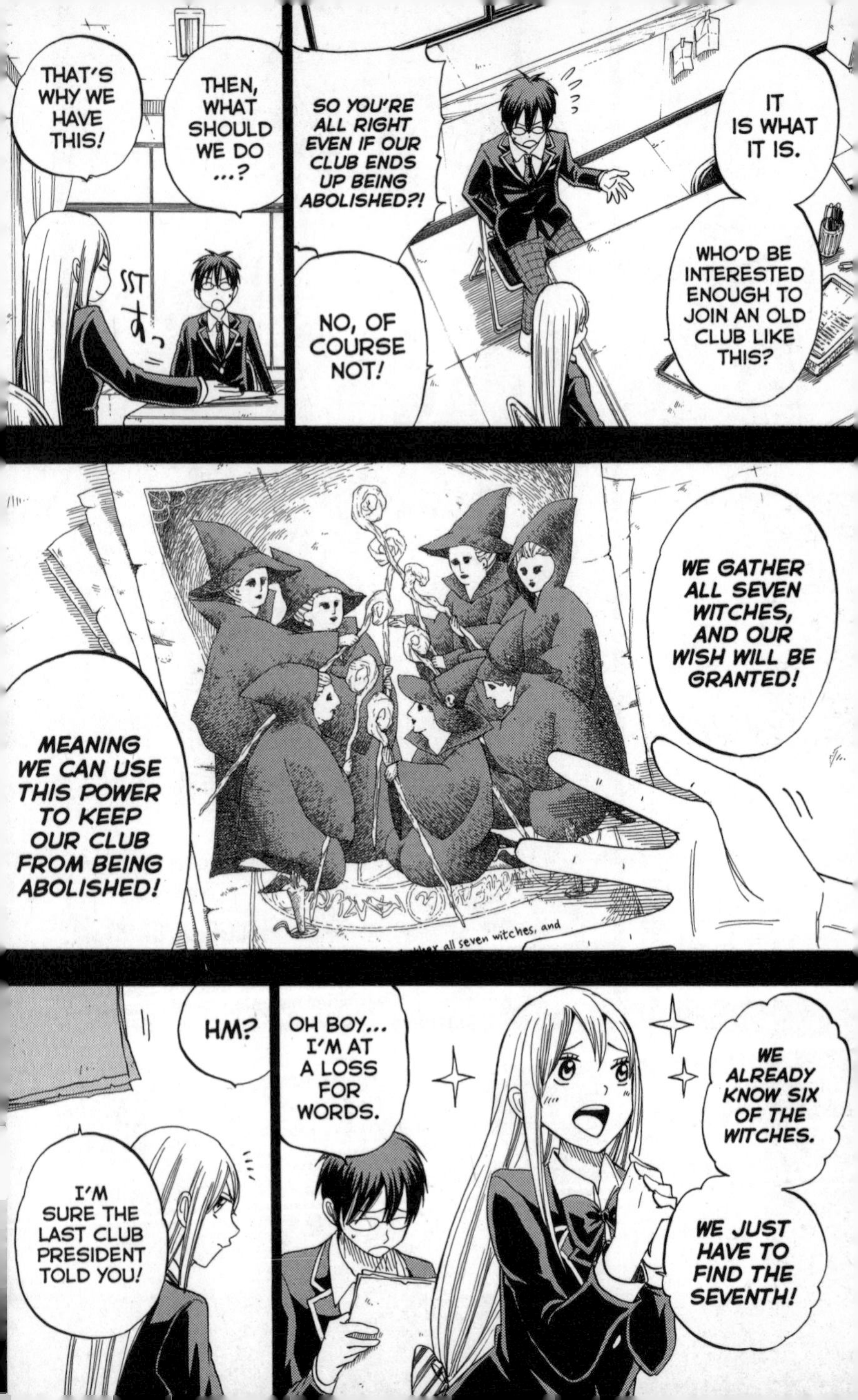
IT IS WHAT IT IS.
WHO'D BE INTERESTED ENOUGH TO JOIN AN OLD CLUB LIKE THIS?
SO YOU'RE ALL RIGHT EVEN IF OUR CLUB ENDS UP BEING ABOLISHED?!
NO, OF COURSE NOT!
THEN, WHAT SHOULD WE DO ...?
THAT'S WHY WE HAVE THIS!
SST
WE GATHER ALL SEVEN WITCHES, AND OUR WISH WILL BE GRANTED!
all seven witches, and
MEANING WE CAN USE THIS POWER TO KEEP OUR CLUB FROM BEING ABOLISHED!
WE ALREADY KNOW SIX OF THE WITCHES.
WE JUST HAVE TO FIND THE SEVENTH!
OH BOY... I'M AT A LOSS FOR WORDS.
HM?
I'M SURE THE LAST CLUB PRESIDENT TOLD YOU!

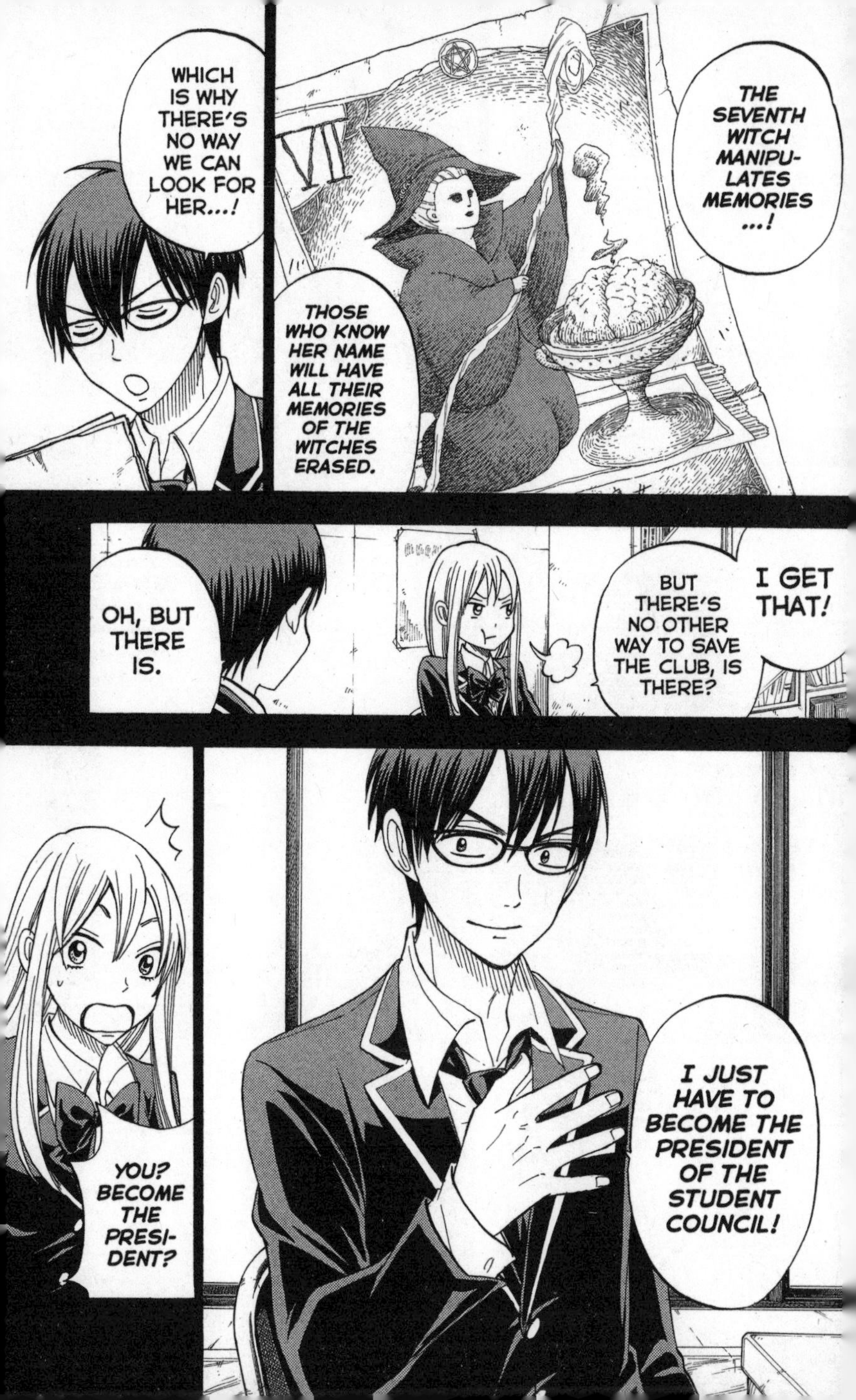
THE SEVENTH WITCH MANIPULATES MEMORIES ...!
THOSE WHO KNOW HER NAME WILL HAVE ALL THEIR MEMORIES OF THE WITCHES ERASED.
WHICH IS WHY THERE'S NO WAY WE CAN LOOK FOR HER...!
I GET THAT!
BUT THERE'S NO OTHER WAY TO SAVE THE CLUB, IS THERE?
OH, BUT THERE IS.
I JUST HAVE TO BECOME THE PRESIDENT OF THE STUDENT COUNCIL!
YOU? BECOME THE PRESIDENT?

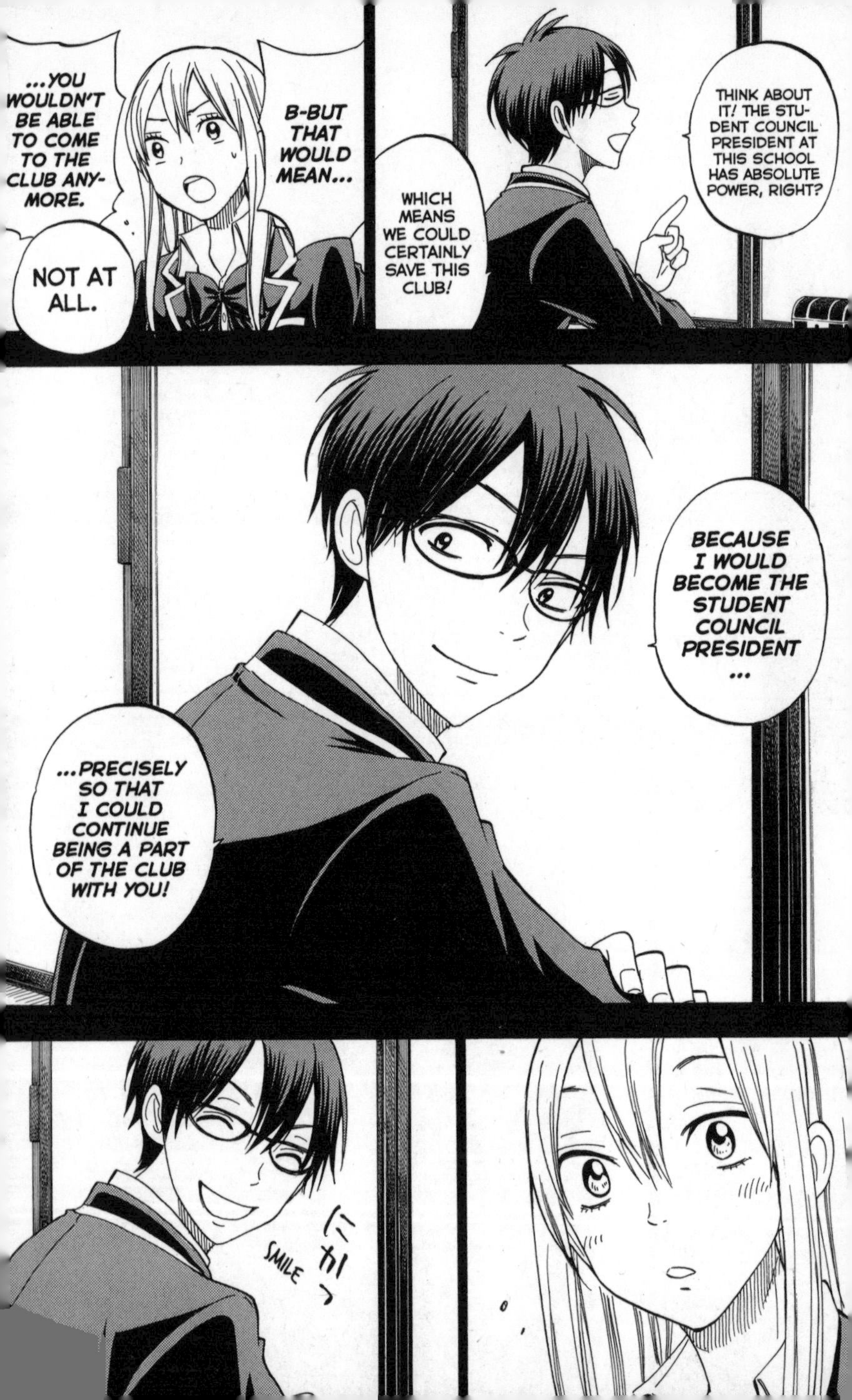

THINK ABOUT IT! THE STUDENT COUNCIL PRESIDENT AT THIS SCHOOL HAS ABSOLUTE POWER, RIGHT?
WHICH MEANS WE COULD CERTAINLY SAVE THIS CLUB!
B-BUT THAT WOULD MEAN...
...YOU WOULDN'T BE ABLE TO COME TO THE CLUB ANYMORE.
NOT AT ALL.
BECAUSE I WOULD BECOME THE STUDENT COUNCIL PRESIDENT...
...PRECISELY SO THAT I COULD CONTINUE BEING A PART OF THE CLUB WITH YOU!
にかっ
SMILE

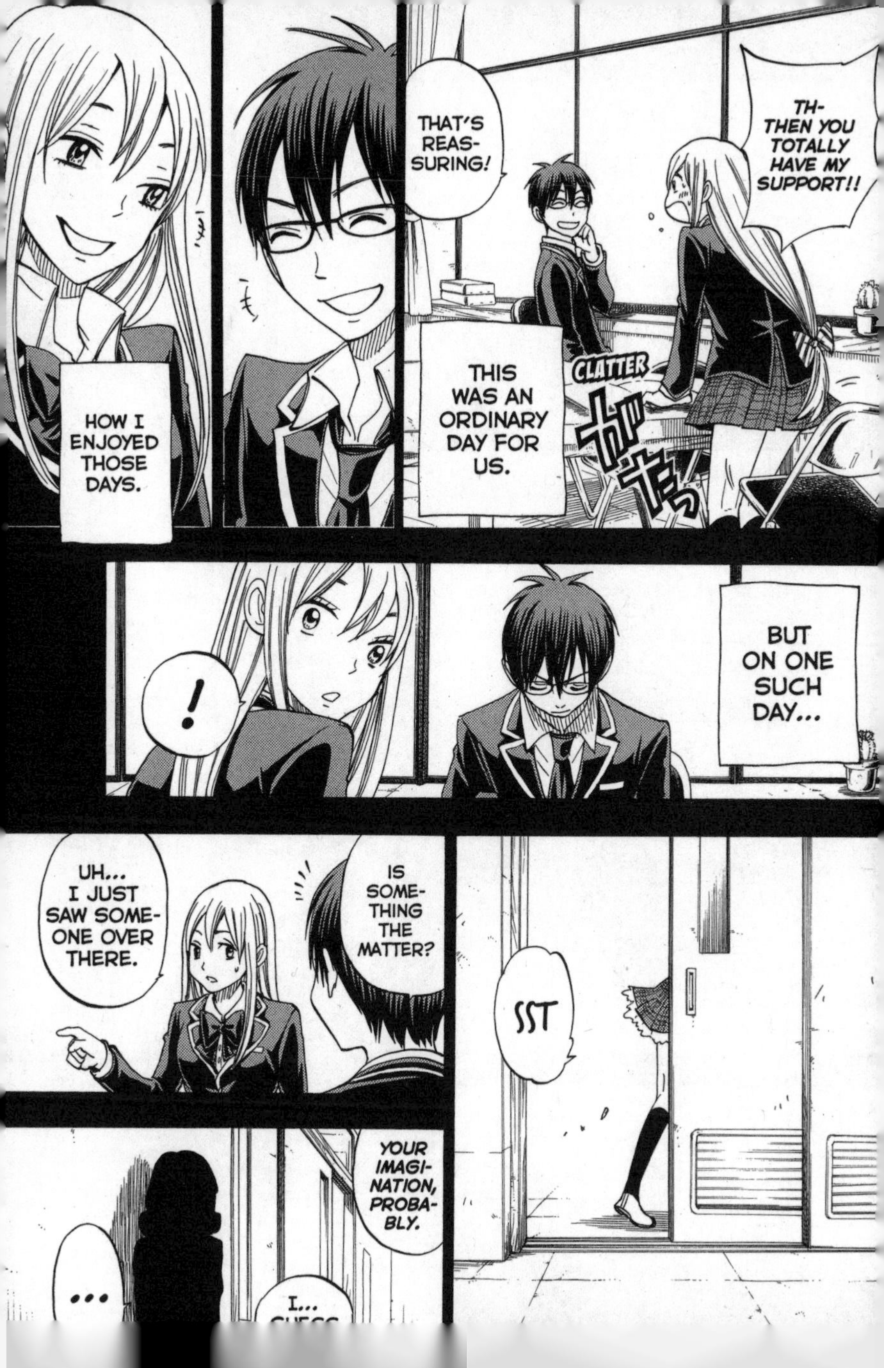
TH- THEN YOU TOTALLY HAVE MY SUPPORT!!
THAT'S REAS- SURING!
CLATTER
THIS WAS AN ORDINARY DAY FOR US.
HOW I ENJOYED THOSE DAYS.
BUT ON ONE SUCH DAY...
!
SST
IS SOME- THING THE MATTER?
UH... I JUST SAW SOME- ONE OVER THERE.
YOUR IMAGI- NATION, PROBA- BLY.
I...
...

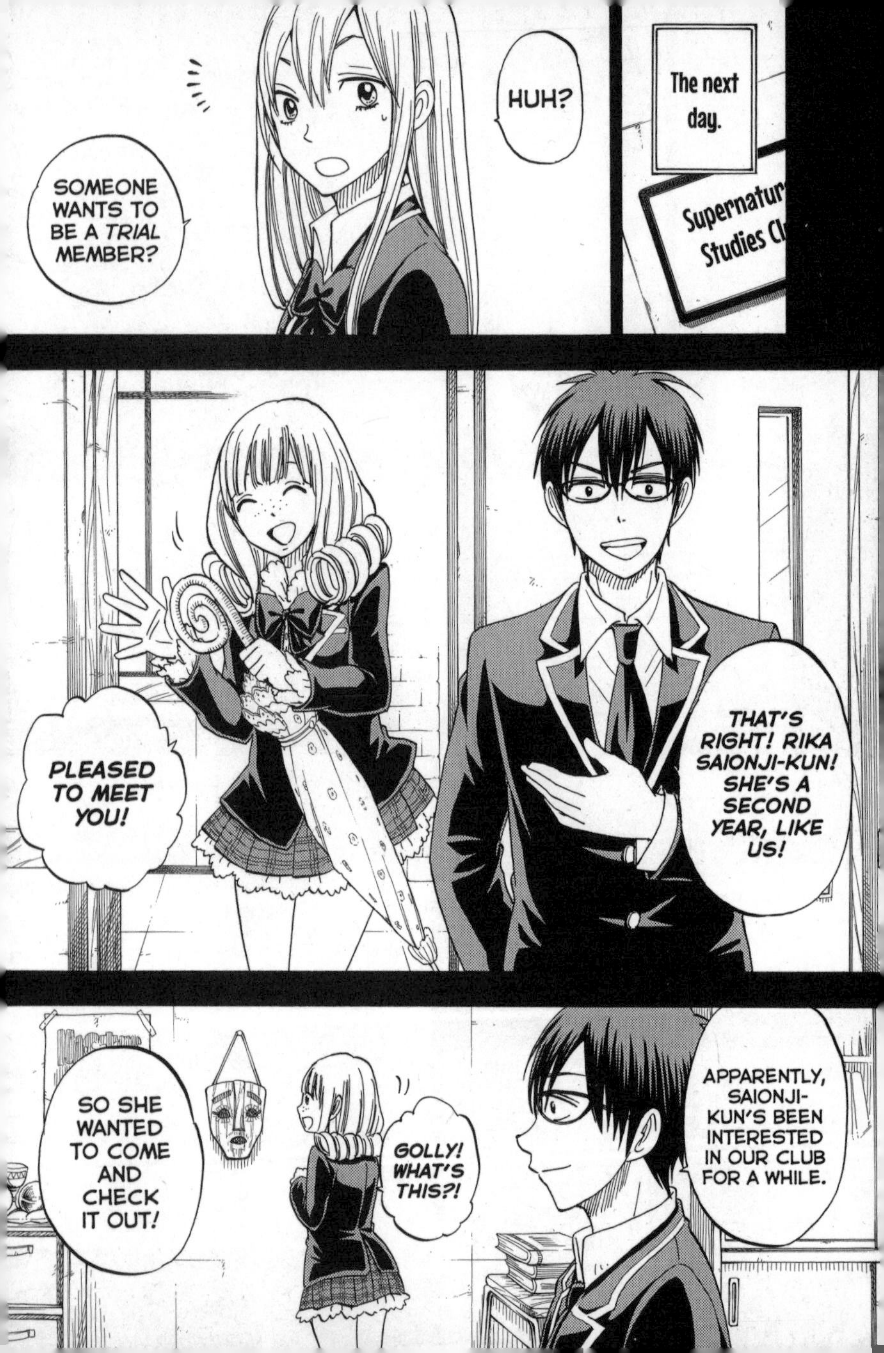
The next day.
Supernatur Studies Cl
HUH?
SOMEONE WANTS TO BE A *TRIAL* MEMBER?
THAT'S RIGHT! RIKA SAIONJI-KUN! SHE'S A SECOND YEAR, LIKE US!
PLEASED TO MEET YOU!
APPARENTLY, SAIONJI-KUN'S BEEN INTERESTED IN OUR CLUB FOR A WHILE.
GOLLY! WHAT'S THIS?!
SO SHE WANTED TO COME AND CHECK IT OUT!

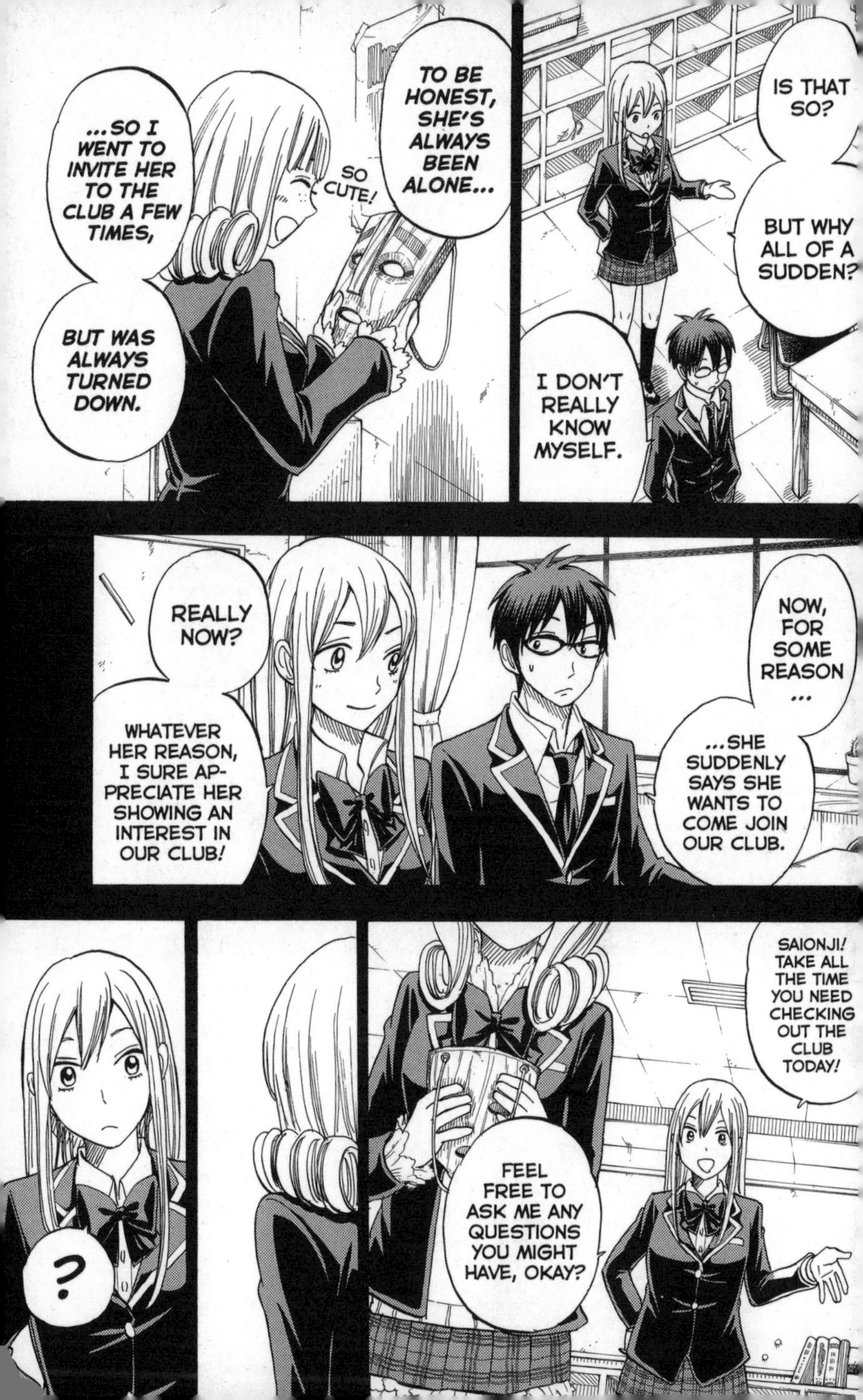
IS THAT SO?
BUT WHY ALL OF A SUDDEN?
I DON'T REALLY KNOW MYSELF.
TO BE HONEST, SHE'S ALWAYS BEEN ALONE...
SO CUTE!
...SO I WENT TO INVITE HER TO THE CLUB A FEW TIMES,
BUT WAS ALWAYS TURNED DOWN.
NOW, FOR SOME REASON...
...SHE SUDDENLY SAYS SHE WANTS TO COME JOIN OUR CLUB.
REALLY NOW?
WHATEVER HER REASON, I SURE AP-PRECIATE HER SHOWING AN INTEREST IN OUR CLUB!
SAIONJI! TAKE ALL THE TIME YOU NEED CHECKING OUT THE CLUB TODAY!
FEEL FREE TO ASK ME ANY QUESTIONS YOU MIGHT HAVE, OKAY?
?

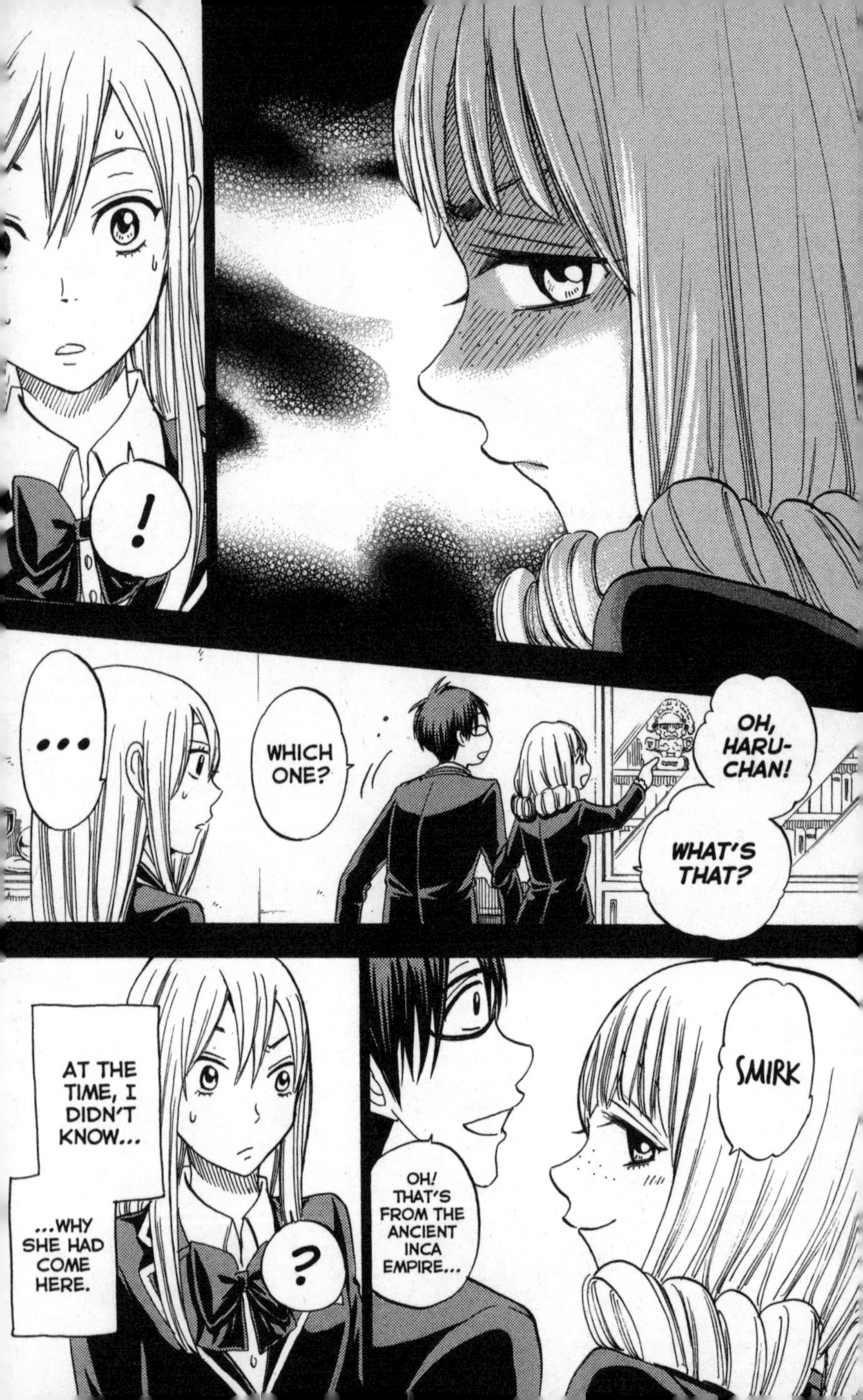
!
OH, HARU-CHAN!
WHAT'S THAT?
WHICH ONE?
...
SMIRK
OH! THAT'S FROM THE ANCIENT INCA EMPIRE...
AT THE TIME, I DIDN'T KNOW...
?
...WHY SHE HAD COME HERE.

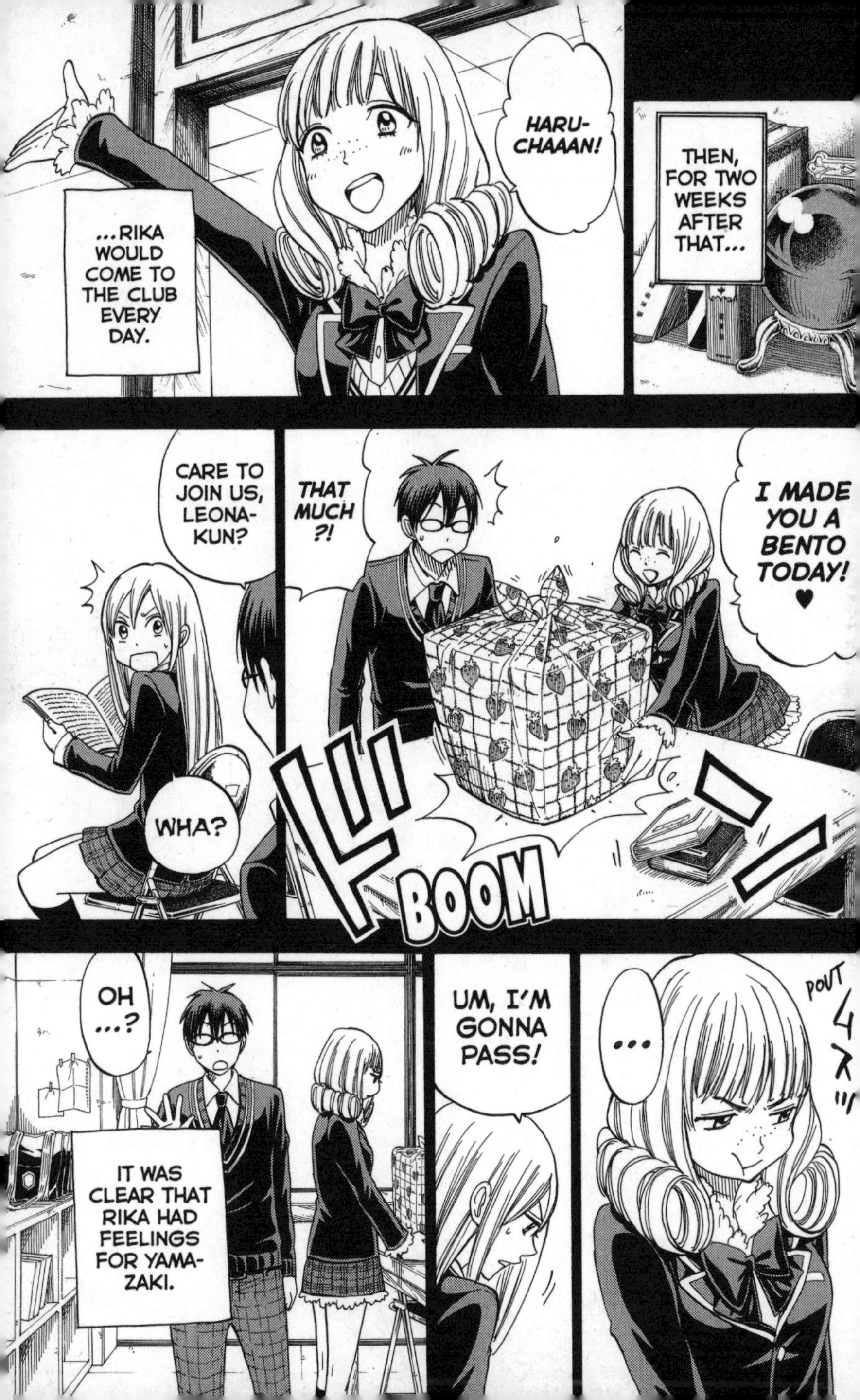
THEN, FOR TWO WEEKS AFTER THAT...
HARU-CHAAAN!
...RIKA WOULD COME TO THE CLUB EVERY DAY.
I MADE YOU A BENTO TODAY! ♥
THAT MUCH?!
BOOM
CARE TO JOIN US, LEONA-KUN?
WHA?
POUT
...
UM, I'M GONNA PASS!
OH ...?
IT WAS CLEAR THAT RIKA HAD FEELINGS FOR YAMA-ZAKI.

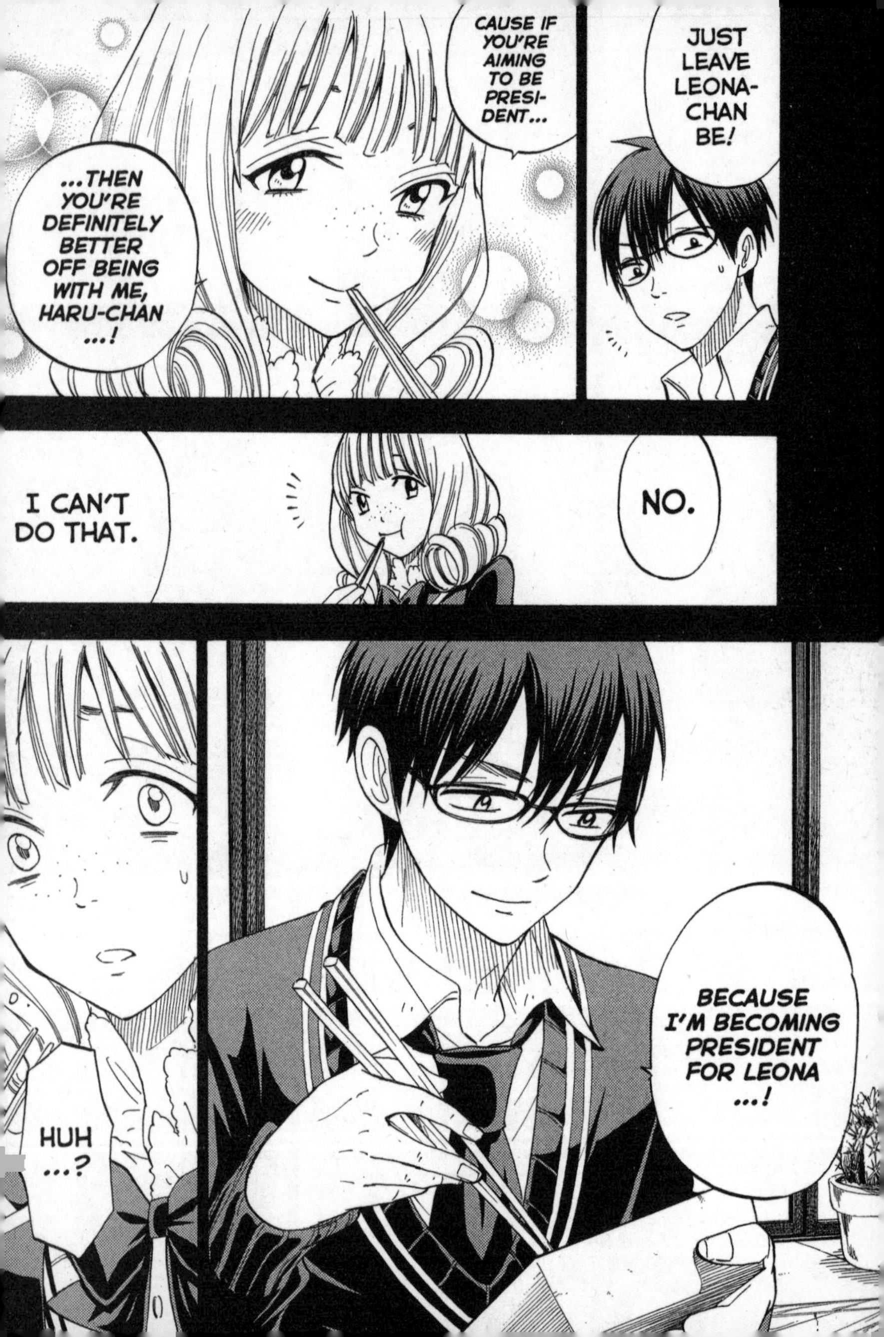
JUST LEAVE LEONA-CHAN BE!
CAUSE IF YOU'RE AIMING TO BE PRESI-DENT...
...THEN YOU'RE DEFINITELY BETTER OFF BEING WITH ME, HARU-CHAN ...!
NO.
I CAN'T DO THAT.
BECAUSE I'M BECOMING PRESIDENT FOR LEONA ...!
HUH ...?

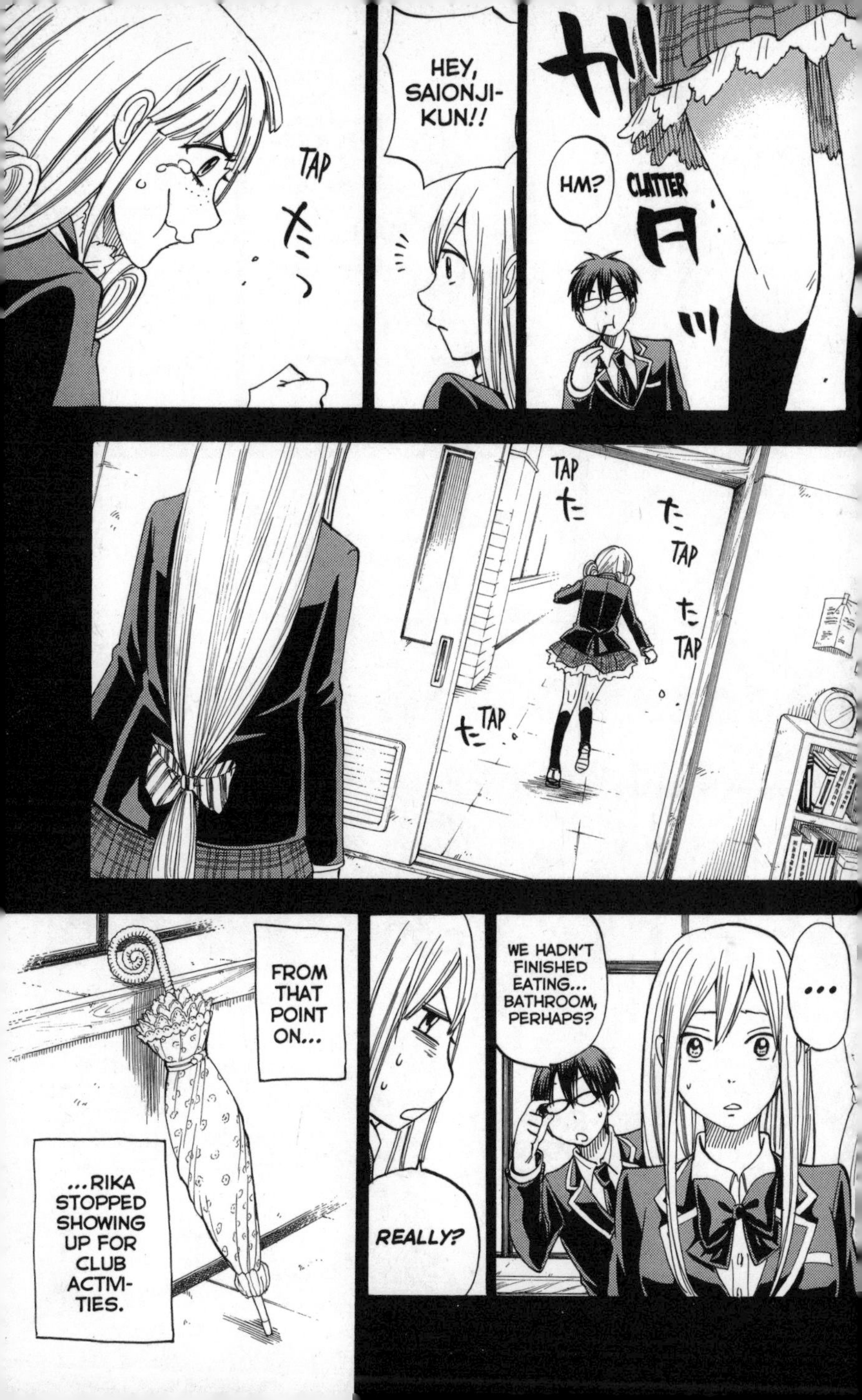
HM?
CLATTER
HEY, SAIONJI-KUN!!
TAP
TAP
TAP
TAP
TAP
...
WE HADN'T FINISHED EATING... BATHROOM, PERHAPS?
REALLY?
FROM THAT POINT ON...
...RIKA STOPPED SHOWING UP FOR CLUB ACTIVITIES.

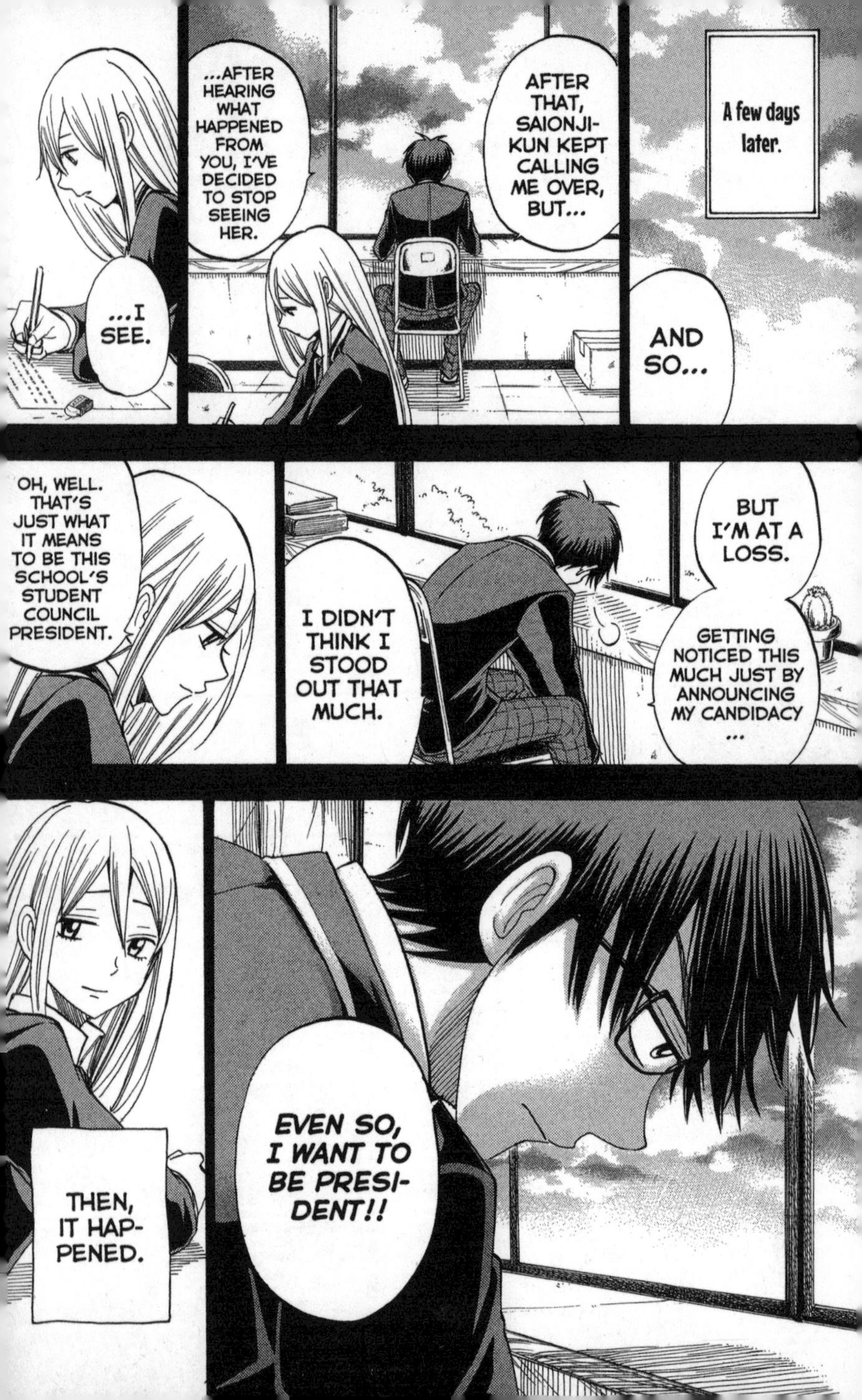
A few days later.
AND SO...
AFTER THAT, SAIONJI-KUN KEPT CALLING ME OVER, BUT...
...AFTER HEARING WHAT HAPPENED FROM YOU, I'VE DECIDED TO STOP SEEING HER.
...I SEE.
BUT I'M AT A LOSS.
GETTING NOTICED THIS MUCH JUST BY ANNOUNCING MY CANDIDACY ...
I DIDN'T THINK I STOOD OUT THAT MUCH.
OH, WELL. THAT'S JUST WHAT IT MEANS TO BE THIS SCHOOL'S STUDENT COUNCIL PRESIDENT.
EVEN SO, I WANT TO BE PRESIDENT!!
THEN, IT HAPPENED.

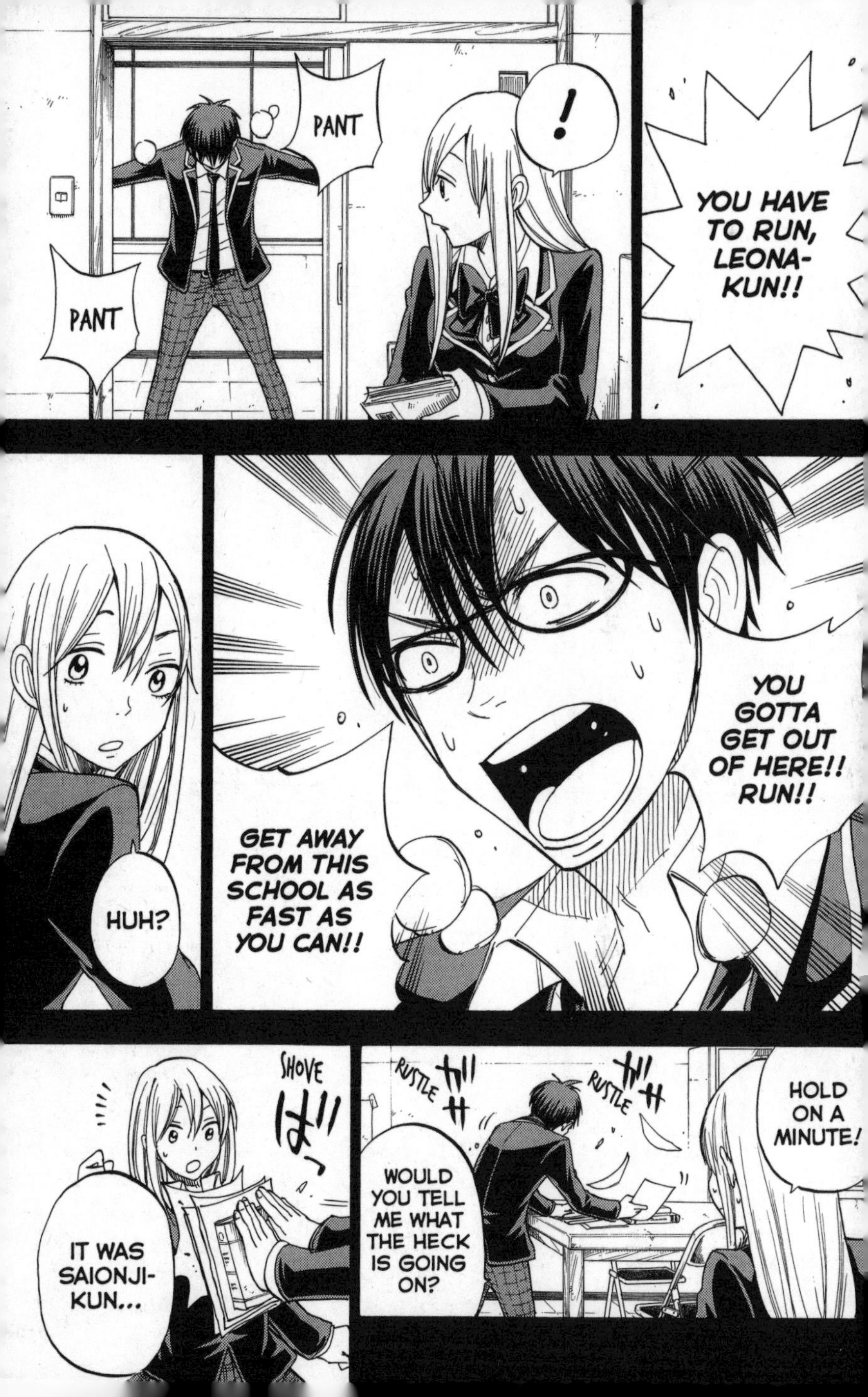
YOU HAVE TO RUN, LEONA-KUN!!
!
PANT
PANT
YOU GOTTA GET OUT OF HERE!! RUN!!
GET AWAY FROM THIS SCHOOL AS FAST AS YOU CAN!!
HUH?
HOLD ON A MINUTE!
RUSTLE ガサ
RUSTLE ガサ
WOULD YOU TELL ME WHAT THE HECK IS GOING ON?
SHOVE ばっ
IT WAS SAIONJI-KUN...

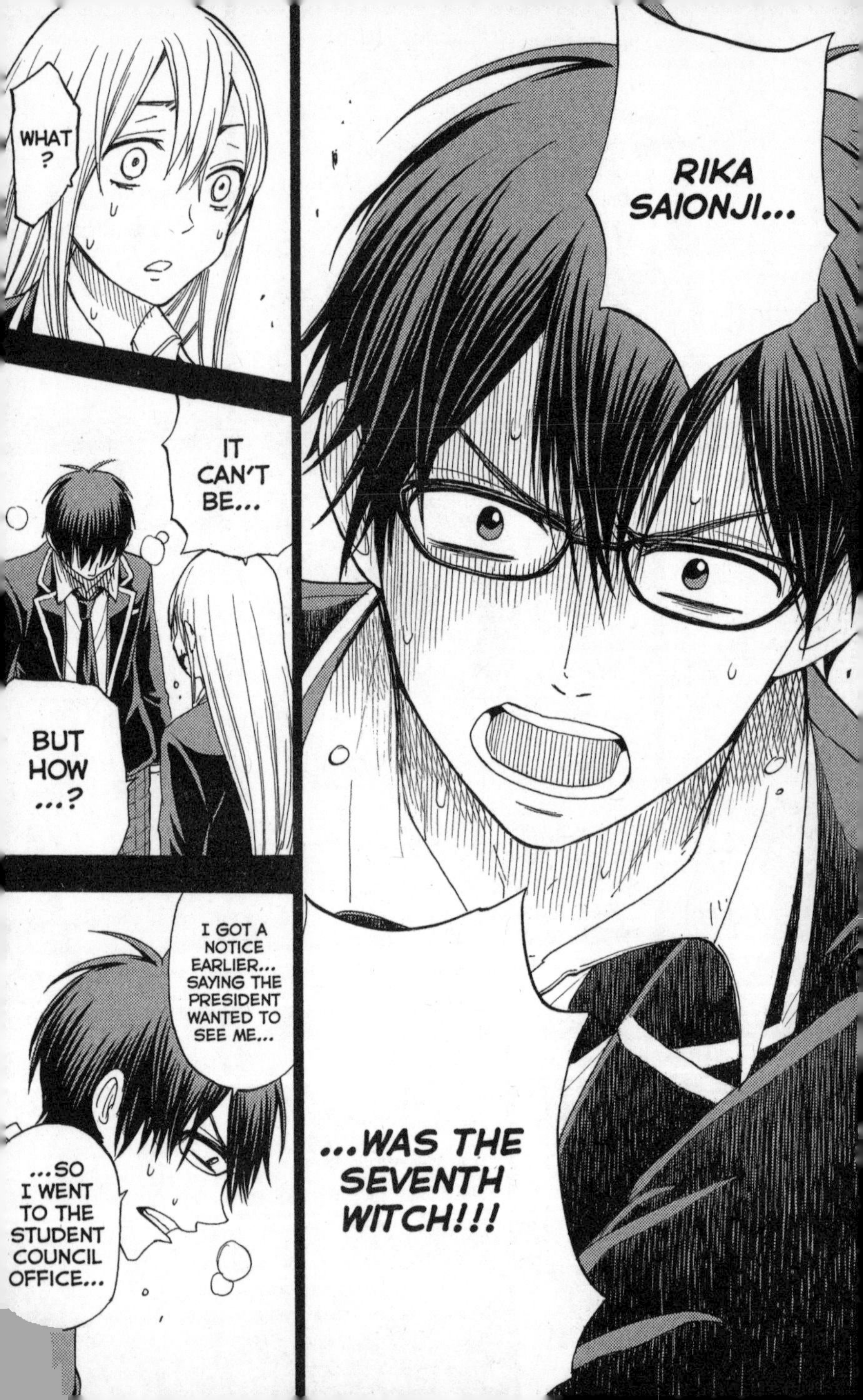

RIKA SAIONJI...
...WAS THE SEVENTH WITCH!!!
WHAT?
IT CAN'T BE...
BUT HOW...?
I GOT A NOTICE EARLIER... SAYING THE PRESIDENT WANTED TO SEE ME...
...SO I WENT TO THE STUDENT COUNCIL OFFICE...

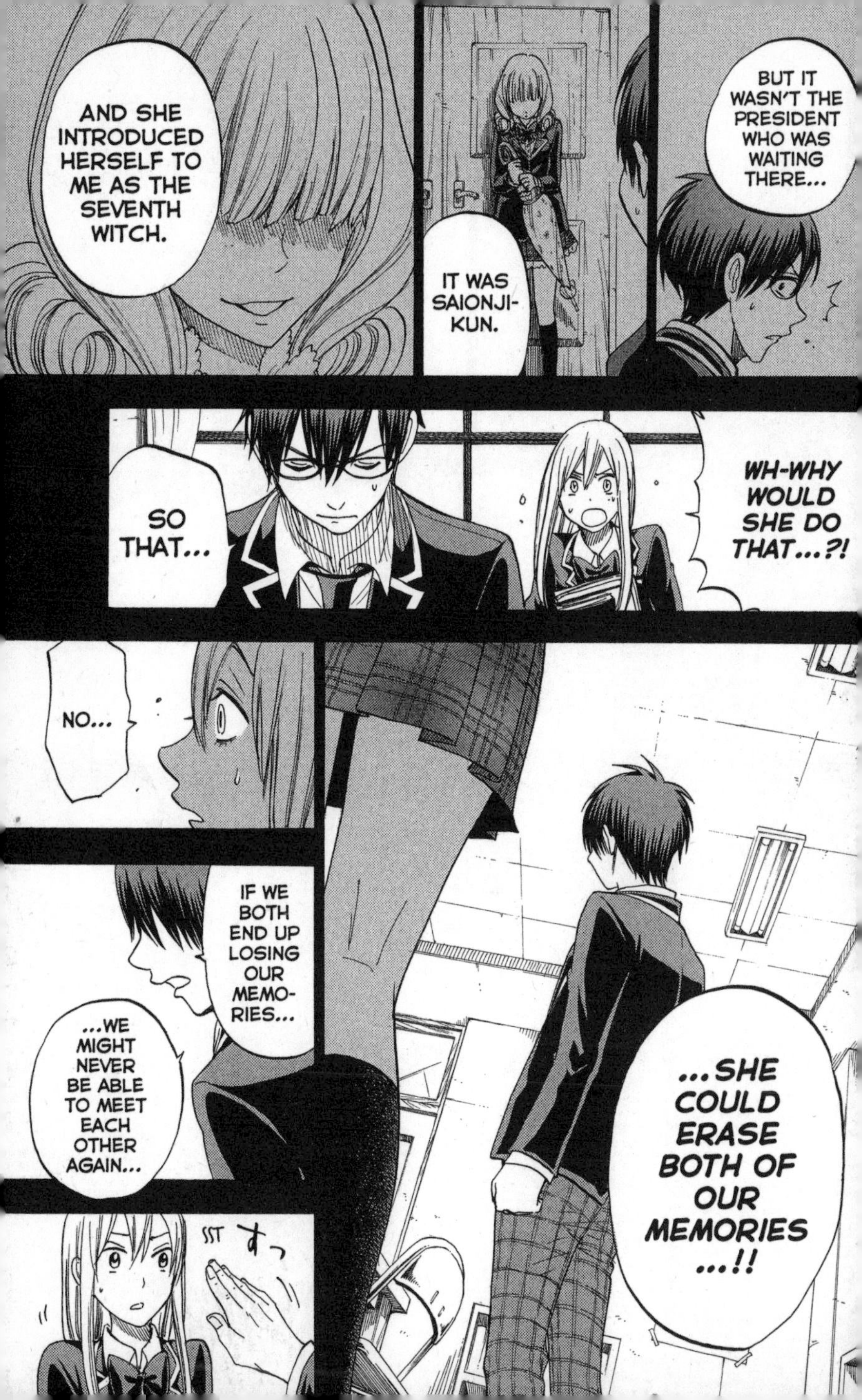
BUT IT WASN'T THE PRESIDENT WHO WAS WAITING THERE...
IT WAS SAIONJI-KUN.
AND SHE INTRODUCED HERSELF TO ME AS THE SEVENTH WITCH.
WH-WHY WOULD SHE DO THAT...?!
SO THAT...
...SHE COULD ERASE BOTH OF OUR MEMORIES...!!
NO...
IF WE BOTH END UP LOSING OUR MEMORIES...
...WE MIGHT NEVER BE ABLE TO MEET EACH OTHER AGAIN...
SST すっ

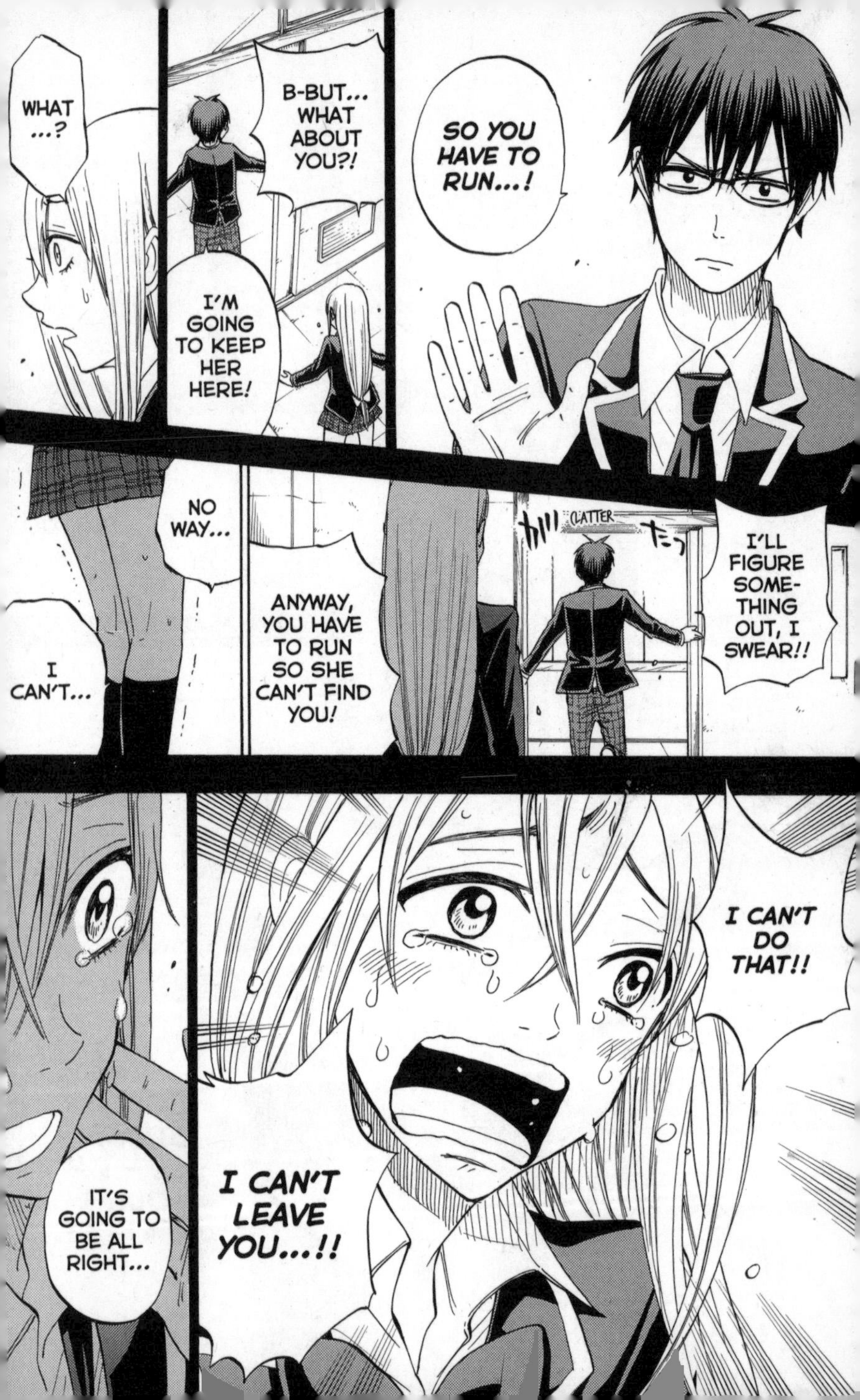
SO YOU HAVE TO RUN...!
B-BUT... WHAT ABOUT YOU?!
I'M GOING TO KEEP HER HERE!
WHAT ...?
CLATTER
I'LL FIGURE SOME-THING OUT, I SWEAR!!
ANYWAY, YOU HAVE TO RUN SO SHE CAN'T FIND YOU!
NO WAY...
I CAN'T...
I CAN'T DO THAT!!
I CAN'T LEAVE YOU...!!
IT'S GOING TO BE ALL RIGHT...

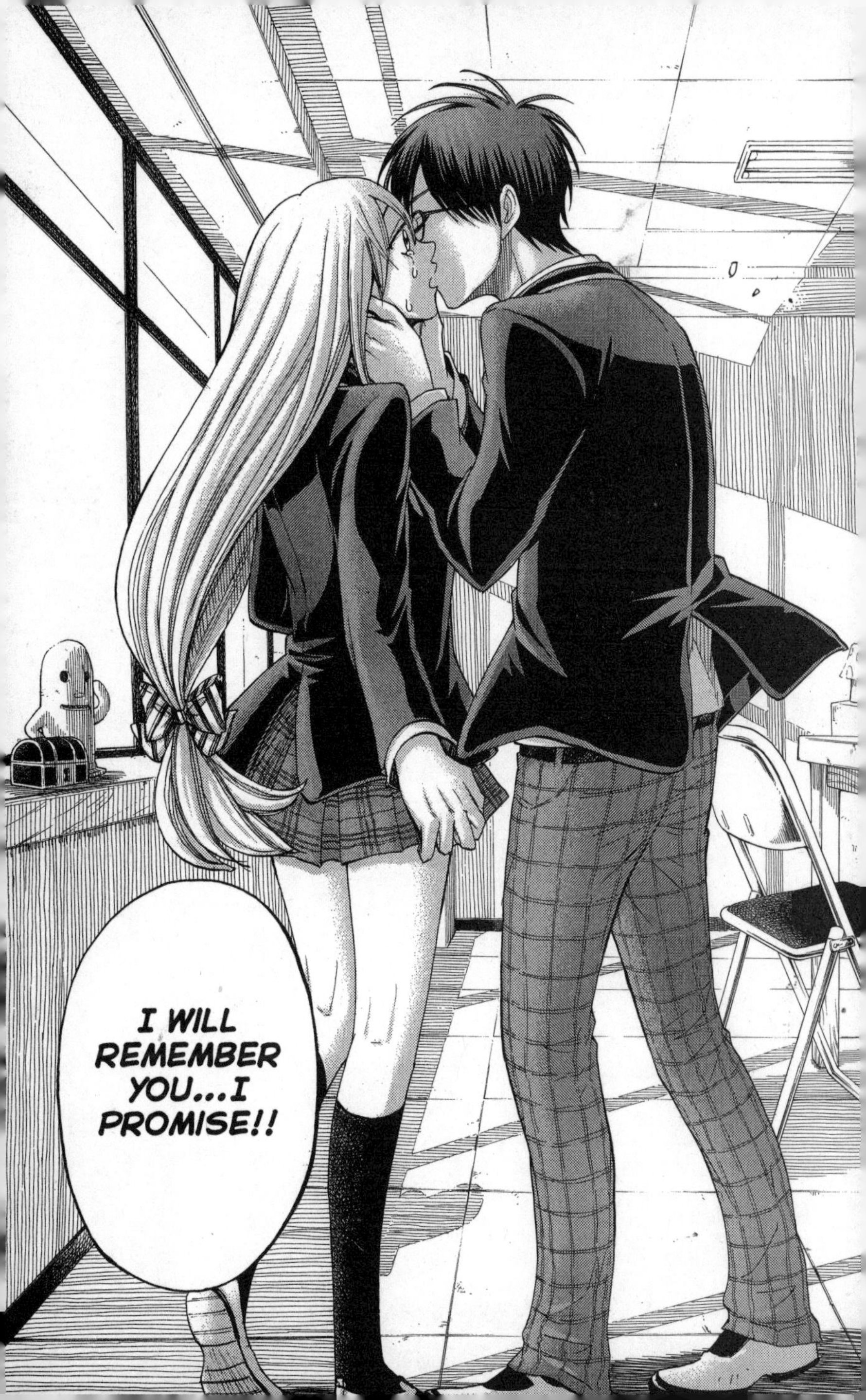
I WILL REMEMBER YOU...I PROMISE!!

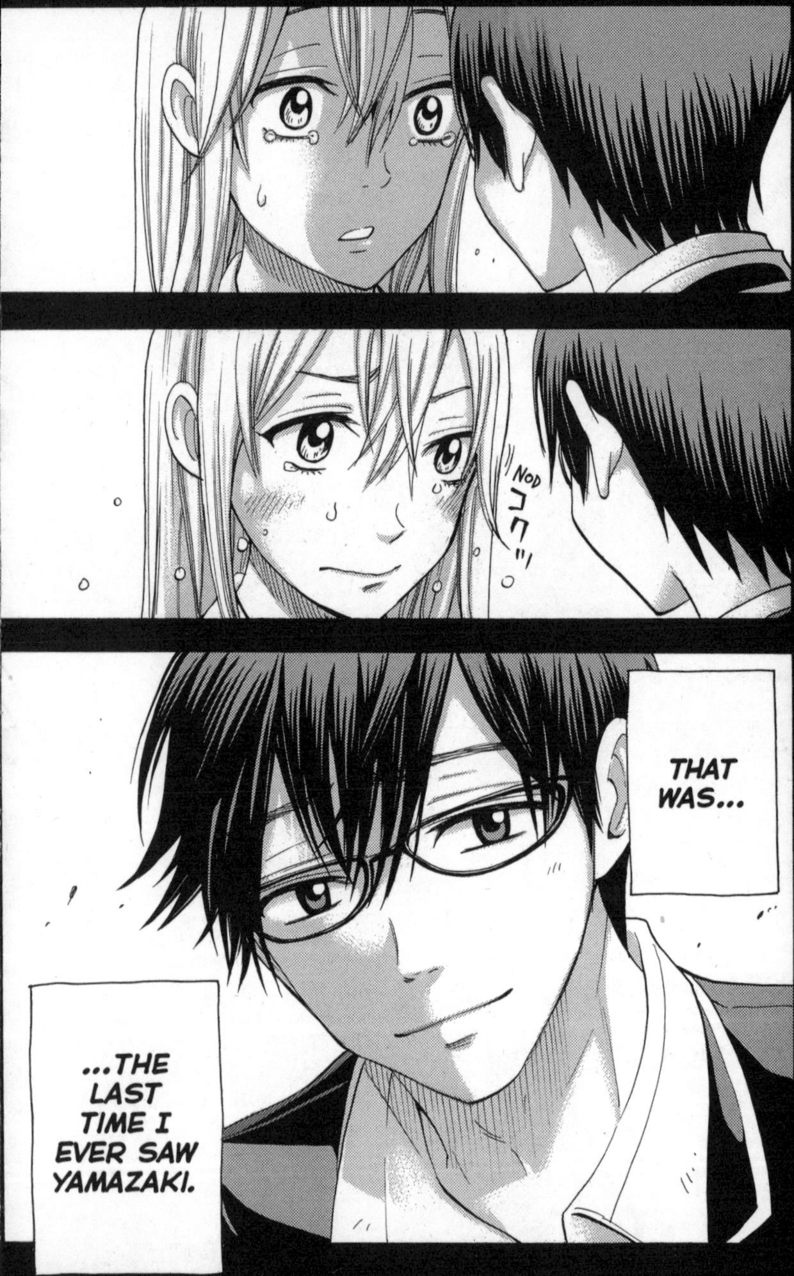
NOD
コクッ
THAT WAS...
...THE LAST TIME I EVER SAW YAMAZAKI.

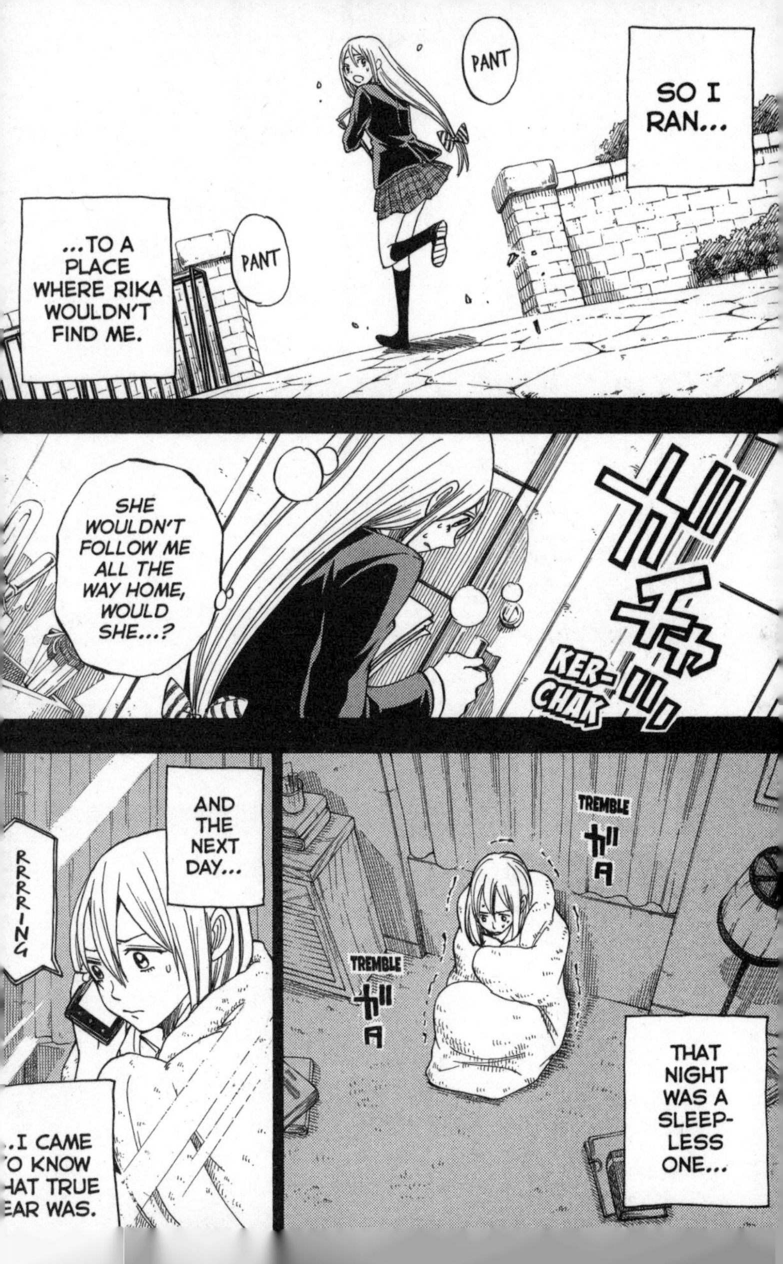
SO I RAN...
PANT
PANT
...TO A PLACE WHERE RIKA WOULDN'T FIND ME.
KER-CHAK
SHE WOULDN'T FOLLOW ME ALL THE WAY HOME, WOULD SHE...?
TREMBLE
TREMBLE
THAT NIGHT WAS A SLEEP-LESS ONE...
AND THE NEXT DAY...
RRRRING
.I CAME O KNOW HAT TRUE EAR WAS.

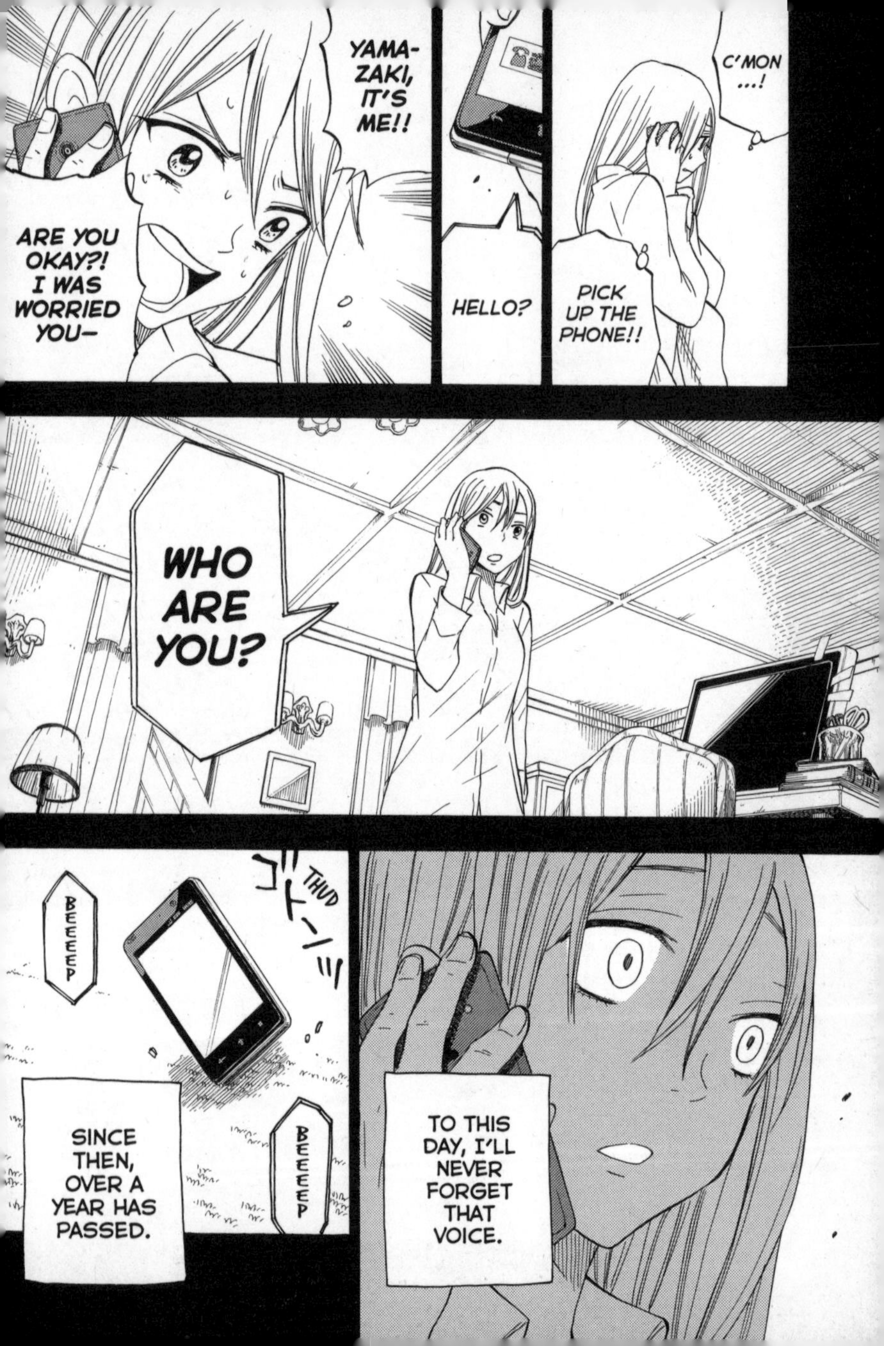
C'MON ...!
PICK UP THE PHONE!!
HELLO?
YAMA-ZAKI, IT'S ME!!
ARE YOU OKAY?! I WAS WORRIED YOU—
WHO ARE YOU?
TO THIS DAY, I'LL NEVER FORGET THAT VOICE.
THUD
BEEEEP
BEEEEP
SINCE THEN, OVER A YEAR HAS PASSED.

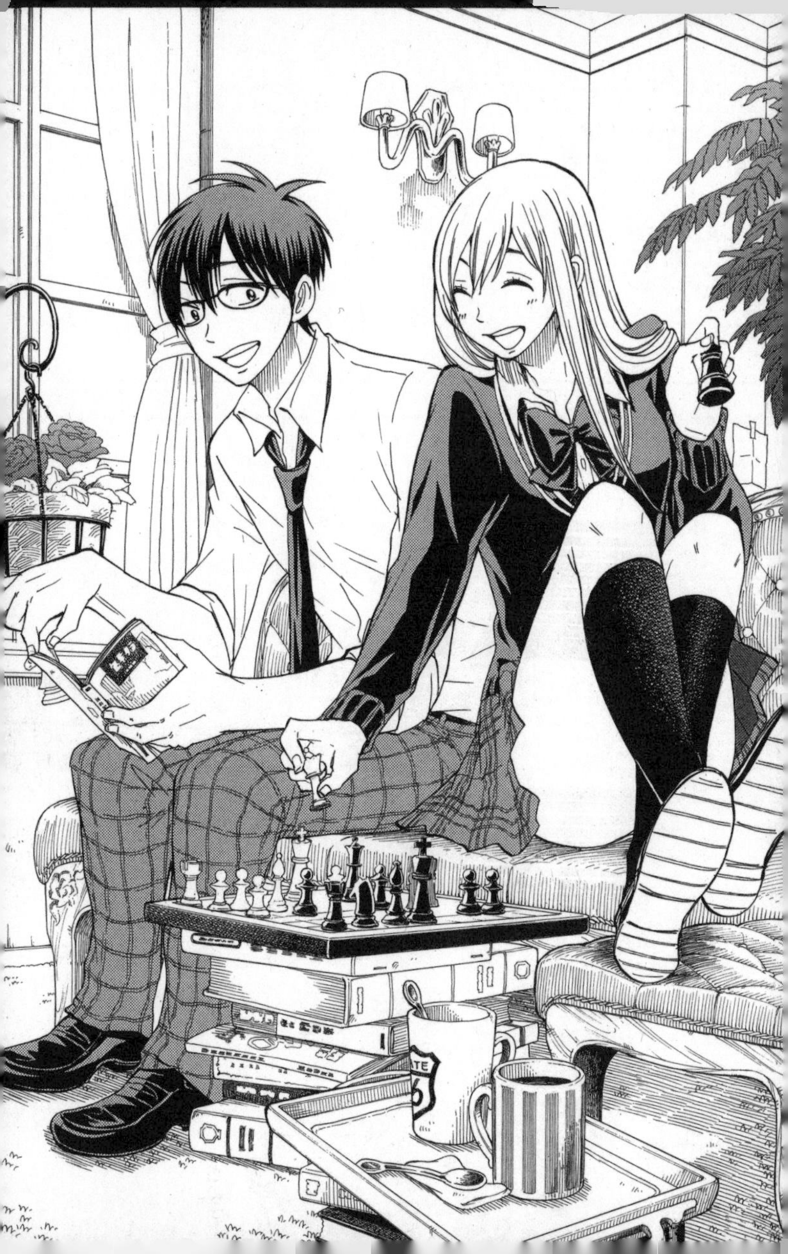

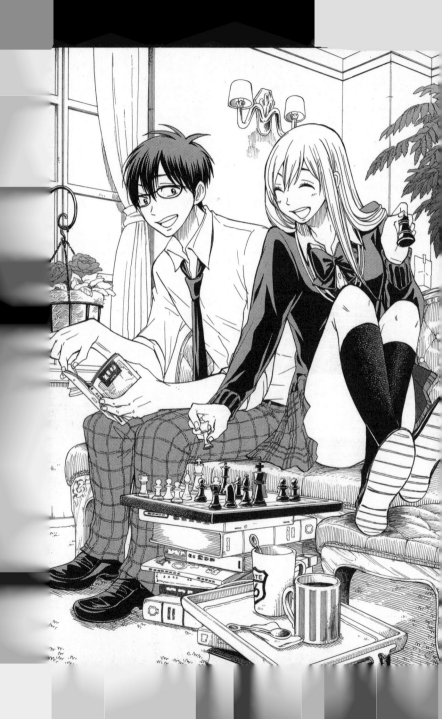

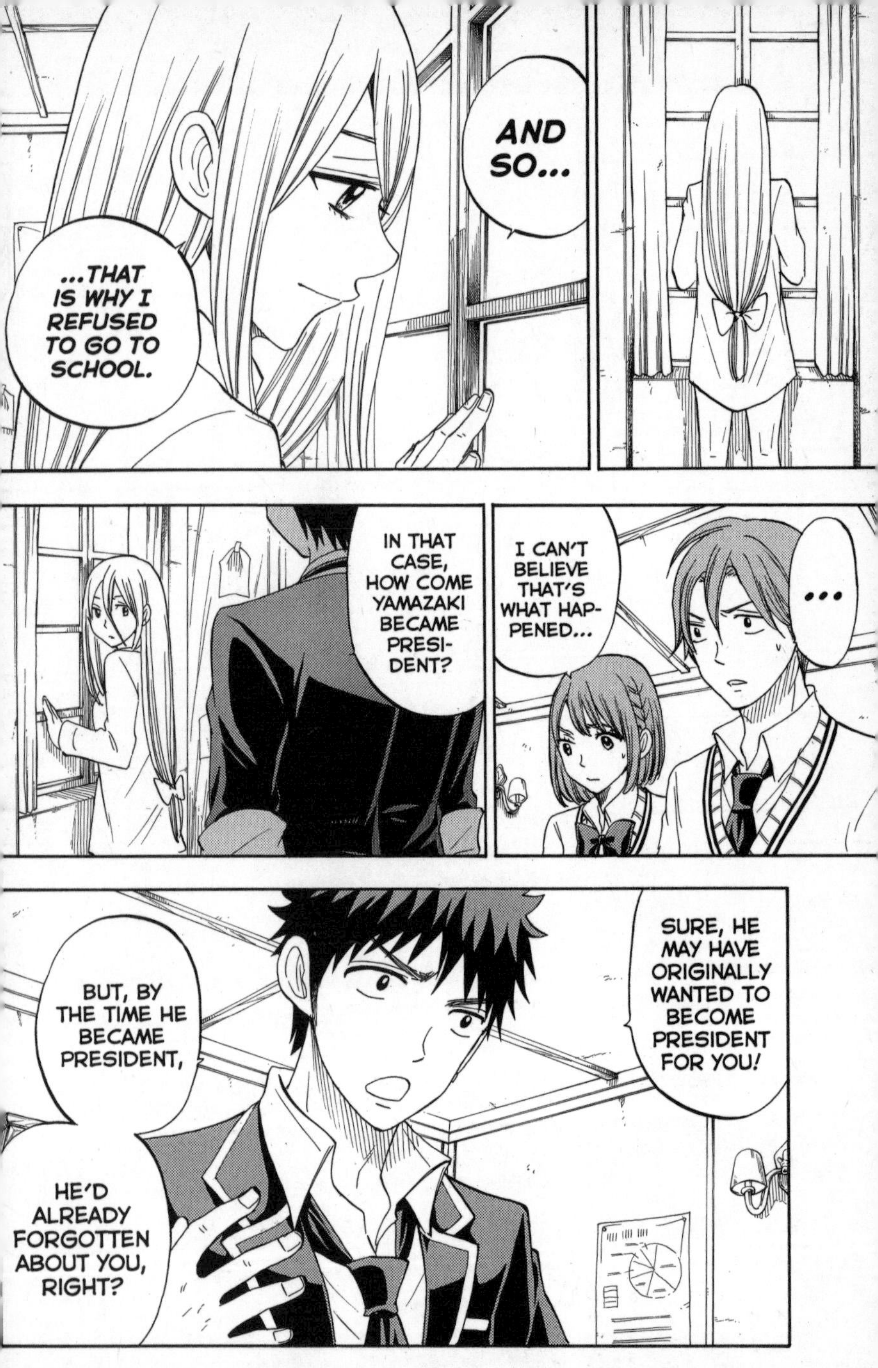
AND SO...
...THAT IS WHY I REFUSED TO GO TO SCHOOL.
...
I CAN'T BELIEVE THAT'S WHAT HAPPENED...
IN THAT CASE, HOW COME YAMAZAKI BECAME PRESIDENT?
SURE, HE MAY HAVE ORIGINALLY WANTED TO BECOME PRESIDENT FOR YOU!
BUT, BY THE TIME HE BECAME PRESIDENT,
HE'D ALREADY FORGOTTEN ABOUT YOU, RIGHT?

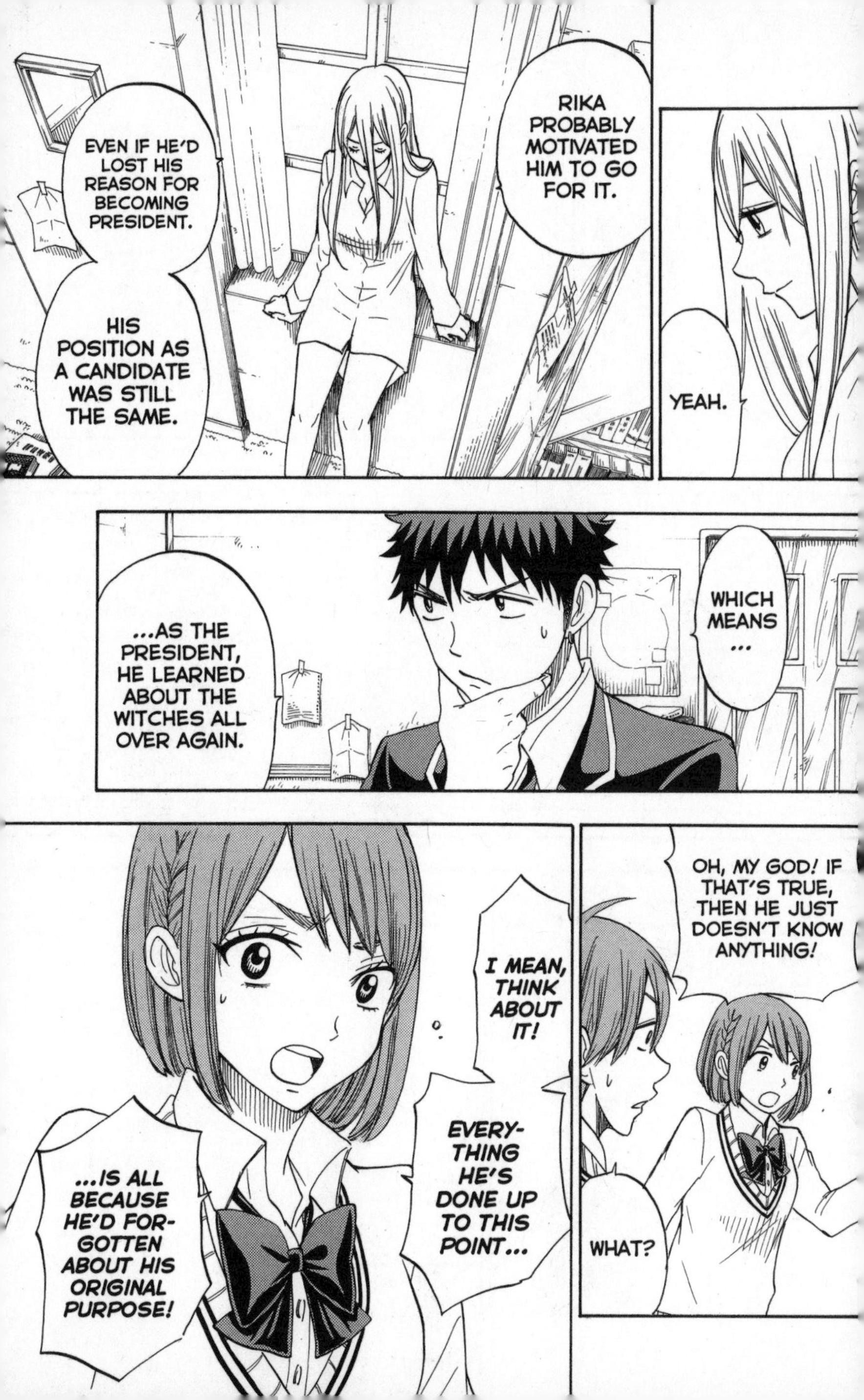
YEAH.
RIKA PROBABLY MOTIVATED HIM TO GO FOR IT.
EVEN IF HE'D LOST HIS REASON FOR BECOMING PRESIDENT.
HIS POSITION AS A CANDIDATE WAS STILL THE SAME.
WHICH MEANS...
...AS THE PRESIDENT, HE LEARNED ABOUT THE WITCHES ALL OVER AGAIN.
OH, MY GOD! IF THAT'S TRUE, THEN HE JUST DOESN'T KNOW ANYTHING!
WHAT?
I MEAN, THINK ABOUT IT!
EVERYTHING HE'S DONE UP TO THIS POINT...
...IS ALL BECAUSE HE'D FORGOTTEN ABOUT HIS ORIGINAL PURPOSE!

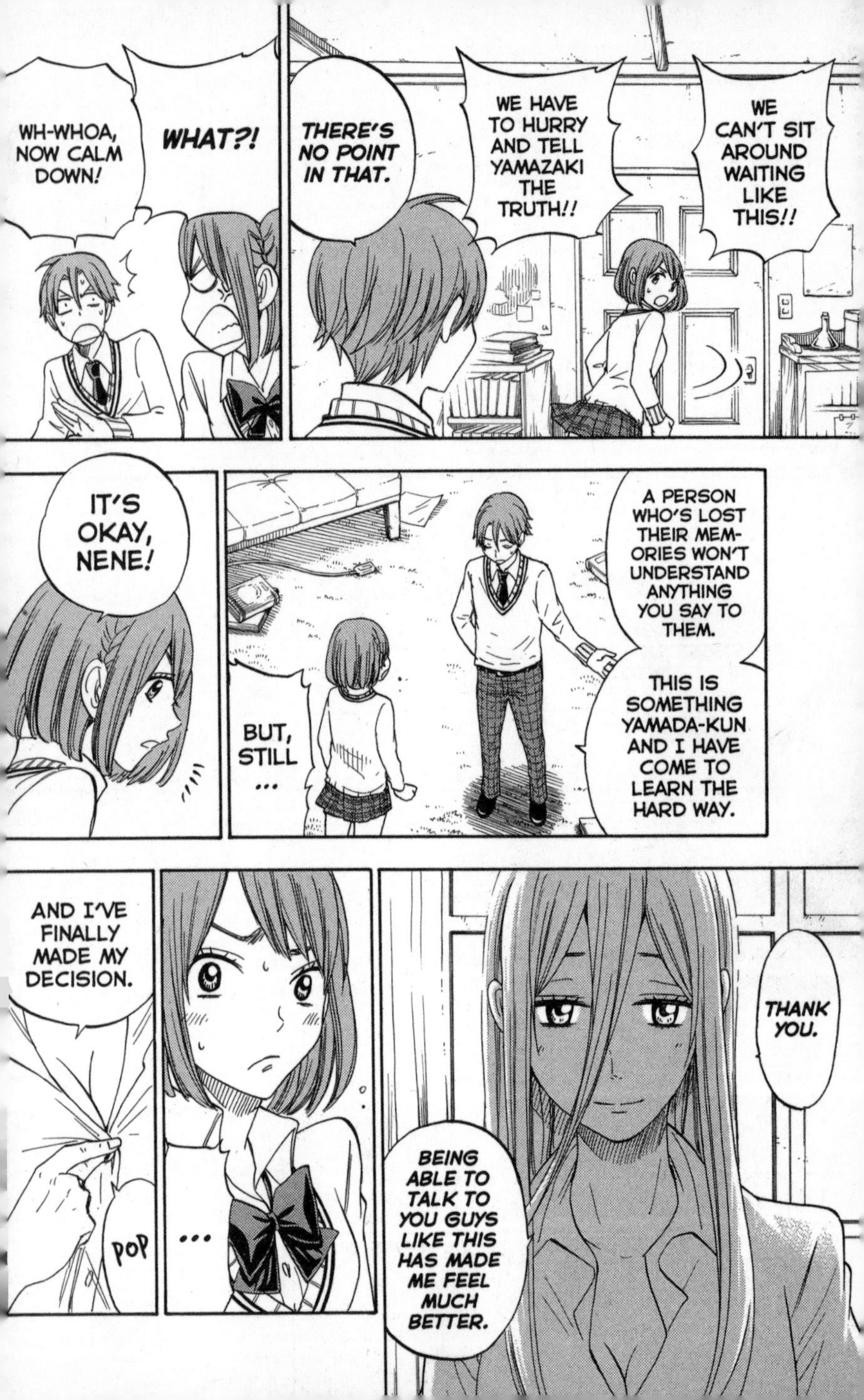
WE CAN'T SIT AROUND WAITING LIKE THIS!!
WE HAVE TO HURRY AND TELL YAMAZAKI THE TRUTH!!
THERE'S NO POINT IN THAT.
WHAT?!
WH-WHOA, NOW CALM DOWN!
A PERSON WHO'S LOST THEIR MEM-ORIES WON'T UNDERSTAND ANYTHING YOU SAY TO THEM.
THIS IS SOMETHING YAMADA-KUN AND I HAVE COME TO LEARN THE HARD WAY.
BUT, STILL ...
IT'S OKAY, NENE!
THANK YOU.
BEING ABLE TO TALK TO YOU GUYS LIKE THIS HAS MADE ME FEEL MUCH BETTER.
...
AND I'VE FINALLY MADE MY DECISION.
POP

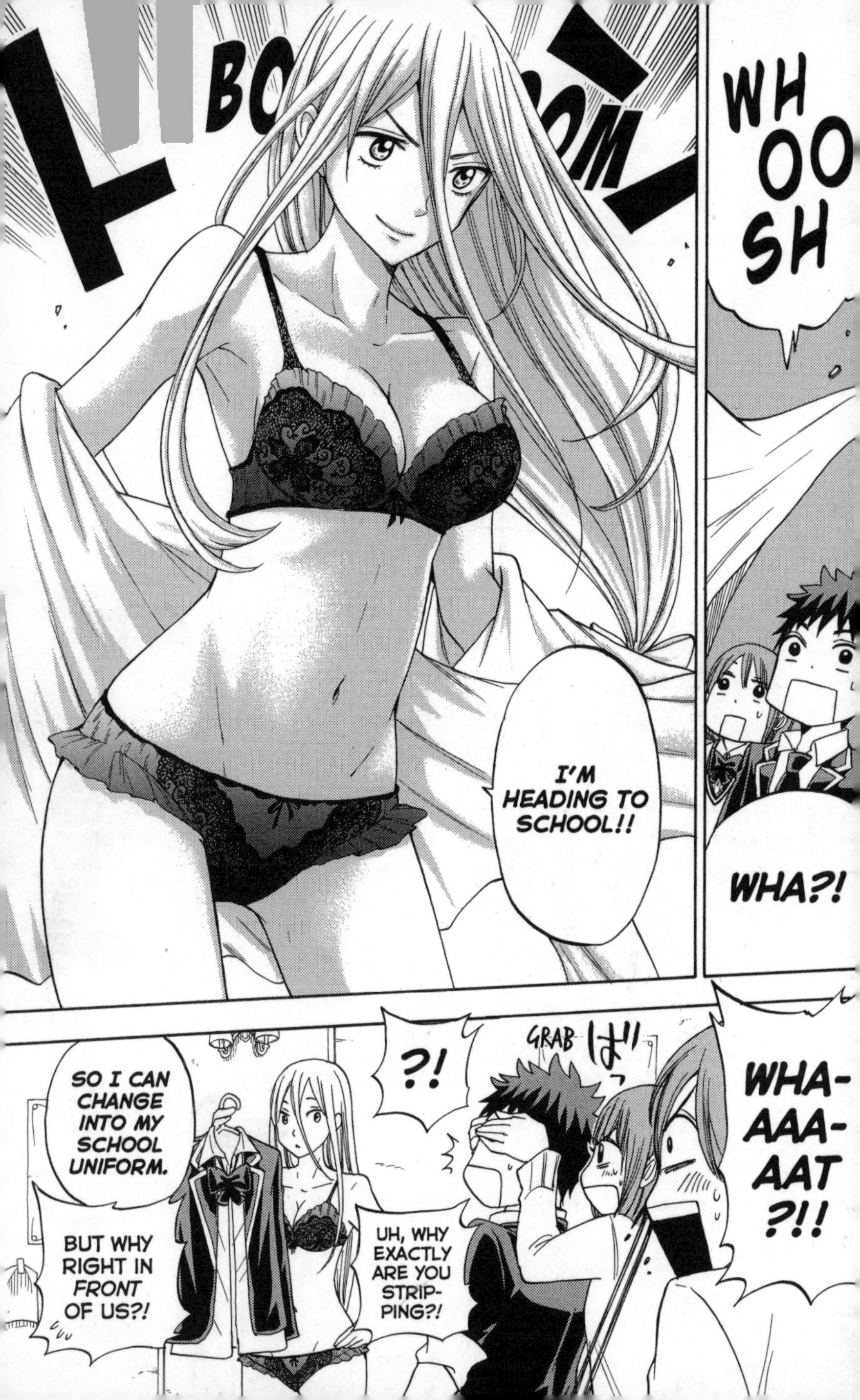
WHOOSH
WHA?!
BO
OM
I'M HEADING TO SCHOOL!!
WHA-AAA-AAT?!!
GRAB ばっ
?!
UH, WHY EXACTLY ARE YOU STRIP-PING?!
SO I CAN CHANGE INTO MY SCHOOL UNIFORM.
BUT WHY RIGHT IN FRONT OF US?!

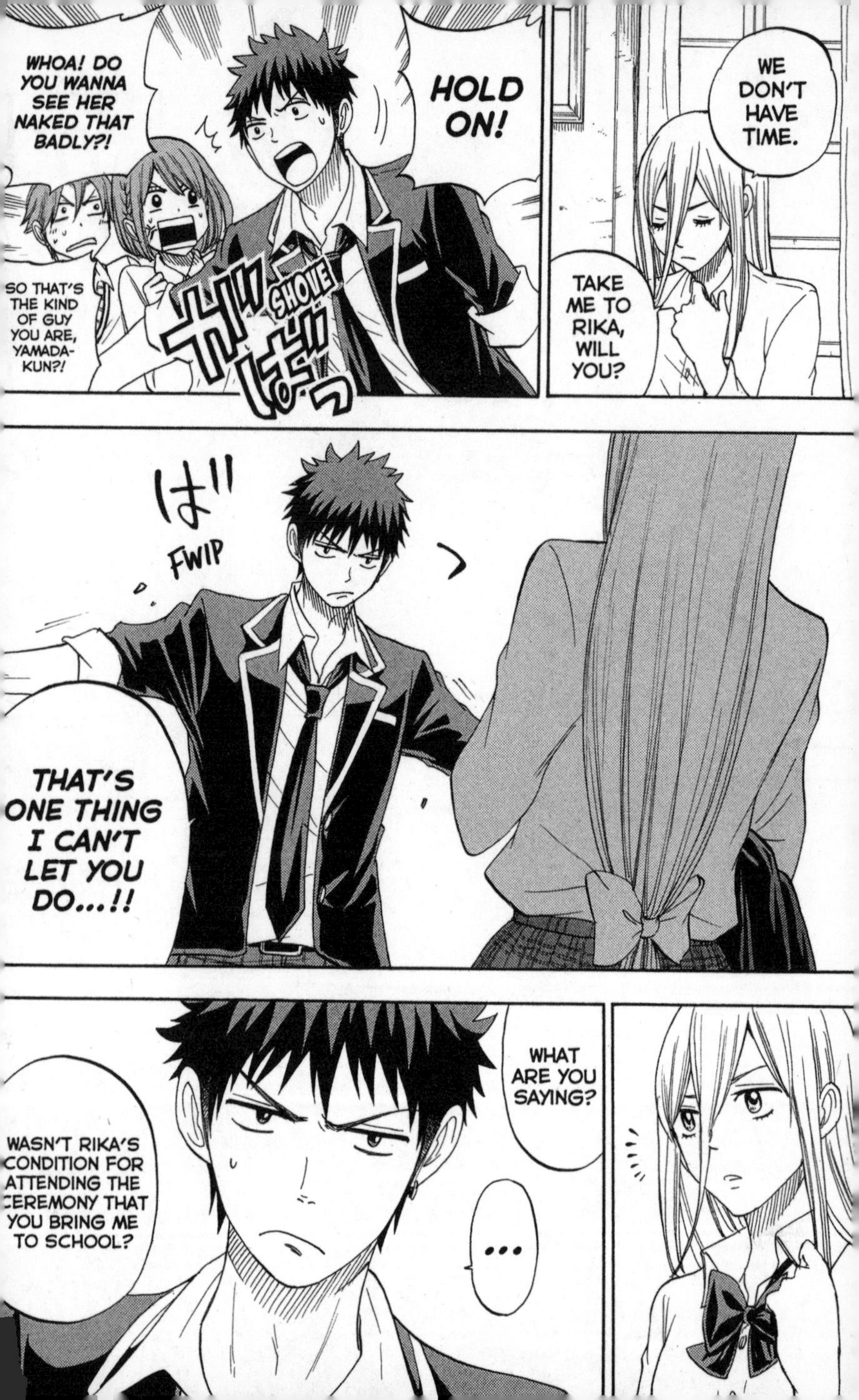
WE DON'T HAVE TIME.
TAKE ME TO RIKA, WILL YOU?
HOLD ON!
WHOA! DO YOU WANNA SEE HER NAKED THAT BADLY?!
SO THAT'S THE KIND OF GUY YOU ARE, YAMADA-KUN?!
ガッ
SHOVE
ばっ
ばッ
FWIP
THAT'S ONE THING I CAN'T LET YOU DO...!!
WHAT ARE YOU SAYING?
...
WASN'T RIKA'S CONDITION FOR ATTENDING THE CEREMONY THAT YOU BRING ME TO SCHOOL?

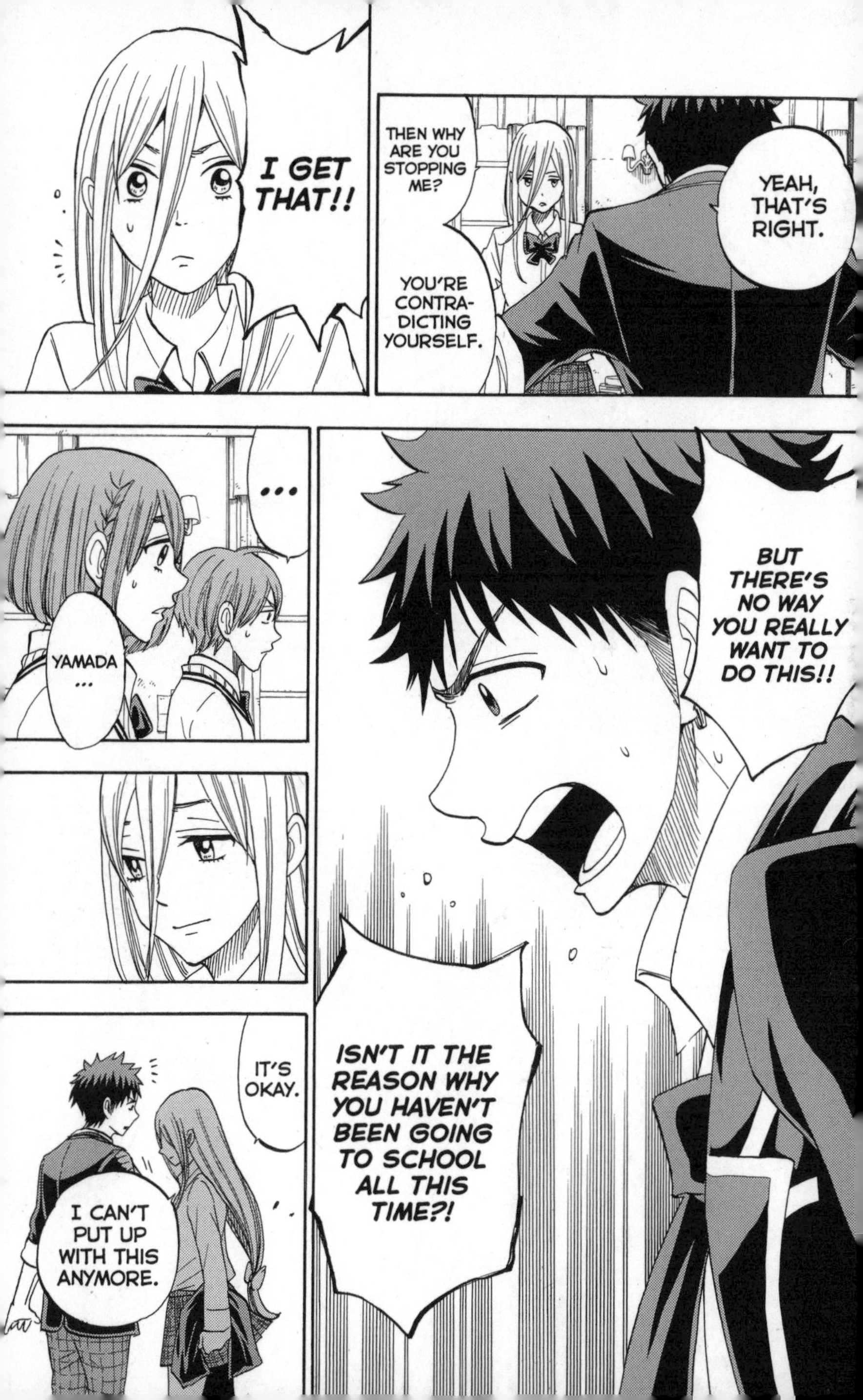
YEAH, THAT'S RIGHT.
THEN WHY ARE YOU STOPPING ME?
YOU'RE CONTRA-DICTING YOURSELF.
I GET THAT!!
BUT THERE'S NO WAY YOU REALLY WANT TO DO THIS!!
ISN'T IT THE REASON WHY YOU HAVEN'T BEEN GOING TO SCHOOL ALL THIS TIME?!
...
YAMADA ...
IT'S OKAY.
I CAN'T PUT UP WITH THIS ANYMORE.

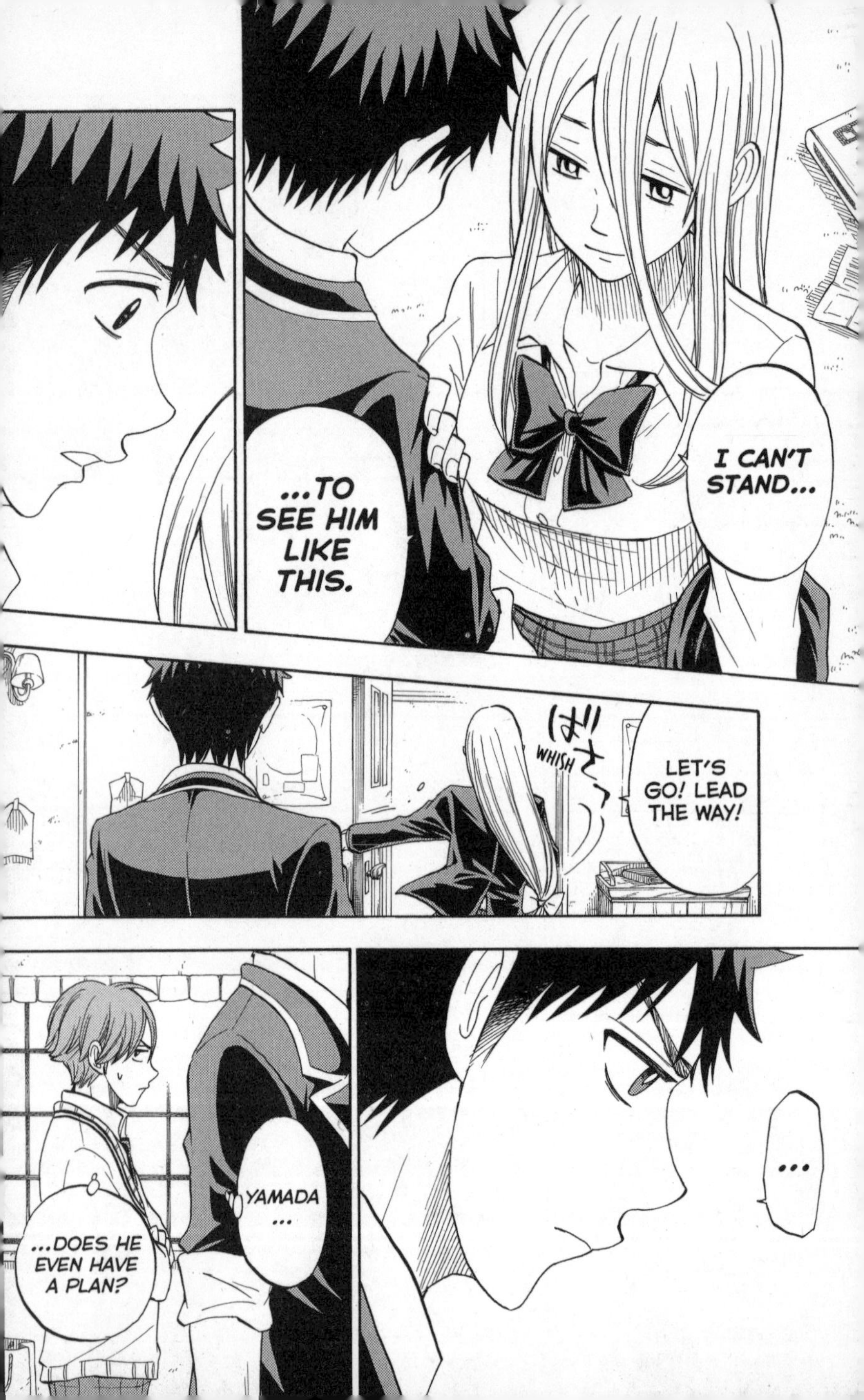
I CAN'T STAND...
...TO SEE HIM LIKE THIS.
LET'S GO! LEAD THE WAY!
ばさっ
WHISH
...
YAMADA ...
...DOES HE EVEN HAVE A PLAN?

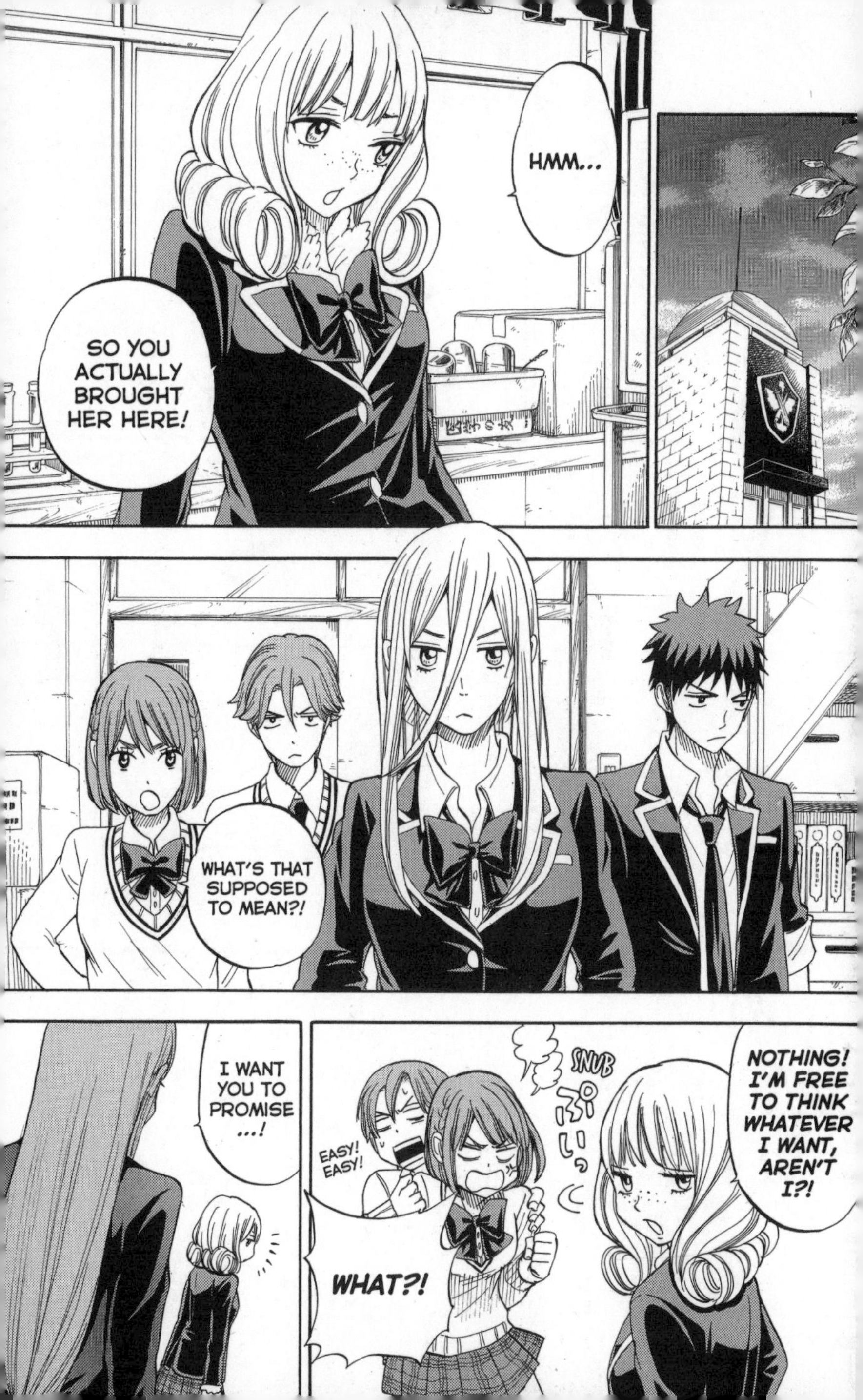
HMM...
SO YOU ACTUALLY BROUGHT HER HERE!
WHAT'S THAT SUPPOSED TO MEAN?!
NOTHING! I'M FREE TO THINK WHATEVER I WANT, AREN'T I?!
SNUB
ぷいっ
EASY! EASY!
WHAT?!
I WANT YOU TO PROMISE ...!

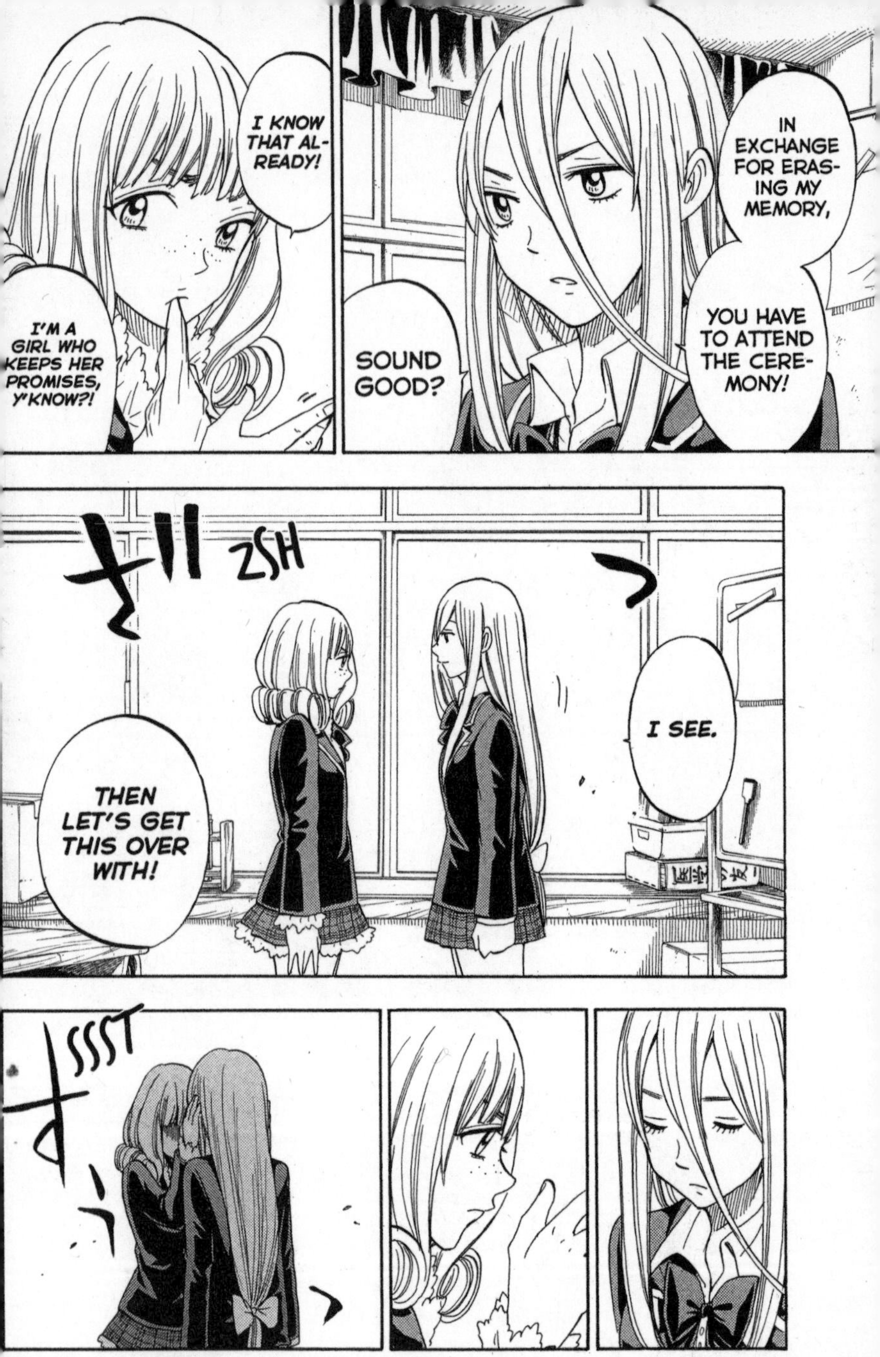
IN EXCHANGE FOR ERASING MY MEMORY,
YOU HAVE TO ATTEND THE CEREMONY!
SOUND GOOD?
I KNOW THAT ALREADY!
I'M A GIRL WHO KEEPS HER PROMISES, Y'KNOW?!
I SEE.
ZSH
THEN LET'S GET THIS OVER WITH!
SSST

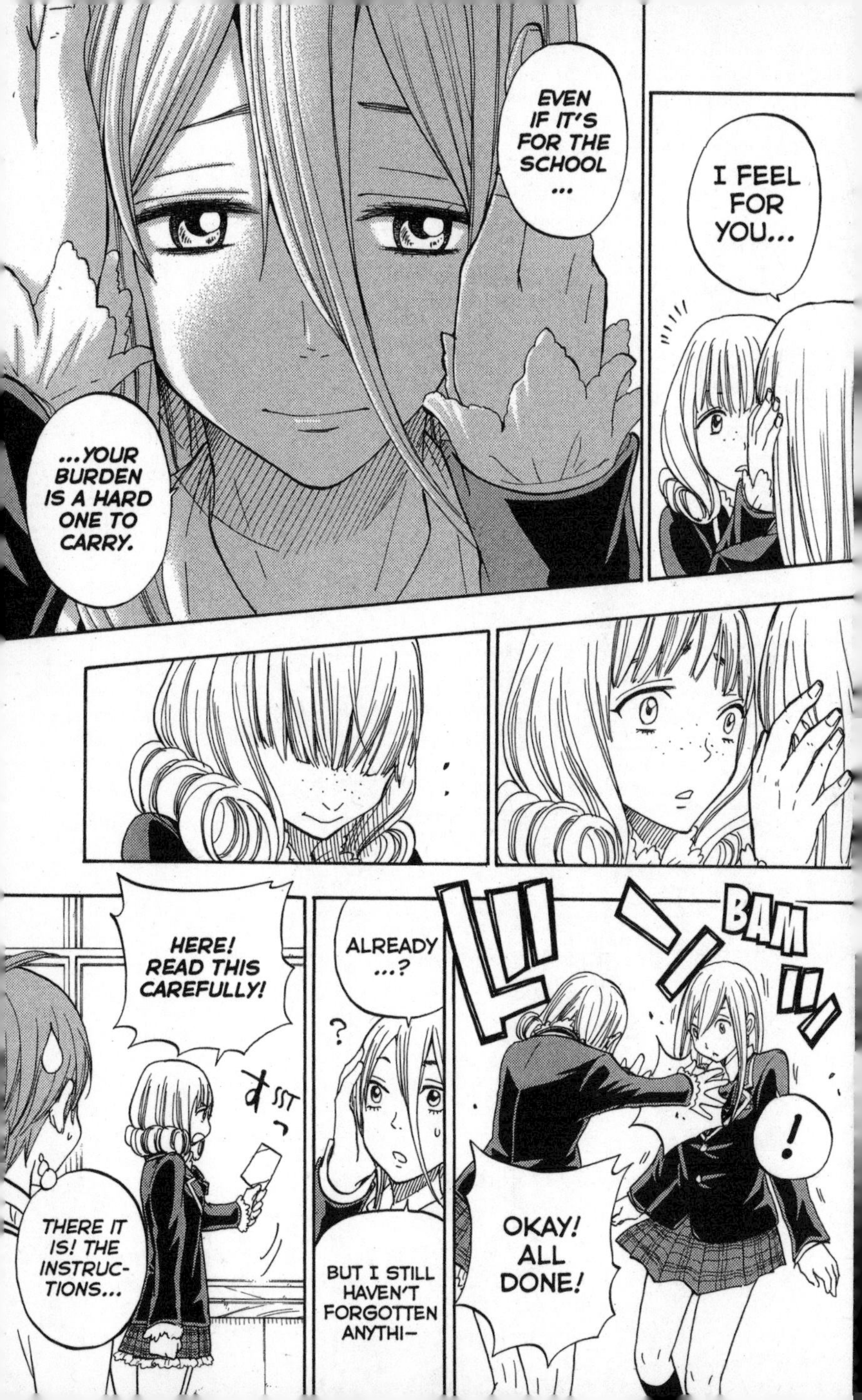
I FEEL FOR YOU...
EVEN IF IT'S FOR THE SCHOOL ...
...YOUR BURDEN IS A HARD ONE TO CARRY.
BAM
!
OKAY! ALL DONE!
ALREADY ...?
?
BUT I STILL HAVEN'T FORGOTTEN ANYTHI–
HERE! READ THIS CAREFULLY!
SST
THERE IT IS! THE INSTRUCTIONS...

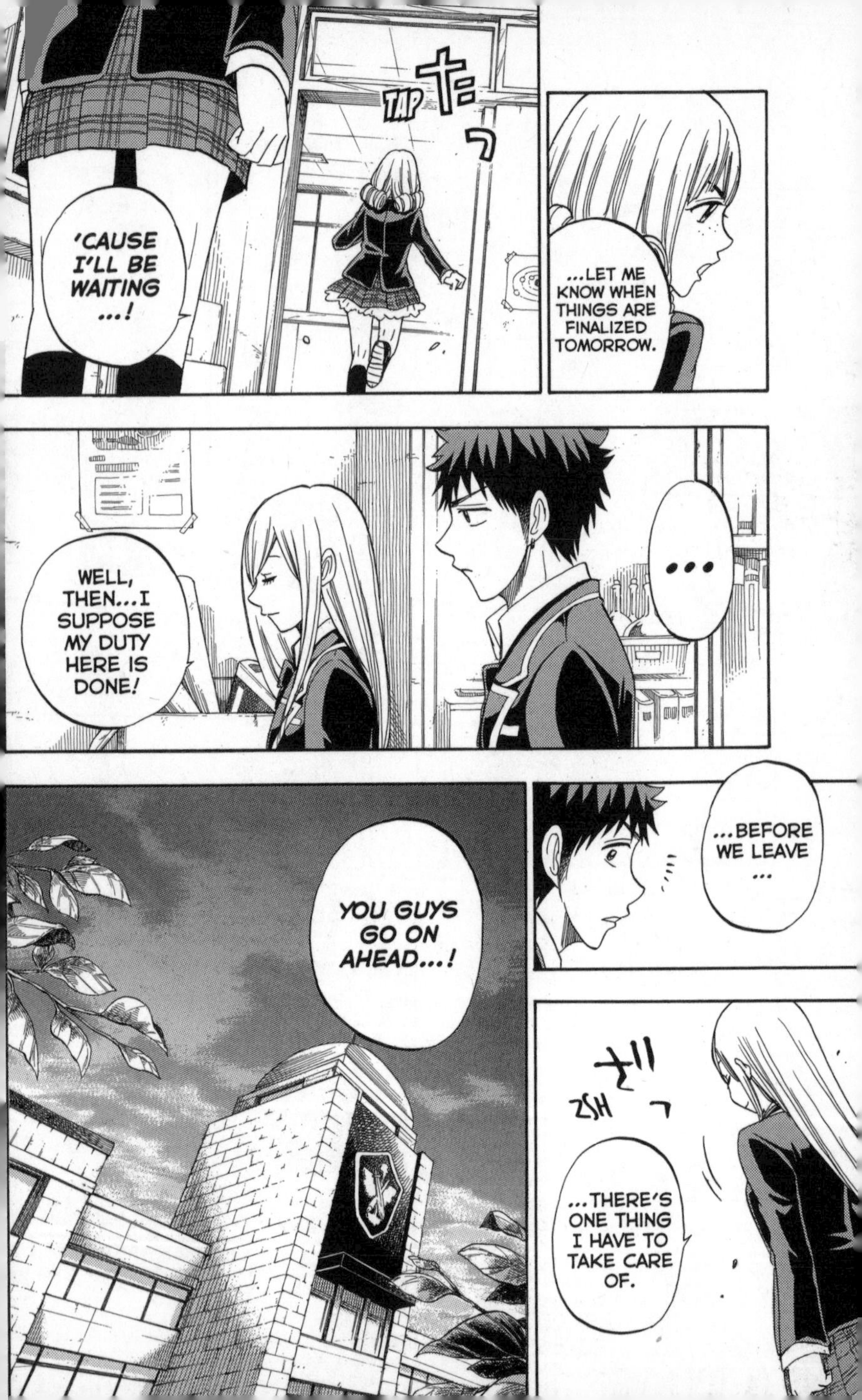
...LET ME KNOW WHEN THINGS ARE FINALIZED TOMORROW.
TAP
'CAUSE I'LL BE WAITING ...!
...
WELL, THEN...I SUPPOSE MY DUTY HERE IS DONE!
...BEFORE WE LEAVE ...
ZSH
...THERE'S ONE THING I HAVE TO TAKE CARE OF.
YOU GUYS GO ON AHEAD...!

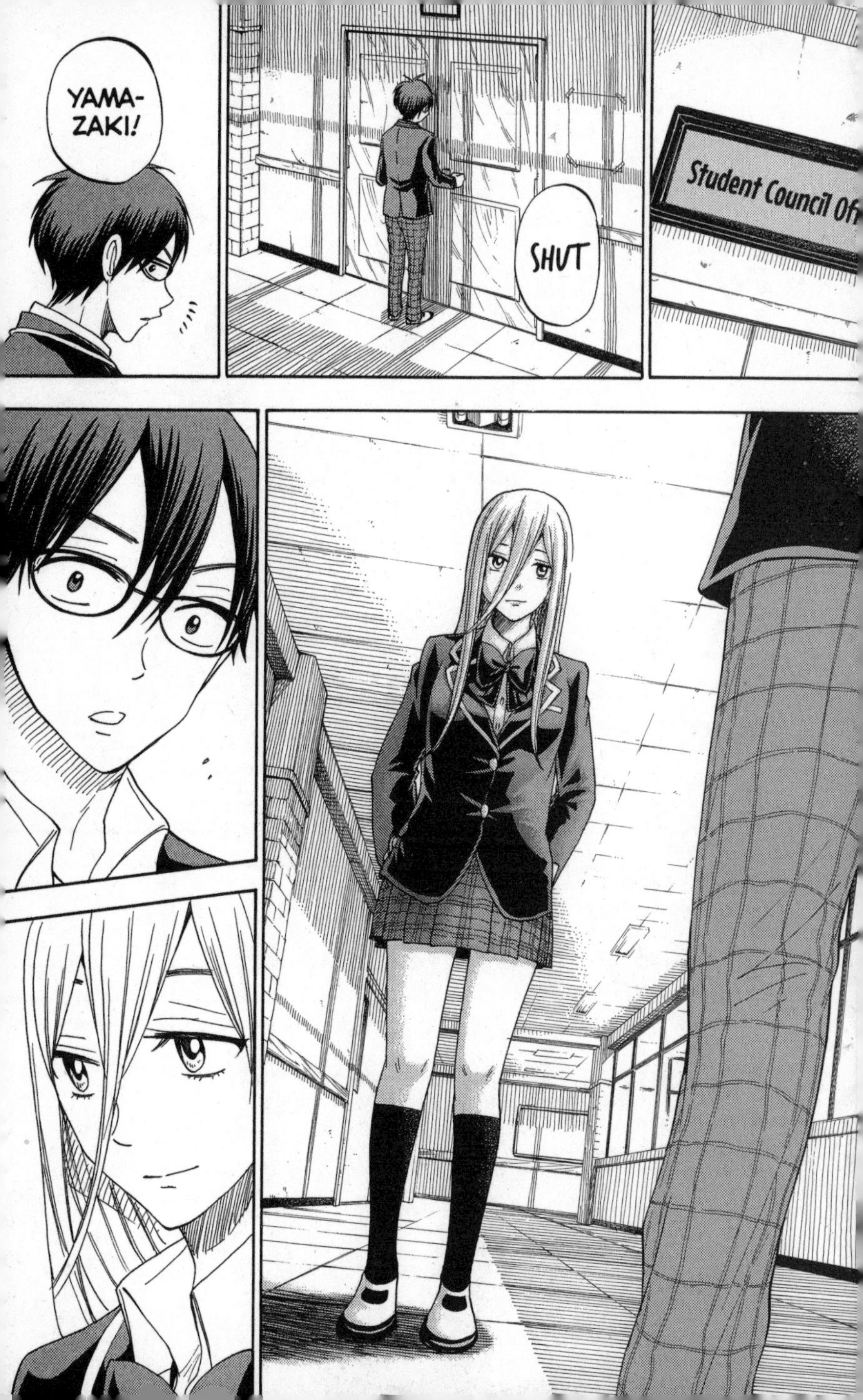
Student Council Of
SHUT
YAMA-ZAKI!

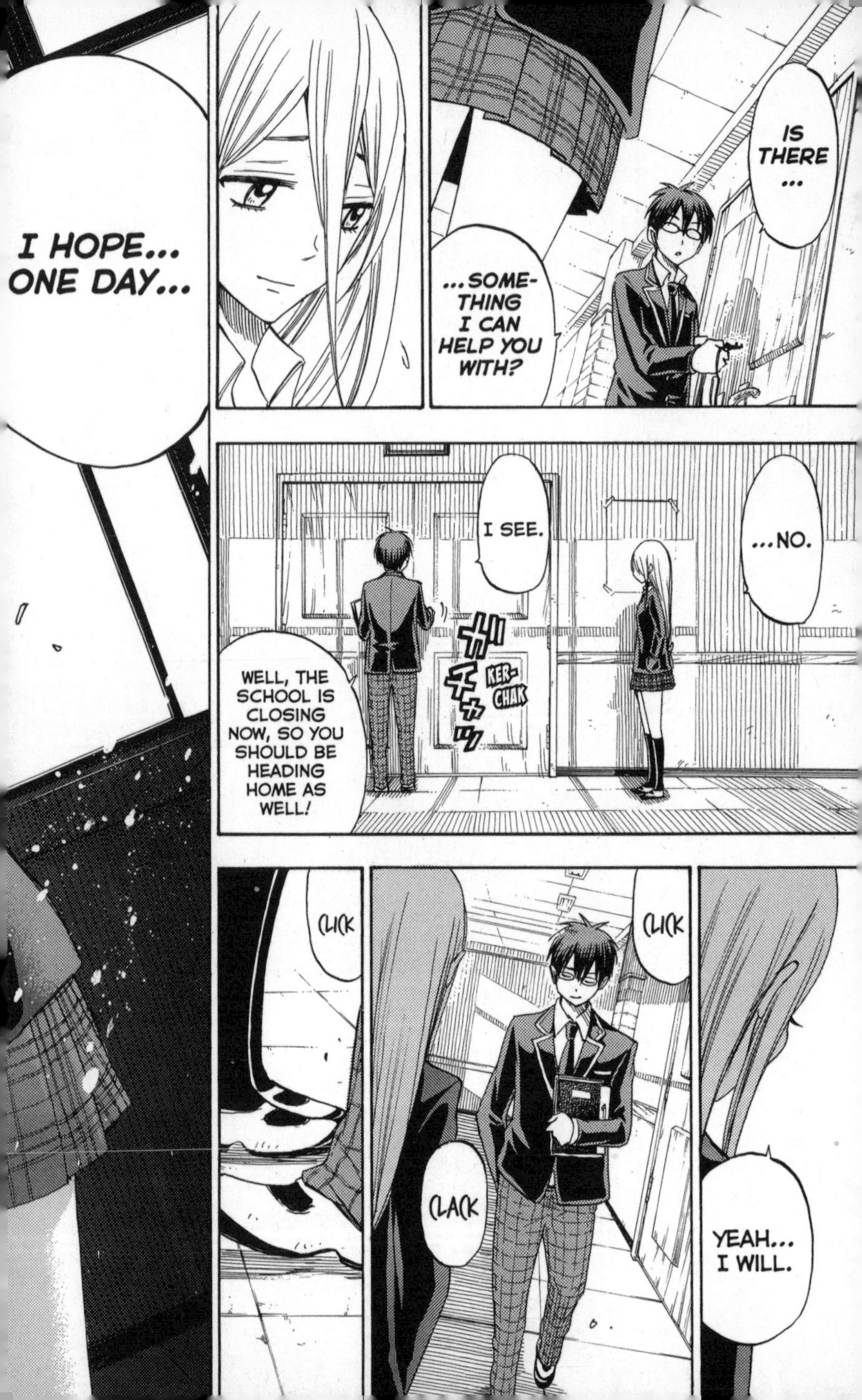
IS THERE ...
...SOME-THING I CAN HELP YOU WITH?
...NO.
I SEE.
ガチャッ
KER-CHAK
WELL, THE SCHOOL IS CLOSING NOW, SO YOU SHOULD BE HEADING HOME AS WELL!
YEAH... I WILL.
CLICK
CLACK
CLICK
I HOPE... ONE DAY...

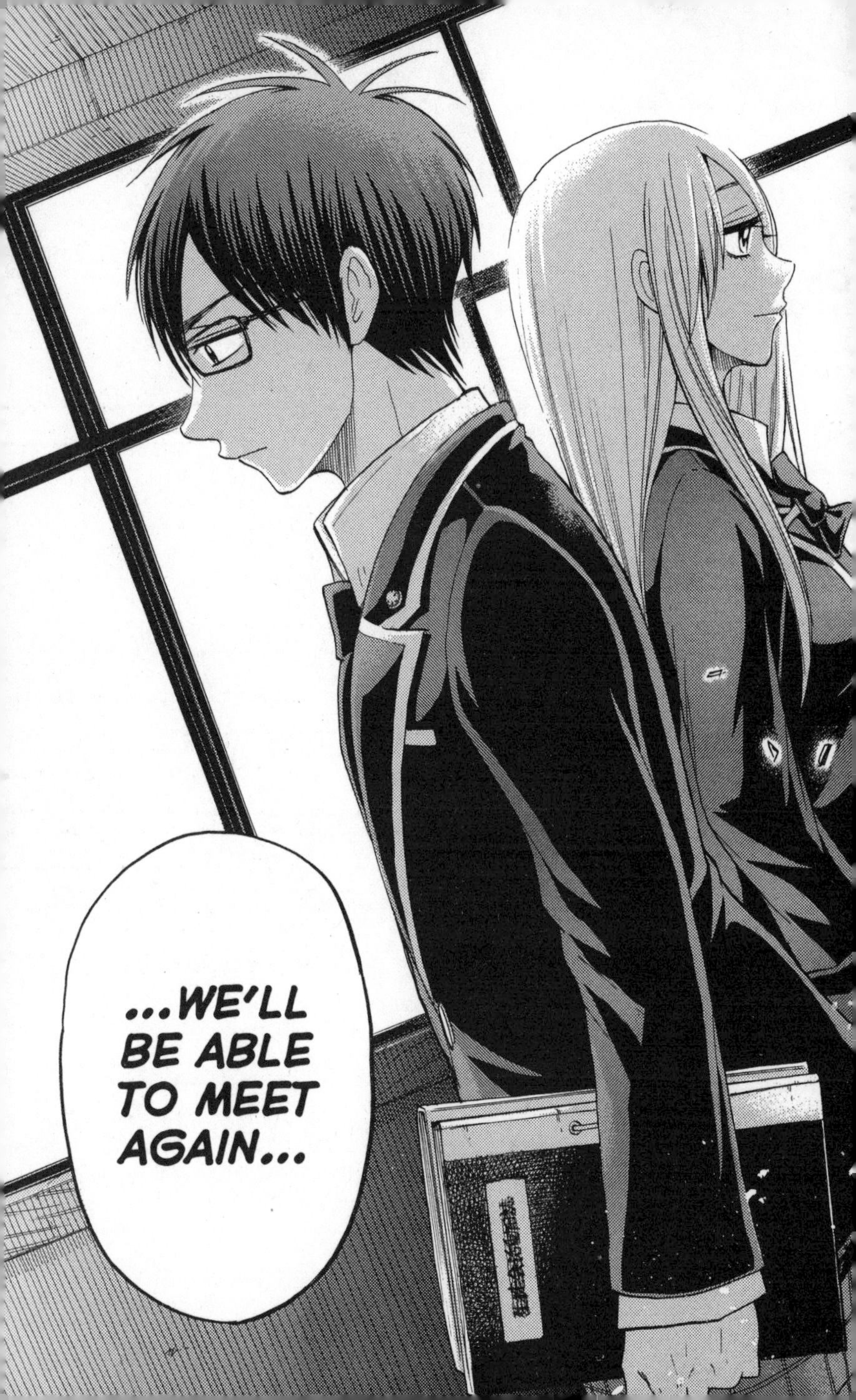
...WE'LL BE ABLE TO MEET AGAIN...

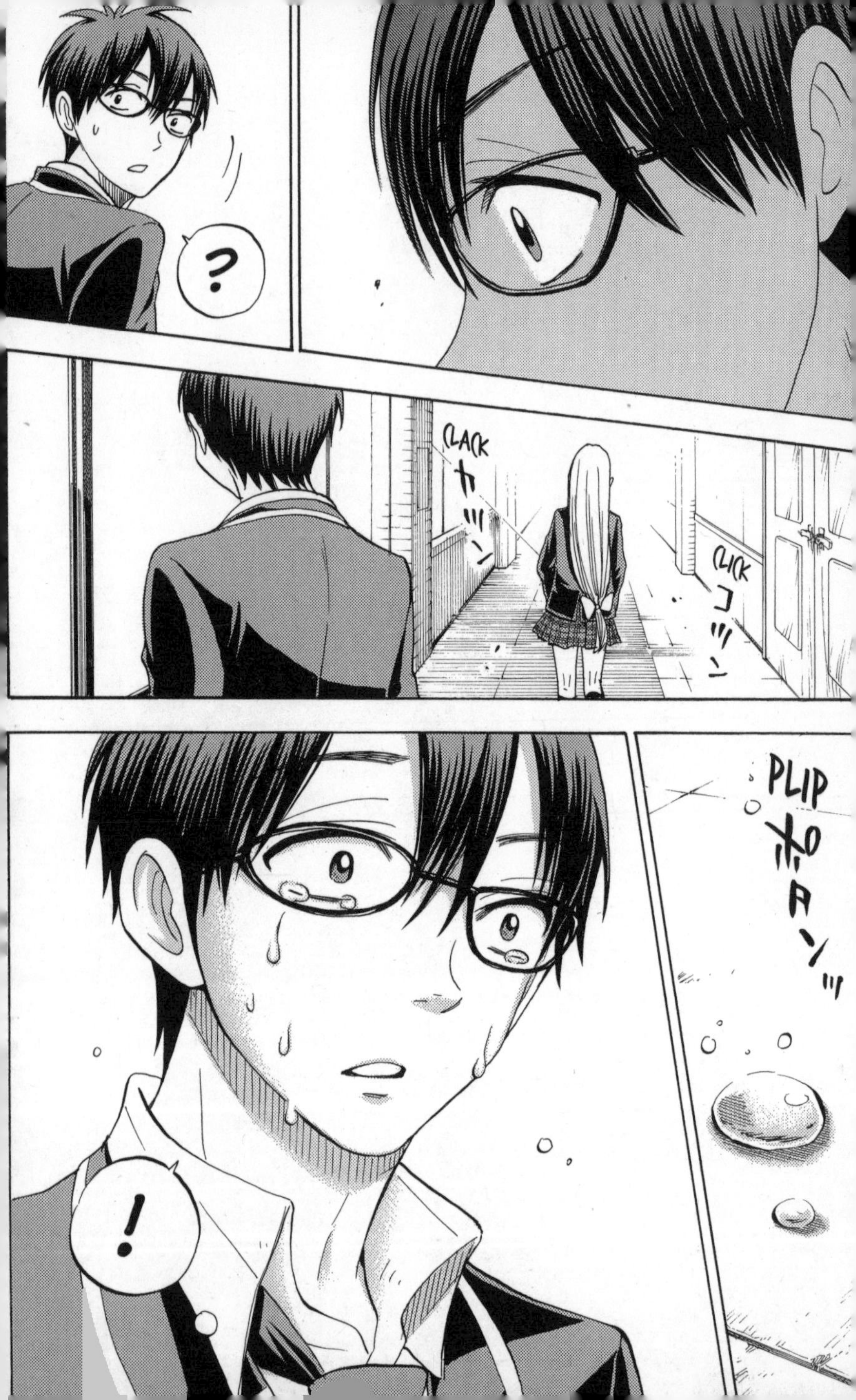
?
CLACK
カツン
CLICK
コツン
PLIP
ポタン
!

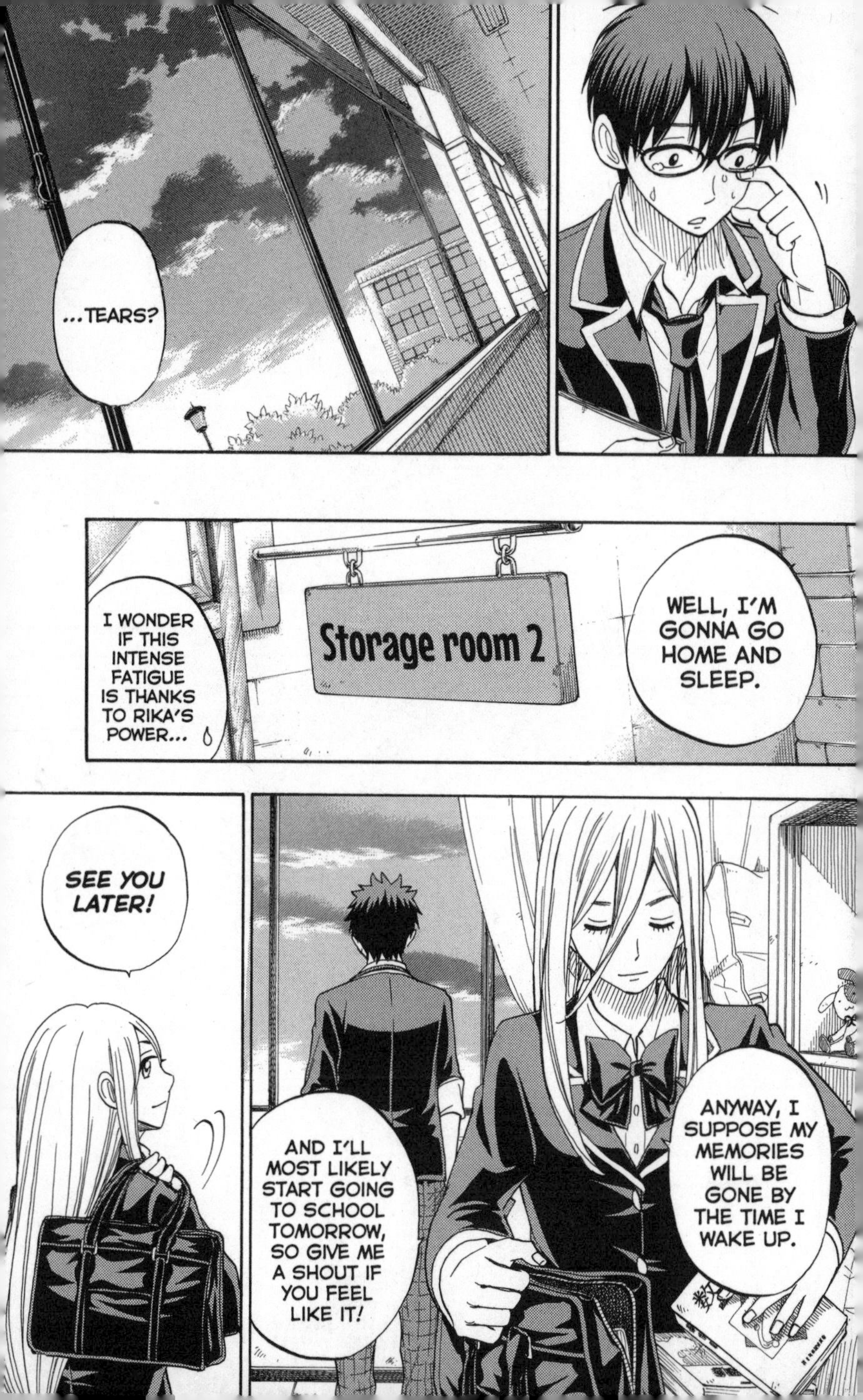
...TEARS?
WELL, I'M GONNA GO HOME AND SLEEP.
Storage room 2
I WONDER IF THIS INTENSE FATIGUE IS THANKS TO RIKA'S POWER...
ANYWAY, I SUPPOSE MY MEMORIES WILL BE GONE BY THE TIME I WAKE UP.
AND I'LL MOST LIKELY START GOING TO SCHOOL TOMORROW, SO GIVE ME A SHOUT IF YOU FEEL LIKE IT!
SEE YOU LATER!

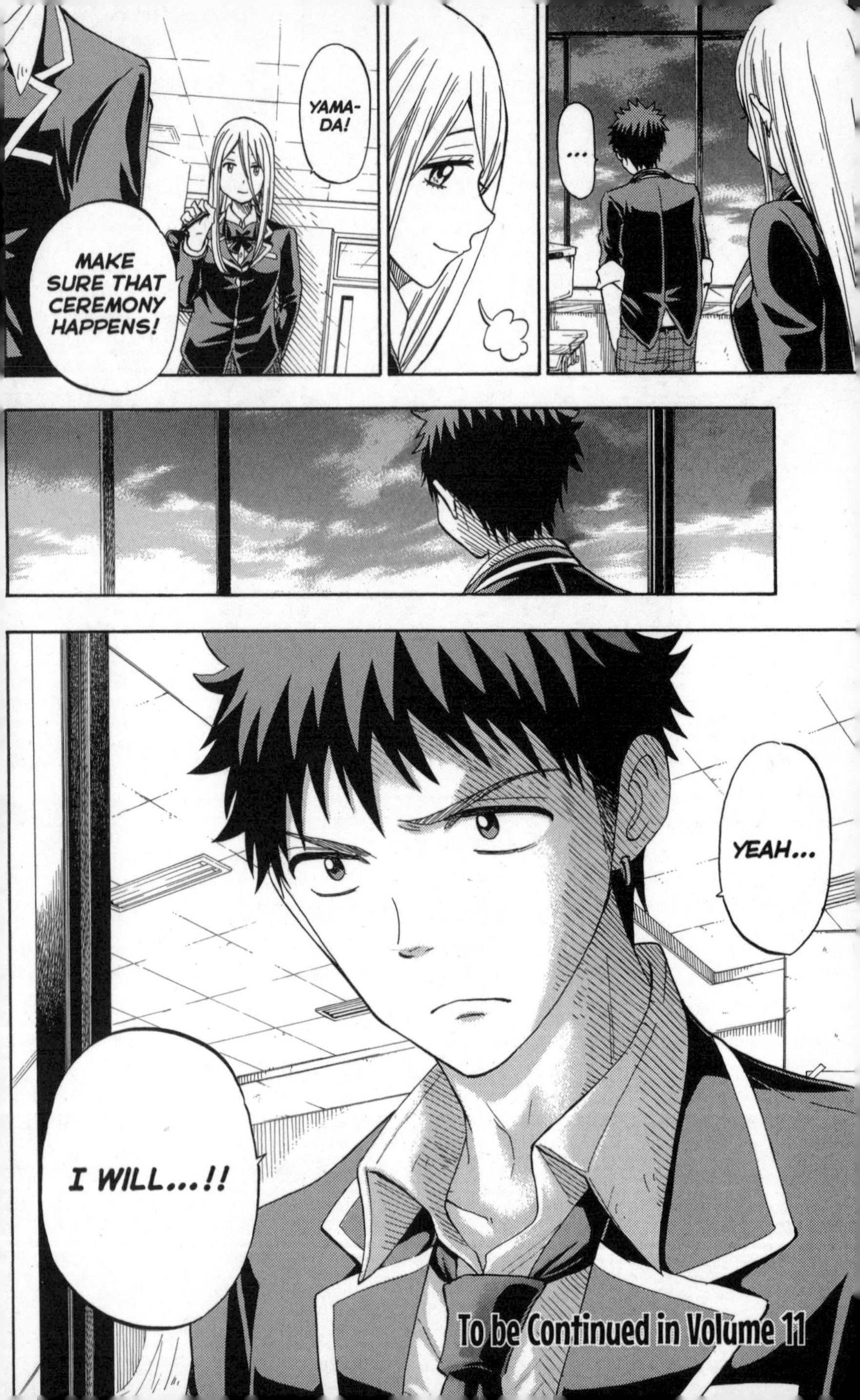
...
YAMA-DA!
MAKE SURE THAT CEREMONY HAPPENS!
YEAH...
I WILL...!!
To be Continued in Volume 11

Yamada's

~~Miyabi~~ Itou's Witch Research Notes

File.6
By: Yamada

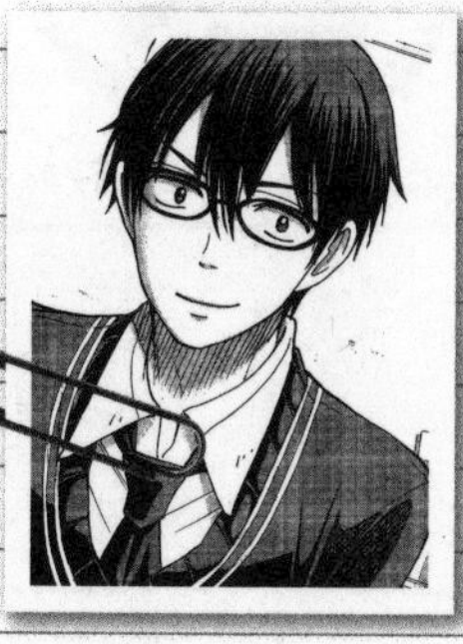

Haruma Yamazaki

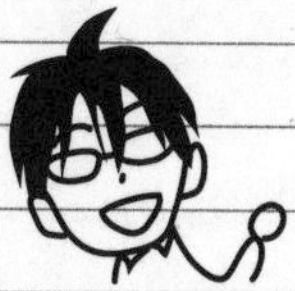

Student Council President

- He knows all witch secrets?
- He was a Supernatural Studies Club member until spring of last year!
- He investigated the witches with Leona!
- His memories were erased by Saionji!
- He learned everything he currently knows about the witches after becoming Student Council president (from Saionji?)
- He used to like Leona...?
- He became president so he could continue the Supernatural Studies Club with Leona. So what's his goal now...?

★ Common rules for the witch powers that I've figured out! A Review!

- One person, one power!
- If a person under a witch's spell is kissed by another witch, the person being kissed will not be affected.
- A witch cannot put another witch under their spell.
- Tamaki and I aren't witches.
- There are always seven witches.
  When a witch leaves the school or loses their power, a new witch is born.

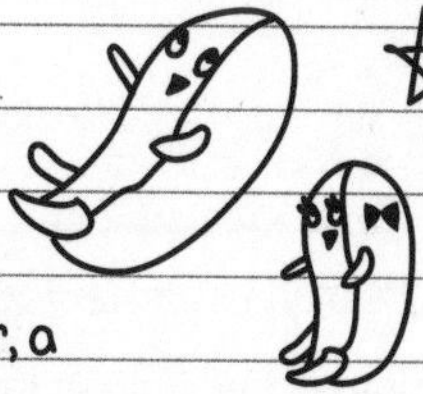

朱雀高等学校 裏ホームページ

SUZAKU HIGH SCHOOL UNDERGROUND WEBSITE

It's time for the 6th installment of our Q&A session!

Uhhh. This is a bit sudden, but we got this question.

Q1. When Shiraishi-san (who was really Yamada) stayed over Itou-san's house, did the cosplay outfits that Shiraishi-san wore belong to Itou-san? Gunma Prefecture H.N Kuroneko-san

Oh…that…

Hm? What's the matter? Who'd have thought Supernatural Studies otaku Itou-san would be into cosplay…

N…no!! Those aren't mine…they're my

mom's!!!

Huhhhh?!! Your mom is into that kinda stuff?!! I'd definitely be down for getting real close with h–

Hey! Don't get any weird ideas!!

My mom apparently has them 'cause she "used them for work a long time ago"!

Wh…what kind of work was that…?!

Q2. When everyone stayed at Miyamura-kun's house, did the clothes that Itou-san was wearing belong to Miyamura-kun by any chance? If so, I'm super jealous... H.N Kana-san

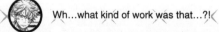

That's right! I borrowed the smallest shirt Miyamura had, but it was still pretty big for me!

That's 'cause you **don't have boobs–**

POW!!

Next question!!!

Q3. What does Kenken-kun always have in his mouth?

Shimane Prefecture H.N Takenokonosato-san

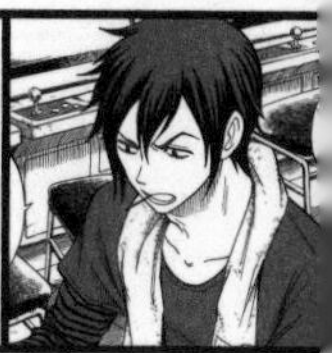

That's clearly a **toothpick!!**

Kenken-kun can set the tempura oil to just the right temperature with that, y'know?

He's always ready to fry up tempura, isn't he?!
All right, then, that's it for this one!

Please send your correspondence here ↓

Yamada-kun and the Seven Witches: Underground Website
c/o Kodansha Comics
451 Park Ave. South, 7th Floor
New York, NY 10016

Please send your letters with the understanding that your zip code, address, name and other personal information included in your correspondence may be given to the author of this work.

※ **Don't forget to include your handle name (pen name)!**

If you have questions for Itou-san's mom, please send them our way! I'll hear those questions out in her place!

N-no! You can't! This conversation is over!

New!

Suzaku Gallery

This is where we'll introduce illustrations that we've received from all of you!

Selected artists will receive an original present from Itou-san and yours truly! When you make a submission, please make sure to clearly write your address, name, and phone number! If you don't, we won't be able to send you a prize even if you're selected! Anyway, looking forward to all your submissions!

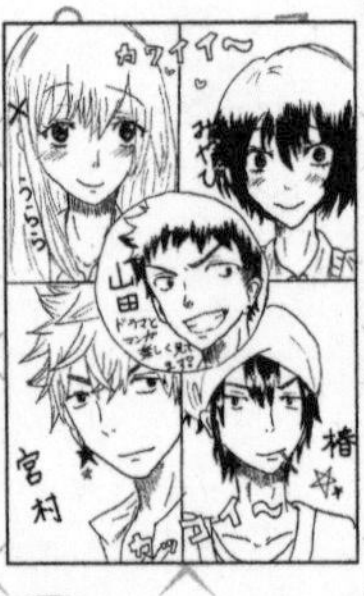
カワイイ〜
山田
宮村
椿

Kagoshima Pref., H.N. Ikepan ☆ Melonpan-san

We're lookin' good! (Especially me!)

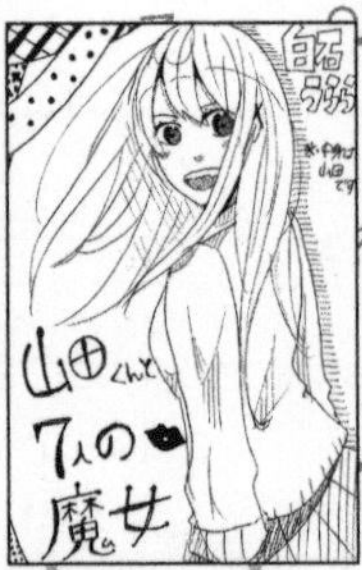
山田くんと7人の魔女

Chiba Pref., H.N. Seimana-san

Even if it's Yamada on the inside, I can't help but fall for her!

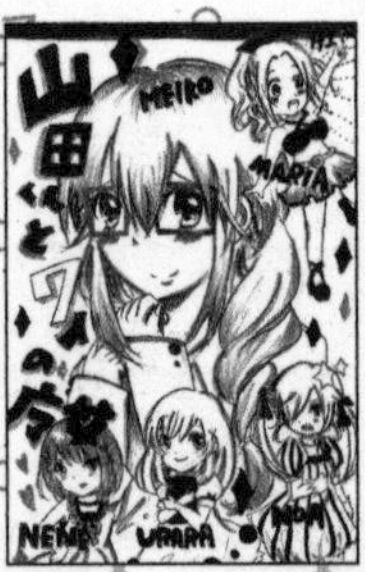
MEIKO
MARIA
NENE
URARA
NOA

Chiba Pref., H.N. Suzume Kaneito-san

Everyone's clothes are like dresses! So fashionable! ☆

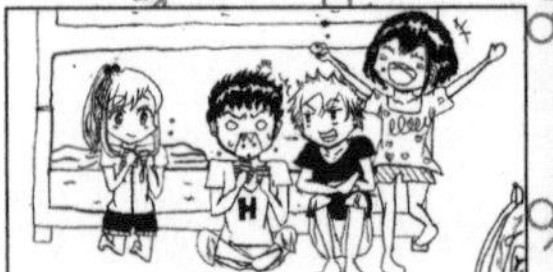

Hyogo Pref., H.N. Hono-san

Yamada-san meets with utter defeat in a game of cards. This is an every-day occurrence for us.

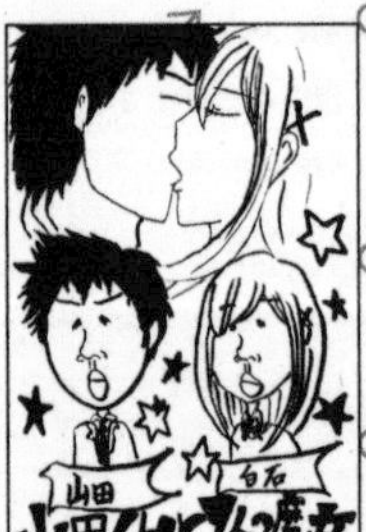
山田
白石
山田くんと7人の魔女

Okinawa Pref., H.N. Johnnyko-san

They get those faces when they kiss?! What a terrible power!

Suzaku Gallery

付き合って ください
え
これからも がんばって ください

Kagoshima Pref.,
H.N. Marina Inoue-san

Shiraishi-san, noooo! Of course you're going to reject Sobasshi, right?

RIKA
WAN
WAN
WAN

Nagano Pref.,
H.N. Nekopunch-san

I can certainly say that Rika-senpai doesn't NOT resemble a dog.

Miya
2人でお泊まり会
パジャマパーティーなう
Urara

Yanagi Pref.,
H.N. Shiho Hoshi-san

I hope to make this a reality with Urara-chan someday! ♥

Okayama Pref.,
H.N. Mei-san

What a bright sense of design. Shiraishi-san's cute, too, of course.

山田くんと
7人の魔女

Ibaraki Pref.,
H.N. Beni-san

Hey, Yamada! Just where do you think you're putting your hands on Shiraishi-san?! Change places with me!!

H.N. Reimii-san

Wow, a load of itty-bitty characters! They're just so cute and pudgy! ♥

Please send your art here ↓

Yamada-kun and the Seven Witches: Underground Website
c/o Kodansha Comics
451 Park Ave. South, 7th Floor
New York, NY 10016

* Please clearly write you address, name, and phone number. If your address, name, and phone number aren't included with your submission, we won't be able to send you a prize.
* And if necessary, don't' forget to include your handle name (pen name)!

Please send your letters with the understanding that your zip code, address, name and other personal information included in your correspondence may be given to the author of this work.

みやむら
いとう

Ryu Yamada-san

Uh…wait a sec! This is a submission from Yamada!! I didn't think he'd seriously send this in. (sweat)

Translation Notes

Light novels, page 54

A light novel is a type of Japanese book aimed at the young-adult demographic, typically featuring illustrations and a shorter word count than a standard novel. Many well-known light novels are originally published online and attract interest from publishers upon gaining popularity. Successful light novels often receive anime and manga adaptations.

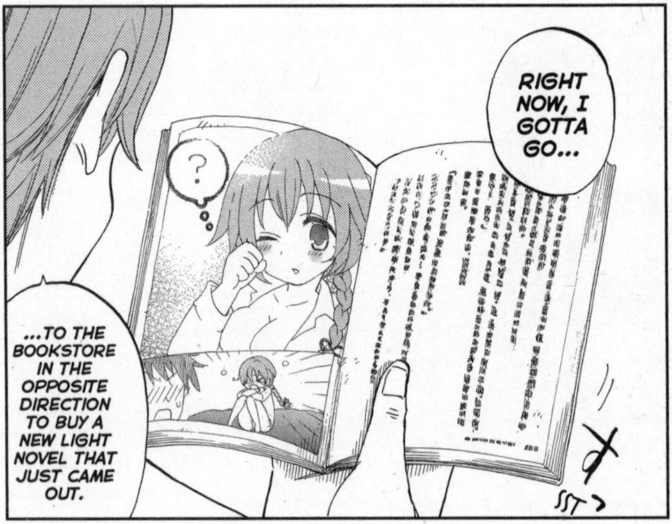
RIGHT NOW, I GOTTA GO...
...TO THE BOOKSTORE IN THE OPPOSITE DIRECTION TO BUY A NEW LIGHT NOVEL THAT JUST CAME OUT.

A Kodansha Comics Trade Paperback Original.

Yamada-kun and the Seven Witches volume 10 copyright © 2013 Miki
Yoshikawa
English translation copyright © 2016 Miki Yoshikawa

Published in the United States by Kodansha Comics,
an imprint of Kodansha USA Publishing, LLC, New York.

Publication rights for this English edition arranged through Kodansha Ltd.,
Tokyo.

First published in Japan in 2013 by Kodansha Ltd., Tokyo, as *Yamada-
kun to Nananin no Majo* volume 10.

ISBN 978-1-63236-139-4

Printed in the United States of America.

www.kodanshacomics.com

9 8 7 6 5 4 3 2 1

Translation: David Rhie
Lettering: Sara Linsley
Editing: Ajani Oloye
Kodansha Comics edition cover design: Phil Balsman